CREATIVE
THINKING

JOHN G. BENNETT

COOMBE SPRINGS PRESS

ISBN 0 900306 10 6

COOMBE SPRINGS PRESS

SHERBORNE HOUSE

SHERBORNE

Glos. GL54 3DZ. England

Contents

Chapter		Page
One	*Living in the Medium*	1
Two	*Real Thinking*	19
Three	*The Levels of Energies*	39
Four	*The Organization of the Sensitivity*	63
Five	*Practical Rules for Creative Work*	81
Six	*Group Creativity*	95

LIVING IN THE MEDIUM

I HOPE TO CONVEY TO YOU something of what I
have been able to recognize over many years'
experience of the factors important to creative
thinking.

What are the conditions for creativity?
First of all, one must be *living in the medium*.
People are not creative in some medium with
which they have no real contact. In that sense,
if we wish to think creatively, we have to be
in the process of thinking. Then we have somehow
to bring into that process additional factors
which will give it the quality of creativity
that we are looking for.

There is the saying that creativity is ninety-
nine parts transpiration and one part inspiration - in other words, that it is mostly very
hard work. But there is no doubt of the importance in creativity of some second element that
we cannot ourselves control. I am going to call
that element 'spontaneity'.

If you read accounts of creative activity - by
scientists, or artists or others - you do see in
these that the spontaneous element is really out

of the person's control. Yet, though it comes unexpectedly, it does not come without certain conditions being satisfied - and the conditions we will come to later.

Let us take one classical example of creativity which has been often reported: Lawrence Bragg's account of the way in which he made a particular step in understanding crystallography when he was working with his father, William Bragg. They came across some experimental work that did not fit into the accepted theory of the crystal lattice. They verified their experiments and they verified what other people had done, and then they were stuck. No combination or adjustment of the existing theories would make it all fit together. Then, one day, - as Lawrence Bragg describes it - when he had almost given up hope of finding the answer without new experimental evidence turning up to give a clue, he was walking down the Backs of Cambridge and *in a flash* the whole thing came clearly in front of him. He was able to go back immediately, do the necessary mathematical analysis with his father, and the whole thing became clear, although it required several months' work before the new theory which they produced was ready for publication.

The actual creative step, as he describes it and as hundreds of other people have described it at different times, came 'in a flash', unexpectedly. One of the questions that we shall have to talk about is whether anything can be done about this or whether it is entirely out of our power and wholly dependent upon good luck, as it is sometimes supposed to be.

LIVING IN THE MEDIUM

There is a third element that enters into all
this, which I shall call by the name of *technique*. Let us take the example of an artist.
Without technique, the moment of creative insight can hardly be made fruitful. The same is
true for the scientist. That means that one
must know the form of thought and expression
that will enable one to clothe the moment of
insight in some expression. First of all for
oneself, so that it may become clear, and afterwards for communication to others.

Let us just take those three factors for the
moment and look at them. First of all that one
needs to be grounded in the subject matter one
wishes to develop creatively; where one feels
that a creative step has to be made. Secondly
there is this spontaneous arising of the new
vision, or understanding, or insight, into the
situation. Thirdly there is the ability to
translate that into something which can be
thought about and expressed.

So far, all of these are concerned with creative activity in general. All of that is equally
true of the artist, of the scientist, or of the
man of action who has to take a creative decision (the general in front of a strategical or
tactical problem, the doctor in front of sick-
ness) wherever there is something that cannot be
dealt with by routine alone and therefore where
some kind of creative step is needed.

I said that the first factor is being well
grounded in the subject that one is dealing with.
But this grounding itself is a special process:
one must know what has to be known about it and
one must put out of one's attention all that is

3

unnecessary. That is to say, this grounding is
itself a selective activity; one must know what
it is that one is going to work at. The artist,
let us say, the painter, must, in this work of
grounding, select, reject and also assemble his
material; that is, he has to decide how he will
treat it. And yet, in all of the work in preparing the ground, he is not called upon to make
a creative step, and even if by chance this
should happen, there is a certain risk that he
will not complete his grounding and the construction will be lacking even if there is the flash
of genius at some point.

When we are concerned with thought, then the
grounding has to be made in our head. There is
no doubt that this part of the work is hard in
the field of thinking. Sometimes, when people
set themselves to understand something or to make
creative investigations of a subject, they proceed to get all the relevant information down in
front of them: they write it down on a sheet of
paper, or they make a card index. Really, this is
not sufficient. It is necessary that one should
do that work of selection, elimination and assembly (as far as possible) *inwardly*. I know from
my own experience that this is a hard discipline
and that there always is an inclination to get it
down on paper or to read it up. But if one wants
to bring it into the sphere of creativity, this
preparatory work has to be done in a special way,
it has to go through the mill of one's own past
experience and one has to come to terms with the
subject. If I have to do such work as this, then
after just a preliminary collecting together of
what I happen to know about it, I sit down and

and try to *put it together in my mind* in order
to see what it is that I really know about the
subject, and what I intend to do with that knowledge. In the course of doing that, I may find
that there is something clearly missing and that
I have to go out and study it or perhaps make
some investigations or experiments. But in doing
this I am only preparing the ground; I must not
be looking, at this point, for a solution to the
problem, and even if I seem to see the situation
more clearly, and am ready to make progress with
it, it is essential to exercise self-restraint
so as not to allow myself to make a premature
step forward in understanding. Thus there is a
special discipline which one has to learn and
impose upon oneself - and I shall certainly be
saying more about it in the course of these lectures. This preliminary stage goes through the
whole process and does not remain static; one
does not merely, as is said, 'mug up' the subject and decide what one knows about it and then
leave it to go on to the other stages. This
ground work *must be kept fluid* so that there can
be a process of transformation. One must constantly remind oneself that it has not yet taken
shape; although we may assemble it and try to
give it a coherent form, so that at least we can
hold it in our minds: this is not the goal, it
is not what we are aiming at.

  This work of grounding oneself in the subject
makes this process different from other sorts of
learning, where it is sufficient to learn what
one has to know about a subject and then fix it
in the mind, either by memorising it or by making the necessary notes so that, when informa-

tion is needed, one can find the necessary sources, or bring it to mind. We are not concerned with learning but with something else. And for that, any kind of fixing is the one factor which can *spoil the whole process*. One caution I must make here is that that which is necessary for creative thinking may be quite harmful, even destructive for other kinds of activity, where it is necessary, for example, to settle upon what one knows and act upon that and stick to the decision that has been made. Those things are very necessary for other purposes, but they are those very things which must be thrown aside when one is trying to make a new creative step.

I find myself that it becomes like a kaleidoscope; patterns of ideas are passing in front of my attention and I do not allow myself to dwell on anything in particular so that other patterns arise. Out of all this I expect nothing of any value to come. And, in fact, it very seldom, if ever does come.

When you are ready to bring in the next factor you have to see that you do provide the necessary conditions; and that is, *you ask yourself a clear question*. In the example I gave you about Lawrence Bragg, there is a clear question here: how are we to fit these measurements of lattice energies in with the present theories of crystal structure? The question was clear enough to know *whether or not it was answered*.

Now, what is to be done about the element of spontaneity? Here I think that I really can offer you something which is not generally understood, which I have gained from my own experi-

6

ence and what I have learnt from others. I am
sure that there is a practical means whereby one
can bring about the conditions for this spontaneous step to be made. Some of you may remember
how we used to speak about thinking at Coombe
Springs ten or fifteen years ago, when there
were questions about 'how to think'. I always
answered this question of 'how to think': "The
way to think is not to think". If you grasp
this, 'the way to think is not to think', then
you will be able to follow what I mean.

If I have some question which I cannot answer
by the ordinary processes, by calling upon what
I know about the subject, and I have satisfied
myself that I do not already know the answer,
then it is no use going on looking for it. I
have become habituated, by doing this for many
years, to quite quickly stop looking for an answer and to go to this other, opposite, condition of putting the whole thing away, save for
the question. I stop all thinking 'about' the
subject, even to the extent of chasing away any
thoughts that may come to my mind about it, and
especially chasing away any thoughts that seem
interesting or suggestive. Even the question
ceases to be present in the form of words, or an
image which I can hold; all that remains is *the
need to find an answer*.

This has to be practised. You must not think
that because I have explained this to you, you
can do it at once. I am going to help you with
this over the series, of lectures, and therefore
you will not have to pick it all up in one go.
But the process, as far as I can describe it, is
this: that having brought the question in front

of me, I then empty my mind of all that I know about the subject. I also have to prevent my mind from wandering off on to other subjects, which of course it will want to do because it abhors a vacuum. And it is really, I suppose, this abhorrence of a vacuum that draws to the mind some new thought or new insight, that makes this creative or spontaneous step that I am looking for.

Several of you have probably quite often done something similar to this when you have had a lapse of memory and you have known, or heard, that the best way of dealing with a lapse of memory is to prevent oneself from trying to remember what one has forgotten. And then somehow, by emptying the mind, this forgotten or lost memory is drawn back into our consciousness. That simple procedure is not difficult when it comes to a memory that is actually latent in our minds but is outside the sphere of our conscious experience at the moment.

The point here is that the same method can carry us much further into attracting into our conscious experience ideas which we have not had before - even ideas which no one has ever had before; that is, truly original thoughts. This will depend entirely upon the strength of one's mind, the power that one has to reject anything which is incomplete which is not evidently the required step forward. There is a tremendously strong temptation, when something comes into the mind which throws light upon the subject and is very interesting, to follow it up. But this means that the step is only half, or less than half, made and though there is an enrichment of

8

our thinking, it is not a truly creative step.

Those who have the real creative power have always this strength of mind that enables them to deny, to reject anything but the truth, the insight or moment of understanding that is required. But all of us can strengthen our mind quite simply by this practice. All that is required is that, having found the theme with which to practise, we then resolutely refuse to think about it.

You all know the famous kind of mental trick which consists in asking someone how long they can not think about a white elephant, and as soon as they try to do it, they find it is impossible; they can think about nothing else than white elephants, and the more they want not to think about it, the more white elephants march up and down in front of them. If you refuse resolutely to think about white elephants, then, who knows, a white elephant may come marching in through the window ... a real one! That is, if your power of thought is strong enough to refuse anything but what you are actually determined to have, it will come, that is in the nature of this power.

This has to be practised in simple things to start with, but you must understand that there is nothing that I can do for you in this particular field. Either you are sufficiently interested or all these lectures can do for you is to give you an interesting theory *about* creative thinking. I am sure of this, that there is no substitute for this particular discipline.

The same effect can be produced unintentionally by fatiguing the mind - for example as in

the case of Lawrence Bragg. He told me about
this himself. Lawrence Bragg so occupied his
mind with the problem that finally his mind got
tired of it and would not think about it any
more. And then, when by sheer fatigue he had
succeeded in not thinking any more about the
question, the answer came. But this in reality
is an extremely clumsy way of doing the job.
Strangely enough, it is almost the only one that
is known to even the best scientists and therefore things very often take much longer than
they need take.

It is true that the mind is fatigued by a process of rejection, but it is not nearly so hazardous, so uncertain and chancy to do it that
way as to try to understand the subject and go
on thinking and thinking about it until at last
your mind refuses to think about it.

There are, as you know, exercises that are
taught by masters of Zen Buddhism, like the
Koan, where the mind is resolutely held upon
some absurdity that it is impossible to think
about. By holding the attention upon something
which cannot be thought about because of its inherent absurdity, a vacuum is finally created -
in this case for the entry of a complete insight
into the nature of man. That is what is called
Satori. But it is all connected with the one essential technique, and that is that *for something to enter, a place must be made for it.*

Gurdjieff used to refer to this by simply saying "Must make vacuum", and he used this technique for other things besides thinking; he used
it as a technique for making money.

But first, if you want to practise this, you

have to practise it for a relatively short time,
without, for the moment, expecting to arrive at
anything spectacular, because this refusal to
think about what you wish to understand is an
unusual thing for most people. And I know, from
my own experience, what kind of inner resistance
there is to it; the peculiar way in which something in us revolts against it and is ready to
take any excuse for stopping this and doing
something else instead. But I have no doubt at
all that this has an extraordinary liberating
effect upon the hidden powers of the mind.

Now the third factor in creative thinking is
the one I called technique. There is a difference between the technicality of the subject itself, which belongs to the first stage (that is,
the marshalling of the data and bringing oneself
really to the point where it is something that
is working in oneself) and what we are now talking about, which is the conversion of the moment
of insight into a usable understanding, or expression. It does happen that by this effort of
non-thinking we see something which really appears to us to be a brilliant clarification, a
light on the whole thing. Then afterwards we
find that it cannot be used because we do not
know how to formulate it and bring it into relationship with the rest of our understanding,
or with what has actually to be done. This is
probably something that applies specially to the
problem that we have here; creativity in thought.
Because art has available the artist's technique
in a relatively usable form. I say relatively usable because if you have some experience of this,
you will realize how always in artistic creation

there is a terrible descrepancy between the moment when you really see what you want to do - for example, in producing a musical sound or in producing an expression, a phrase, a way of condensing a certain experience into words or painting - and what you actually achieve. This is over and above deficiencies in the ground constructive technique.

In the realm of thought this is very important indeed. It is necessary to find a way to express what one has seen in a way that can afterwards be worked with and used. It has to be conceptualized or one can say it has to be *formulated*. It has to be put in a form in which it can be attached to some words, or symbols, because these are the instruments of thinking. Whereas in art it has to be attached to some sound, or sight, form, colour, and in action it has to be brought into a deed. But usually - this is the advantage of creative work in the field of action - the creative step itself is a vision of the deed that has to be done. At the same time, of course, the technical skill here is a very necessary factor.

When I had to study the campaigns of Napoleon, as we had to do in the military academy, and go through battle by battle and see just what he did at what moment - one always felt it was all very fine, but how on earth did he know that that was the moment to do it! But the third part, that is, the actual deployment of the forces, the ferocity with which he saw to it that his vision was actually brought into reality, is something that can be followed. One can say that this power is observable because one sees it exercised.

There is then something of this kind: a determination to bring the moment of vision into a workable form. This is a quite different discipline from the first one, the preparatory discipline that I have spoken about. If this third part is neglected, there is a very great likelihood that the whole thing will be sterile, however successful the other two may have been.

In the course of these lectures I will be explaining the use of *systematics* in the third stage. Only you must not expect - and no doubt you do not expect - that systematics by itself will be a substitute for the spontaneity that is necessary. There is no substitute for that; no technique whatever will take the place of this element.

I now want to suggest a theme which is accessible to everyone for a preparatory experiment: that is, *the present position in Cyprus*. There is at the moment a certain critical situation in Cyprus between the Greek and Turkish communities between the Greek and Turkish governments, the British and American governments, the NATO administration and the United Nations, the Greek Orthodox Church and the Islamic religious organization. There is an economic, and an overriding large and a local small military problem. All of those can readily be brought together, but it is necessary to do so with a little bit of reading from *The Times,* or whatever paper gives a reasonably reliable picture of these things, with a view to asking yourself the question: what could be a solution to this problem? If you put yourself that question, you are put-

ting yourself a question that has been asked by
the governments of the world, and they would
probably be very glad to have an answer!

I chose this as an exercise because it is a
problem which has a remarkable degree of isolation and can be looked at reasonably well on
the whole. I do not mean by that that it has
not got repercussions far beyond Cyprus itself,
because of course it has. And I do not mean by
that also that I can ask of you to have an intimate understanding of the character of the
Greek and Turkish people. I have lived for
years among both of them and I therefore have
an advantage over you in that. And I am also
only too familiar with the peculiar fanaticism
of both the Greek and Turkish communities,
but this does not matter, really. You can get
yourself fairly well into this picture.

The exercise that I propose to you is that
you set yourself, by a reasonable amount of
reading and enquiry into this study, to see it
as it is at this moment and as it develops
from day to day, and set yourself every day, for
five or ten minutes, *not to think about it* ...
nor about anything else either. This is because this exercise in non-thinking has to have
something to non-think about!

QUESTIONS.:

Q.: You spoke of the process whereby the mind
became tired giving the empty period in which
some inspiration could arise. What would you
say of the process whereby this is done deliberately, that is, when you 'fling the book' at
it and hurry the process along in that way, and

then reach the blank period in which something
real can come?

J. G. B.: For this to happen, there has to be
an *emotional involvement;* that is to say, there
has to be an emotional force strong enough to
make this 'throwing of the book' something which
is an authentic revolt, not just a gesture.
There has to be an emotional involvement which
produces despair if you do not get the answer,
but it cannot be simulated. It is no use pre-
tending that you are desperate; if you are not
desperate, it does not work. So that that method also has the limitation that you cannot deliberately control the conditions. In this case
the finding the answer has to really matter so
much that there will be a break-through. But
this way is not a very sure one, although of
course it is well-known that it does happen in
that way also.

Q.: Can circumstances be artificially stimulated, in which externally an answer is demanded of one, coupled with the realization that
one does not have the answer from the date
which one is in contact with, and also a sense
of urgency, so that something sometimes comes
through because of this external demand that an
answer must be found? I wondered to what degree
this could be artificially stimulated? But does
it also depend on the emotional force you have
just spoken of?

J. G. B.: Here the important thing is urgency.
It can happen that one sees the answer at the

last moment, when the urgency has piled up. A
great many actions, which require a certain element of spontaneity, fail to be performed until
the last moment. You have to write something ...
common sense tells you that you have to sit
down and write it now. If you do, nothing happens. When you know that it has got to be delivered tomorrow, you will do it. That is also
connected with this emotional pressure. Being
put in front of a questioner and being aroused
also has this sense of 'I must but I cannot'.
The actual clash of 'must' and 'cannot' also
produces this vacuum state, a suspension of
one's own thinking. But these sort of shock-
tactics, in my opinion, have something artificial about them and they cannot always be produced. Whereas what I am talking about has much
wider application and has a more progressive
character. If you practise like this, you become more and more open to spontaneous insights,
whereas the various shock methods, in my experience, do not produce the same.

Q.: Could you tell us what is the difference
between not thinking about Cyprus and not thinking about white elephants?

J. G. B.: In either case there has to be a
great resolution, by this rejecting. If you refuse to think about white elephants for long enough, I say that something about white elephants
will happen, but the difference is this: you
have no question about white elephants, and
therefore it is a sort of sterile activity to
refuse to think about them. In the case of

Cyprus, there is a question.

Q.: Could you explain what you mean by not thinking? Do we just sit and do nothing? You also said to think about nothing else. Do you mean *think* nothing else? Or do you mean to go about one's daily life and whenever that crops up to push it away?

J. G. B.: No, no. Just to sit still and not think about Cyprus. But you must be sure that it is *Cyprus* that you refuse to think about, that it is *Cyprus* that is knocking at the door and if anything else comes, you must say: you must not even knock at the door!

Q.: One of the most crucial steps to me is getting sufficient contact with the question so that 'not thinking' is not a process of letting the mind wander, but that the mind really wants to get to grips with it, it is somehow involved.

J. G. B.: The first step, the first element is indispensable. You cannot do this just 'in the air'. You could not sit down now, if the question of Cyprus has not engaged your attention, and do anything useful with it. I chose this on purpose because it is a burning question of the day, and rightly so, because if something goes wrong over this it will be very, very awkward.

Q.: You formulate the question ... ?

J. G. B.: Do not formulate the question in
words. In this case I formulated the question
for you: what is to be done? What could be
done at the moment to create a new situation in
Cyprus? Funnily enough, when I was preparing
this question, I saw myself what could be done.
But I will not tell you ... or the government.

REAL THINKING

I WANT YOU TO DISTINGUISH between two activities, both of which are called thinking, but
which are really quite different. In fact, what
we usually call thinking is not thinking at all
in the sense that we are trying to understand it.
And what is real thinking is hardly ever noticed
or understood.

Real thinking is the spontaneous arising, in
the inner awareness, of an image that gives us a
contact with some part of reality. Such images
take their own form and, being spontaneous, cannot be forced or produced artificially.

The inner awareness where images are formed
can be compared to a sensitive screen, like a
cinema screen on which pictures are thrown. Images may be thrown on to this screen from different sources, and we now understand this to be a
very complex process. We must distinguish between the various sources if we want to understand the nature of real thinking.

The old idea about the way in which the content of the mind was formed was that this inner
screen took impressions from all sensations that

reached us from the outside, which collected to-together and formed little by little the content of the mind. This picture of the mind as a purely receptive substance coated from outside does not agree with what we now know about the formation of the mind in children, which shows that there is a much more active cooperation be-tween the mechanism of the mind and the incoming impressions than the old simple picture would allow. The mind, or this sensitive screen, is not initially a clean slate written on by life - as for example William James describes it - but is more a sensitive substance that is constantly renewing itself, transmitting images to a much more complicated recording mechanism that is out of the focus of our awareness. The recording ap-paratus is associated with the main part of the brain, where quite an elaborate work of assoc-iating and sorting and registration and so on takes place - much more elaborate than the sim-ple registration as was formally thought. But we are not concerned with this at the moment, we are concerned just with this sensitive screen upon which the impressions fall.

It is possible for this sensitive screen to be restored to a state of simple receptiveness, so that it does correspond to the old idea of the clean sheet or the clean plate. This consists in quietening the mind or stilling the thoughts. When the thoughts are still, then real thinking can begin; that is, there can be a really spon-taneous arising of images in the mind. But when there is not that state of stillness, then the process that we ordinarily call thinking takes place, and then the images, instead of being

fresh and spontaneous, are simply the revival of
previous impressions. It is mainly due to language that we go through this complicated process of reviving and combining old impressions
rather than receiving direct impressions.

In order to understand the difficulty of our
problem in coming to creative thinking, we have
to see something about the rôle that language
plays. It is, to some extent, quite indispensable, but also the main obstacle to the state
of creative thinking arising in us. Words are
formed in the registering part of the mind by
the association of impressions and a certain
mechanism that forms these associations, called by Gurdjieff the 'formatory apparatus',
which should keep them in reserve, not con-
taminating the screen until called for by an
act of choice or an act of attention. If we
could work in that way, then we would have the
spontaneous arising of images in the mind and
be able to bring them into verbal form *after*
the images themselves have been brought into
focus and have given us the fresh contact with
some portion of reality that we were looking for.

But we do not work that way; we have become
habituated in fact to working very differently.
There is never, or very seldom, a state of stillness, there is a constant interaction between
the impressions that are coming in from the outside and the impressions that have previously
been registered in the apparatus. And then what
happens is that instead of having fresh impressions, we simply have the arousing of already existing images which usually takes the form of
what is called an inner conversation, so that

words interfere all the time. This habit of in-
terposing words and images equivalent to words
is so strongly ingrained that some people have
even thought that it is impossible to think without words or without images of that kind.

Thinking with words cannot be creative thinking because words only give us the contact with
what is *already there* in our minds. No word can
ever contain anything new or express anything
new unless that something new is added on to it;
and that very seldom occurs because we very seldom have a condition in the mind where adding on
is possible. The result of this is that we are
constantly and all the time re-thinking combinations of old thoughts, because we are constantly
using words with the meanings that they already
have for us, and in that there is no enrichment
of the content of our minds, only the addition
of more and more impressions and memories and
what we call facts and experiences and so on.

Now let me try and make this as clear as I can
because it is a difficult and yet quite simple
notion. Real thinking is spontaneous; that is to
say, it does not come from anything that is already present in us. But in order to have spontaneous thinking, there must not be interference from what is already present in us, which
means that there must not be interference from
words. When there are words, then there is the
other kind of thinking which Gurdjieff calls
'formating'. Whatever descriptions we give to it
you have to understand that all that we can ever
do when we use words is to make combinations of
what is already there. If anything new is to come
it has to be outside of words or outside of any

22

fixed symbols or images that are equivalent to
words.

So we can put it in another way: there is verbal thinking and non-verbal thinking, and it is
the non-verbal thinking that we are after. But
this non-verbal thinking is very hard to recognize, chiefly because we have this very strong
habit of verbal thinking but, more fundamentally, because of the inability of most people to
bring their inner sensitive screen to the state
of empty receptiveness, unencombered by words.

Now you may ask: if real thinking is non-
verbal, what is it then that happens? What are
non-verbal thoughts? If you can answer this
question, or rather if you can see the answer
to this question, then you are half-way home in
this search for creative thinking, and I do not
expect you to find the answer so easily. The
first thing is to understand the distinction I
am trying to express to you. This in itself is
hard enough, and I suspect that if you begin
to ask yourself questions about this, you will
see that the whole time you remain in words,
and if words stop, then everything seems to
stop.

But let us suppose that you do manage to stop
verbal activity in your mind. This is not really so difficult. What you will then find is
that images begin to appear on this screen; for
some people just visual images, pictures like
in dreams. With other people, who do not have a
strong visual activity, there will be other
kinds of representations which will attract
their attention. This is still not the spontaneous thinking that we are looking for, though

it is a stage towards spontaneity that we have
to learn how to reach. If you set yourself for a
minute or two to keep your mind free from words,
just observe what comes into your mind in the
way of images of various sorts. And again, do
not allow yourself to associate any words with
those images. A further step will be to stop the
images altogether from coming into your mind,
and then it begins to be really difficult. Therefore we have to ask ourselves the question: why
is it so difficult to produce this state, which
is really normal for man, where this sensitive
place in ourselves is free from any verbal activity and free from any kind of pictures or images?

This I am going to speak about during the second half of this lesson today. I am going to
stop here for a little time, because what I have
been saying up to now is very important and I do
not want you to let it pass with only half an
idea of what I am talking about. If any of you
cannot follow this or cannot recognize what I
have been saying, will you speak about it now,
and then we shall come back to the next stage,
that is to answering the question.

QUESTIONS

Q.: Is it the same as a completely blank mind
where you see nothing, hear nothing, no words
come ... ?

J. G. B.: How does it come, how does the completely blank mind arise, appear in you?

24

Q.: It takes a moment or two, it is not really
black it is just blank. It doesn't last very
long.

J. G. B.: How long do you keep yourself in
that state, what do you mean by not very long?

Q.: I have never timed it, but I should be
very surprised if it were more than a minute
and a half.

J. G. B.: So would I. Why have you tried this?

Q.: It started ages ago, when we were reading
a book by Huxley, *Grey Eminence*, when I was
fifteen.

J. G. B.: Can you say how you set about this?

Q.: Well, I just stopped talking to myself and
stopped things coming in ... and then there was
a blank. I think I used to build up with a certain amount of tension with it, but not nowadays. Then I had to stop this thinking. Sometimes I was absolutely sweating with the effort
but now it is not like that.

J. G. B.: Now you have to be careful about
this because you produced a partial change that
is on the way to what is required, but at the
same time you have done it negatively, that is,
simply by exclusion, and now you have to learn
how to do it without this shutting out of everything. The awkwardness about some of these practices that are recommended by eminent people is

25

that they do not always take into account what
will happen if people do them ...

Q.: Oh, it is not recommended, it was a novel.

J. G. B.: Yes, I remember it. It was when
Huxley was coming to Ouspensky's lectures. A lot
of that novel was very much influenced by
Ouspensky. Ouspensky was very keen at the time
on this stopping thought, and Huxley and Gerald
Heard practiced it for a year or two. In stopping inner conversations, stopping the images
coming into the mind, it really only produces a
kind of build up of this energy, which then after a certain time you have to let go and the
normal thought activity begins again. But it
does not open the door to spontaneity unless
you know what to do beyond this. I am glad you
have spoken about this because I think I will
be able to show you what to do in order to make
this productive.

Q.: Before going to sleep it happens sometimes
that I have some kind of pictures which emerge
from a background of whirling clouds or something. This is when there is no inner talking.

J. G. B.: The difference between this and day-
dreaming is that you are stopping inner conversations, and in this case the day-dreaming becomes more like the sort which you have at night.

Q.: I wonder if it is really possible to free
oneself from images and words entirely?

J. G. B.: P. told us that she has practiced this and finds that she can for a time. I am sure it is possible that she does come to a state where there is simply a cessation of thinking and a cessation of images also. I am sure it is possible, because I know I can produce that in myself. The only thing that you must understand is that this, by itself, does not produce what is wanted. You can, with practice, also bring yourself into a state where you are simply aware of this inner sensitiveness, when nothing disturbs it and you are not aware of outside sounds and sights. If you can cut yourself off from impressions coming from outside as far as this sensitivity is concerned, they all remain on a reflex level. It does not mean that sensations cease, but you cease to be aware of them.

Q.: Is relaxation necessary?

J. G. B.: It is not just a question of relaxation. I shall come to the necessary conditions later.

Q.: Can this spontaneity also arise in physical action, for example, driving a car in a difficult situation where you do something new or different?

J. G. B.: Yes, this moment that you speak of here does correspond to the authentic process that we are looking for. The moment in which you see *how* and not only just see *what*. This happens with the motor functions when there is a certain

pressure for the acquisition of a greater skill
in doing something; for example some kind of
pressure from the feelings, or pressure from
time, or pressure from danger; sometimes it will
happen in one moment that one sees what has to
be done. But it is only relevant here in helping
you and any other people who can recognize what
you are talking about to see the difference between being able to do something better because
you see, at that moment, a different way of doing
it. It is unverbalised, and as far as the motor
functions are concerned, it is quite unnecessary
to tell ourselves what we are doing. But our
motor skills are registered in the same way as
impressions associated with words and so on;
there are also different parts of the brain
which serve to register all kinds of motor functions. As far as registration is concerned,
there is no particular difference; for we simply
call upon habitual functioning - whether it is
in the motor, or thinking, or even in our emotions and feelings.

We may think that we have some spontaneous
feelings, but in fact no one ever - or very seldom - has spontaneous feelings. Nearly everything we feel is simply a recall of something we
already felt before, which simply attaches more
or less to that particular situation. When there
is real spontaneity in the feelings, it is something quite extraordinary, and one at once recognizes it as extraordinary. One can have very
strong feelings but there is nothing spontaneous
or new about them, they are simply the repetition of feelings we have had before, with simply

a bit more energy flowing through them. The actual form of the emotions is already there and the
form of the movement is already there.

Just occasionally it happens that something
changes and then we have the kind of experience
you describe: we see a way of doing and we realize a new skill has come into that particular
thing. That is how it is with moving processes.
With emotions, they are recognizable by the
sense of astonishment and surprise which accompanies any spontaneous emotion. When we realize how seldom we have this astonishment at what
we are feeling, we should realise how little
spontaneity there is in any part of our lives.

Q.: I was wondering how we could really think
without bringing anything of the emotions or
feelings into it, because it seems to me that
for this spontaneity which you advise something
has to go on in the subconscious because of this
need or urge either for a solution or some kind
of answer.

J. G. B.: You are speaking now about how all
this can happen. Before we speak about that, I
want to make sure you recognize what it is we
are talking about. Do you all feel now that you
recognize the difference between thinking with
the forms of thought that are already there
mainly words and ideas connected with words –
and the other, which has associated with it the
quality of astonishment when we experience it,
and a sure conviction of seeing something new
and in a new way? What you probably do not easily realize is that when this does happen, it

29

happens without words - if words come in, they
come in perhaps so quickly that we do not notice that the moment of seeing did not depend
upon words or images.

How to do something about it? Now to speak of
the conditions that make it possible. Someone
asked whether, for this tranquil state of the
mind, relaxation was desirable, and somebody
else said that it seems that there has to be
some emotional urge, or need to produce this.
The truth is that the different functions, or
centres, are linked in such a way that we cannot have one kind of state in one of the centres, or functions, and a totally different
kind of state in another. For example, if we
are making movements, or if we are in some posture which is habitual to us, that is to say,
which corresponds to past experiences that have
already been registered or fixed in us, then it
will be very difficult to be in a state of spontaneity or quietness of the mind. This is where
people make a mistake that prevents them thinking spontaneously, and they make it over and
over again; that is, when they wish to think
about something, they make themselves comfortable and sit in a chair, let us say, and begin
to think about some problem that they wish to
understand. But the very way in which they are
sitting and holding their body is habitual, and
in this habitual bodily posture it is almost impossible to do anything but think habitual
thoughts. If your moving centre is occupied with
some activity which demands a certain amount of
attention, then it is easier to free the mind
from its influence. That is why many people find

that they are able to think better when they go
for a long walk, for example. But this is not
always possible and it may take a long time to
find oneself in a state where one's thinking has
become free. If you have to think about some problem while you are in your own room, then the
great thing to avoid is to settle down in some
comfortable posture that is habitual to you.
This does not mean that relaxation is not good,
but the relaxation must be of an active and not
a passive kind. If you relax passively, then
your body will enter into its habitual associations, many of which are unnoticed, or nearly
unnoticed, or nearly all of which are unnoticed,
and connected with them there will also be habits
of thought, particularly habits of verbal thought.
   It is also true about the feelings. This is the
reason why people find that when they particularly want to think about something, they cannot,
because as soon as the feelings become engaged
in the process through wanting something, there
are always liable to come habitual states of anxiety or tension, or haste, or even - what appears to be very necessary - an interest, concern in what one is doing. But whether the emotional state is a negative one - such as a state
of anxiety or fear that one may not be able to
do what is required - or whether it is simply
interest or excitement and concern in what one
is doing, all of this is nearly certain to be
habitual. And because the emotional state is a
habitual one, it will engender also habitual
activities in the thinking apparatus, and therefore, for this reason it is necessary to try to
find how one can produce feeling states that are

not habitual in oneself.

The main thing to be understood about this psychological investigation of creative thinking is the need to free the instrument of thinking which has to be set free from the habitual influences of the thinking apparatus itself and the instinctive and moving processes and of the body from habitual emotional states. Creative thinking sometimes arises in states of despair, when one is on the point of giving up, when there is exhaustion of the habitual emotional reaction. With that exhaustion the pressure of the habitual emotional states is diminished and the mind becomes for a moment free. Often, in that moment of freedom, the necessary spontaneous vision arises in the mind.

I want you to understand the various ways in which we can interfere in this state in which the mind can have spontaneously arising images. Coming right back to the sensitive place in the mind itself, you have to realise that if you try to produce a state of vacuity, or emptiness by force, then you will come just to a state of blankness, as P. described. But you must understand that this blankness is really produced by the fact that you are using pressure in the mind in order to hold back the thinking and the image-building.

What is required can be got in a simpler way than that. It can happen, of course, that people discover for themselves various conditions that make it easy for them to return to this state of inner quiet. There are special techniques that are taught in schools in the East, various sorts of mental exercises, the repetition of

phrases or mantrams, as they are called, but
there are also the production of various physical sensations. For example, if I remember rightly, it is said that Wagner found that music
could only compose itself for him if he was
stroking velvet. This always seems to people a
sort of exaggerated, almost unseemly kind of behaviour, but in reality it corresponds with the
practice of many people who have found a way to
make a link between physical sensations and a
state of receptiveness in the mind.

There are various postures that are good for
this purpose - I am not recommending this any
more than I am recommending you to invest in
velvet cloth - especially the well-known posture with the crossed legs that is used by
people for meditation in the East. This posture
proves, when you are able to take it without
discomfort and without strain, singularly favourable for producing that state of peace of
mind. This I have verified for myself. There is
unquestionably a close linkage between the postures, movements and states of the body, of the
physical sensations, of sight, hearing, touch
and so on, and the condition of this inner sensitive place where spontaneous thinking can
arise. With some people music is conducive to
spontaneous thinking, with others it is an obstacle and just occupies the mind in such a way
that they are not able to think freely. Therefore, if one were to use any methods of this
kind, they would all have to be specially
studied for each individual to discover for himself what is most favourable for him.

But really the best and simplest method of

doing it is by a combination. If one, to a certain extent, takes the body out of its habitual
postures - for example by sitting a little differently from what one is accustomed to or by
holding one's hands in a slightly different way
from what is habitual for us - then this is sufficient to reduce the interference of the bodily
posture to quite a great extent. If one finds
that this does not work, then it is necessary to
exercise the body by some energetic physical
work which will relieve and remove physical ten-
sions in the body which one has not been able to
notice. But it is no use simply relaxing in
order to bring oneself into a passive and relaxed state, for this will only produce a condition
of day-dreaming. The body must be held in such a
position that a certain alertness is maintained.

All I want to say at this stage is that it is
then possible to allow the mind to quieten down,
to still itself without attempting to force
thoughts out of the mind or forcibly to stop inner talking. By keeping oneself in such a posture and keeping a degree of attention upon the
particular theme in connection with which one
wishes to have some spontaneous thoughts, then
usually the mind will quieten down.

I would like you to practise this a little bit
by seeing if you can understand what is meant by
saying that *true thinking is spontaneous*. If you
can see this, as I said earlier this evening,
you are already half way towards understanding
the problem, and therefore it is well worthwhile
setting yourself to see what this means. At the
moment when you hear it, you hear it in words

and you will think about it in words, and this
will not get you anywhere. What you have to try
to achieve is where you see at least something
which cannot be expressed in words. You do this
every day for a little time - it is no use doing it for more than three minutes - by selecting a time where you will not be disturbed for
say five minutes. You put yourself into some
posture which is deliberately taken as out of
the ordinary habits and then set this theme before your mind. Certainly do not talk to yourself about it, but do not *forcibly* drive out
words, because this will only produce a state
of blankness, where you will not be able to
make a step. What there has to be here is a
very sincere wish that your mind will become
quiet. The wish for a quiet mind is - I am
afraid for most people - quite an unusual emotion, and therefore you can safely adopt this
as likely to be free from interference from
habits.

When you begin to see what it can give you,
you will wish this very much. Do not worry at
all if it does not give any results at first.
If something interesting and relevant does come
into your mind, then really you have to take a
firm hold on yourself not to begin expressing
it in words. That is really quite a hard act of
self-denial in oneself. You must not only resist the temptation to express it in words but
especially resist rehearsing the way you will
talk about it to somebody else and tell them
what a wonderful thought you had. That must be
avoided like the plague!

Q.: Even if we know you are going to ask us?

J. G. B.: I will not ask you ... just as I have not asked anyone to tell me about Cyprus! I will certainly not expect you to produce results here round the table. It would be fatal for what we are trying to do. Whatever you see must, as far as possible, be kept as your own momentary vision, not to be brought into verbal form or any kind of expression. And if nothing whatever comes, do not worry at all, because at this stage of the proceedings, what I am really wanting for you is that you should begin to catch the technique of getting your mind quiet without forcing it. We have four more lessons before we finish this course and later on I will be able to tell you what to do when something does happen.

Q.: I am interested in this feeling state in trying to get to the receptive stage, because I can recognize what you mean in saying that the feelings get too involved in wanting to get an answer, not giving us a chance, including enthusiasm in the ordinary sense, which might be a more positive sort of feeling - at the same time it is not a non-feeling state although I feel totally inadequate to say anything about this.

J. G. B.: Yes, there is something that could be called elation, which is certainly different from excitement. If you really know what a state of elation is, then you know it is not habitual. Actually the state of elation is the state one has when one is not in the grip of a habit, and

therefore if you are elated, you know that is
right - but you must know what elation really
is.

Q.: How does this fall in place with represen-
tation? Someone experiences something and simultaneously achieves this state usefully, without it necessarily being in retrospect ... ?

J. G. B.: What we have to learn is to keep
separate the moment of vision and the connection of this with what we already know, which
can be said to express it in words or communi-
cable images. To hold those two steps apart even
for a short time, is the only way in which we
can really preserve the quality of what we have
seen, otherwise we tend to lose it, and it is
only on special occasions that something really valuable can be made of it. Holding back
from putting it into any form is the important
thing here. This does not only apply of course
to mental work or to images that can be put
into word form. Supposing that in the work of
an artist he sees something and without any sort
of self-restraint he immediately tries to bring
it into expression, then he will lose something.
It is that moment of holding that is necessary.
Here I am not very concerned about that part of
it, I am really only concerned that you should
practise taking this notion that true thinking
is spontaneous, to see whether you can come to
the point where you really see that this is
true. You may think it is obvious, but believe
me, when you see it you will see it is not at

37

all obvious.

THE LEVELS OF ENERGIES

IN THE LAST TALK I spoke of the sensitive receptor in ourselves where images are formed which constitute what we ordinarily call the 'stream of consciousness', or the stream of awareness. I also said that there are two different origins for the material which appears on this screen. One is already stored impressions and the other is from images which come to it spontaneously. Now, I want to go more deeply into this and show you what I believe to be the basic structure of all the various activities that we have in life.

This can be represented in a very simple way if we consider the different streams of activity which are going on at the same time in us, rather than trying to analyse the activities themselves. One of the difficulties of understanding the way we work is that people generally try to arrive at it by studying just the instruments and not the conditions under which these instruments are used, when the conditions make more difference to the results than any other factor. For this study of creativity it is essential to keep our attention especially on the conditions of our inner working.

One of the ways we can speak of the conditions of the inner working is to look upon these conditions as different sources of supply to the activity, as different fuels or different kinds of food, that enter to nourish and sustain the activity that is going on. We shall call these different fuels or foods, *energies*. I shall have to clarify the notion of energies a little in order to explain the structure we are concerned with.

It is quite legitimate to say that everything that happens, of every possible kind, is a transformation of energy. This is true of the physical world, it is true of life, it is true also of our mental processes and it is probably true of these higher levels of existence that we do not know, perhaps shall never know, anything about. If transformations of energy are present in everything that goes on, then, to understand about energies is something that is going to help us to follow the processes and to see how they can be controlled.

There are the material energies connected with material transformation. Energies like motion, heat, electricity and so on. There are also energies connected with matter that we know about like the energy of the nucleus, or atomic energy as it is sometimes called; there are energies connected with surfaces and there are also energies arising from these surface energies by which everything is held together. Now those energies all fall outside of our experience; they are unconscious, or at any rate they are unconscious in

THE LEVELS OF ENERGIES

any sense in which we can understand the word
consciousness.

Rising out of these energies and probably capable of being produced from them even, are the
energies of life. It seems very probable that
all the energies upon which our life activity
depends have been produced from these first kind
of energies, that is, the material energies. In
order to produce them, a special sort of apparatus is necessary, and the only kind of apparatus
of this sort that we know at all well is the
living organism. There may be others, and maybe
man, in making transformations of energy, produces the same energies as those of life, but he
does not seem to recognize what he is doing or
know how to use these energies.

I am saying this because I do not want to suggest that the energies of life are something
totally different from the material energies,
but they have one important distinction, and
that is, as soon as we reach the energies of
life, we do also reach the threshold of consciousness or of experience. It is not yet possible to prove this, but it seems very likely
that every kind of life is associated with some
sort of experience. We have no doubt that there
is experience present in animals, even quite
primitive animals. It seems quite sure that
there is experience present in insects, perhaps
in forms of life that are extremely simple.
Also there is a certain kind of experience present in our own bodies which is too diffuse,
too vague, to enter into our ordinary awareness
but which we can recognize from general states
of the organism, such as states of well-being

41

or states of lethargy; when we say we have, or
we lack, vitality. It even seems likely that
this kind of energy, which we call vitality, can
be transmitted from one person to another, so
that we sometimes observe how a person will give
vitality to others or suck vitality from others.
All this happens without one being aware of what
is going on except as a vague well-being or
vague discomfort, according to which way these
vital energies are flowing.

I am saying all this to show you that we come
by stages towards the energies which are concerned in our conscious experience. It certainly
does not seem as if there is any abrupt change
from the material energies to the vital energies
or from the vital energies to energies that have
some kind of experience or awareness associated
with them, but rather a scale of transformations.

After this vital energy which we vaguely experience, there is certainly some kind of energy
that works in the nervous system of the higher
animals, and of course in man also, by which all
our automatic functioning is maintained. This energy has a certain power of keeping connections,
of doing more than just make the apparatus work,
for it also takes a direct part in the working
or the regulation of it. This kind of energy
seems to have a certain power of storing the results of past actions and is therefore able to
learn and be trained. This is the first one of
the energies which concerns us in our search for
an understanding of creativity. I call it by the
word *automatic* because it is the energy by which
all our automatic functioning is maintained.

In our bodies, all the time, there is an

enormously complicated working of the automatic
activities. The simplest action requires coordination of millions of nervous discharges.
Just to see an object like a piece of chalk en-
tails an almost incredibly complicated work:
collecting together the impressions that reach
us in our eyes, transferring them through the
various mechanisms of the optic nerve and building out of them a visual image, and then connecting that visual image with past visual
images so that we recognize the particular visual image we see, not merely as a lump of matter, but as a piece of white matter and as a
piece of chalk. All of that is achieved without our being aware of it at all - at the most
we are aware of the final result which enables
us to recognize that we have a piece of chalk
or a glass, or an ashtray in front of us. The
important thing is that all this complicated
work is done without our being aware of it until
it reaches the end-product, which may be a sensation, or perhaps an idea, or maybe a feeling.
What happens when this enters as a visual image or a thought? It is then that we come to
what we talked about previously ; that is, the
sensitive screen, which is itself made of another kind of energy which I am going to call
the *sensitive energy,* because that is its main
characteristic. The sensitive energy is the
carrier of our ordinary awareness. When this
sensitive energy is stimulated, or set in motion
we become aware of whatever happens to touch it,
such as a visual image. If the visual images,
or other sense-impressions do not come in contact with the sensitive energy, we are not aware

43

of them. All the time, as we are sitting here,
various sensory impressions are entering us,
through our eyes, ears, through the skin,
through all the tactile nerves of the surface of
the body - feelings of warmth, pressure and so
on - and we are only aware of a minute fraction
of all of these, only that fraction which is
actually coming in contact with our sensitive
energy. But, as I have said at our earlier lectures, this sensitivity is not the true consciousness of man because it does not make him aware
of himself.

There is another energy which does have that
property of making a man conscious of himself as
well as of what is going on round him, of what
appears on this sensitive screen. If you look
at that analogy of the sensitive screen, you will
see that it is not sufficient that images should
be thrown on the screen, it is necessary also
that there should be someone looking at the images, and the looking-at-the-images, comes from
the next kind of energy, the *conscious energy*.

The range from sensitivity to consciousness,
which can be put as the horizontal arm of the
tetrad for all human activities, represents what
we ordinarily call our conscious experience, or
consciousness. This conscious experience has two
parts; one part is the sensitivity and the other
part the consciousness. People do not usually
distinguish between these two, for the reason
that in the ordinary state of man, consciousness
is absorbed into the sensitivity and there is no
standing apart one from the other.

So we can say that in the ordinary way man can
be aware of what is going on, but he is not con-

scious of being aware of what is going on. Sometimes he does involuntarily separate the two and then he is aware that there is something else in him from the experience going on in his sensitivity.

We use, strangely enough, the word self-consciousness in two different senses, both of which are quite right, and the difference between them is that one is voluntary and the other involuntary. Involuntary self-consciousness is the state of embarrassment we feel when we are aware that our sensitivity is out of our own control; that is, when our behaviour continues to produce images on our sensitivity without our being able to control them. Then we feel awkward, and very often this produces various physiological changes in the body, such as blushing. That kind of self-consciousness is quite a genuine separation between the conscious and the sensitive energies, and we are aware in that state that there is something in us which is sensitive and something that is conscious of our sensitivity. But this condition does not lead us very far, because when that arises, there is no control over the situation, in fact it really is an awareness of our inability to control what is going on at the sensitive level.

But it is also possible for us to have an intentional separation between consciousness and sensitivity. Then that produces a state of real consciousness of self - we are able to stand apart and observe what is going on in the sensitivity, and then even have a possibility of directing and controlling it. But the important thing at this moment is to see whether you really

can recognize that there are two distinct states
in us which are sometimes merged and sometimes
separated: one a state of sensitiveness and the
other a state of consciousness. And also whether
you can recognize that for nearly all the time
our consciousness is simply carried along by our
sensitivity and there is no inner detachment or
observation of what is going on. The merging of
consciousness and sensitivity produces a state
in which there is no power to alter what is happening and in that case we are largely under the
control of the automatism; that is, of the automatic working of the nervous system.

Now supposing that we want to understand some
problem. This problem may be presented to us
from outside by somebody speaking to us, in
which case it reaches us through the senses, or
it may arise from our own memories of the past,
or by a combination of the two. In any case it
comes into our awareness by the path that leads
from this automatism to the sensitivity, because
the automatism is connected to the outside world
through the senses. What I am saying now enters
your awareness through your automatism of hearing, mixed with associations of other impressions and memories. The automatism is like the
counter from which we go and buy everything that
we need, where you can get both what comes from
outside and also what is stored in the shop.

When a problem has been presented to our
sensitivity, then we either accept or reject it;
it either interests us and we wish to find an
answer, or it does not interest us and our sensitivity fails to respond to it, and other impressions and other ideas drive it out. But supposing

that this problem arouses in us some reaction of
interest, or desire to find an answer to it. What
usually happens then is that the problem remains
as a series of mental images on the screen of the
sensitivity, which then recalls from the automatism various impressions of the past. It may do
so without being aware of it, because there are
automatic ways of thinking to which we have been
so habituated that we call on them without even
noticing it; or we may recall particular facts,
as we call them, or events, or else we seek for
information from outside by reading, by studying,
by asking questions, and by observing the situation. In other words, we may try to solve this
problem with the help of material that we can
call on through our automatism. Some problems can
be solved quite adequately just by this means a-
lone. In fact, most problems that arise for us
from day to day, are of a kind that can be solved
just with the help of our past experience and our
knowledge of what is going on around us. When the
problem is thrown up from our sensitivity of providing food for ourselves because we are hungry,
the thought that it is now time for a meal enters
the sensitivity and the problem is solved because
we know where to go for a meal, at what time, and
how to set about it. But of course, from time to
time, problems arise that cannot be solved in
this way. Then it becomes necessary to make connections that the sensitivity is not able to make;
that is, the ready-made material is, as it were,
scanned by the sensitivity, fails to provide us
with the solution to the problem. It may be
necessary to see new connections that we have
never seen before. This can only happen if there

47

is a separation between sensitivity and consciousness. And it happens because the consciousness has certain properties and powers
that the sensitivity lacks.

The nature of the sensitive energy is such
that it works entirely on the stop-go, yes-no
mechanism. If something is presented to it, it
can be interested or not interested and if it
is interested it accepts, if it is not interested, it rejects. It is presented with possible
solutions to the problem and it can say yes or
no - like with the problem of food: "Shall I go
to this place or that place?" It confronts this
with the amount of money I have in my pocket
and it says yes or no to it in terms of putting
one factor against another, either accepting or
rejcting. Not always in this kind of factual way
but sometimes in terms of feelings. We may want
to go to an expensive restaurant, and yet we
cannot afford it, but between the 'I want' and
the 'I can' there is just again a kind of direct
yes or no, and one or the other will prevail.
You must understand that a very great part of
our lives is spent just with this 'yes-no',
'start-stop' working of the sensitive energy. It
has scarcely any power beyond comparing things
in twos; pairs of ideas, pairs of feelings, likes
and dislikes and so on. In other words, it is
dualistic in its working.

Consciousness has a much greater connecting or
integrating power. When the conscious energy is
really liberated from the stream of awareness,
it is able to see many things of real importance
according to the degree of freedom which is achieved. In order to see, you must stand away,

48

otherwise you will not see the wood for the trees. That not seeing the wood for the trees is really characteristic of the sensitive energy, whereas seeing the whole, the wood, is characteristic of the conscious energy. There are problems which are intractable on the level of sensitivity, which can be solved on the level of consciousness. In this state they are not solved by bringing in anything which was not there before, but by seeing connections, and meaning, and significance, that we did not see before.

When we have that kind of experience of seeing what we did not see a moment ago, a kind of opening of the inner eye of the understanding, then this is the sign of the working of consciousness. For this to happen, we must either have a bit of luck through the consciousness liberating itself long enough to produce this condition of integrating the awareness, or we have to know how, by some technical way, to bring ourselves into a state where we can stand aside from the problem. A great deal of that is connected with what I spoke about last time; quietening the mind, allowing the images that arise in the sensitivity to settle down. But these methods can only produce for a short time a state of detached consciousness. It can be produced for a much longer time, also with a greater intensity, through various harsher practices which can, paralyse the working of the sensitive energy. Such a paralysis can of course be produced by drugs and in various conditions of narcosis there is an enormous increase in the field of vision, inwardly and outwardly, together with a sense of integration, of seeing things as a whole, and especially of seeing meanings and significance in everything. The narcotic breaks the link between consciousness and sensitivity by suppressing the sensitivity. The interesting part about these narcotics is that they very seldom have any real objective value, but it illustrates a property of the conscious energy: that in itself it is not a contact with things as they really are; it is really a deeper contact with oneself that makes things matter to one in a much sharper and intense way. For it so often happens that when we have such a momentary liberation of consciousness - whether in transition between sleep and wakening, with the action of a narcotic or in states of fever - we have the conviction that we see things that are of cosmic importance, truths that are ultimately real, then, if by chance we write them down, we afterwards find them to be nonsense, or something quite impossible to interpret. It is confirmed by all the studies that have been made of these artificially induced conditions - because it shows why these conditions are not really a help to creative thinking, although people sometimes have hoped that they would be.

In order to see how it is possible for something of a different kind to enter, we have to go beyond these levels of conscious and sensitive experience and understand that there is in man another level, a fourth kind of energy, which I shall call simply *creative energy*, because what we observe of the working of creativity must be ascribed to something which cannot be accounted for on the level of our conscious experience, even the artificially intensified conscious experiences that are produced by drugs or special kinds of practices.

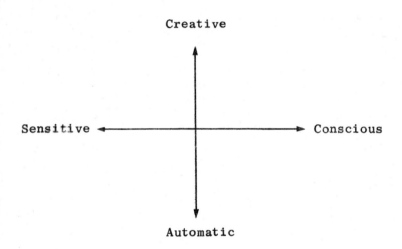

ENERGY TETRAD

The creative energy is at the opposite pole from the automatic in the structure of the working of man's mind. Its chief characteristic is that it unites directly with things as they are instead of having to pass through some kind of transmission mechanism. Another characteristic, almost as important as this one of direct contact, is the synthetic, or unifying action of the creative energy whenever it comes into play. A third characteristic of the creative energy and

perhaps the most surprising one, is that it is
not conscious, it is really beyond consciousness.
This is surprising because it seems that the more
conscious an experience is, the more the element
of integration and creativity can enter into it,
but I have satisfied myself that this fourth energy really belongs to a supra-conscious level in
the working of man. This is by no means a new
idea, it is an idea that has always been held,
particularly in Hindu psychology, where it is always taught that the unitive energy by which man
comes in contact with reality is reached only in
a state of complete unconsciousness as far as the
ordinary functions are concerned; the state that
is called Turiya. There is also a phrase which is
used in Western tradition; that is, the 'Black
Light'. Black Light is used to describe figurati-
vely a consciousness which is beyond consciousness, a light which is not seen as light.
   Sometimes people think that this fourth state
of consciousness is really so brilliant a state
of consciousness that it blinds us, as in the
Republic of Plato, where he compares the ordinary state of people to men in a cave chained with
their backs to the opening and looking at shadows
thrown on the wall (which corresponds no doubt to
this sensitivity which we have been speaking about earlier) and he says that if somebody were
forcibly taken away from the cave and brought into the sunlight, he would only suffer, his eyes
would pain and he would wish to be brought back
into the darkness because he could see nothing in
the light of the sun. That supposition that this
fourth state of consciousness, or fourth state,

is really a higher state of consciousness to
which we are not yet accustomed, may or may not
be right, but we have to remember that we live
the whole time on this central line between
sensitivity and consciousness, and chiefly just
in the state where consciousness is merged into
sensitivity, when there is no awareness of anything else than just the images passing on the
wall of the cave, or the sensitivity.

So far I have spoken about three characteristics that we associate with the creative energy: the first is that this creative energy
is a direct contact and not an indirect one,
which in Plato's simile is the difference in
seeing the shadows thrown on the wall and seeing things in direct sunlight. The second characteristic is that it is synthetic or unitive.
Whenever it works in man, it produces a syn-
thesis of his experience; things which were
separate come together. The third characteristic
is that it is beyond consciousness or supra-
conscious. That last characteristic is certainly experimentally true, for when anything
enters us from this higher source, it appears
as if it came from nowhere. It just has that
quality of spontaneity about which I was speaking.

You may remember that I said that if we practise quietening the mind, the first thing to
happen is that the mind is filled with a stream
of thoughts, chiefly in the form of words,
verbal mental associations, a kind of inner
conversation, and at the most, accompanied with
certain images of what has been or is going on
around us. That is the ordinary state of the
sensitivity. If we succeed in quietening that,

than images of a different kind enter the mind,
with much higher significance, that enable us to
understand things that we could not notice or
understand at all before. That is when the consciousness is working. It is very difficult to
go beyond this, but if one can come to a state
of real stillness and there is a genuine problem to be solved, then the solution of this problem can of itself appear upon the screen of the
sensitivity.

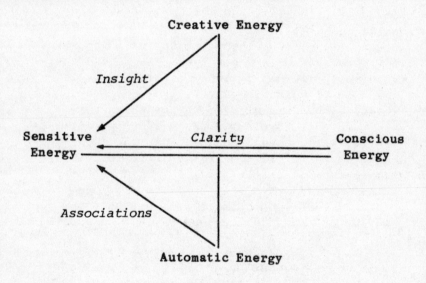

INTERCONNECTION OF ENERGIES

The first associative state corresponds to a
link between automatism and sensitivity; the

second state, of clear understanding, corresponds to the working of consciousness on sensitivity, and the third, the creative state, to the creative energy acting in the sensitivity. Only when the sensitivity has really been brought to a state where it is not cluttered up with the sensations and associations that arise from the automatic level, subconscious or unconscous, and when it is also freed from the integrative action arising from our own consciousness is it able to receive impressions of a quite different kind that do not come from us at all, but appear as if they were flashes of unaccountable inspiration. The important thing about these flashes of inspiration is that they bring in elements that are not provided by the material we have at hand for dealing with the problem. Sometimes they provide a missing link without which the problem could not be solved, and this explains why it is that so long as we are looking for the answer to a problem in what we know, there is no chance of solving it; something has to enter that we did not and could not know.

All the great scientific discoveries have an element of this kind in them, and the same is not only true of the scientific activity but of the creative activity in art and in the affairs of life.

Now the question is whether there is also a connection to be made on the right-hand side of this diagram; for example, between the creative energy and the consciousness. Here it seems as if this is connected with confidence, with the conviction, in front of an impossible situation, that there is a way out of it. Or even confidence

in the more ordinary sense, that is, that which
keeps us in our search for a solution of our
problems even though there is nothing to tell us
that we shall find that solution.

It is as if there were in us something that is
already in contact with the goal towards which
we are striving and so long as we do not lose
our connection with that, we shall not lose
heart, we shall continue to strive. Yet another
way of looking at this connection on this side
is that it does give a certain flair or intuition, as it is sometimes called, for what should
be done in front of a situation with a problem.
Very often great scientists have what people
call an uncanny insight into the experiment that
should be made, or the line of investigation to
be pursued in order to find the answer. Whereas
it would be almost impossible to arrive at the
answer by plodding away, trying out all possible
or all logically sensible ways of solving the
problem, these men manage to see what is really
needed and try something that would not occur to
anyone else. They find what is necessary for
solving the problem in a way that seems really
unfair to the others who perhaps have more knowledge, better techniques, and so on, but just do
not happen to have this in their power. I am
sure that plenty of instances of this kind will
occur to you if you studied the lives of great
men in any field. It seems as if that which
characterizes a great man is that this connection is stronger in him than it is in ordinary
people.

The remaining connection between the consciousness and the automatism is also important for

our understanding. This connection gives the
disciplined working that is one of the elements
in all successful activities. It is this that
provides the necessary information and also
keeps the body itself occupied with what is necessary for the solution of the problem instead
of losing touch with it. Where this is particularly well developed, many problems can be solved and unnecessary difficulties avoided, just
because the consciousness can see connections
in the store; that is, in the subconscious or
automatic levels, that would be missed by the
sensitivity. This can also be seen, I think, in
the form of skills, though I am not quite sure
where one can put this. What really matters as
regards this connection is that there has to be
a certain self-directed regulation of the automatism, that we call discipline.

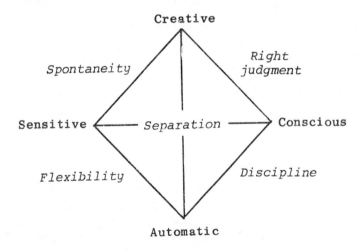

OPERATION OF ENERGIES

CREATIVE THINKING

On the left-hand side, where the connection
goes between the automatism and the sensitivity,
there is also something to be done, but of a
different kind. Our sensitivity is not something
that is just given once and for all in the way
that a cinematograph screen is given, where you
just vary the images that are thrown on it, but
not the quality of the screen itself. Our sensitivity is much more highly organized. I think I
mentioned that at the end of the last lecture,
when I said that it is sometimes taken that the
sensitivity is just like a clean slate on which
nature writes, whereas the work of modern psycholo-
gists of children, such as that of Piaget, have
shown how very much more the sensitivity co-
operates in the formation of the mental images
and the development of the automatisms than is
implied in the 'clean slate' picture of it. In
fact, our sensitivity is like a body within the
body. That is why this sensitivity is sometimes
even called a second body (the 'astral body')
to indicate that it can have an organization
which is so complete that it is capable of an
independent existence. I am quite sure that
there is a lot of truth in this view that the
sensitivity itself can be organized to become
an independent body, but that is hard to demonstrate. What is quite easy to demonstrate is
that our sensitivity is capable of being trained
and organized, and that our effectiveness, in
any kind of work we have to do, is very much
influenced by the organization and receptiveness
of this sensitive level of our working.
It is quite a different sort of training from
the training that is suitable for bringing up

58

the automatic powers. We can train the automatism
by repetition, by pressure of attention, by suf-
fering and so on, to certain kinds of skills.
All of this really is of the same category as
Pavlov's conditioning of reflexes, and that is
really all you get on the right-hand side. But
on the left-hand side it is something quite different, if this is brought about on the level of
the sensitivity. If the sensitivity is trained,
it has to be trained by the consciousness. This
cannot be attained by just conditioning, and it
is really attained by the very reverse: by de-
conditioning, by setting the sensitivity free
of the habitual reactions from the automatism.
This is very important for understanding all
processes of training and learning. Because we
do not keep these different parts of the human
totality clearly separated in our actions with
children and with ourselves in our own training,
we can produce quite lamentable results; we can
even condition the sensitivity so that it becomes almost incapable of receiving new impressions or responding to anything new, and it will
lose contact not only with creativity but even
with our own consciousness.

What is required is that all conditioning and
training should be transferred directly to the
automatism. This cannot work in any other way,
and it requires to be conditioned, but it must
be conditioned in such a way that the sensitivity is not conditioned at the same time. This is
something which I will have to speak about
during the next two or three lectures because it
is very important. Over the rest of the course I
will probably be speaking about how it is pos-

sible to bring our sensitivity towards the state
of non-conditioning, while at the same time not
losing all the powers that come from a well-
conditioned, well-trained automatism.

QUESTIONS

Q.: Does the conscious energy play a role in
visualizing something?

J. G. B.: Yes, visualizing is a projection of
images on the sensitivity from the consciousness
instead of from the automatism. If you say: "I
will see a lemon suspended in mid-air there in
front of me", and you begin not only to see a
lemon, but your mouth begins to feel the taste of
lemon, all that is produced by a projection of
the conscious energy onto the sensitive screen.
But the experience, the taste of bitterness of
the lemon and the shape and colour of it all,
that is actually experienced in the sensitive
energy.

Q.: When that comes from the automatic energy,
in the case of a lemon, is it somehow like a memory?

J. G. B.: Yes. Nothing will come from the automatism that has not come into it from the senses,
and I think it is probably true also to say that
if we are going to produce an image like this of
a lemon, and the taste of a lemon, it is something
for which we have to make use of the material that
is available in the automatism. It can be that one
can set oneself to produce some image or experience of a new kind, but that is something else.

Q.: Is there not one property of this sensitive
part which is something like the following: that

if there is some new insight, then it seems to produce a very rapid proliferation of things around it in this sensitivity, which happens extremely quickly; if one consciously can see a new connection, then very rapidly this connection is transferred to a number of other related domains. There is a danger that this becomes out of hand because it has this expansive quality.

J. G. B.: It is quite true, and it comes because of the lack of the power to hold these two apart. This is connected with the actual strength of the person concerned. A weak man can have flashes, but then it will all collapse onto the sensitive energy and will be simply experienced; there will be excitement and interest and, as you say, a proliferation of images, all sorts of connections will begin to be seen. But there is something lacking, and that is the withdrawn consciousness which is able to make judgments as to what shall be permitted and what shall not be permitted. Your having said that reminds me that when I spoke of the conscious energy I did not refer to one of its most important properties, which is that the power of judgment is associated with it.

Q.: I would like to ask a question about the separation on the horizontal plane: I found that in moments of really getting to see something. there appears to come a very strong force which acts against the separation and attracts them together ... it is difficult to bear.

J. G. B.: Quite right. Because there is a very

strong polarity between the sensitive and the conscious energies; they are really like male and female powers and they attract one another very strongly. This is really our difficulty; if we try to what is called 'remember ourselves', which means to keep separate the consciousness and the sensitivity, we see that as soon as we take our eyes off them, at once they go into a guilty embrace!

The most useful exercise you can do now is to see if you can verify for yourselves the distinction between sensitivity and consciousness. Once one is really clear and sure about this, a whole lot of things fall into place permanently and certain confusions will never again arise. One way of studying this distinction between sensitivity and consciousness is trying to stop thoughts; that is, trying to empty the mind of thoughts. That, by itself, requires that you should have this separation between awareness and consciousness of being aware. Being conscious of being aware of what is going on can arise spontaneously and involuntarily with no action on our own part. To maintain this intentionally is very difficult, but even doing it only occasionally will help you to begin to see what is meant by that separation.

ORGANIZATION OF THE SENSITIVITY

L ET US RETURN to the tetrad of energies and
see how we can translate this into practical procedures.

You may have noticed that I use the word sensitive energy, or sensitive screen, in place of
the word that is commonly used - 'mind'. Nearly
all uses of the word mind refer to the sensitive
energy. When we speak of things 'going on in the
mind', or we speak of mental images, or mental
processes, we are nearly always referring to the
condition of the sensitive energy in us. But when
we refer to mind as consciousness, then we are
being rather inaccurate in the use of language,
as consciousness is really consciousness of the
process of the images passing, as we way 'through
the mind', not just awareness of the images themselves. The trouble is that the word mind is used
in a number of ways, and because it is not used
precisely, it is sometimes even said that there
is no such thing as the mind, and that the word
does not refer to anything at all. There even is
a school of philosophy which rejects the notion
of mind as meaningless. That is probably due to

the failure to make the distinction between the two energies of consciousness and sensitivity. Attempts to describe man and his activities without some notion of mind must fail, and I

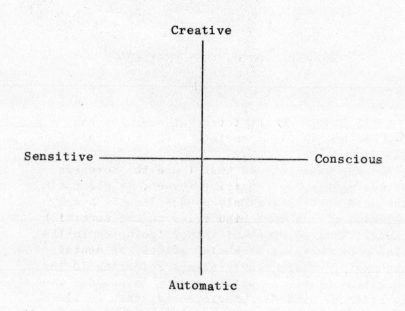

ENERGY TETRAD

think it is generally agreed that the attempts made during the past twenty-five years to exclude the mind from philosophy have really come to nothing. At the same time, those philosophers

who rejected the idea of mind had got hold of
something important, because they could see that
the conception of the mind as a being, as a person, as the man, or, as one philosopher called
it, "the little god in the mind", is all wrong,
because we are not speaking here of something
which is the person or the man himself, but simply of a part of the instrument which we use, or
is used, in the activity.

In one sense the notion of mind has got to be
expanded to include all that is shown on the
diagram. The whole of this can, in a certain way,
be called mind. But since, nearly always, it is
the sensitive energy which is being referred to,
I think it is better to use it only in that
sense. If in the course of this lecture I shall
speak about mind and mental images, it will be in
reference to the sensitivity.

The simplest practical proposal that can be
made for a better working of the energies together is that we should empty or quieten the
mind of sensitivity. I have said that one of the
secrets of thinking is to know how not to think,
or how to make the mind available to thoughts
that arise spontaneously. I suggested the exercise of first occupying your mind with a particular subject (for instance the political situation in Cyprus) and then setting yourself to
empty your mind with the subject itself somehow
in the back-ground. That was a preliminary experiment to show you how the usual processes of
automatic associations prevent us from using our
minds for constructive work, and also prevent
our minds from being used for creative work. Unless the sensitivity can be freed from automatic

associations, we can neither act on it construct-
ively from the consciousness, nor can it be acted
upon creatively from the creative source, which
is represented at the top of the diagram. This
sensitive part can play a positive role in the
creative activity, including creative thinking,
because it is capable of being organized, and its
organization will then enable it to respond to
the other three sources. I want also to speak
about the mental training which is really an
organization of the sensitivity.

There is, first of all, the training which
consists in improving our capacity for perception
working on the connection between the sensitivity
and the automatism. Unless something is done
about this, the connection tends to work only
automatically. There is no selection except the
inherent likes and dislikes, yes and no reactions
of the sensitivity and our being interested or
not being interested in what we see, hear, think
about and so on. This is a very weak activity,
and it needs to be strengthened by training and
practice, so that we can relate ourselves to our
sense-impressions and also to the associations
that arise in the automatism (which is below the
threshold of consciousness) according to our own decision and choice, and not according to whether they
happen to interest us or whether they provoke some
reaction of like or dislike. In other words, we
should have the power to attend to the impressions and associations by choice and not by reaction. This is a matter of training, which is
necessary for professional work of any kind. A
man cannot do his professional work just on the
basis of what happens to interest him or what

he happens to like or want to do, and therefore
he develops a certain power which could be called professional attention or professional competence, which enables him to hold his attention
on what has to be done in terms of its objective
significance and not only in terms of how he is
reacting to it and whether it interests him or
not. But the limitation of this professional
training is that it cannot be transferred, and
it is very noticeable how, outside of one's own
professional training, one's attention reverses
to the reactional mechanism: we attend to what
interests us, we react according to our likes
and dislikes, and the selection is no longer
intentional.

It is very interesting and worthwhile to study
professional attention, for a man some specialized job, for a woman her housework or family.
He or she will see that in their own field the
power of noticing becomes very acute and does
not require any conscious direction. For example,
a woman whose attention is wholly engaged in
something else, will immediately recognize, from
the sound of a child's crying, whether it needs
attention from her or whether it does not. A
professional man, in his own job, will recognize
quite small indications as something that requires to be dealt with; he will automatically
and constantly be interpreting his impressions
in terms of his professional experience.

I saw this particularly vividly, twenty-five
or thirty years ago, when I was engaged in the
coal trade and I used to have to travel about
quite a lot in England. As I was travelling in
the train, I once noticed that every time I

passed some line of coal trucks, I immediately knew the collieries from which they came, what quality of coal was in the trucks, where it was likely to be going and what it was going to be used for. Throughout the journey, whenever I saw trucks in sidings or passing on the line, I would find myself being connected with all parts of the coal industry and coal-consuming industries. Any man who was deeply engaged in the coal industry would do the same. If I had been a farmer going on that journey, I have no doubt that I would have noticed in the passing countryside such things as the kinds of herds grazing in the fields or what crops were being grown. One can notice in this acute way without any effort or direction of one's attention just because of professional training in a particular field, which is really a connection between sensitivity and automatism. If you understand that, you will see that it is not transferable. Though I could tell at a glance, from catching sight of a few letters of a word on a passing truck, the place from which it came and its probable destination, the sight of a herd of cows would tell me nothing, whereas a farmer could immediately have told their breed and history.

Now is it possible for us to develop an equivalent power of connecting our sense-experience and mental associations with a definite purpose outside of a field of special training? It is indeed possible to do this by a very simple kind of exercise: that is, by accustoming ourselves, when we are in contact with different sources of impressions, to interpret, to try to see the

meaning of the different things in front of us.
For example, when I noticed that all my interest
was connected with coal trucks, I then began to
oblige myself not to look at coal trucks but to
look at farms instead, and then I found myself
beginning to feel that I had to learn the difference between, let us say, an Aberdeenshire and
an Ayrshire herd, which would of course have
been obvious from the tip of the tail of a cow
to a farmer.

Loosening up narrow concern with one's own professional interests is therefore quite a good
line of training if one wants to develop a more
free and creative power in one's mind. A highly
trained professional attention, that is, a professional connection between sensitivity and
automatism, can become quite a serious barrier
to creative thought in the very field where one
had developed it. This can be seen, for example,
with professional people who begin to notice less
and less of anything that is unexpected or unusual in their profession because they become so
very good at dealing with all the kinds of situations according to a certain established reper-
toire. We must not underrate the value and importance of professional competence, but we must
also see that it has the limitation of restricting one to the particular kind of field in which
one is trained. Why is that? It is in the nature
of the automatism not to be adaptive and not to
be capable of transference; that is, whatever one
is automatized to do, one will do very well, but
one will not be able to do something else.

Now, let us consider what can be done about
developing the sensitivity itself. Here I want

you to understand that I am referring to the organization of the sensitivity and not to the organization of the connection between sensitivity and automatism, which I am calling 'competence'. This distinction is very important, and usually it is neglected. Nearly all training is directed towards the application of competence, or perhaps even towards the relaxation of the fixity of one's own competence in order to make one adaptive so that one's capactiy for attention will not be confined to the professional field. But what is not usually taken into account is the condition of the sensitivity itself. This is commonly taken for granted, and yet it is really much more fruitful to have a highly developed and organized sensitivity than to have simply a well-trained connection between sensitivity and automatism. The development of the sensitivity is achieved by working directly on it, and there is nothing particularly mysterious about this. This is obtained by various kinds of mental exercises; that is, exercises which make demands on the sensitivity itself rather than demands upon the connection between sensitivity and automatism. I will come back to this later.

You must understand that in this case, everything is constructed within the mind. Nowadays there is a certain improvement in the methods of teaching with regard to the sensitivity; for example, in the increased demand in schools for doing mental arithmetic without the aid of written symbols (which act through the automatism). There is also a certain improvement in educational procedures in some forms of teaching where visualization of situations is required. But, on

the other hand, there is also a weakening of the
work on the sensitivity through the use of various aids which enable work on the sensitivity to
be dispensed with. It is therefore necessary to
be clear about what kinds of teaching are useful
for the developing of the powers of the automatism, such as, for example, what I call hypno-
teaching procedures, which are methods of teaching not involving the consciousness or even the
sensitivity, working directly on the automatism.
Such procedures are quite sufficient for developing memories that are fixed in the automatism,
as for example, in learning languages and whole
arrays and orders of facts. For those purposes
all kinds of mechanical devices that enable the
sensitivity to be eliminated, the action going
directly to the automatism, are quite useful.
But on the other hand, it is also indispensable
that there should be work on the sensitivity itself, which can certainly start with the use of
mental problems, mental representations. But
this does not usually go far enough.

I was very fortunate that when I was about
twenty years old, with the army in France during
the First World War, I met someone who was particularly interested in this development of the
sensitivity. He had experimented with various
kinds of mental exercises for this purpose and
persuaded me to try some experiments in this
field. The particular kinds of mental exercises
which we tried at that time were mainly to hold
a number of ideas together in the mind. A simple
way of doing this is, for example in solving
equations with a number of unknowns simultaneously, which requires that one should hold

certain matrix patterns in one's mind long
enough to be able to make calculations from
them. But any kind of exercise which requires
that one should bring into the sensitivity
several different ideas or images simultaneously can really help in this direction.

Another way in which the sensitivity can be
strengthened and organized is through developing the power of visualization, or the conscious
creation of mental images. When this is done, we
transfer the action on the sensitivity from
something arising from the automatism - that
means the senses, seeing, hearing and so on - to
a direction coming from the consciousness. For
this kind of exercise, one has to prepare a particular complex pattern up to the limit of what
one is able to hold, and project this onto the
sensitivity until a clear image of it is formed.
For some purposes one can take just abstract
ideas, such as mathematical formulae, or abstract geometrical patterns. Or else one can take
a situation where there is life and movement and
produce in the sensitivity the experience of
this life and movement, of these moving images,
and with the same degree of vividness and sense
of reality as one would have if they were actually coming up through the automatism, through
the sense impressions. When this is done, the
line from the automatism to sensitivity is cut
off, inhibited, and the sensitivity is then put
at the disposal of the consciousness to receive
images that are projected onto it.

This is quite a different kind of work from
the work which trains one in attention, trains
one in noticing, as in the example I was speak-

72

ing about earlier. The difference is that in
the case I was talking about, you deal with material that is given to you either from outside,
in the form of sensations, things you see and
hear, or else with mental associations that arise
from the automatism; memories, for example. Pro-
fessionally you are able to recall or to remember
the kind of facts, formulae, methods, techniques
and so on that are required for your professional
work; that is, to call them up from the store in
the automatism. The material with which you are
working is there, your professional attention in
the sensitivity simply strengthens your power to
select and recognize and make connections with
this material. But when you are working in the
way I am now talking about, on the connections
between consciousness and sensitivity, you construct the material, you form the material, you
produce it voluntarily by a projection from your
consciousness onto your sensitivity. Or you can
say, you intentionally produce mental images, images in the mind.

You may wonder what is the value of this power
and why one should take the trouble to develop it.
I shall not overburden you with more than two
reasons for this study.The first power enables
you to hold in the mind, or sensitivity, a greater
number of concepts, images, or thoughts than by
automatic training. Therefore you develop a constructive, integrative power not ordinarily obtainable. The second power connected with this is
really much more extraordinary. It is that when
the sensitivity begins to respond to the consciousness, then we are able to withdraw the sensitivity
from the constant influx of sense-impressions

and associations that arise automatically, the
sensitivity becomes available to a number of
new, almost unknown functions and power. For
example, it is possible to see things that cannot ordinarily be seen. We usually suppose that
it is not possible to see the future, and the
reason for that is that we attribute anything
we see to the working of the sensations and
automatisms, and it is perfectly true that a-
long the line of competence everything has to
come from the past. But along the line that
connects sensitivity and consciousness, there
is not the same time dependence; there is a
different sort of connectedness. People very
seldom appreciate what is happening, but sometimes they get glimpses of the future or glimpses of things that are happening in a different
place; various sorts of connections arise in
their minds that they are not able to explain
in terms of the connections between the automatism and the sensitivity. There is nothing
mysterious about this; it is simply that there
is a different kind of connection along the
horizontal line that enables one to see in a
different perspective. One can see more ideas
together; one can also begin to see, in a strange and different way, backwards in time. One
can even see what is going to happen as well as
what has happened.

This connection has a property which is very
important in relationships between people, for
people begin to understand one another and to
be able to share experience in a way that cannot happen through the other connections. It is
difficult to find a single word to cover all the

powers that are developed through the work on
the sensitivity. One word which expresses a good
deal of this is *understanding* - understanding in
the true sense of the word, that is, seeing the
relevance of anything in relation to the whole.
This belongs to a right connection between consciousness and sensitivity. It is through this
that one is able to see the meaning and significance of ideas, that would be missed by competence alone.

It is possible that this power of the sensitivity is retained in spite of faulty education
procedures and in many people continues to be
quite active say up to the age of thirty-five
years. However it usually begins to diminish after this, chiefly because the sensitivity has
been far too tightly linked to the automatism,
and the rôle of sensitivity begins to be played
by competence. But this hardening of the sensitivity is totally unnecessary and can be avoided
by such simple practices as these sort of exercises of visualisation, of mental alertness,
which I referred to before. I think that anyone
who constantly exercises his mind to see a great
deal and to make connections between ideas that
at first sight seem to have no connection, will
not only retain this power right through life
but can even develop it to such an extent that
quite new and unexpected faculties arise with it.

So certainly it seems to play an important part
in the development of creative thinking. People
who have shown to a marked degree the power of
creative thinking, or creativity in general - not
only in science but also in art and in practical
affairs - are what are called men of vision, and

a man of vision, properly speaking, is a man
whose *inner vision* is developed, and not whose
senses are highly developed, who is very compe-
tent in his work. For all that to be accomplished, you have to bring about in yourself the
power to separate sensitivity and consciousness;
that is, what is called self-remembering, self-
observation, or self-awareness. But people who
have never even heard of these terms acquire
these powers if they have a certain initial advantage by a natural capacity for the inner
vision. They begin to exercise this power because it is so obviously intrinsically worth
having. Anyone who experiences it finds joy in
it and feels himself differently related, so
that he will tend to develop this power if he
can. But unfortunately there is a serious snag
or pitfall here, for it is possible for this to
become a kind of mental self-indulgence which
everyone is well aware of in the form of day-
dreaming or automatic image building. It must
be understood that the true man of vision does
not daydream, does not have idle fancies.
Those arise only too easily in the sensitivity
when there is no real separation between the
sensitivity and consciousness. The true power
that we are speaking of here is an intentionally
exercised power that makes a very big demand. I
can speak for myself as I have been interested
in this pretty well all my life and I have at
all times tried to exercise myself in this. I
know very well how very much less I have done
in this field than I would have liked to do just
because of the natural laziness of people, which
made me abandon it when it became really too

difficult.

So that you must not suppose that this organization of the sensitivity is a simple and easy matter. In reality it is considerably harder than the development and the acquisition of competence, because although competence itself requires hard work, it is work of a less demanding nature than the organization of sensitivity. I would, however, like to recommend to you that you should, between now and the next meeting, make some experiments of your own. Set yourself to experiment with the formation of intentionally constructed mental images. There are all sorts of methods of doing this. If I remember rightly, the very first one I ever came in contact with was a book by Hinton, about the fourth dimension. I know I came across it at school and how fascinated we all were by the exercise he gives to enable you to visualise four-dimensional figures. One simple kind of exercise of this kind, which I would recommend to you, is to see why it is not possible to tie a knot in four dimensions. Set yourself to see clearly how in four-dimensional space it is not possible to have a knot. It is an extremely simple notion, but very hard to actually see for yourself. One says, of course one cannot tie a knot, of course things will slip through, but to really see how you can only have knots in three dimensions of space requires a certain steadiness of the inner attention in your sensitivity, until you bring it to the point where it is steady enough really to see this happening. If this is too difficult, try to visualise constructions in your mind, and see if you can actually build the

construction. Or try visualising a specific
action and see if you can carry through in your
mind just all that is required for doing some
action with which you are quite familiar. For
example, let alone failing to tie a knot in four
dimensions, see if you can visualise what happens when you actually do tie a knot in three
dimensions. But in that case you have to reproduce the whole process just as mental construction, cast from your consciousness upon your
sensitivity. You could also try to reproduce in
your mind the whole of the action that is required for some simple operation, like washing
your hands. It so happens that this has also got
an extra dimension, because when you actually do
it, your body is taking care of the sequence in
time and you do not realise all that you are doing when you are washing your hands.

Try to wash your hands in your mind's eye, and
really do everything that you do when you are
washing your hands, and you will see how difficult it is.

This sort of practice is, I am sure, very useful. Among other things it does liberate the
mind from quite useless day-dreaming and mental
associations, but its ultimate benefit is very
much greater than that. I have only given a kind
of simplified version of this because the sensitivity itself has got different constructional
materials. It has got thought, it has got feeling, it has got sensation and so on, and out of
these different materials we can construct a
whole world. In fact, I personally have been
quite astonished, I had not quite realised until
I began to take stock of it all some time ago,

of what it is that you obtain when you really
work on the organization of the sensitivity, and
nobody knows - at least I do not - what are the
potentialities of the organization of the sensitivity in man. You learn how to keep that quite
separate from the training of your attention and
your powers of dealing with the presented material. It is most important for this to see very
clearly the distinction between the use of attention in dealing with what we see and hear and
thoughts that arise in our mind (memories and
the rest of it) and construction and formation
of images in the mind by a direction that comes
from the consciousness.

Now we have to consider another role of the

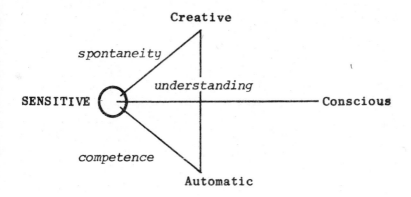

ACTION OF CONSCIOUSNESS ON SENSITIVITY

consciousness in the horizontal line. Consciousness has the power to bring the sensitivity to a

state of stillness and emptiness and, what is
more, without wishing or looking for anything.
This is a different practice - which I have already spoken of in the first lecture in this
series - that enables the sensitivity to receive spontaneous images. It is also a useful
practice, which I personally consider everyone
should spend a certain amount of time on every
day. I am quite sure for myself that it is
quite indispensable for me to spend ten minutes
or longer if I can manage it every day in just
bringing my sensitivity to a state of emptiness,
not projecting anything onto it and keeping it
clear from the automatic associations.

That gives three different actions on the
sensitivity. One concerns its connection with
the automatism, with the subconscious and unconscious processes; the other concerns its own
organization, the development of the powers
that are inherent in the sensitivity itself; and
the third concerns learning how to make the sensitivity available for the arising of spontaneous images. Each of these requires different
kinds of training and discipline.

PRACTICAL RULES FOR CREATIVE WORK

VISUALIZATION - *Abstracts from questions and*
answers

Images of sensation: "In the problem of all
that is involved in some familiar activity or
motion, if the person is me doing it, I cannot
do it by sight, I *feel* it. Say I am mounting a
pony; it is my hands, it is the feeling of the
leather ... But if I am thinking of someone else,
then I see them from some viewpoint. It seems
absurd to see the back of my own head, cleaning
my teeth".

Picturing: "I used to do solid geometry in my
head, just for fun. But visualising an *abstract*
thing does not mean an awful lot to me".

Concepts: "I would like to try and clarify this
difficulty of non-visible visualization. I find I
have an almost negligible capacity for forming
what I would call pictorial images, but if I am

looking at an idea, or trying to see what happens when you put two ideas together, something happens. I was very interested to read in a book on neuro-physiology that some people seem to have a very strong pictorial visualization, and others just cannot do it".

J. G. B.: I cannot understand what people even mean when they say they can have visual images. I cannot picture to myself what it is like to see something I am not looking at with my eyes. The idea that one can close one's eyes and evoke a picture of something! I believe it because people say they can, but nothing like that ever happens to me. It does seem as if the two types are mutually exclusive. That means that people who relatively easily form abstract concepts very seldom can form visual images, and the other way round.

Operations in the mind: "How can you detect the presence of an abstract concept?"

J. G. B.: You can operate with it. There is no picture. There may or may not be words. For example, if I wanted to multiply 75 by 91 in my head, I do not see the figures in front of me, I simply hold the numbers in front of me and perform the operation, that is all.

Training: There is this very marked difference in the way people form and operate with mental images. I am not at all sure that one cannot, by practice, develop to some extent the forms of mental imagery that one is not naturally endowed

with. I think I can get pictures a little better,
but they are very much *constructed*. I cannot evoke a picture in front of my mind, but I can lab-
oriously build one up. I see it made bit by bit
in front of me. I can evoke in front of myself
the sense of handling an object and knowing what
its shape is like. I can picture myself going
through a city that I have been in, without seeing images in my mind. I remember an enormous
number of cities that I visited and I can mental-
ly find my way about in them although I do not
see anything at all. I can give someone precise
instructions how to get from one place to another
in hundreds of different cities or towns, but I
do not *see* them at all.

Practical rules for creative work

You have to ask yourself, when you are in front
of a problem, whether it is something which you
can solve by knowledge alone. You may not have
the necessary knowledge in you, but you can set
about finding it. Even when the problem is complicated, it may still be possible to find the answer by using what is already known, though this
may require one further step than just obtaining
the information. Take, as an example, what has
come up in our discussion: the different types of
mental images. If I am satisfied to know what has
been discovered by people who have studied perception and mental images, then all that I shall
have to do is to find the suitable references,
look up the books and see who has done experimental work in this field and what they have found.
That is just the information-seeking stage. But

it may be that I want to apply this information
to, say, the classification of my own mental
processes. In that case I have to conduct some
investigations. I can carry out certain experiments indicated in the books and give myself the
appropriate rating or classification. In this
case I go beyond simple information-seeking to a
step of obtaining data acquired by establishing
conditions in which it can be available to me. I
could, for example, put myself into the experience of playing chess games in my mind and observe my method of holding the pattern of the
game in front of me without the help of a board
to refresh my memory. One person does it in one
way and another person in another way. The experiment once made gives me the information and
I can classify myself as someone who works by
visual memory, by form, by enumerative memory. In
that there is nothing more involved than *putting
together information and observation*.

If I want to go further and add something to
the understanding of the process of performing
mental operations, I shall have to *devise* other
kinds of experiments. In this case I shall have
to, what is called, *construct a situation*. This
situation-construction is an act of my own that
comes over and above the previous stage where I
take a ready-made situation, one recommended in
a text book. But it still need not have in it any
creative step. I can have been trained in that
kind of situation-construction. For example, if I
am trained as a chemist, I will know from my
training how to devise experiments or to make the
tests that are required for obtaining information
that I have not got and I cannot get out of a

book of reference.

Situation-construction of that kind can be just a matter of training, but it does involve something of *my own,* because *I* have to be trained in this way, *I* have to do a constructive step over and above the application of routine methods.

In trying to solve some problem which is really going to require a step of understanding there is much beyond even this. I will take an example which I choose just because it is so difficult: *understanding time.* Clearly I can go about the first three steps quite easily; I already have the ordinary available information about time, I can quite easily make measurements and observations about time - I have learnt to do so from childhood by using a watch and I have all the experience of my life that tells me that different operations require different periods of time. If I want to go further, for example, if I want to be able to correct and verify time-measurements, then I have to be able to go to the constructive stage. I have to understand how, for example, a watch works, how watches and time-keepers are regulated. I can learn this from text books on chronometers and I can also devise steps to find out about the measurement of time, but when I have done this as far as I am able, I ask myself: Now, how much has all this really taught me about time? I see immediately that there is a mystery which I cannot grasp.

I am dealing with time in one way only by this process of information-seeking, observation, constructive experimentation. I could arrive at the utmost accuracy in the measurement of time, I could come to a great deal of knowledge, and that

is no small thing, about the connection between
time and motion and between time and various
sorts of processes. I could carry that such a
long way that I would eventually have to catch
up with Newton and Einstein in order to understand about time and motion, and I would also
have to catch up with a great deal of biological
science in order to understand about life processes and time. However far I carry this kind of
information-seeking, observational and *constructional* study, I am still only dealing with one
side of time: what can be known about it. In
front of the problem of time I can see a way of
study which will eventually give me an immense
amount of information and, what is more, this information will penetrate into everything, because
time enters into everything that I can know about.

But if I then say to myself: Is this really going to satisfy me, am I going to *understand* time
in this way? I realise that this cannot help me
because I am concerned with *something else;* I am
concerned with what time *means to me,* and why
there is this peculiar *quality* in the experienc-
ing of time that is different from the *observation* of time. When I observe time, it appears to
be measurable and regular, and subject to laws
which, however difficult they may be, such as in
relativity, they are, nevertheless, all in the
end reduceable to information that can be verified, transmitted, shared and subjected to constructional treatment. But when I turn to my *experience of time* this measurableness, this regularity and clarity about time vanishes. Moments
become hours, hours become moments, time sometimes presses heavily, sometimes it seems to

disappear altogether and the beginnings and ends
of things always have a mysterious element that
cannot be measured, as in our own birth and
death.

As I bring this before me, I see that in my
attitude towards time there is one procedure
which can be called *information-seeking* and another which can be called *striving to understand.*
Obviously there is a difference between seeking
information about time and striving to understand time, but this is true not only about something so tremendous in our lives as time must
be, but even about much simpler things. Because
we can always tell that however simple something
is and however easy it is to reduce it to information, there remains in it something which cannot be understood: what it means for our experience, *why it is unique and personal* as far as we
are concerned, why it has *come to our attention.*

I happen now to have my attention drawn to the
glass before me. For the last half hour I have
been sitting in front of it without noticing it.
I can trace the information about that glass as
thoroughly as I wish to do so in all directions;
in its origins, its material construction, its
uses, its ultimate destiny, its geometrical
shape and so on. But when I say to myself: How
is it that this glass has now become part of my
experience and yours in a way that it did not
before? I begin to enter something which is no
longer reduceable to information. It is connected with *what we are,* and *what the glass is.* It
opens up all sorts of new fields about things.
*What is life, what is experience, what is con-
sciousness?* Why are things related to us?

This is the second step in creative understanding. *The first rule* for any problem is to look at it in terms of information-seeking and decide how far we need to carry this. You can follow that information-seeking route along the ways of what you yourself happen already to know, what you can easily find from available sources, then through various observational procedures on to constructional procedures.

The *second rule* is to ask yourself: What does this mean, in what way can I hope to understand it? What is it that links me to this particular problem? I would say, from my own experience, that this rule should be applied more often than we usually do; even in what appears to be quite ordinary situations it is very often worth while stopping - even if it is only for a few moments, or perhaps minutes - to hold our attention upon the two sides of information and understanding, the *knowable and the mysterious* in the situation until the situation has really become *alive* for us.

It is worth doing because the practice produces a certain *change in ourselves* which is a necessary preliminary to applying the *third rule*. After you have looked at the problem first of information and secondly in terms of understanding, you look at it in terms of action: What is it that I am going to do? You do not ask yourself what ought I to do or what is the best thing to do or how is the problem to be solved. It is not a matter of choosing what to do because *what you are going to do is very largely already conditioned by the fact that you put yourself in front of the problem*. You ask yourself: Am I going to carry this further? Very often, at this point, there is some astonishment because you may see that you are not really going to take this problem seriously and you may as well cease to concern yourself with the attempt to solve it. Or you may see that you are really committed to going further.

Let us come back to this big problem of time. What am I going to do about the problem of time? You may see very well that you are in fact not going to do anything more than you have already done because you have no idea how to make any step which is going to give you anything else but either a lot more information about time or an increasing sense of the strangeness of the world that exists in time, with no idea of how to come any nearer to understanding it.

Sometimes you have got to do something - you have a practical problem of life where action is going to be taken whether you are properly prepared for it or not. If you see for yourself that you *are committed,* then you can go forward towards another step. But if you do not do this, then there is great probability that you fall into imagination or day-dreaming about it and that is useless. It will not bring you anything of practical value nor a step forward in creative understanding. The third step must be taken *now.* Far too often we let imagination creep in at this point; we imagine that we are taking the problem seriously, or we take some action and then continue to think of what we shall or ought to do about it. In other words, *the action has parted company with our own mental process.*

To bring and hold together the mental process

and the action is the necessary condition for achieving something - in abstract studies such as science and philosophy as well as in practical fields. One can think about a problem and be doing nothing about it, or do something purely through knowledge and the emotional commitment of the moment - desire, fear, excitement or interest - that will take charge of the action so that understanding comes to a stop.

The commitment to action can be very painful or onerous. Only when we have really faced the realities of the situation and made the commitment do we come to the *fourth rule*. We have to see the problem as *having a solution*. This can be called the *stage of confidence*. We have no solution, we do not know what to do, we have realised that there is something mysterious and intangible about the problem and we also may have realised that there are severe limits to our information capacity, but yet we have committed ourselves to doing something about it. We must have hope, and the basis of hope is that *a problem which can be envisaged is a problem which can be solved*. The state of conflict and the sense of impotence or ineffectualness in front of the problem is only something temporary: we shall come to a solution of it. This is based on a very simple act of faith; that the world contains the solution of its own problems. We know very well that it is quite beyond us to solve the central ultimate problem of time: Why should this peculiar condition of existence be imposed upon us? Yet this is not totally impossible; there is a real answer to this question not only "What is time?" but "Why is time?" Because of that it must be possible to take *some* step.

Suppose that it is a more immediate, practical problem: what are we going to do with some intractable personal relationship? It we act, we shall do one kind of harm; if we hold back and refuse to act we shall do another kind of harm. We are helpless in front of this, but we must still say to ourselves: "There is a right action". There is a dilemma only because we do not yet see enough.

Or supposing it is something of a much more abstract nature, such as a problem in the interpretation of some scientific experiment, where the present theories do not make sense. We can still say to ourselves "There is a way of looking at this which does make sense if I am strong enough in my mind to be able to hold all the necessary elements together". Experience shows that if this step is deliberately taken and we hold on to the assertion that there is a solution to this problem for long enough - in some cases it may be a matter of minutes but in other cases days or weeks during which we have to reinforce the conviction - then this pre-disposes us to making the break through. It is as if at this point we have to invoke the help of a state which we have not yet reached or a step which has not yet been made. If I try to go forward without having applied this rule, I shall not do anything except turn over the existing material.

I think that this is not only true for a mental process, I have also seen it in dealing with personal problems. If I attempt to deal with the problem before I have convinced myself that there is a *right* way of dealing with that particular problem anything that I do will be of a routine,

almost automatic character. I have to deal with
someone; I see that I am not going to take this
peoblem seriously forward. In that case it is
quite simple, I will deal with that person only
according to my information and the understanding
I have, and that will be that. But if I realise
that in dealing with the person I am going to
commit myself, then I have to convince myself
that something important can be done here, which
does not occur to me or anyone else to do.

Sometimes it is possible to realise this fourth
stage by 'visualising' it; how, if I were really
a wise person, there *would* be a way of dealing
with this. If a really wise person could deal
with it fully and properly, I can at least deal
with it to some extent and need not be defeated.

I must remind you that this step that I call
the stage of confidence, *cannot be applied until
you have gone through the other stages.* If you
try to boost up your own courage by saying to
yourself that it will be all right without having
first prepared yourself by passing through the
three initial stages, then nothing significant
will happen.

The *fifth stage* that follows I have talked
about in the earlier meetings. Now you have to
open yourself to the possibility of a creative
action. Having gone through the self-disciplining
process involving a 'conditioning' of yourself,
you have to stop and empty it all out. The ground
has now been prepared; either you must put the
whole thing out of your mind and deal with something else, or you have to sit and bring yourself
into a state of emptiness, vacuity of the mind.
This is not abandoning the problem. You must

promise yourself to accept nothing except the step that is unmistakably a step forward; you are either going to understand better or do nothing further. The fifth rule is determination to go forward in understanding, in the realisation that you can no longer do anything about it.

SUMMARY OF THE RULES

The first rule is to seek information. The second rule is to ask the question: But what do I understand here, personally and directly? The third rule is to ask, quite mercilessly, the question: Am I going to take this problem seriously or not? The fourth rule here is an opening to the confidence that something can be done and there is a way through; I have not awakened to it, but *it is there*. Having convinced oneself that the problem can be solved, one is ready for the fifth rule, the stage of emptiness, to allow the arising of a spontaneous element that is outside of our own control. This vacuity of mind must be combined with clarity on the goal that is desired. Something significant is wanted; not just any ideas - these will come anyhow and it is necessary to deny oneself and refuse to take the second best. Whether this is a sixth rule or whether it is part of the fifth, I do not know, but there must be a resolution to accept only the treasure.

These stages I have been describing are often wonderfully pictured in fairy stories. At the last stage of the hero's search he must not succumb to temptations drawing him to accept something other than the solution that he has set out for. I can say, speaking from my own experience, that this is a temptation that I very easily fall into. One becomes tired at this stage, and various things suggest themselves - interesting ideas - and it is very easy to snatch at what come along and do something with it. Of course something will happen, but perhaps comething very much bigger has been missed.

GROUP CREATIVITY

WE TOOK AS THE TITLE of our lectures *Creative Thinking* and not *creativity*. I want to draw your attention to the fact that creative thinking is a special form of creativity. It is a creativity that works and expresses itself through mental images which in turn can lead to action, but not all creativity has to express itself through mental images and we must distinguish between creativity as a universal or cosmic activity, and creative thinking as but one way in which this activity enters our human life. In the wider sense, creativity can be called play. It is play as a universal or even a cosmic process. This, as many of you will recognize, is described in the Hindu conception of the world as the play of Brahma, and very great significance is attached to play in the cosmology that comes from the Vedas. The spontaneity of play, the free delight of creating, is akin to the element of spontaneity in creative work which I described in the first lecture. Creative activity is never without this taste of delight, and of course also the taste of surprise and unexpectedness, because if

it were not surprising and unexpected, it would
be something coming from the past. Whereas all
true creativity arises out of nothing, in the
moment.

Is there *any evidence at all* that there is such
a thing as this spontaneous creativity? I put
this question because I was reading the other day
two interesting papers by W. Ross-Ashby on intelligent machines and the brain, based on the notion, which is quite valid, that there is no difference whatever between the human brain and certain machines that can be devised, and that machines can be made which are in principle as
intelligent as the human brain.

Ross-Ashby starts with the postulate that all
intelligence is nothing else but the seeking of a
goal, and this is what distinguishes intelligent
action from unintelligent action. Machines can
be made that are goal-seeking, and not only goal-
seeking, but goal-making; that is to say, a machine could be so divised that it does not have
its goal or its aim fed into it by a human operator, but be able to learn from its environment
to decide what it wants to achieve and set itself
to achieve this as its goal, performing the most
economical operations in order to do so. Hitherto
it has generally been supposed that machines can
do very complicated operations but that they can
hardly be expected to decide what it is they want
to do. I think it is now evident that it will be
possible to devise machines able to select goals
which could not have been foreseen at the time
they began their operation, because the goal itself will, to a great extent, be derived from
the experience that enters the machine and is

stored up in it in the process of its moving towards a sort of preliminary, provisional aim.

This is all very different from the way we looked at machines not so very long ago, but it is of course not at all different from the ways Gurdjieff has looked at the human brain since he first began to expound the notion that man is a machine, and that machines are not different from men.

I am saying all this because I think it is extremely important that we should clarify for ourselves all that cannot be brought into the scope of creativity. To propose to oneself an aim and to set about intelligently to achieve it is not evidence of anything creative. All of this can be done by a machine for which we can now establish the principles of construction, chiefly because new ways have now been found of storing information, of learning from the environment in mechanical devices, and of making combinations so rapidly that perhaps more than a hundred million could be tested in a second - which is not very much different from the way our human brain works.

Ross-Ashby asks: "Can anyone produce any evidence of there being any operations that occur in man which could not occur in a machine ideally constructed in this kind of way?" No one has so far produced any evidence of this, and therefore let us take as our basic postulate that everything that exists - everything living, including human beings - is identical in its nature with the kind of machine that we are able to construct. This view is very widely held by very intelligent people, and obviously there is no reason why one should not suppose that the whole of life, including man with his body and the working of his brain, has not been coming to existence by a series of what you call 'self-optimising processes' until at last a kind of machine has developed that is able to select its own aims and, what is more, modify and adapt them as circumstances change. It is very interesting, in my opinion, to push this right through to its logical conclusions and ask ourselves: can we suppose that there is anything which could not be brought within this picture? It cannot be said that machines could not enjoy themselves because it seems quite clear that machines can be constructed that *will* enjoy themselves - just as certainly as there are already machines that get tired and bored, and when they are obliged to do an operation that requires more capacity than they have, they become nervous and psychopathic and have to be rested or treated very carefully in order to bring them to behave properly.

If we face up to all this, we see the importance of answering for ourselves the question: Is there something, a real creativity, which is not reduceable by any conceivable ingenuity to the operations of a machine? I am sure there is no way of answering that question by means of positive evidence, by the very way it is reduced, it brings it within the scope of this kind of mechanical intelligence. I do not believe there is any way by which evidence could be produced that creativity is something not mechanical.

So that in talking about creativity we are already entering the domain of faith. Just as we can take as one kind of assumption or postulate that intelligence, in the sense of the successful selection and pursuit of goals, can always be reduced to a set of mechanical operations, we can also make another kind of assumption and say there is something different from that and that is genuine spontaneity or playful creative activity. It is an assumption which cannot be proved by reference to the other assumption.

For some reason the importance of this free creativity has not been recognized very much in our Western thinking, as far as I know; not so much as it has in the Indian philosophies, for example. That was the reason I had to refer to them. I think we should say something of this sort; there is, everywhere, a creative activity, a cosmic play. We men can participate in that play.

It even seems that it is quite natural and universal because children have almost always the capacity for play or an unconditioned activity which is spontaneously created. Little by little this is overlaid by the conditioning of education and the necessary requirements of social life. It also seems as if this kind of creative play is preserved in artists.

Some work has been done in the United States on the connection between creativity and intelligence as measured by various sorts of intelligence tests, which give a very low correlation between the creative power and intelligence. One result is that under the ordinary conditions of education where intelligence is considered the important function, those with intelligence come to the fore and those with creativity are almost always placed under a social disadvantage. With an increasing recognition of the importance of creativity in human life, we still continue to follow procedures, educational and social, that tend to give all the advantages to those with intelligence and put in a position of inferiority those who are creative, with the result that comparatively rarely do people with powerful creative ability succeed in bringing this to bear upon their life problems. Very often they become in fact social failures, life failures, although they were potentially creative elements of society, desperately wanted in a world that is having now, more and more, to face incessant change and incessant innovation. Does this mean that there are two kinds of people; intelligent but not creative and creative but not intelligent? Certainly not. There are probably people who are neither the one nor the other, but this means neither the one nor the other to a very marked degree.

I think I said it before, but I certainly want to emphasize it again now, that my own conviction is that creativity is as natural for man as the different powers that we call intelligence, and also the more mechanical powers connected with memory and ease of conditioning, or the ability to undergo successful training in the acquisition of skills. It seems to me that the fostering of creative ability is going to be one of the most important problems of the future that will mean a great change in attitude towards the processes of education and also of social organization.

Let me here just say one thing in parenthesis; obviously, as we can see only too well from recent events, one of the greatest problems of our age is the use of leisure and the kind of destructive

activity that enters human life when there is no
right use of leisure. There cannot be any doubt
that the right use of leisure is play, but play
itself must be creative, otherwise it is not authentic play, it is a kind of imitation, or
false play. There seems to be no doubt, also,
that there is a negative creativity which is destructive, and that if the positive creativity is
not given its chance to function, then the very
same creative energy flows into destructive activity. Where play is not given its full scope
and other powers of man are brought into operation where creative play would be appropriate,
there is a certain unbalancing of the human
nature. This seems to me to be evident in the
artificial stimulation of interest that occupies
most leisure time. Passive participation in spec-
tacles and stimulation from the outside holds in
abeyance the creative play activity of the individual concerned, which then, almost inevitably,
breaks out and produces a destructive response.
 Sometimes people think that I am absurdly pre-
judiced and narrow-minded because I do not like
television. I do realise that there is an exaggerated prejudice in my own mind against television and radio and other things of that nature
where people receive impressions passively and I
am aware that many people tell me what wonderful
educational procedures are available by these
methods, but what has impressed me so terribly
over these years that these things have been developing is the way in which this works upon a
certain level of man and does not give scope to
the level which really belongs to his free expression. Although it seems admirable that people

should greatly increase their knowledge of the world and their understanding (I would not be so sure about understanding) and their acquaintance with many different things through these presentations, I personally remain convinced that the price is too high for the very reason that it occupies the time of people where there could be a free play of the creative activity. It is not at all certain that this could always be compensated by bringing creative activity into professional work.

Now let me come to the theme of this evening's talk, which is creative thinking in groups as distinct from creative thinking in the individual. The notion that you can have a creative group seems very strange, and I must say some time ago I would have thought it strange myself because of the well-known and well-proven saying that God does not vouchsafe originality to committees. Everyone who has had to work with committees knows how painfully true this is and how it always seems that any attempt for a number of people to get together to produce something which is an original and creative solution to problems is doomed to failure and all that is produced is something on the level of the combined skill and experience of the members, even when they work together in harmony.

I myself, during my professional time as director of scientific research - when I was really very keenly interested in the question of scientific creativity and looking where and how it could be fostered among young scientists - saw only too well that very often those who had a creative power were unable to be team workers.

GROUP CREATIVITY

It is commonly said that you must not expect from
your creative workers that they should also be
good team workers, and I am afraid it is true.
But why is it true? I think it goes back to the
years at school and even college, when the unus-
ually creative boy or girl was an awkward customer, able to see things that perhaps even the
teachers did not see in various situations - a
most irritating trait in children - and able to
look at things in a way that the fellow pupils
or fellow students could not do, always tempted
to be sarcastic, sharp or sometimes over-clever
because their creative ability was not allowed
to find an outlet under the restrictive conditions of ordinary teaching. There is a very special irritation for a young person with creative
power in seeing others, with intelligence only,
getting to the top of everything. I believe that
it is this which brings about the anti-social behaviour of creative people and causes them to be
trouble-makers in forming teams for creative
work.

I am thinking now particularly of the great
problem in scientific research where team work
is more and more indispensable on account of the
impossibility for a single person to use all the
necessary skills and collect the necessary data
for solution of the greater part of the kind of
problems that natural science deals with today.
This problem could undoubtedly be overcome if
these things were better understood and there
was an acceptance of the difference between people in respect of the different powers. And also
if it were realised that very often there can be
a creative step brought forward from a source

that is ordinarily looked upon as not creative. What often happens is this; you can see, in a team of people working together, a creative idea coming from someone. The idea will be lost if the person is regarded by others and has come to regard himself as non-creative, and he will not trust an idea that has come into his mind if it is different from what the other people are suggesting or thinking about. But everyone can have some part in the cosmic play. For that reason it is important, when people come together in front of a problem requiring creative steps, that everyone should be prepared to listen to anything that the others have to say; not only the ones who always seem to have what are called the bright ideas. Because if one looks closely at these bright ideas, very often they are only intelligent ideas and not creative. Through following intelligent ideas it can very easily happen that the whole activity of the group is set upon a model which will make the solution of the problem impossible.

So if we become engaged at any time in this kind of work, we have to be on our guard against being deceived by intelligence. Does this mean that intelligence has no part in creative thinking? Of course not. The step that has to be made from the flash of creative insight to its formulation is an intelligent act. Here is where extraordinary mutual help can often occur between people, and why sometimes - when the group is really inspired to a level of creative activity - things can be accomplished that none of the individuals could do alone. For example, an insight comes in an almost inexpressible form to one person, who may not even recognize its significance. Another, working

on the level of intelligence - or what we called
in previous lectures consciousness, will see the
value and the point of this suggestion. Then
comes a quite separate work involving testing,
verifying, bringing the idea into coherent form
upon what we call the level of skill, or sensitivity, and also of relating it to the body of
existing knowledge, to the whole structure of
the problem with which we are engaged which is
on the level of the automatism that we have
spoken about in previous lectures. All of these
things are necessary in order to have creative
thinking as distinct from creativity pure and
simple. Because creative thinking is already a
more complete process than simple creativity;
it is creativity that has penetrated into life
and taken shape and begun to produce action and
results.

As I said right at the beginning when I spoke
to you about the importance for creativity to be
able to put aside ordinary thought-processes, so
it is here. We prevent the entrance of anything
that is outside the power of intelligence when
intelligence is too strongly engaged. Intelligence has to abdicate, stand aside for a time,
in order to allow the other to enter. As I am
speaking there are bound to occur to you such no-
tions as 'becoming as little children' and the
notion of emptying oneself and 'the things that
are hidden from the wise and prudent are revealed to the babes'. These point the finger to the
possibility for man to become connected with
regions that are really outside of human experience.

How can we give the right place to our

intelligence and the right place to our skill
and the right place to our conditioning, so
that this fourth power, the spontaneous power,
can come into play and allow something really
new to enter when a group of people are working
together rather than an individual wrestling
alone with a problem?

It seems that the condition for this kind of
group creativity is that one should be able to
combine a condition of mutual acceptance, readiness to listen to one another, with a certain
tension of the atmosphere, a certain kind of
excitement, which seems to be able to draw away
the activity of the mind from its ordinary functioning. I am saying this because experience
shows that free and easy conversation, which is
admirable from the point of view of mutual acceptance - just talking together and everyone
expressing their opinions on the problem in
hand - very seldom results in any spontaneous or
creative addition to the activity. But sometimes
it happens that we are shocked out of this easy-
going kind of freedom and the tension is stepped
up; the people in the group become aware of
there being something just behind the veil, of
something important which they could come to.
That is the moment when the mind and the intelligence must not interfere.

Very often, at such a moment, the excitement
when we feel 'We are on the point of making a
real step now' occurs and then we try to use the
ideas that are arising and build something out
of them rather than waiting. Then it is necessary to introduce something that is similar to
the exercise of stopping the thinking which I

have recommended in my first lecture, and this
means going through the three distinct phases:
first of all allowing trivial associations to
stop, secondly to put aside interesting ideas
that come into the mind - which tempt you to
accept and to follow them - by saying 'No' firmly to everything that comes in that way; thirdly
a moment can come - indeed, if one is strong enough in one's mind it will come - when one sees
the right thing, when all doubt disappears, when
there is complete clarity on what has to be done
or what has to be understood at that moment. The
difference between the interesting ideas and the
complete clarification of the mind is quite unmistakable.

It can sometimes happen that the equivalent is
obtained in a group, though by different procedures because it is not possible to produce this
cessation of thinking in the way that one does
inwardly, because the group has to exchange, and
it has to exchange by communication, by language
and so on. But I have seen people - who are particularly skilful in this and understand the requirements - produce the stepping-up by a kind of
shock that is given to the condition of the group
at a certain moment - perhaps by presentation of
some outrageous notion, or by a very illogical
rejection of something interesting which is put
forward which would normally be followed up. It
is only by such means that a group can go beyond its own intelligence and something happen.

If this procedure is not available, or if no
member of the group is able to play ruch a rôle
in it, then the only alternative is patience and
understanding of the principle that what will come

will not come through the intelligence. But the
patience has to be a very alert patience; it
can happen that *the* creative suggestion is made
and not noticed. There is a great difference between a group and an individual in that there is
very seldom a common consciousness in a group
which enables others to see with clarity what
has been seen by one. And if that one is not
able to express and formulate what he sees in
such a way that the others can be confronted
with the same experience, then it is possible
for this flash of insight to be wasted.

This sort of work that I am speaking about now,
the work of a group which is committed to the
task of creative thinking, will not arise very
easily. It usually arises through some very
powerful need or very powerful stimulus, which
overcomes all the conditioning and limitations
of the lower levels of our experience. Before
we had this last meeting I had wondered whether
it would be possible to make an experiment in
creative thinking together, as a group, and I
saw that this cannot be done artificially, that
it would really be against the whole conception
of what I am trying to put forward if we tried
to do this just for the sake of doing it. You do
not, in my opinion, ever arrive at creativity
under artificial conditions. That really is the
last point I particularly wanted to make about
this question.

You must not expect that anything you may
learn about creativity - even if I were to know
a great deal more about it than I do and were to
propose to you various kinds of practical exercises of the kind that I found valuable for

myself - will enable you to bring your creative
powers to bear where they are not actually necessary, because it is in the nature of creativity
that it will not allow itself to be *used* by man.
It belongs to a higher level in the hierarchy of
reality than our ordinary human selves, and our
place is rather to serve the creative power than
to make it serve us. It will do things for us because it is man's nature, or destiny, to be a
creative factor in the universe. Man is so made
that he can be a channel of the creative power,
but this is not at his disposal.

I have used the words 'play' and 'spontaneity',
and that may have given you the impression that
I meant something quite arbitrary and without
purpose or meaning. I do not mean that. You may
have thought that when I spoke of children's
play I was comparing creativity to something
which is itself meaningless and transient in
human life, but that is not so. Children's play
is not meaningless and transient; the play of
children is something more than just a preliminary to the development of their own intelligence and powers and the taking over of their
reason. Children's play is a means whereby the
contact between man and the creative power is
constantly being renewed. One has to see that
when children play they are touching something
which is out of the reach of our ordinary consciousness, not something meaningless or arbitrary. If by any tragic misfortune children began
to be born and were so conditioned that they
were without the power of play, the whole human
race would degenerate within a very few genera-
tions. You may think that this is a very strange

and arbitrary thing to assert, and or course it
is so, but if you could understand a little bit
better from your own vision and insight what
creativity is, then you would see that this is a
reality.

This does not of course mean that the kind of
play children enjoy has simply to be preserved in
that form. The ideal thing for man, which does
occasionally occur, is the gradual transformation
of this play-creativity into the creative power.

I think I must, before I stop, return again to
the question of leisure, which is probably going
to become one of the key themes of human history
if, as seems probably, we can remove from human
life and transfer into machines a great deal of
what has in the past taken up time and energy. It
may well be that the solution to the problem of a
human society of the future will be the opening
up of new creative channels. At the present time
we are trying to fill the gaps which are created
in our lives by the removal of drudgery by activities that belong only to the level above automatic functioning, that is, activities on the
level of our sensation. This does not really work
or only works to a limited extent.

With the increasing complexity of human society
the need for a creative adaptation to situations
is going to grow. There is no other way to keep
pace with complexity. I can well believe that
within a hundred years maybe, the ordering of human activity can be largely transferred to machines. The production of the necessities of life
and the means of diversifying our experience -
that is, travelling and transferring experiences
from one place to another - could be handled by

GROUP CREATIVITY

mechanised systems, but into these systems there
will have to enter a quality that is equivalent
to the quality of life or they will become oppres-
sive to man. The only way I can imagine that this
can be done is if far greater attention is paid
to the creative powers of a far greater proportion of people. Clearly, this cannot be done in
isolation, and therefore we shall have to find
methods (which I have only been able vaguely to
suggest because I have so little experience of
this myself and I think very few people in the
world have very much experience of it) and new
and better techniques for bringing about creative
group work. A lot of so-called creative group
work in schools and adult societies for the oc-
cupation of leisure are terribly artificial. They
do not really enter into the field of true creativity because it is closed by a certain kind of
conditioning.

QUESTIONS:-

Q: In the chapter "My Father" of Gurdjieff's
Meetings with Remarkable Men, when Father Borsh
walks into the workshop and starts off: "Where is
God now?" - is this not a form of creative play?

J. G. B.: Yes, certainly. I think that this book
is really in many parts an allegory of this process. In his *Meetings with Remarkable Men,* a lot
of the absurdity of the chapter called "Material
Questions", if you look at it more closely, belongs to this category.

Q: Could you give us an example of creative groups in history?

J. G. B.:   I was talking with somebody about this today, mentioning as an example Rutherford who was in Manchester University when there was a real explosion of discoveries in the field of experimental physics, and also a remarkable freedom of the professor-student relationship. From descriptions I have had of the people, of their work, it seems to me really an example of creative work in the field of natural science. A suggestion night come from almost anyone and because of Rutherford's special quality, he would spot the suggestion and see what kind of experimental work could be done and, as was notorious, he would then get some string and sealing wax and set up an apparatus that would nowadays cost a hundred thousand pounds! Shocks and astonishments of the kind I have spoken about would come from Rutherford and I think from Bohr also. It was much the same at the Cavendish, but already it was getting more intelligent.

Someone described to me the Göttingen group of about the same period, and it had the same kind of quality of permitting the creative suggestions to come from anywhere. It was not considered that only the professor was able to think.

Another period of extraordinary creative activity was the period - you will say this is not thinking, but it is, it belongs to this same category of things - of Spanish mysticism. Amongst St. John, St. Teresa and others there was an extraordinary readiness to listen to each other and to accept ideas that could even give

great shocks to people. Very profound influences
came from that relatively short period of what
amounted to group creative activity because they
had such a big influence on one another. There
was certainly a period of the Cinquecento in
Florence which was very remarkable in that way,
and whatever one may think of this, it undoubtedly poured into the world all sorts of forma-
tive influences.

Much later, in Florence, at about the end of
the nineteenth century, were the pre-Raphaelite
groups. They had something remarkable. Not only
were people like Richard Burton and Strickland
of *The Times* there, but the group also had a
readiness to listen as well as a readiness to
accept different kinds of shocks. This I heard of
from my mother who was brought up in that environment, and certainly I think one can say that
Richard Burton was not backward in giving shocks!
Nor was Strickland from what I have heard of him.

Q.: Does there not have to be something quite
beyond the group to really knit them together in
an unusual way; something bigger than an individual interest?

J. G. B.: Yes, that is so. That is why I say one
cannot produce it artificially. As I said, I
would very much have liked to make an experiment
together, but it cannot be done like that. My own
belief and conviction in this matter is that there
is a creative process incessantly at work; the
continuous creation of St. Augustine is a reality.
Creation never ceases, and we can participate in
it through something greater than we are, greater

113

than the whole group.

Q.: What do you mean by the word intelligence?

J. G. B.: I used the word intelligence just because it happened to be in my mind today and I apologise if I do not make use of any stable terminology. I used the word intelligence purely for convenience, so as not to be too pedantic. Really both sensitivity and consciousness - that is, both the element of skill and the element of judgment - enter into it. Judgment has to be brought to bear in the creative experience; skill has to be used in order to give it expression and form and realize it, but judgment itself will not create. Even understanding is not creative. I take 'creativity' quite literally, in the sense that I understand the word. Without beating about the bush, by creating I mean *out of nothing,* that there are no antecedents. When there is a creative step, there is nothing beforehand which can explain why it should have occurrred. It is in that sense *ex nihilo.* You may say afterwards: "Oh yes, it was obvious there was a 'Zeitgeist' or something, it was in the air, it had to happen when it did happen". All that may still be true, but it still does not mean that it developed out of the past. It comes in a different way.

Q.: But we cannot create except out of the elements of our experience?

J. G. B.: In other words, creativity is nothing but a fresh combination of what is already existing? That is the crux of the matter, and I would

114

say that it is not so; that is post-creative.
The creative step is not simply seeing a new
combination; the creative step is seeing something which was not there before. After that has
happened, then there is putting it into form,
then you have to use what is already there and
you have to judge it and do all sorts of things
in terms of experience and your understanding
must be brought to bear on it. Unless we go the
whole hog and say that creation is creation,
that when there is a creative step something has
come into existence which was not there in any
shape or form before that moment, then we shall
be bound to come back in the end to say that
everything is a machine and that it can all be
produced by super-cybernetics. There is no es-
cape from this except to believe that it is possible for something to come into existence out
of nowhere. That is why I say that creativity
is inseparable from faith.

Q.: But surely the new combination makes something new?

J. G. B.: No. If it were that, then a machine
could do it. A machine can make a new combination that has never been made before. If creativity were no more than new combinations, then in
the end machines will get ahead of us, and many
people believe that.

Q.: Of course there is an emotional quality as
well in creativity ...

J. G. B.: There is no reason why we could not

have emotional machines. Our problem has nothing to do with that. I think myself that this very difficult question can only be resolved in accepting that there is something which is absolutely irreduceable to machines. If you do not accept that, then in the long run you are bound to admit that a machine could be devised to do anything you can describe. Logically everything new is no more than a new combination. On any kind of realistic basis, 'new' means a new combination. If you say creation is more than a new combination then you are saying something which does not make sense at all. But allow me to finish with the words "So what?".

DATE DUE

LOGISTICS
IN
MARKETING

LOGISTICS
IN
MARKETING

edited by   ## Jerry Schorr

Director, Distribution Planning and Research,
Eastern Airlines

Milton Alexander

Professor of Marketing,
School of Business Administration,
Fordham University

Robert J. Franco

President, Gilbert Shoe Company

PITMAN PUBLISHING CORPORATION
New York · Toronto · London · Tel Aviv

PREFACE

PHYSICAL distribution may represent the third largest cost of doing business, but traditionally it has been *the* neglected and disembodied function in the study of marketing. So, too, texts on "transportation management" have tended to lag about a generation behind technological and managerial advances in the field.

This lag has grown all the more pronounced since the advent of "management science" with its newfangled array of mathematical and analytical techniques for the solution of logistical problems within an integrated system of free markets. As the new breed of logisticians see it, the chronic failure to catch up is responsible for much of the present-day inadequacy in managerial decision-making.

The rapid-fire changes in the theory and practice of physical distribution during the past decade have nevertheless wrought a revolution in distribution methods. And business enterprise as a whole has been impressed by the possibilities in marketing logistics: the promise of minimizing risks in planning and implementing marketing programs, of maximizing profit, and of sharing the benefits with consumers.

As might be expected, the burgeoning, multifaceted field of physical distribution has been gradually split into a number of interrelated specialties: transportation, inventory control, warehousing, packaging, order processing, and materials handling. Potentially, at least, each of these specialties is richer in marketing content, more demanding in its mastery of quantitative techniques, more sophisticated in its analytical calculus than all of the traditional facets of "transportation" put together (preoccupied as it has always been with rates and routes within fairly fixed areas of action).

This proliferation has created a critical need in business schools and in industry for a book that incorporates the substance and tone of the "new" marketing logistics—one that updates the thinking, planning, and implementation of the diverse theories and practices; one that applies this new, sometimes recondite knowledge to the practical world of business enterprise. As intimated above, the advances have seemingly been neglected in pedagogy for sundry reasons: a conceptual failure to recognize the importance of physical distribution; a lack of opportunity costs; and more recently, a formidable problem of assimilating brand-new ideas and methods and presenting them in a way that does justice to the infant science, making it understandable and useful to typical graduate students in business administration and to ambitious but "nonmathematical" businessmen.

In such an arcane and complex field, in this period of unprecedented change, we have had to draw on the skills of thinkers and practitioners in several of the physical distribution specialties and, with their gracious permission, we have sought to assimilate each contribution into a meaningful whole.

Our intent has been not only to bring together and update the numerous concepts and techniques of theory and practice, but to make them directly applicable to problems in marketing. Partly as an earnest of this, we present nine problem cases (see Part VI).

We wish to express our gratitude to the organizations that so kindly gave us of their time and talent to make this book possible: the American Management Association, Inc.; the American Telephone and Telegraph Company; Arthur Andersen & Company; Arthur D. Little, Inc.; Booz, Allen & Hamilton, Inc.; E. F. Macdonald Stamp Company; Honeywell, Inc.; the Interstate Commerce Commission; McKinsey & Company, Inc.; Price Waterhouse & Company; REA Express, Inc.; S. D. Leidesdorf & Company; the Sperry & Hutchinson Company; and the Union Carbide Corporation. In particular, we wish to thank Gerald Winston and Ralph Oravec, of Price Waterhouse & Company, for contributing Case 1, "The Small-Order Problem."

In a collaborative book, some errors of substance and of literary grace are perhaps unavoidable. We have conscientiously tried to eliminate them; but for this very reason, we must be held solely responsible for all shortcomings.

Jerry Schorr

Milton Alexander

Robert J. Franco

CONTENTS

Part One   THE SETTING OF LOGISTICS
IN MARKETING

1   Introduction   3
Milton Alexander

2   Organization Theory and Practice in
Physical Distribution Management   17
Milton Alexander

Part Two   PROBLEMS IN MARKETING
LOGISTICS: A FUNCTIONAL
APPROACH

3   Logistical Factors in Transportation   33
Jerry Schorr

4   Location Analysis   45
Donald J. Bowersox

5   The Optimization of Distribution Centers   61
Jerry Schorr

6   Forecasting and Inventory Control   69
Allan Vesley

7   Aggregative Inventory Standards
for Management Decision   81
Granville R. Gargiulo

8   Marketing Logistics, the Order
Processing Cycle, and Computerization   99
Paul R. Saunders

9   A Logistical View of Packaging   129
         Nelson R. Jantzen and Milton Alexander

10   A Logistical View of Containerization   157
         Fred Muller, Jr.

**Part Three   LOGISTICS: THE COMPOSITE
               PICTURE**

11   A Profit Improvement Approach to
         Marketing Logistics   171
         Marvin Flaks

12   Communications: The Catalyst   211
         Warren Billings

13   Systems Analysis in Logistical Planning   221
         Martin L. Ernst

**Part Four   QUANTITATIVE TECHNIQUES FOR
              SOLVING LOGISTICAL PROBLEMS**

14   The Application of Operations
         Research to Problems in Logistics   239
         Robert A. Hammond

15   Special Applications of
         Linear Programing   257
         Jerry Schorr

**Part Five   ISSUES AND PROBLEMS OF
              PUBLIC POLICY**

16   Computers and Government Regulation
         of the Transportation Industry   279
         Robert L. Calhoun and Ernest Weiss

**Part Six   SELECTED CASES IN
              MARKETING LOGISTICS**   297

Case 1:   The Small-Order Problem

Case 2:   The ASME Manufacturing Company—
A Study in Logistical Reasoning and Planning

Case 3:   The ABC Corporation

Case 4:   The Apex Manufacturing Company

Case 5:   The Barnes Manufacturing Company

Case 6:   The Alexander Hamilton
Electric Company

Case 7:   A Short Problem in the Total
Distribution Cost Approach

Case 8:   Using Linear Programing to
Dispatch Vehicles

Case 9:   A Short Problem in Linear
Programing for Distribution Costs

Appendix A   Introduction and Background
to the Transportation Function   359
Robert J. Franco

Appendix B   Functional Components of
Materials Handling   375
Jerry Schorr

Bibliography   381

Index   393

Part
One

**THE SETTING
OF LOGISTICS
IN MARKETING**

1

Milton Alexander

Introduction

If one could personalize a business enterprise, "physical distribution" might well be regarded as its central nervous system; pursuing this analogy further, one could add that the developing system has recently assumed supreme co-ordinative command over the marketing process. Physical distribution is now the third largest cost of doing business (raw materials and labor are the first two), clear evidence of its ascendance in an increasingly technological business environment.

Yet, historically, to the extent that it figured at all in the history and practice of marketing, physical distribution meant "transportation"—a dismal calculus of rates and routes of commodities in conventional channels of distribution. The auxiliary functions in this unassembled jigsaw puzzle— e.g., warehousing and storage—were at best treated disparately, while other functions, such as inventory control and packaging, were not even regarded as parts of the puzzle.

Accordingly, consideration of opportunity costs in physical distribution was at best confined to manipulation of the four factors in the basic trans-portation problem, namely, commodity, source, destination, and unit cost. It is all the more remarkable, therefore, that the once backward, peripheral area of "transportation" has since the end of World War II become the spearhead of "marketing science" and the nerve center of interrelated pro-motional and physical systems of exchange (as reflected in the schema of "pipeline flows" of time, place, and possession utilities shown in Figure 1.1).

As a matter of fact, only in the mid-1950's was physical distribution recognized as a pivotal business cost—for its impact on marketing strategy and planning, on redistribution of wholesale and retail trade, and on the concomitant redistribution of industrial and consumer markets. Only since then has it entered the age of electronic computers, linear programing, and systems analysis—to the point where it may now be defined as an arm of business management responsible for the movement of raw materials and finished goods and for the development of movement systems. Its major functional areas embrace materials handling, inventory control, transporta-

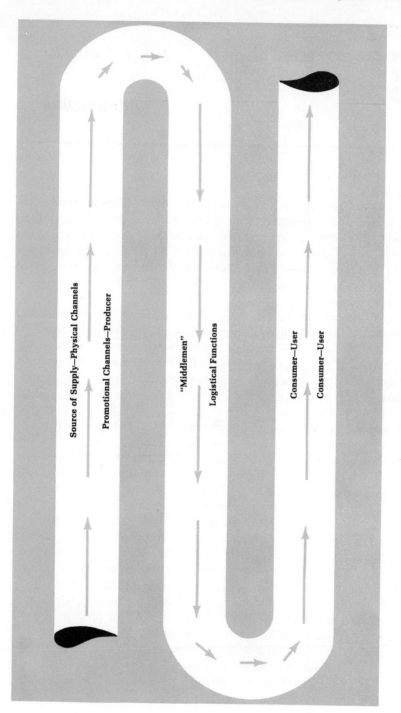

FIGURE 1.1

The marketing distribution pipeline

tion, packaging, order processing, and plant and warehouse location. The aim of physical distribution management is to coordinate all marketing and marketing-related activities so as to minimize the *real* cost of distribution for the firm.

The seemingly abrupt transition from "traffic management" to "physical distribution" is in fact rooted in certain recent phenomena in American economic history. Among these are:

1. The sharp rise in the cost of handling and distributing commodities. This reflects the greatly increased bargaining power of labor unions, the enlargement and dispersion of markets, and the growing service orientation of the economic system as a whole. Handling alone is now said to account for approximately 80 per cent of all indirect labor costs!

2. The phenomenal growth of electronic computers since the mid-1950's. The staggering volume of multivariate data generated by the quantification of distribution problems can now be processed.

3. The urbanization of American life. Markets have proliferated but populations, plants, and buying power are clustered in and around the so-called standard metropolitan areas. Some 67 per cent of the population is now found in 225 standard metropolitan areas, representing over 75 per cent of personal expenditures for commodities. As a result, there has been a rapid rise in intercity freight rates. (In fact, until the end of World War II and the beginning of the suburban movement, distributors were mired in decaying central cities by heavy investments in land, building, and transportation facilities.)[1]

4. The trend toward free-price competition in transportation service. Especially since the Transportation Act of 1940, the federal government has been groping toward this goal. Its aim has been an optimum allocation and utilization of economic resources among the carriers and agencies that comprise the nation's transportation system.[2] The trend toward

---

[1] The basic and overlapping pattern of the typical metropolitan traffic impasse has two parts: (a) a stream of traffic moving in and out of the city, embracing the collection (concentration) and distribution (dispersion) of goods through numerous terminal points; (b) on top of all this, the intra-area movement of goods. While this traffic is preponderantly vehicular, much of it requires the terminal facilities of other modes of transportation, especially railroads.

[2] If the prevailingly inadequate profits of transportation companies are any criterion, our economy suffers from overinvestment in transportation. At present, relatively few railroads are able to recover the full economic cost attributable to the transportation function. In any event, there are many plans afoot for pretesting free rate determination—including experimental freight rates, new combinations of services, and variations of existing systems of freight classification.

free intercarrier competition has been hastened by legal decisions which seemingly outlaw uniform delivered pricing.

5. The dynamism inherent in physical distribution within a free, flexible society of mass consumption. It is reflected in the expansion and redistribution of markets, the changing competitive structure of industries brought on by their ever-increasing size, the emergence of new modes of transport and handling, and product susbtitution (both in the raw and finished state). Since the end of World War II, decentralization of manufacturing has been further promoted by the fact that rates on manufactured goods have increased faster than those on raw materials. Nearness to markets, therefore, has become all the more essential. Also, the ubiquitousness of commodity components (including "raw" materials) has tended to draw industry even closer to metropolitan areas.

6. The diversification of product lines, for example, through conglomerate mergers and innovation. This, of course, makes for a disparity of products, and so demands varying distribution systems.

7. The change in management orientation from production to marketing. The "new marketing concept," also a post-World War II phenomenon, has placed special stress on customer service,[3] a task obviously fit for the logistician rather than the old-line traffic manager.

What next? Toward what ultimate goal of profitability is the infant "science" of physical distribution headed? In all likelihood, toward a massive system completely automated from receipt of order to shipment of material.

Is physical distribution going to do for marketing what the assembly line and rationalization did for industrial management? Is it going to be stripped down to a science of preplanned computerized tradeoffs in decision-making, including even the function of persuasion (as it already does in at least one of the sectors of physical distribution, namely packaging)?

In physical distribution, a discipline where change is still the order of the day—and where there is still much room for disagreement as to precisely what the subject embodies and where it belongs in the organization structure—it is well to begin by asking some stock questions. First, semantics. What are the functional boundaries of physical distribution in theory and in practice? How does physical distribution compare and contrast with "transportation," the term it has begun to supplant? What is the underlying

---

[3]Hence the fairly recent spread of manufacturer branch warehouses, as distributors have insisted on curtailing their investment in inventory.

concept of the discipline as a system? What are its goals? From the perspective of business history, what is its genealogy? Let us now consider each question under its respective heading.

1. Historically, as is self-evident, physical distribution is an outgrowth of transportation and traffic management of those simple days when the rigidity of law and the virtual absence of competition among many kinds of transportation precluded any notion of optimization. If any figuring was required as between alternative carriers and routes, it involved little more than a straight-line computation of which method of shipment offered the quickest delivery at the lowest cost per ton-mile—measured against the need to deliver at a specified time.[4] In the 1930's, however, this relatively inert stance of "traffic management" was jolted by the new gospel of managerial decentralization. And through the medium of "interdisciplinary" management committees, the old-line transportation department made contact with other related (but still detached) physical distribution functions, particularly warehousing and storage.[5]

2. Functionally, "transportation," like "physical distribution" today, has been found on both the administrative and operational levels of management. However, in earlier days its jurisdiction was sharply limited, as noted above.[6] Transportation was commonly treated as an auxiliary to production.

As already suggested, physical distribution began to break out of its "traffic" cul-de-sac long before the entrepreneurial switch from production to marketing orientation. And by the mid-1950's, physical distribution practitioners actually began to turn tables on the other segments of management—thanks, in large part, to the many fruitful applications of operations research techniques and electronic data processing, and the emergence of an all-inclusive "management science." In a real sense, physical distribution may be viewed as a corollary of the curiously belated recognition that buying-selling transactions are the basis of economic

---

[4]In any case, the prevalence of "exceptions rates," "tapering principles," zoning, delivered pricing, and the like—all sanctioned or tolerated by government—would have dampened the ardor of old-time optimizers.

[5]The fruits of this contact began to appear in the literature in the late 1940's. See, especially, Paul E. Holden, Lounsbury S. Fish, and Hubert L. Smith, *Top-Management Organization and Control*, Stanford University Press, 1947.

[6]The straight-line opportunity costing of the past is in sharp contrast with today's advanced computerized approach to solutions of the basic transportation problem used by up-to-date firms, which is discussed in Chapter 16.

life: With time the most crucial element in business planning and doing, physical distribution became the focal point of entrepreneurial activity.[7]

With the emergence of a worldwide market system, decision-making became more complex and infinitely more hazardous. Quite naturally, new and more advanced tools of prediction and measurement were brought to bear; and, in these circumstances, physical distribution inevitably became a rather esoteric discipline, requiring the talents of mathematicians, statisticians, operations researchers, and communications experts.

In short, physical distribution has, in the past decade, become the first of the marketing functions to be brought under the quantitative constraints of decision premises and principles of choice.[8]

3. Conceptually (and adventitiously, as happens so often in economic history), a number of theoretical and engineering breakthroughs have enabled business management to optimize its decisions, in real time, under conditions of uncertainty.[9]

All these developments, eagerly embraced by the new breed of theoreticians and practitioners in physical distribution, culminated in a regrouping of functions within the firm and in new (albeit tentative) boundary lines for the various specialties: transportation, inventory control, order processing, materials handling, communications, warehousing, packaging, storage, and law.

What of the present status of physical distribution in the typical American firm?

First, as we will see in Chapter 2, physical distribution is increasingly conspicuous on all levels of management, both conceptually (as a systemic approach to problem-solving in marketing logistics) and functionally (as a bundle of interdependent technical skills).[10]

---

[7]A central theme, incidentally, that is implicit in Wroe Alderson and Paul E. Green, *Planning and Problem Solving in Marketing*, Irwin, 1964.

[8]A brief but incisive analysis of the underlying decision theory will be found in John A. Howard, *Marketing Theory*, Allyn & Bacon, 1965 (especially Chapter 3, "Normative Decision Models").

[9]The uses to which this new generation of measurement tools is being put is, of course, the theme of much of this book, in particular, Chapters 14–16.

[10]Top management's point of view regarding the importance of physical distribution is perhaps most sharply reflected in the periodic surveys by leading trade publications in the field. See, for example, the findings of the survey "Physical Distribution Management, How It Is Organized," *Transportation and Distribution Management*, October–November 1963.

Second, as the concept of "channel of distribution is widened and, in fact, split so as to include a confluent physical flow of goods, the physical "pipeline" is becoming increasingly differentiated from the traditional legal-promotional channel. In the modern view, *both* flows are propelled by an interdependent and successive series of market transactions.

In fact, so pervasive by its very nature is the physical distribution function that it has become enmeshed in numerous interrelated activities of the business firm. This is evident from the following description of the subject matter of each of the seven major specialties of physical distribution:

1. Transportation: The movement of raw materials and semiprocessed and finished products (either through private or common carriers), which commences with the purchase of raw materials and ends with the delivery of the product to the ultimate consumer or user (see Chapters 3 and 4). Here, linear programing techniques (as we shall see in Chapter 15) are now crucial in minimizing transportation costs.

2. Inventory control: The maintenance and storage of optimal levels of cycle and safety stocks in order to assure adequate servicing of customer orders and a minimum of stockouts (see Chapters 8 and 9).

3. Order processing: The processing of all documents pertaining to internal and external transactions—sales orders, shipping manifests, invoices, loading forms, payments, receipts, warehouse storage data, pallet-loading forms, etc. (see Chapter 5).

4. Materials handling: The internal movement of raw materials and finished products through plants and warehouses. Here, mechanization of handling equipment, geared to unitized shipping, has become imperative for the modern business firm (see Chapter 14).

5. Communications: The liaison component between the various "line" sectors of the physical distribution system (see Chapter 12).

6. Warehousing: The storage of goods within private and/or public warehouses to insure an optimal level of delivery service. (Ideally, "scientific" warehousing tends to equalize opportunity costs between marketing areas—as will be discussed in Chapters 5, 6, and 7.)

7. Packaging: Methods of coating, wrapping, and boxing goods which provide the necessary protection for commodities, and yet are consistent with common carrier regulation, and which minimize handling costs (see Chapters 12 and 13).

Third, reflecting this pervasiveness of physical distribution, the old organizational structure of "transportation" must be completely realigned.[11] As yet, there is no "one best way" by which to fit physical distribution into an organization. However, a number of significant interfunctional relationships have begun to emerge, and will be treated at some length in Chapter 2.

Fourth, physical distribution is the principal key to profit control: (1) Its costs can be controlled; (2) it bears directly on the cost of production as well as marketing (and as the "value adding" catalyst to both, its optimization of product movement is inevitably reflected in the profit performance of both functions); (3) it is one of the larger cost factors.

Clearly, however, the branches of physical distribution are still in flux and proceed at different rates of development, for they are variously affected by different organizational environments and respond in varying ways to operations research treatment.[12] And no wonder. For the so-called marketing management concept itself, which predates the physical distribution approach but is basic to it, is still conceptually ambiguous, although, as a distinct area of top administrative and operational management, it goes back to the 1920's.[13]

Hence, many concepts of physical distribution must be clarified if logisticians are to fulfill their "mission" in management science. Physical distribution must be freed of makeshift numerical constraints, lagging acculturation of the work force, and often archaic marketing policy and practice. Let us briefly review the nature of each of these remaining tasks.

BUSINESS PHILOSOPHY

Inasmuch as physical distribution deals with a functional area that is rife with tradeoff possibilities and opportunities, it is necessary to decide at the

---

[11]Some logisticians may well take exception to this "rule." One of them, employed by one of the nation's largest diversified industrial corporations, would actually reverse the "rule." Referring to his firm's adoption of a logistical approach to marketing, he summed up his experience as follows: "The broad organization of the marketing function of our business could not be dictated by physical distribution considerations. Instead, we felt that our charge was to use fundamental principles of logistics to develop a system of physical distribution that was most adaptable to and compatible with the organization structure extant."

[12]It is ironic that the often breakneck speed of advances in management science and computer technology has frequently served to retard the logistician's "real-time" response.

[13]It is noteworthy that physical distribution, like the "new" marketing concept, must initially contend with the hostility of vested job interests, due to widespread fears of technological disemployment through rationalization and automation among old-timers in traffic management. Once a physical distribution system is installed, it is quite generally freed from obstructionism, unlike the case of the "new" marketing concept, where interpersonal friction persists long after the fact, especially in the area of persuasion.

outset, on a micro basis, what shall be the policy constraints between cost on the one side and customer service on the other. Therefore, philosophy and approach must take precedence over quantitative techniques of problem-solving (which, after all, are only the tools of management), and planning and profit objectives over action. As is pointed out in Chapter 5, there is much more to optimization than the much touted tradeoff.

Basically, insofar as a "philosophy" of physical distribution is concerned, the "solutions" depend on how far one wants and/or needs to go in providing consumer satisfaction. This rule is illustrated in three (of many) applicable marketing problem areas:

1. *In marketing planning*   Here, marketing (including physical distribution) action depends largely on management's perception and appraisal of opportunities and threats (to its market status) under conditions of uncertainty, as, for example in:
    (a) selection of optimal combinations of operating, financial, and systemic inputs and outputs;
    (b) integration of subsets of relationships affecting the marketing system over time and in space—external (consumer, trade channel, and competition) and internal (involving marketing and other departments); and
    (c) profit objectives, particularly those of the middle range (three to five years).[14]

2. *In marketing innovation*   Presumably, marketing management is oriented to the consumer point of view, in accordance with the needs-satisfaction theory of selling. But in the absence of rules and standards of procedure —say, for introduction of new products—this managerial philosophy posits many more questions than it answers. Hence, the unavoidable subjectivism (on the part of many managements) in solving such problems as: Which time and place utilities (of existing products) is the new product designed to supplement or supplant? How will the new product, at least initially, be distributed, and to what extent can the projected physical and promotional flows of goods be controlled? What is the anticipated impact of physical distribution on the basic life cycle of the new product (and vice versa)? Will the distribution channels and advertising media change as the product evolves? Is the relative density of product flow measurable, and if so, how does one test for capacity of channels (including the interaction between physical and promotional flows)?

---

[14]The author is indebted to the late Professor Wroe Alderson for some of the ideas presented in this section.

3. *In locating a new store* Here, the retailer is confronted by a large number of countervailing pressures stemming from socioeconomic characteristics of the population (including buying power and propensity to consume), the structure of retail trade, the nature of competition, differentials in rent, "attainable" sales volume, traffic flows and trade affinities, custom, the distribution of prospective consumers in the area, physical accessibility to sources of supply, and (if a chain unit) nearness to other units of the firm, to corporate headquarters, etc. An increasing number of such problems can be solved, as we shall see in Chapters 14 and 15, through "new" techniques of operations research. But even so, the retailer must *first* take an audit of his capabilities, his financial resources, the merchandising and service policies he intends to pursue, and (above all) his *net* objective—in short, an audit of the reasons for and against opening the store at the particular site.

ORGANIZATION

It may be right and proper to assume (as do champions of the marketing management concept) that all functions of the firm are interrelated *under the hegemony of marketing*. But as we already have noted (and will detail in the next chapter), there are both pros and cons for positioning physical distribution in one or the other of several places on the chart; the pros and cons vary according to size of firm, share of market, length and width of channel of distribution, nature of product, required and available skills, and a host of other variables.

As previously stressed, the first need in solving this problem is a clear statement of principles, objectives, and a semantic consensus. Who does what? Which functions properly belong under the general heading "physical distribution"? How many of these functions may be shared with others? It will, of course, be helpful to visualize these relationships via the marketing management concept by charting the interdependent functions.

However, one cannot overstate the need for prudence in organization planning. It is just as bad for a firm to extend physical distribution to the point where it encompasses everything, as it was in the old days of "transportation" to restrict it to one aspect only of the distribution problem. Not only have human skills and aspirations yet to catch up with the elaborate functional structure that is scientific marketing management,[15] but dynamic forces now agitating the economy must also be taken account of.

---

[15]For an up-to-date review of the underlying precepts of scientific marketing management, see Henry H. Albers, *Principles of Organization and Management*, 2nd ed., Wiley, 1965.

1. The multifaceted complexity of international trade, as reflected in shifting shares of foreign markets; production and distribution activities originated abroad (by American and local businessmen); the Common Market and other regional blocs on the one hand, and countervailing trends toward freer trade on the other; the competitive and legal challenges to established rate structures in international shipping; the advent of automated order processing and materials handling; the uncertain market potentials in the so-called developing regions of the world, etc.[16]

2. The rather recent growth of competition in all of the seven sectors of physical distribution—between carriers, routes, sources of supply, markets, and alternative institutions and methods for handling, storing, and packaging. (The resultant freedom of choice for users, of course, broadens the scope of optimization in marketing decisions.)

3. The steep rise in size of the firm and in the expansion of domestic markets. Two of the by-products of this trend are economy of size and decentralization of management. But as another result, management must contend with the sharpened uncertainties of sluggishness in organization and in human acceptance and mastery of the new technocracy.

4. The acceleration of advances in communications and transportation—electronic data processing (enabling management to make logistical decisions "on the line" and in "real time"), containerization, TOFC, automatic warehousing, dataphones, and the rest. Yet, as one authority has pointed out, these advances have inevitably pushed physical distribution practice into *new* problem areas.[17]

ACCULTURATION

While the framework of some business school curricula in "transportation" has been broadened to take in related specialties (i.e., the other segments of "physical distribution"), many students are still being prepared for old, often obsolete "traffic management" skills. In fact, only some 34 of the

---

[16]Logistical problems peculiar to international marketing are treated in a large number of new books, among them: Richard D. Robinson, *International Business Policy*, Holt, Rinehart & Winston, 1964; John Fayerweather, *International Marketing*, Prentice-Hall, 1965; Wendell C. Gordon, *International Trade—Goods, People, and Ideas*, Knopf, 1965; Paul V. Horn and Henry Gomez, *International Trade—Principles and Practices*, 4th ed., Prentice-Hall, 1959; Max J. Wasserman, Charles W. Hultman, and Russell F. Moore, *The Common Market*, Simmons-Boardman, 1964.
[17]See Chapter 12.

nation's 2,000-plus colleges and universities offer a full four-year curriculum even in transportation.[18]

Perhaps related to this cultural lag is another problem, expressed in the increasingly common view that the new quantitative techniques have been sprouting so thick and fast that they have left managerial concepts and semantics far behind. True, this type of "lag" tends to slow the progress of all new disciplines, but it must not, for this reason, be treated with complacency.

A third problem in the further growth and development of physical distribution is found in the dynamism of the over-all marketing process, described earlier in this chapter. Naturally, all such ferment places a severe strain on the human and technological resources of an infant "marketing science."

SELF-OPTIMIZATION

The problem of measuring the effectiveness of physical distribution, given its conceptual and practical complexities, as described above, is substantial.[19] Some champions of physical distribution may contend that continuing self-evaluation is not necessary inasmuch as the best minds in marketing have yet to resolve that perennial issue of "does distribution cost too much?"; or even to measure *net* effectiveness of such relatively well-established marketing expenditures as advertising.

Yet, if the discipline of physical distribution is to attain the level of social importance and professional recognition that logisticians seek, it must be subjected to the acid test of profitability—namely, What is the contribution of physical distribution to the net profit of the firm?

The answer to this question provides more than a yardstick of performance (of the old ways versus the new, and of differences between sets of alternatives), more than a resolution of the old argument between cost control and cost reduction. Involved is a fundamental principle in the management of the firm: balance and synchronization between the activities of top management (concerned with problems of conceptualization, planning, direc-

---

[18]This figure is based on a recent national survey conducted by Northwestern University, confirmed by observations of Charles J. Prange, director of personnel development, REA Express, Inc., and by the author's own canvass of business school catalogs.

[19]For a brief "how to" treatment of this problem, see Ward A. Fredericks, "Techniques of Planning and Control in Physical Distribution Management," *Transportation and Distribution Management*, September 1964, pp. 30–35.

tion, and control) and of operational management (concerned with pro-graming and implementation). In fact, the answer itself opens up still another (and rather embarrassing) subject, the gap in internal communications. One operations researcher has frankly posited this communications issue in the age of computers as follows:

> [One of the crucial problems in computer-based simulation] is the absence of what might be called "well-defined structure" in many of the problems we deal with as managers. If two men cannot agree on the exact nature of a problem, let alone on the best approach to solving it or on the criteria by which alternative solutions are to be evaluated, a tool as rigid as the computer is today won't help very much. To make more use of computers, we shall have to find better ways of formulating our problems, our objectives, and our criteria for evaluation—a development, incidentally, which may prove eminently worthwhile even without there being any role involved for the computer . . . .
>
> [What is needed, therefore, is] a better means of communication between the manager and the computer. Today, even after the problem and the data required for its solution are completely agreed upon, a programmer—whose activities are slow and time-consuming—must intervene, in effect, between the question and the answer. There has been talk of a man-machine language that would permit direct "dialogue": the user, without detailed technical training, being able to ask questions of the computer in everyday language and being able to follow them up with other questions based on the answers to the first—all without a programmer . . . intervening.
>
> . . . If I had to rank the barriers to effective use of [such] computers for management purposes, I would put our own limitations as users first; machine language, or software, problems second; and hardware considerations a distant third, well behind the others.[20]

We who practice and/or preach physical distribution ought not to be unduly self-conscious about our "growing pains." After all, it took advertising practitioners some 75 years to recognize the imperative need to measure their productivity! However, because of the numerous cumulative complexities in the marketing process, discussed above, we cannot (and should not) count on such a protracted period of grace. Nor, as we shall see in later portions of this book, can we count on the reversibility of faulty and costly managerial decisions. Perhaps optimization of the physical distribution approach requires that at this particular point in time, we make haste slowly.

---

[20]From "Changes in Management and the Management of Change," a talk by Walter Klem before the I.O.M.A. Annual Conference, New York City, September 30, 1964.

But in any event, if logistics in marketing is as good as its promise, then its benign influence will transcend the interests of particular firms and industries and will promote the cause of economic freedom. For a mature systemic approach to physical distribution would ultimately unlock the secrets of success in logistics (as was previously the case with rationalization in manufacturing) for all; and would enable entrepreneurs (at least potentially) to compete on technologically equal terms. Accordingly, market competition, at least on this account, would tend to be equalized; and this, in turn, might well lead to a renewed quest for distinctiveness in other aspects of production and marketing strategy—perhaps with fresh emphasis on *genuine* differences in product performance and consumer satisfaction. Therefore, other things being equal, physical distribution could ultimately be expected to maximize the national dividend.

2

Milton Alexander

Organization Theory and Practice in Physical Distribution Management

Problems of functional design and human relations, of authority and power, of centralization versus decentralization, chain of command and span of control, bureaucracy and crosswise relationships, etc., are pervasive in industrial organization. But they prevail with particular force in the realm of physical distribution because of the dynamism attending its precipitous growth. Technological leapfrogs have virtually precluded the orderly assimilation of organizational ideas; and in fact, marketing logisticians have scarcely found the time even to seek the proverbial "best way."

Beyond the birth pangs of a new discipline, organizers of physical distribution must grapple with two resultant problems. The first, familiar to readers of management literature, involves the "human equation" in structuring functional interrelationships—whether in terms of psychological balance, linear allocation of human resources, or marginal gains and losses. Quite obviously, the behavior of people does not readily lend itself to probabilistic simulation. The failure to achieve a consensus as to the conceptual nature of physical distribution, noted in the previous chapter, is therefore not surprising (see Figures 2.1A, 2.1B, 2.2, and 2.3).

The second of these organizational problems is rooted in the second industrial revolution, still underway, and has, in fact, given rise to a wholly new cybernetic system of precise, lightning-fast communication and computation, by means of which managerial policy may be translated into optimal action in and between sources of supply, factory, warehouse, and market place.

It will be recalled that the first industrial revolution, some two hundred years ago, was more or less confined to innovations in manufacturing: first, interchangeable parts and standardization of machines, run by steam power and later by electricity; then, the assembly line and mass production. All else

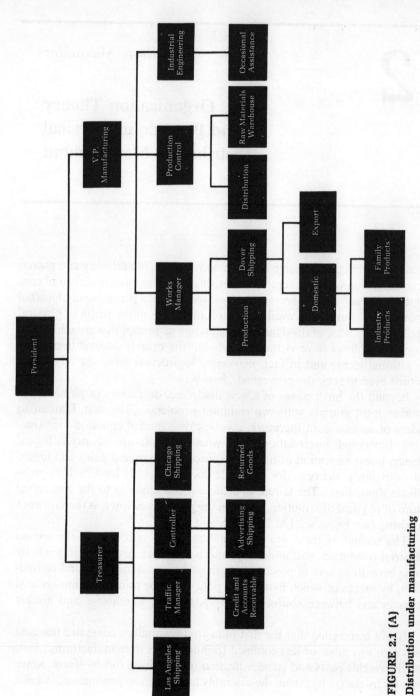

FIGURE 2.1 (A)

Distribution under manufacturing

SOURCE: *Management Report No. 49*, American Management Association. By permission.

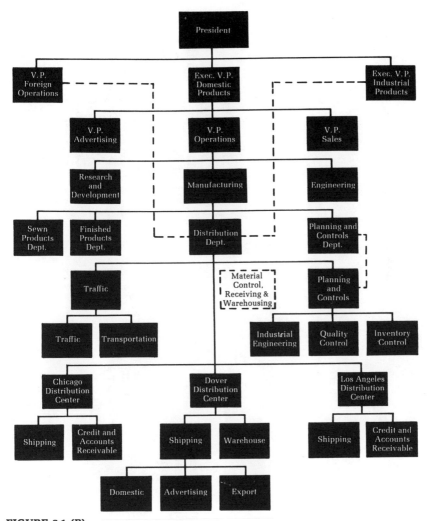

FIGURE 2.1 (B)

Distribution under manufacturing

SOURCE: *Management Report No. 49*, American Management Association. By permission.

in the micro organization, including sales and finance, was left virtually untouched by the revolution during its first hundred years. Under these circumstances, it was relatively simple to organize the satellite functions around production. And all the more so, since differentiation between the four basic elements of the structure—production, finance, sales, and engineering—was

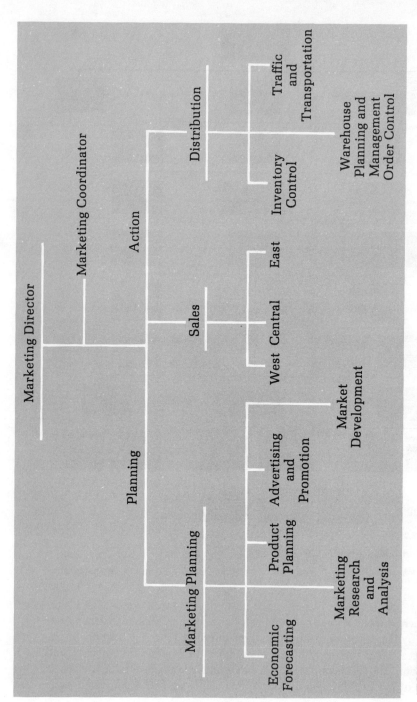

FIGURE 2.2

Distribution under marketing

SOURCE: *Management Report No. 49*, American Management Association. By permission.

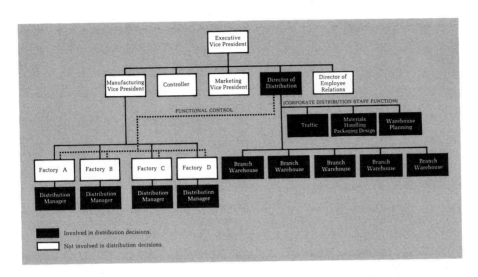

FIGURE 2.3

Distribution as an entity

SOURCE: *Management Methods.* By permission.

clear; and little staff activity was involved. Finally, the predominantly line structure of the organization assured direct and prompt communication between and within levels of management, along closely defined chains of command.

All this is in contrast to the second industrial revolution, which has not only revolutionized manufacturing methods all over again (through automation); but in addition has, as described in Chapter 1, also unsettled the marketing process. The center of gravity in marketing, meanwhile, has shifted more and more from origin to destination. This shift has complicated the task of the logistician who, in an unstable market, must choose between an ever-increasing number of alternatives, representing different tradeoffs between service and cost.

By the same token, however, nothing seems to stick nowadays—neither title nor function, nor especially "system" of organization—in this convulsive environment of scientific change. On top of this, there is much semantic confusion, which makes it all the more impractical to classify and label the different organizational patterns that have evolved.[1] Hence, the futility of organizational comparisons between firms and even between industries.

---

[1] It used to be that an organizational structure was made to last for fifteen to twenty years; nowadays, one year, in the words of one observer, "is about as much as a firm dare expect."

For these very reasons of uncertainty, conceptualization of a firm's logistical organization clearly must come first. In fact, from a marketing management point of view, there is an even more compelling reason for such priority. Namely, all short-term and intermediate decisions relating to the structure of the firm tend to be final, binding management to get the work of physical distribution done through others via one particular system of functional relationships, both line and staff. Quite obviously, a firm must analyze its basic transportation problem and the resultant organizational requirements for optimal flow of its goods to market long before it can hope profitably to utilize the sophisticated techniques examined in this book. And as a start, top management must re-examine many of the seemingly hackneyed issues of a consumer-oriented enterprise. To wit:

1. What business are we in?[2]

2. What is our business philosophy? (especially as this relates to the weighing of customer service and cost).

3. What is (are) our market(s)? And how is this total market and its various segments penetrated most economically?

4. To what extent, in terms of human, financial, and physical resources, do we utilize operations research methodology in our particular marketing process?

5. How do we best organize to achieve our goal—i.e., how do we plan, direct, coordinate, control, and staff the physical distribution complex of functions?

The amount of sincerity and skill applied to this formidable task of conceptualization will in large part determine whether management runs physical distribution or physical distribution runs management!

Unfortunately, however, there are no finite solutions for problems of human organization in physical distribution or any other functional area of business enterprise. True, in a disembodied state, such solutions (even under conditions of uncertainty) may be found for organizing the logistical "mix" of materials, plant, and equipment in the pipeline flow between origin and destination. But the human imponderables (say, of industrial discipline) cannot be precisely measured or simulated. Hence, the quest for the "best way" is in part *qualitatively* stochastic: that is, it must continually reconsider

---

[2]A question that first received conspicuous treatment by Theodore Levitt, "Marketing Myopia," *Harvard Business Review*, July–August 1960.

people, business climate, competitive conditions, and other independent "human" variables.

Also, in retrospect, the evolutionary development of physical distribution organization seems to have followed a course radically different from that of the other major functional areas of business enterprise. These others—production, finance, engineering, even persuasion—were first "scientifically" structured at the turn of the century, in a relatively static period in socioeconomic thought and technology. Physical distribution, on the other hand (as stressed above), was born of a technological upheaval which seeks to automate the production and distribution of goods, thus to optimize probabilistic options in business decision-making. It is, in fact, part and parcel of an emerging management science. All of which adds up to a grinding process of rationalization that shows no sign of abatement.

Hence, any organization plan for physical distribution must be, at best, tentative; that is, subject to the ever-changing demands of technology, law, and countervailing micro- and macro-economic pressures. (See Figure 2.4.) It follows, therefore, that our inquiry must for the present be confined to an analysis of largely inductive concepts and principles, drawn from the experience of firms and industries in organizing for physical distribution.

Philosophical, financial, and competitive factors being equal, the functional design of physical distribution is naturally determined by a particular firm's product flow—some variant of the generalized schema which is shown in Figure 2.4.

This generic product flow, in turn, provides the framework for a firm's channel of distribution. Basically, then, organizational structure is a function of a firm's transportation needs, as these pertain to a specific commodity or group of commodities at a given point in time.[3]

The simplicity of such a direct approach to organization is somewhat deceptive, however. And this is largely because of the fragmentation and proliferation of the logistical functions in the firm. In the first place, as has been apparent to text writers and chartists almost from the start, physical distribution is *inherently* part of production, marketing, accounting, engineering, finance, and even top management—at one and the same time.[4]

---

[3]With a rising trend toward diversification and conglomerate mergers in industry, it is quite obvious that varying and perhaps conflicting needs of marketing and marketing processes must be reconciled. In terms of optimal organization, however, such reconciliation is often quite impracticable since it may require (at least theoretically) a different structure for each different flow of product and channel of distribution.

[4]For an early yet incisive analysis of this problem, see Paul E. Holden, Lounsbury S. Fish, and Hubert L. Smith, *Top-Management Organization and Control*, Stanford University Press, 1947.

FIGURE 2.4

Physical distribution organization changes

SOURCE: Reprinted by permission from *Business Management* magazine. Copyright 1960 by Management Magazines, Inc.

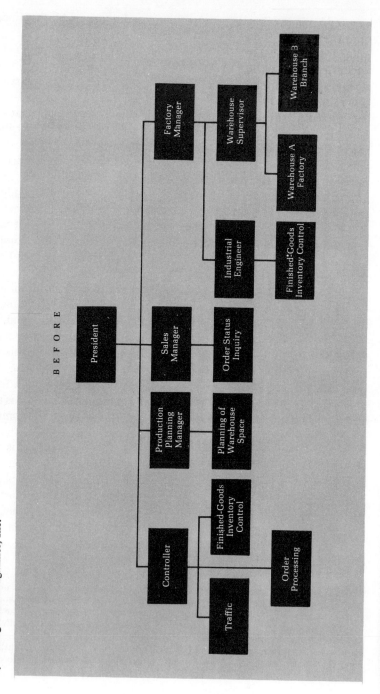

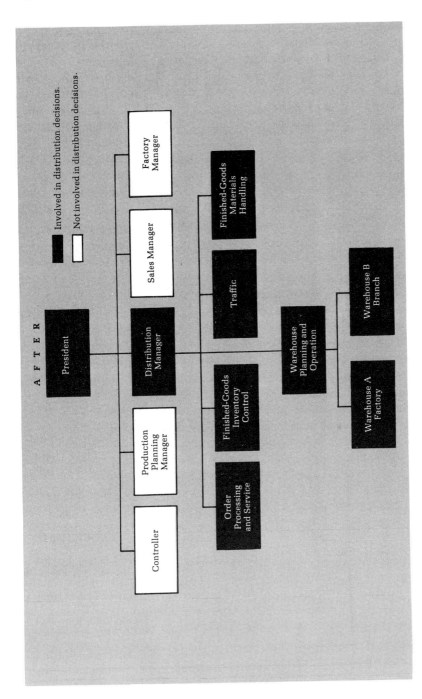

AFTER

■ Involved in distribution decisions.
□ Not involved in distribution decisions.

President

Controller

Production Planning Manager

Distribution Manager

Sales Manager

Factory Manager

Order Processing and Service

Finished-Goods Inventory Control

Traffic

Finished-Goods Materials Handling

Warehouse Planning and Operation

Warehouse A Factory

Warehouse B Branch

In the second place, physical distribution itself is a catch-all term for six related but distinguishable functional areas. And atop these "natural" complications have been two others, "man-made" since the end of World War II: the concept of marketing management, a "system" of only partially controllable inputs and outputs, encompassing a scattering of relationships up and down and across the organization chart; and the advent of cybernetics, as reflected in the large-scale applications of electronic data processing to business decision-making.

These revolutionary developments have played havoc with traditional organization theory and practice; and in due course, have brought attempts to refine and reconcile the differing expedients. So far, only one thing is certain—namely, that the traditional emphasis on transportation by academic and business analysts is foreign to any systemic approach to optimization of physical distribution.[5]

However, it is not enough to pay tribute to the relationship of transportation to the other segments of logistics and to the need for managerial coordination. The question remains: Where does physical distribution belong in the organizational structure of the firm? And the answer (albeit simplistic) boils down to one of three choices—production, marketing, or by itself. These three possibilities are shown in Figures 2.1[A], 2.1[B], 2.2, and 2.3.

Clearly (at least to the eye well-versed in business administration), there is something to be said for and against each of these three alternatives. But while it is hard to generalize on *the* best and *the* worst, one must conclude that physical distribution organization preferably should represent a compromise between the second and third alternatives. Where the consumer- (or buyer-) oriented concept *really* holds sway, physical distribution belongs under the marketing vice-president; and where this is not the case, the physical distribution manager should occupy the middle (balancing and coordinating) ground between production and sales; and all three should report as equals to a common line superior. For obvious reasons, it is not wise to "load" the physical distribution function with a sales bias or (what is probably worse) a production bias.[6]

As with all organizational problems throughout the annals of business history, it has been the heuristic lessons of trial and error experience rather than those of theory that have been implemented by the individual firm. And characteristically, drastic action has been taken only *after* the firm's diagnosis of organizational weakness.

---

[5]And with good reason—inasmuch as "transportation" accounts for less than 25 per cent of the total physical distribution cost.

[6]For the reasons why, in review, see "Physical Distribution, the Neglected Marketing Function," *Industrial Marketing*, October 1961, pp. 102–107.

Apart from the spread of marketing management as a way of entrepreneurial life, the impetus for reopening the long-neglected issue of logistical organization sprang from a number of interrelated events in the micro–macro economic environment. These events were discussed in Chapter 1.

That there are many different and apparently feasible ways of structuring physical distribution has been evident from the start of the new management science in the late 1940's. The course of organizational development since then is shown in Figure 2.4. As the reader will note, the sequence is depicted in five stages:

1. The traditional production-oriented approach, whereby "transportation" (along with marketing) is treated rather primitively as more or less of an appendage of manufacturing (see Figures 2.1[A] and 2.1[B]);

2. The impact of the managerial process of decentralization (which actually goes back to the 1920's) in an emerging marketing department with some responsibility for a number of fairly distinct specialties, including some which are now encompassed in physical distribution, such as transportation, warehousing, inventory control, and packaging (see Figure 2.2);

3. The predawn of physical distribution consciousness, as reflected in the Stanford study;[7]

4. The transition from "transportation" to "physical distribution" (linked to the advent of marketing management), depicted in several pioneering case studies by the American Management Association in the late 1950's (see Figure 2.3); and

5. The novel forms and shapes of physical distribution structures, incorporating most or all of the constituent specialties, all of which mirror the ferment of continuing change in physical distribution concepts and techniques (see Figure 2.4).

Can we now project from these evolving expedients to a generalized pattern (to the "best way") of logistical organization? Clearly not, in the author's view, for several reasons:

1. The conceptual framework of marketing management itself, into which logistics must be fitted, is much too elastic for objective comparisons of alternative organizational solutions.

---

[7]Holden, Fish, and Smith, *op. cit.*

2. The necessarily systemic, split-level approach to physical distribution has so far failed to crystallize the functional relationship between persuasion and logistics, and between administration and operation.

3. The new quantitative techniques for solving logistical problems have still to be digested by the infant discipline. Hence, even if industry could agree on "who does what" in physical distribution—e.g., in the implementation of operations research and communications theory—we have still to chart the flows of authority and responsibility. Having failed to do this seemingly prosaic chore, the "tail" continues to "wag the dog." That is, technicians instead of administrators often call the policy turns in many a firm overly anxious to "go modern."

4. More so than in other spheres of management, the perennial problem of "getting work done through others" is hobbled by poor communications—between the tenuous (because new) loci of relationships between supervisors and subordinates, internal and external. It is, of course, understood that there are more complex causes than newness of physical distribution systems behind the communications gap; and, in fact, that these other causes are often more important in resolving the issues of organization for physical distribution. Basically, in trying to optimize between alternative opportunities for sending and receiving goods, and for trading off considerations of customer service against those of cost, we are confronted by a set of conditions quite unique in marketing history. First, there is the managerial confidence that, unlike traditional marketing problems in persuasion, solutions for logistical unknowns are quantitatively feasible. Second, there is the somewhat countervailing yet intimate relationship with the persuasion function scattered throughout the firm (a function, parenthetically, which may well continue to defy quantification in a free, untrammeled consumption society). Third, there is the firm's communications problem in interpreting and adjusting to governmental fiat, which in the case of physical distribution affects the key segments of transportation, warehousing, packaging, and even inventory control.[8]

It would be foolhardy at this early point in the evolution of physical distribution systems to piece together organizational principles from a bevy of experiences and expedients under diverse conditions of business un-

---

[8]For a lucid exposition of the positive side of this subject, see the treatment of communications in Chapter 12. For a theoretical view, see Adrian W. McDonough, *Information Economics and Management Systems*, McGraw-Hill, 1963; Wroe Alderson and Stanley Shapiro, *Marketing and the Computer*, Prentice-Hall, 1964.

certainty. However, one generalization can be made with reasonable assurance; namely, that regardless of the special configurations that organization charts will ultimately assume for business logistics in general and for the individual firm in particular, physical distribution will inevitably come under the hegemony of marketing. The reasons, which will become increasingly clear in reading the selected cases later on, may be summed up as follows:

1. Survival of the firm is of course the first and foremost goal of its management. Hence, the pervasiveness of marketing management with its gospel of consumer satisfaction, and its determination to exploit the firm's market potential to the maximum. This being the case, management quite naturally seeks to optimize above all the physical flow of input and output of the marketing process—in line with the needs-satisfaction theory of selling.

2. The physical and promotional channels of distribution are closely interrelated and interdependent. That is, physical flow has no economic reality without a corresponding (if not necessarily concurrent) promotional flow of transactions. (See Figure 1.1.)

3. A number of key segments of physical distribution are so closely related to functions of persuasion as to make the two organically inseparable: e.g., packaging (silent selling), inventory control (merchandising), and warehouse location (market penetration). In fact, in many modern firms, physical distribution—through its rationale of optimization, and therefore its promise of improved lower-cost service—is itself used as a tool of persuasion.

4. There is no site in the organization chart for physical distribution other than marketing. The waning influence of production in management councils almost precludes its use as a vehicle for directing and controlling physical distribution activities.

This brings us to the third possible solution for the problem of organizing physical distribution, namely, placing it "on par" with the other basic and autonomous departments in the firm. While the idea of autonomy appeals to some high-placed physical distribution practitioners, it seems to be unworkable, given the present state of the organization art and the all-out emphasis in the marketing process on the provision of time and place utilities. Unlike other service departments structured in the past (such as engineering and personnel), physical distribution is *on a continuing basis* interlaced with the buying, selling, and manufacturing activities of the firm. Further, physical distribution must be viewed in the interest of profit maximization as a controlled and regulated physical flow of goods, confluent with the firm's promotional flow of transactions. To turn physical distribution "loose" under these circumstances would (1) slow down the marketing process; (2) place an unbearable burden of detail on the chief executive officer, to whom the head of physical distribution would presumably then report; and (3) further fragment and/or duplicate a number of "common" functions, such as packaging, inventory control, data processing, materials handling, etc.

Above all, one must avoid the rather common error of confusing the logistician and his team with the physical distribution system so as not to upset the delicate formulas of "human relations" within the firm. Given the present state of technological disequilibrium (including of course job skills and titles) and the vicissitudes of the business environment, it is doubtless futile to seek an optimization of organization structure—in effect, treating men as machines. The most sophisticated planning and controlling of techniques and instruments cannot completely cope with the "human equation" in a free society.

To paraphrase Alexander Pope, the study of business, even in this age of incipient cybernetics, is still mainly the study of man.

Part

Two

PROBLEMS IN MARKETING LOGISTICS: A FUNCTIONAL APPROACH

The evolution of logistics in marketing, discussed in the two intro-ductory chapters, points up the significance of transportation, inven-tory control, order processing, materials handling, communications, warehousing, and packaging as integral parts of an emerging system of physical distribution. The "traditional" function of transportation, however, retains its pre-eminence, at least in terms of value added— accounting for between 25 and 75 per cent of total distribution costs, depending on the type of product that is shipped.

Chapter 3 deals with the transportation function, and describes and explains, from a managerial perspective, the methods employed in optimizing the physical movement of goods from origin to destina-tion: linear programing, break-bulk, electronic data processing, simulation, and containerization.

3

Robert J. Franco / Jerry Schorr

Logistical Factors
in Transportation

Experience has shown that "traffic and transportation" managers, who typically still control this single largest cost component of the distribution function, can no longer treat transportation as a separate entity within the corporate framework, because this treatment excessively raises the cost of distribution. For example, the traffic manager who selects rail as his "best" mode of transport on the basis of its low cost may well have to cope with the consequences of slow movement: construction of new warehouses, acquisition and storage of huge inventories, more expensive forms of packaging, and escalation of order-processing costs.

In brief, a seeming reduction of transport costs may actually cause a substantial increase in total distribution costs. Clearly, the modern transportation manager must coordinate his role with each of the managers responsible for the other corporate distribution functions. The advantage of such coordination is illustrated in Figures 3.1–3.3. The charts show that air, while having the highest transportation cost, yields the lowest distribution costs at most weight increments, because the two high-cost distribution functions of warehousing and maintaining large inventories are not needed when using air but are required when using rail or motor truck. In this example, if the transportation man deals solely with transport costs, he will select rail, one of the highest total distribution costs. The following section of this chapter presents recent transport innovations that are consistent with the thinking of modern transportation personnel.

MODERN TRANSPORTATION METHODS

The following are among the many transportation problemsolving techniques introduced during the past two decades.

33

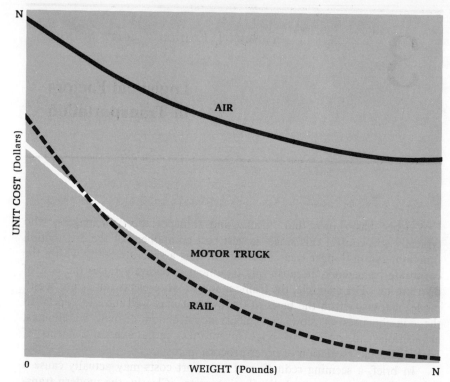

FIGURE 3.1
Transportation costs

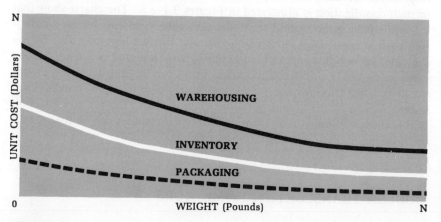

FIGURE 3.2
Other distribution costs

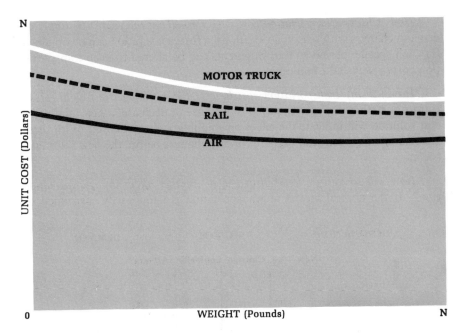

FIGURE 3.3
Total costs

1. Linear programing

2. Simulation

3. Containerization

4. Break-bulk

5. EDP (electronic data processing)

[1] Linear Programing

A transportation system that uses linear programing and other statistical techniques to lower costs is not merely reducing the existing cost of transporting commodities; it is utilizing powerful tools to obtain essential facts for long-range management decisions which may involve hundreds of thousands of dollars. The following are some of the many questions you can ask a linear program.

How will my transportation cost vary throughout the year? If supply or demand changes with seasonal variations, a forecast solution can be obtained for each specific period so that shipments can be altered to keep transportation costs always at a minimum.

How will my transportation cost be affected by changes in freight rates? If transportation rates are expected to increase or decrease, a new minimum-cost solution will indicate the effect on shipping and total costs. With these answers, management can prepare for any changes before the new rates take effect.

How will strikes, national disasters, or weather affect my transportation cost? If the normal means of transportation is temporarily suspended or

DESTINATION	SOURCE				DEMAND
	New York	Chicago	Louisville	Atlanta	
Miami	($10)	($11)	($6)	4 ($5)	4
New Orleans	3 ($12)	1 ($11)	3 ($7)	($8)	7
Minneapolis	($9)	3 ($2)	($4)	($8)	3
Baltimore	2 ($2)	($10)	($5)	($4)	2
SUPPLY	5	4	3	4	= 16

FIGURE 3.4
Using linear programing in the transportation area
(dollar amounts show cost of shipment per unit*)

*Lowest-Cost Solution

Source	Destination	No. of Units	Cost per Unit	Total Cost
New York	New Orleans	3	$12	$36
New York	Baltimore	2	2	4
Chicago	New Orleans	1	11	11
Chicago	Minneapolis	3	2	6
Louisville	New Orleans	3	7	21
Atlanta	Miami	4	5	20
			TOTAL	$98

discontinued, a new minimum-cost solution can be obtained, using the rates for an alternate method of transportation. If the suspension can be anticipated, any changes can be put into effect exactly when needed.

What is the lowest total cost solution for distributing my products? Whether or not customer service requirements preclude the use of the lowest total cost, it is always worthwhile to know the lowest total cost and to back off from this optimum point only where necessary. The lowest total cost can be determined by using linear programing. The construction of the matrix (explained in Chapter 15) shown in Figure 3.4, using demand, supply, and costs, is an example of the use of linear programing in the transportation area.

Should I build a new plant or expand an old one? It is often necessary to determine the relative merits of building or expansion. By analyzing various combinations of increased supplies at existing sources and new supplies at new sources, a correct decision can be made, based upon greatest reduction in net costs (see Chapters 5 and 14).

Which of my production facilities should be expanded? If an existing source of supply is to be expanded, a forecast solution will show what the altered shipping pattern will be, and how much the total transportation cost will change. Comparing solutions for different sources will indicate the proper one to expand.

Where should I build a new factory or warehouse? If another source is to be added to an existing system, various locations can be analyzed to determine which location produces the greatest reduction in total transportation costs. The cost reduction will indicate how long it will take for the new facility to pay for itself.

Linear programing methods for solving the above transportation problems have been thoroughly tested for practical use and have yielded substantial cost savings to many corporations. These methods are shown in Chapter 14 of this text.

[2] Simulation

The simulation method is employed to derive definitive costs, advantages, and disadvantages of alternative transportation and/or distribution systems.

As an example, a traffic manager must select the optimum cost transportation methods consistent with two constraints: The methods selected must (1) tie into the lowest total distribution cost method and (2) provide an acceptable level of service. In order to solve this problem, the traffic manager determines all feasible transportation methods including:

Inbound to plant—(1) rail, (2) motor, (3) air.
Outbound from plant—(1) rail break-bulk, (2) motor truck break-bulk, (3) air break-bulk.

The traffic manager determines the break-bulk locations, break-bulk quantities, and delivering carriers, and sketches these alternative transportation methods as shown in Figure 3.5. He then selects an average shipping period for the year and *simulates* the cost of each shipment—through the pipeline—via each alternative transportation method. The resulting lowest cost consistent with the two constraints will be the transportation method recommended by the traffic manager.

Thus, the simulation method uses a representative shipping period to choose—beyond a doubt—the correct alternatives in terms of economy and customer service requirements.

[3] Containerization

Most traffic and transportation personnel have been conditioned to the fact that transportation costs and weight are tied together. In fact, almost all common carrier tariffs quote transportation rates in terms of per hundred-weight or a flat charge on shipments of less than x number of pounds.

Since we recognize that the common carrier considers many factors, including that all-important area of weight density (pounds per cubic foot) before establishing a rate, why not have transportation rates quoted on something other than a weight basis? The first steps have recently been taken in quoting common carrier rates on a space (or container) basis, rather than on a weight basis. Table 3.1 gives examples of REA Express container tariffs. The use of containers in transportation is becoming more widespread because it offers shippers and carriers many advantages, including:

A. *Loading during down time on the platform or dock* Ordinarily, a number of packages must be loaded on the transport vehicle when it arrives (usually at a busy time of day). The container, however, can be loaded during a slack period. Then one unit, rather than many packages, can be loaded when the transport vehicle arrives.

B. *Handling numbers of packages as one unit instead of handling each package individually* In a typical operation, packages first are separately picked from stock. Second, they are assembled at some

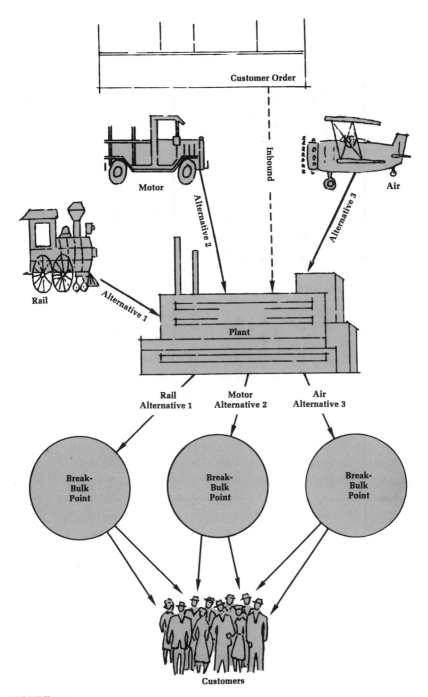

FIGURE 3.5
Alternative transportation methods

TABLE 3.1

Examples of REA Express Container Tariffs

COLUMN 1	COLUMN 2	COLUMN 3	COLUMN 4	COLUMN 5	COLUMN 6
	Maximum not exceeding Height—44″ or Length and width combined—56″ or Gross weight—600 lbs.	*Maximum not exceeding Height—54″ or Length and width combined—80″ or Gross weight—1200 lbs.*	*Maximum not exceeding Height—60″ or Length and width combined—88″ or Gross weight—1600 lbs.*	*Maximum not exceeding Height—60″ or Length and width combined—96″ or Gross weight—1900 lbs.*	*Maximum not exceeding Height—60″ or Length and width combined—108″ or Gross weight—2300 lbs.*
WHERE THE CHARGE PER CONTAINER Is:	THE	CHARGE	WILL	BE	
75	19	37	48	56	69
76	19	37	49	57	70
77	19	38	49	58	71
78	19	38	50	58	72
79	20	39	51	59	73
80	20	39	51	60	74
81	20	40	52	61	75
82	20	40	52	62	75
83	21	41	53	62	76
84	21	41	54	63	77

point. Third, they are moved to the dock. Fourth, they are loaded on the transport vehicle. Thus, each package is separately handled four times. By placing the packages in containers during the picking operations, each package is handled just once and the container is handled three times. If one container holds, say, 100 packages, the number of handlings can be reduced from 400 to 103 by "unitizing."

C. *Definite costs for handling one unit of known size* A container takes up just so much room and is handled as one piece—size and weight are fixed. Thus, it is easy for both the shipper and the carrier to calculate the space and handling cost. For example, a motor carrier has many different costs for handling products which now have the same Class 100 rate. But by loading these different Class 100 products in a container, the carrier will have approximately the same cost for handling each product. The shipper gains his advantage through a flat charge for the container, and he is allowed to load up to x number of pounds in the unit. Thus, shippers with a high weight density can load higher weights—at the same total cost—than shippers with a lower weight density who now have the same class rates. Reductions in loss and damage are also obtained through the use of containers.

D. *Break-bulking many shipments in a container* The use of containers allows the break-bulking of lighter-weight shipments, as described later in this chapter.

Present-day containers may be either disposable (to eliminate back-haul problems) or nondisposable and may be either collapsible or noncollapsible.

The wise modern transportation manager employs some method of unitizing his products in order to reduce transportation costs and also to reduce substantially plant and warehouse costs.

[4] Break-Bulk

For many years traffic and transportation managers have employed break-bulk methods for large motor truck shipments consigned to a multiple number of customers at one or a small number of destinations. Almost always, the total weight of the break-bulk shipment fills a rail car or a truck. These break-bulk techniques have resulted in substantial transportation cost savings.

The modern trend is also to use break-bulk methods for an aggregate of shipments which weigh as little as 150 pounds. Since the cost per pound of small shipments is substantially higher than the pound cost of larger shipments, break-bulking low-weighted shipments usually yields lucrative economic savings.

Small-shipment break-bulking usually takes the following forms:

A. *Air parcel post break-bulk* Combine present parcel post shipments weighing 25 pounds or less that are consigned to a particular destination post office (parcel post local zone) and also within 150 miles of the destination post office (parcel post zones 1 and 2). Forward these shipments via air as one shipment to the destination post office, where they are metered for local zone and zone 1 and 2 delivery and break-bulked to customers. This break-bulking method usually yields cost savings (even after adding on pickup and post office delivery costs) and a substantial improvement of service.

B. *Air break-bulk* Combine motor truck minimum charge shipments weighing 50 pounds or less which are consigned to destinations within 25 miles of each other. In most cases the cost of two motor truck 50-pound shipments is higher than the total air cost. Divert the subject motor truck shipments to air to attain a cost savings and a substantial improvement of service.

C. *Containerization* Place products having a density of 12 pounds per cubic foot or more in a container. The products can belong to a number of shipments but the container should be destined for one city (although the shipments may be consigned to many customers in that city). Substantial improvements in costs and service will result from this break-bulk method.

[5] EDP

Traffic and transportation managers can now use electronic data processing to perform more efficiently in transportation areas (see Figure 3.6):

A. *Program and schedule carrier arrivals and loading times,* using a computer readout of scheduled arrivals and estimated departures of transport to allow efficient use of dock space, dock labor, and materials-handling equipment;

B. *Print weight break points on the shipping document,* eliminating the time-consuming task of checking the routing guide for each shipment;

C. *Estimate and print shipment weight on shipping document,* eliminating the costly task of weighing each shipment, as well as eliminating overweight errors;

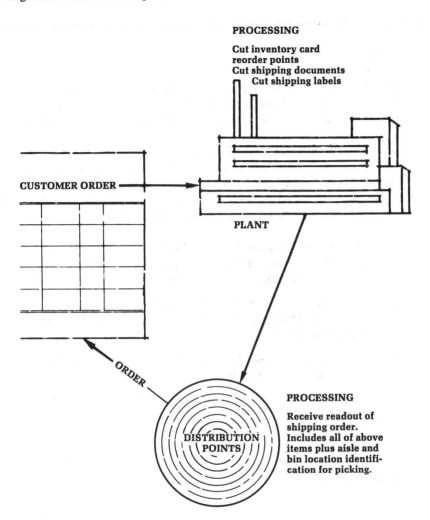

FIGURE 3.6
Using electronic data processing in transportation areas

D. *Print carrier selection on shipping document,* permitting shipments to
be automatically sorted into carrier groups and eliminating a separate
sorting function;

In this chapter, modern transportation concepts have been stressed,
rather than basic transportation facts. The more important of the transportation innovations of the past two decades, described briefly here, are
fully detailed within the total distribution framework in later chapters.

ANOTHER basic function of logistics in marketing is location analysis for the purpose of optimizing the geographic placement of distribution centers—factories, warehouses, bulk plants, etc.

Such optimization of the number, location, and size of distribution centers is obviously of prime importance to the firm, both in terms of costs and of customer service requirements. It follows, therefore, that almost any location analysis of distribution centers will pose certain "systemic" questions. For example:

1. Will the construction of an additional distribution center reduce the average shipping weight to other distribution centers, and thereby result in additional transportation costs?

2. Will the location of the new distribution center reduce the shipping distance to the consignee, and thus allow a reduction of transport costs?

3. What types of materials-handling equipment are to be used in the new distribution center?

4. What will be the effect of an additional distribution center on paperwork costs?

Chapter 4 deals with the evolution of scientific location analysis; Chapter 5 reviews the quantitative techniques for solving location problems.

4

Donald J. Bowersox

Location Analysis

Concern with the selection of distribution center locations has increased substantially since World War II. General interest in the concept of utilizing distribution centers to decentralize inventory may be traced to (1) the logistical experience gained from wartime military operations; (2) the realization that strategic location of forward inventories has marketing implications far greater than those traditionally embodied in the warehouse static storage concept; and (3) the postwar profit squeeze, caused in part by the constantly increasing cost of physical distribution.

Much literature on the location of distribution centers has appeared in the past decade. In general, these studies differ from plant and retail location analyses in two basic ways. First, most studies describe the various techniques for selecting distribution center locations, but direct very little attention to reasons for using distribution centers as opposed to other methods of product distribution. For the most part, the problem of designing an optimum network of distribution center locations has been neglected. Second, almost all analytical techniques concentrate on the fundamental importance of minimizing transport cost but generally neglect other costs that influence the choice of location.

Postwar business experience reflects an over-all deficiency in selecting the number and location of distribution centers. One major business concern has increased, contracted, increased, and now once more is in the process of contracting the number of distribution centers utilized to support logistically a relatively stable marketing situation. Countless other firms, analyzing their logistical systems, have been forced to examine the proper role of distribution centers without much help from pertinent literature.

DERIVED NATURE OF DISTRIBUTION CENTER LOCATION

Distribution centers, per se, represent only a segment of a firm's total strategy for creating time and place utility. The dependence of distribution center locations upon manufacturing and retail or customer locations must be visualized. From a total corporate viewpoint, retail or customer locations represent the final point of product distribution[1]—the apex of the total marketing effort. Thus, the distribution center location is subordinated and perhaps only justified, to the degree that it increases sales impact at the point of final product transfer.

Over the years, a relatively refined body of knowledge has emerged concerning the location of manufacturing facilities. Today, firms can draw upon sophisticated analysis tempered by sound theory so as to select plant locations offering maximum economic and competitive benefits.[2]

Distribution centers enter a logistic system only when a degree of differential advantage results from their inclusion between manufacturing site and final product destination.[3] The exact location selected for a single distribution center or a network of centers is properly viewed as part of the logistic strategy of the firm. Differential advantage gained by adding distribution centers culminates in achieving a distribution cost and/or service advantage in a market segment. The particular distribution center location strategy desirable for a firm depends greatly upon the degree of product differentiation enjoyed, basic product-line width, competitive structure, and the logistical mission of the distribution center. A few common business situations are examined here to illustrate the derived nature of the distribution center location decision.

Distribution Center Location Strategy with Nondifferentiated Products

In the case of an industry characterized by nearly identical products, little consumer loyalty is commanded by individual firms. The industry demand curve is relatively elastic. Fundamentally, individual firms may attempt to differentiate their products by location dispersion. Under these conditions, Lösch's hexagon and generalizations concerning location patterns are likely to be experienced.[4] The major firms in the industry seek plant locations in prime markets and at low-cost production points. Smaller, high-cost firms normally find economic justification by selecting locations in marginal

---

[1]For a detailed review of retail location literature, see Bernard J. LaLonde, *Differentials in Supermarket Drawing Power*, Marketing and Transportation Paper No. 11, Bureau of Business and Economic Research, Michigan State University, 1962.

[2]For a review of plant location literature, see Edward W. Smykay, Donald J. Bowersox, and Frank H. Mossman, *Physical Distribution Management*, Macmillan, 1961, Chapter VI.

[3]*Ibid.*, Chapter IX.

[4]August Lösch, *The Economics of Location*, Yale University Press, 1954.

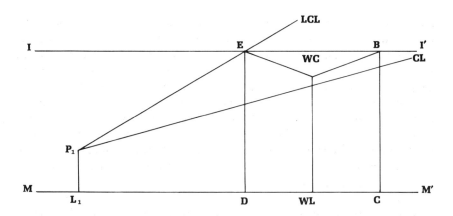

FIGURE 4.1
Market extension by use of a distribution center
SOURCE: John H. Frederick, *Using Public Warehouses*, Chilton, 1957, p. 81.

markets contained in space islands; these islands are created by the inability of major producers to place products at a competitive price. It is equally possible that major producers located in prime markets may utilize distribution centers to service marginal markets. By locating distribution centers in space islands, major producers may extend their effective method of coverage. This type of market extension creates entry barriers to the location of high-cost producers in space islands.[5]

Consolidation of shipments is a basic economic principle underlying the utilization of distribution centers to extend market coverage to secondary areas. The major producer may initially sell f.o.b. mill over his entire market area. Each customer is shipped products directly from the production point by some method of less-than-quantity shipment. The consolidation of product shipments to a distribution center substantially reduces transportation expense. Thus, the monopolist can move large quantities of his product into market areas, previously beyond his reach, at a total cost considerably below the consumer's price acceptance level. The savings must be sufficient to cover the cost of facility operation and inventory. Products may then be distributed f.o.b. distribution center in all directions to a point where total product price reaches the level of consumer indifference.

Figure 4.1 contains an example of market extension through a distribution center. The case of the spatial monopolist is illustrated in only one

[5]For an extended discussion, see Smykay and others, *op. cit.*, pp. 151–161.

direction for the linear market. Under conditions of direct shipment, the monopolist can sell only as far into the market as point *D*. At the line *ED* the total cost of his product reaches the consumer-indifference price level. Beyond line *ED* the high-cost producer could exist in a marginal market. By placing a distribution center at some point in the market beyond *D*, the monopolist can consolidate shipments to the distribution center at a landed cost within the consumer-indifference price level. Shipments are then returned toward the production point and farther into the market area until total price once more becomes prohibitive to the consumer. The total market expansion achieved by utilizing a distribution center is expressed in the linear diagram by the area *DC*.

Furthermore, locating a number of such distribution centers around the total market area initially served by the spatial monopolist will produce again a system of Lösch hexagons, and stability will exist. However, marginal markets are now served by distribution centers controlled by the major producer rather than by competitive high-cost producers. Thus, one function of distribution centers is to extend prime markets under conditions of nondifferentiated products.

Distribution Center Location Strategy with Differentiated Products

Distribution centers often are vital to the expansion of firms that sell differentiated products nationally. Since products offered by all firms are differentiated in the consumer's eyes, the neat theories of spatial monopoly break down. Each firm is forced to sell over a larger total market area in order to realize sales volumes sufficient for survival. These conditions probably will compel large producers to concentrate product plants where low production costs and much industry demand exist. This is necessary since no individual submarket demands a firm's total production. From such concentrated locations, each firm may be characterized as playing a waiting game.[6] Each can meet the service capabilities of competitors, and all confront nearly similar transportation costs. Under these conditions, the industry initially settles down to conventional tactics of nonprice competition in order to achieve differential advantage.

---

[6]Basically, this type of location strategy represents a game in which each player possesses perfect information concerning opponents' *ex post* moves. Consequently, each player is content to maintain *status quo* until an allocation alternative offering a definite payoff is discovered. For a discussion of the logic of game theory in competition, see Martin Shubik, *Strategy and Market Structure*, Wiley, 1959, pp. 3–18.

The dynamics of spatial competition enter the industry when differentiated products begin to gain acceptance in distant markets. The firm finds it desirable to decentralize physical facilities when sales volumes become sufficient in submarkets to justify distribution centers and, then, branch plants. The transportation principle justifying the use of distribution centers is the same as in geographically dispersed industries. When total demand in a given market segment becomes substantial enough to consolidate shipments, the resultant economies may justify a distribution center. Thus, a second economic force leading to the use of distribution centers is the normal expansion of firms selling differentiated products nationally.

Once a major producer obtains sufficient volume to support a distribution center in a market segment, the waiting game which earlier characterized such a concentrated industry is abandoned. In addition to transportation economies, firms that operate distribution centers also gain a service advantage in these market segments. These select firms then replenish consumer inventories more quickly than can major competitors. For customers this means faster special order handling and an over-all reduction of basic inventories. Thus, the firm with distribution centers has one more method of gaining a differential advantage. The counterstrategy is for all major firms to neutralize this location advantage by developing a competitive system of distribution points when sufficient sales volumes are obtained.

Distribution Center Location Strategy
with Multiple Products

Distribution centers may also provide an economic function for many firms engaged in producing and marketing a broad line of highly differentiated products. Industrial location theory points out that plants producing a particular type of product often must locate near required inputs.[7] For production economy, firms may need geographically decentralized production plants; but for marketing control, they may prefer a convergent marketing program for the multiple-product line.[8]

Under conditions of joint marketing, a distribution center may be operated as a collection point for various products produced at decentralized locations. By centralizing all products, a firm can deliver mixed shipments. Mixed shipments allow customers to realize economies of consolidated transport and faster replenishment of all products normally purchased only in

---

[7]Melvin L. Greenhut, *Plant Location*, University of North Carolina Press, 1956, p. 113.
[8]Thomas A. Staudt, "Program for Product Diversification," *Harvard Business Review*, November–December 1954, p. 125.

quantity lots. Besides gaining a competitive advantage by providing these additional services, the firm offering mixed shipments may combine slow-moving products with faster movers and, thereby, offer the total product line at consolidated transportation rates.

The average retail store, whatever its size, does not have sufficient demand to order inventory in consolidated quantities directly from manufacturers. Retail product lines, manufactured or processed at widely scattered geographic points, are usually extensive. In order to obtain rapid inventory replenishment of this heterogeneous product line, the retailer normally requires some form of distribution center.

The basic purpose of the distribution center is to consolidate purchase from distant procurement points and replenish inventory to retail outlets. A distribution center intended to provide a cost-and-service benefit to retail stores is best located near the outlets it serves. This allows maximum advantages of consolidated shipment with relatively short local delivery. Therefore, retail store location modifies distribution center location. Thus, a third economic justification for distribution centers is the need to engage in joint marketing of a multiple-product line.

These few illustrations serve to emphasize the dependent nature of distribution center location upon the characteristics of the industry and the manufacturing and/or retailing location decisions made by each firm. Upon this foundation, it is possible to summarize the logic underlying distribution center location.

DISTRIBUTION CENTER
LOCATION LOGIC

A dichotomy appears in historical marketing literature concerning the role of traditional warehousing and the function of product distribution. In early writings, storage is viewed as an ancillary function—it is merely to match supply with erratic demand.[9] The warehouse was considered a location for product storage until demand became sufficient to support distribution. The creation-of-time-utility principle was used to justify this type of economic activity.[10] This tendency to consider storage as merely a required facilitating function generally resulted in criticism of efficiency

---

[9]H. H. Maynard, T. Beckman, and W. Davidson, *Principles of Marketing*, Ronald, 1957, p. 473.
[10]Hugh B. Killough, *The Economics of Marketing*, Harper & Row, 1933, p. 101.

with little appreciation of the broader distribution spectrum in which storage played a vital role.

A few early writers, Ingersoll, Cherington, Clark, and White, did attempt to generalize the physical distribution function. In 1919, Wilber Ingersoll directly attacked the question of distribution inefficiency by stressing the importance of distribution systems.[11] He illustrated the economic reasons for several marketing steps to distribute goods produced in large quantities at a factory or farm. He stated that distribution systems were necessary to satisfy consumer demand and concluded that relatively few commercial points could justify wholesale centers. He also pointed out the need to disseminate products to tributary territories from each of these commercial centers. Ingersoll's fundamental argument was that countless economic enterprises of different sizes were required to distribute products. These would be located in various areas, depending upon demand, with the scale of the enterprise proportionate to the intensity of demand—a concept surprisingly similar to the theoretical contentions of spatial economists.[12]

In 1921, Paul Cherington broadened the perspective of storage and transportation by acknowledging the necessity for adjustments in place.[13] He clearly separated the flow of paper and the flow of physical products from production to consumption.[14] With a system of circles to represent market demand, Cherington illustrated the attraction of distribution facilities to the points of demand concentration. Unfortunately, he spent little time considering the nature of distribution systems and the relative importance of product storage.

Fred Clark, in both of his basic marketing books, was probably the first writer purposely to use the term "physical distribution" in discussing the process of market logistics. In his *Principles of Marketing*, he included such facilitating functions as transportation, materials handling, and storage as fundamental in distributing products.[15] In his *Readings in Marketing*, the subjects discussed under physical distribution were expanded to include more detail on the warehouse operation.[16] This reader was left with the impression that Clark gained significant insights into the basic forces influencing distribution systems; however, he did not clearly relate this to the marketing strategy of the firm.

---

[11] *National Civic Federation Review*, June 5, 1919.
[12] *Ibid.*, p. 3.
[13] *The Elements of Marketing*, Macmillan, 1921.
[14] *Ibid.*, p. 93.
[15] Macmillan, 1924, pp. 293–324.
[16] Macmillan, 1924, p. 481.

In 1927, Percival White advanced the integration of basic marketing functions into a system of market action.[17] Writing probably the first book on managerial marketing, White visualized traditional marketing functions as sequential steps in the broader process of product concentration and dispersion.[18] His general thesis was that although marketing is normally concerned only with the process of broadcasting commodities, it deals with commodity reception as well as transmission. White's classification of marketing functions included three main categories: (1) concentration, (2) dispersion, and (3) facilitation. Concentration was assumed to include the traditional functions of assembling and grading. Dispersion included demand, creation, and merchandising. Facilitation included storage, communication, transportation, and financing. White's conception of marketing is presented in Figure 4.2.

Following White's basic diagram, marketing is concerned with the process of product flow from production to consumption. Of particular interest is the central position occupied by storage. No longer is storage considered a necessary evil; rather it assumes paramount importance in the marketing process. White saw the storage function in its broader perspective.

> Storing occupies a position midway between the functions of concentration and those of dispersion. It helps to take care of the inevitable lack of coordination between production and consumption. It will include not only the control of finished stores at the factory, but also the provision of suitable stocks, *properly warehoused, at strategic points throughout the market territory.*[19] [Italics added.]

White's major objective was to illustrate that managerial marketing embraced considerably more than merely advertising and selling, which, he felt, received undue emphasis to the detriment of other vital functions. As a by-product, he considerably improved the role of physical supply in the marketing process.

Modern treatment places the distribution center concept in clear perspective. Those like White, who viewed product distribution and storage as basic marketing functions, more closely approximated modern physical distribution systems. The meaning of storage, as used by these earlier writers, has been redefined because of modern technological advancements. Based upon improved sales-forecasting, production-scheduling, and inventory-controlling techniques, storage has become a temporary function. Writers who concentrated upon storage, without reference to the economic

---

[17]*Scientific Marketing Management*, Harper & Row, 1927.
[18]*Ibid.*, p. 72.
[19]*Ibid.*, p. 75.

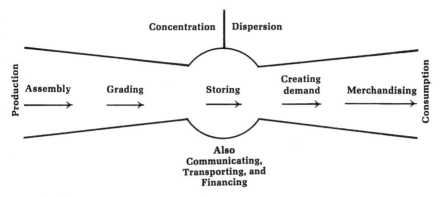

FIGURE 4.2

White's conception of the marketing process

SOURCE: Percival White, *Scientific Marketing*, Harper & Row, 1927, p. 73.

and service aspects of distribution centers, succeeded in explaining a secondary and relatively unimportant part of modern distribution—namely, permanent storage. Due to special conditions, products may be retained in a distribution center longer than the normal inventory replenishment cycle. Such permanent storage may result from seasonal production, product conditioning, or the realization of special quantity discounts. In the concept of modern distribution, such permanent storage is considered the exception rather than the rule.

This evolution of marketing thought, coupled with the various economic justifications supporting distribution centers, helps explain the logic of such distribution points. The distribution center, viewed as a vital link in the dynamics of market logistics, renders service or cost advantages to a firm in a given market segment. The geographic location of a distribution center is controlled by production locations and markets to be penetrated. Logically, three types of distribution structure evolve when a distribution center is adopted. Under Hoover's plant location classification, these may be identified as being market-positioned, production-positioned, or intermediately positioned.[20]

Market-Positioned Distribution Centers

The basic function of a market-oriented distribution center is to replenish inventory to retail stores and facilitate merchandise delivery to consumers.

---

[20]Edgar M. Hoover, *Location of Economic Activity*, McGraw-Hill, 1948, p. 35.

The distribution center located near ultimate product consumption affords maximum transport consolidation economies from distant shipping points with relatively short product movements locally. The geographic market area served from a market-oriented distribution center is determined by the required speed of inventory replenishment to customers, size of average order, and cost per ton of local delivery.

Market-oriented distribution centers may be retailer-, manufacturer-, or independently owned. The mission of the distribution center will vary, depending upon the ownership arrangement. Retailer-owned distribution centers are designed to serve as break-bulk points for various products purchased from different sources. Since the product line processed through retailer-owned distribution centers is extremely wide, the magnitude of demand for a given product need not be much of the center's total volume.

The market-oriented, manufacturer-owned distribution center may represent an extension into submarkets when the industry is characterized by differentiated products. Under these conditions, the manufacturer must enjoy sufficient sales volume in the market to operate a distribution center. In the case of an industry selling nondifferentiated products, a market-oriented distribution center may help extend sales territories into marginal markets. Under these conditions, volumes need not be as extensive as in the case of differentiated products; however, they must be sufficient to realize consolidation economies and cover the cost of distribution center operations. The volumes required under both cases of manufacturer-owned distribution centers may be substantially lessened by public warehousing; but this system is readily duplicated by major competitors.

The independently owned, market-oriented distribution center may function primarily to replenish retail inventory or to act as distribution point for manufacturers. When the primary function is retail inventory replenishment, the distribution center is normally owned and operated as an independent wholesale establishment. Such business enterprises take ownership as well as physical possession of products and may assume full responsibility for the sales effort. When independently owned distribution centers act primarily as distribution points for manufacturers, they are commonly called "public warehouses." The typical pattern of operation is for public warehouses to take physical possession of products while assuming no responsibility for sales. The ownership of such products is retained by the manufacturer or a middleman.

This description of market-oriented distribution centers represents only a few combinations of physical movement. The basic point, their location close to the market served, rests upon the need to replenish customer inventory rapidly and the desire to achieve product distribution at lowest cost.

Production-Positioned Distribution Centers

A production-oriented distribution center is located close to production plants in order to act as a collection point for many products manufactured at different plants. The fundamental reason for using production-oriented distribution centers is the manufacturer's desire for maximum service to customers. Quantities of products at each plant are shipped to the collection center, from which customer orders are filled.

Upon order receipt, merchandise is shipped in the combination that is necessary to satisfy consumer requirements. Location near manufacturing plants allows mixed carloads to move to customer locations under volume transportation rates. Under carload conditions, a consolidated order often may be shipped to a customer more quickly than smaller quantities, thereby allowing rapid replenishment and lower basic inventories. This mixed carload service stimulates purchase of products which normally move under less-than-carload rates. Therefore, the advantage of a production-oriented distribution center is its ability to furnish superior service across the total product line offered by a firm. To the degree that a manufacturer can offer all products in consolidated quantities at volume transportation rates, a differential advantage is obtained in serving customers.

Intermediately Positioned Distribution Centers

Distribution centers situated between customer locations and production locations are referred to as intermediately positioned. These centers, like those that are production-oriented, find economic justification on the basis of increased service. They serve as mixing points for manufacturers engaged in the production and marketing of a multiple-product line. The earlier discussion, concerning the derived nature of distribution center locations, pointed out that manufacturing facilities often must be located near the source of raw materials or power. Under these conditions, firms engaged in manufacturing disparate products probably will have manufacturing locations spread over a large geographic area. Consequently, the most economical grouping point may be an intermediately located distribution center. From a distribution location which minimizes inbound transportation cost from all plants, the firm can most economically provide mixed-carload service to customers.

THE SINGLE-LOCATION SOLUTION

At least two general mathematical methods are available to aid the selection of a distribution center location.

The first method involves various formulations for averaging transport costs within a predetermined market area. The fundamental system of orientation is based upon Cartesian coordinates; the techniques employed are those of analytic geometry. Several alternate formulations, depending upon the specifics of the problem confronted, are available.[21] All solutions represent essentially a weighted average of a given number of independent variables, such as delivery locations, annual tonnage, and delivery time; the dependent variable is the distribution center location.

The Cartesian format may be utilized on a point-to-point basis or may be modified into a grid coordinate. The variables used determine the method. In special situations, where either inbound or outbound transport cost tends to dominate the problem solution, formulations to emphasize only that critical factor are available.[22]

In the outbound-transport-dominate problem, when private transportation is utilized, formulations which integrate running time as a delivery cost determinant have been developed and tested.[23] Each of these location solutions is most readily determined using a point-to-point formulation. For more generalized location problems, requiring a balancing of inbound and outbound transport costs, the grid approach is more efficient.[24] With the grid, common carrier rates are easily introduced into the solution.

The techniques built upon analytic geometry have the advantage of simplicity. Location problems covering as many as 100 retail outlets can be solved without the aid of electronic data processing. No assumption covering the final distribution center locations is required under the point-to-point or grid approach, since the mathematical process seeks the single best location within the search area. A deficiency of the analytic-geometrical approach is inability to expand the analysis beyond transport costs. Consequently, the application of this technique is limited to single-location solutions in which transport expense predominates.

---

[21] See "Warehouse Location Based on Trucking Costs," *Materials Handling. Manual No. 1*, Boston Publishing Company, 1955, pp. E84–E86; Donald J. Bowersox, *Food Distribution Center Location Technique and Procedure*, Marketing and Transportation Paper No. 12, Bureau of Business and Economic Research, Michigan State University, 1962, pp. 9–32; and C. G. Eneborg, "How to Plot the Ideal Location for a Warehouse," *Management Methods*, January 1958, pp. 52–55.

[22] For a complete discussion of available alternative formulations, see Bowersox, *op. cit.*, Chapter III and Appendix B.

[23] Bowersox, *ibid.*, pp. 18–19.

[24] Smykay and others, *op. cit.*, Chapter VIII.

The second method currently popular for solving distribution problems is linear programing. It is possible to determine the distribution center location through a modified version of the transportation or distribution model.[25] This requires the assumption of an array of possible locations to isolate the least-cost location within the array. The general technique, given an array of potential locations, is to use a controlled system of substitution for selecting that location which minimizes transportation cost.

The real least-cost location may not be included within the original array. Consequently, the solution may not represent the single best location available. In more advanced applications of linear programing, this deficiency may be eliminated; however, the technique becomes unduly complicated for the single-location solution.[26]

The mathematical programing technique of location selection has the advantage of more readily handling a total cost analysis than do the various geometric techniques. In other words, the problem of how many distribution centers and where each should be located may be solved with advanced linear programing. However, linear programing appears less efficient for the multiple-solution problem than simulation, which will be discussed in the next section. The most efficient application of linear programing is in optimizing transport equipment utilization, given a series of locations. For example, the transport model provides a comparatively simple method of determining which distribution center should be used to meet a customer's requirements during a given shipping period.[27]

THE MULTIPLE-LOCATION SOLUTION

The most promising technique for determining the optimum number of distribution centers is system simulation.[28] The potentials of simulation are

---

[25]Robert Dorfman, Paul A. Samuelson, and Robert M. Solow, *Linear Programming and Economic Analysis*, McGraw-Hill, 1958; Dakota Ulrich Greenwald, *Linear Programming*, Ronald, 1957; Nyles V. Reinfeld and William R. Vogel, *Mathematical Programming*, Prentice-Hall, 1958.

[26]Greenwald offers a technique using the simplex algorithm, which appears adaptable, although it is unduly complicated for the problem at hand (*op. cit.*, pp. 9–12).

[27]For a simplified discussion, see Reinfeld and Vogel, *op. cit.*, Chapter III. For an advanced discussion of routing contributions, see Stanley Zionts, "Methods for Selection of an Optimum Route," *Proceedings, American Transportation Research Forum,* Winter Meetings, 1962.

[28]To date, little has been written on the application of simulation to the specific problem of distribution system design. For some early works, see W. J. Baum and P. Wolf, "Warehouse Location Problem," *Operations Research*, March 1958, pp. 252–263, as well

exciting because broad-system experimentation with alternative customer service levels and corresponding distribution costs places the derived nature of distribution center locations into an analytical framework. In simulation, a working model of all significant factors relevant to a particular firm's distribution requirements is formulated. The objective of simulation is to consider simultaneously all possible distribution designs to ascertain a system for profit maximization.

Under simulated conditions, various distribution configurations are tested until that system capable of providing necessary customer service at lowest total cost is isolated. Basically, three strategies of distribution flow between plants and final sales point are available. First, a wide network of distribution centers may be created. Second, products may be shipped directly from manufacturing plants to final destination. Third, a combination of distribution centers and direct shipments may be employed. Under simulated conditions, the combination of these strategies which best fits a firm's marketing requirements is determined.

The main advantage of simulation is the capability it provides to study the location problem on a total cost basis. As noted earlier, the outstanding deficiency of techniques available for selecting individual sites is their singular emphasis upon transportation cost. In a simulation study, the over-all problem is studied on a total cost basis. The typical procedure is to establish element costs for such critical factors as transport, labor, inventory, communications, etc. If the research objective is only to study distribution system configuration, such factors as plant location, customer locations, and sales forecasts are quantified and held constant. Desired service standards are developed as management constraints. For example, one parameter may be to service all accounts over a given dollar sales volume or profit contribution within a specified period after an order is received. Another may be to ship 95 per cent of all requests on the original order within a specified period.

Once the model is constructed, the simulation exercise proceeds to determine the minimum configuration of distribution centers that will meet the specified managerial objectives at the lowest total cost combination of all critical elements. From that point forward, the simulated results may be used to evaluate alternative costs of various other managerial objectives or standards of performance. For example, how many additional dollars of

---

as Leon Wester and Harold H. Kantor, "*Optimum Location Allocation*," Sixth Annual Meeting of the Operations Research Society of America, May 16, 1958. The most significant recent applications of simulation have been developed by Harvey N. Shycon. His work with the Heinz and the Nestlé companies is reviewed in a five-part article "Operations Research—Tool for Better Distribution," *Transportation and Distribution Management*, November 1962–March 1963.

cost would result from a decision to increase service capabilities by twelve hours? To the degree that costs of alternate service policies can be related to potential sales, a simulation offers an analytical approach for studying service elasticity of demand.

Advanced simulation still remains in the development stage.[29] Simulation's fundamental limitations are expense, complexity, and the immediate practicality of experimental results. Rarely, if ever, can a firm optimize all economic locations at a single point in time. The more normal situation is a series of suboptimizations which result from seeking the best location for a specific type of facility at a specific time. The practicality of simulation will advance with the development of techniques for a dynamic model of a firm's geographical adjustment to demand and competition over an extended period.

CONCLUSION

Traditional location concepts, modern marketing distribution, and analytical techniques have been summarized in order to review information about distribution center location. All forms of location are established as important strategic elements in a firm's total marketing plan. Differential advantage, by virtue of astute location, varies from the advantage obtained by other marketing tactics because of the time element. Once a firm is committed to a location, its ability to maintain flexibility is limited. Therefore, it must move cautiously in selecting locations. Once superior locations are obtained, a firm enjoys a differential advantage that is difficult to duplicate.

---

[29]Although not directly related to distribution center location, an excellent example of the potential of simulation is F. E. Balderston and A. C. Hoggatt, *Simulation of Marketing Processes*, IBER Special Publications Series No. 1, University of California at Berkeley, Institute of Business and Economics, 1962.

5

Jerry Schorr

The Optimization of
Distribution Centers

In order to determine the optimum number, size, and location of distribution centers for any location problem, one must follow a logical, mathematical approach.

To facilitate use of the location tools and techniques, the mathematics of this chapter has intentionally been kept simple without sacrificing accuracy.

Here are examples of the procedures, techniques, and tools used to determine the optimum number, size, and location of distribution centers.

STEP I

Determine present distribution areas and total costs within each distribution territory, area, or region.

The total distribution cost within each region includes five categories: transportation, inventory, storage, labor and materials handling, other.

STEP II

Determine the optimum number of warehouses.

The optimum number of warehouses may be (1) fewer than the present number, (2) more than the present number, or (3) the present number.

In order to find this optimum number, first determine if fewer than the present number of warehouses is needed. If not, then determine if

61

more than the present number of warehouses is required. If this also is not correct, it therefore follows that the present number of warehouses is the optimum number.

Determining Whether Fewer Warehouses Are Needed

1. List the present distribution territories in order of total annual weight volume:

New York	10,000,000 lbs.	Los Angeles	5,000,000 lbs.
Chicago	8,000,000	Houston	4,000,000
Atlanta	6,000,000	Portland	2,000,000

2. Eliminate the distribution territory having the smallest total annual weight volume. (In this example, eliminate the distribution location in Portland, Oregon.)

3. Determine the new total annual distribution cost of using five, instead of six, warehouses (Table 5.1).

Transportation cost. The total transportation cost has risen as a result of the reduction from six to five warehouses, as shown in Table 5.1.

Portland, Oregon, and its distribution area would be served either from a company plant or from surrounding warehouses.

For a simple method of determining which warehouse should serve the Portland distribution area, apply the "compass method" (Figure 5.1).

Semicircles from each warehouse are drawn into the Portland, Oregon, distribution territory. Straight lines are drawn through the tangent points of the semicircles; and the Portland, Oregon, distribution territory is divided among the Los Angeles, Houston, and Chicago warehouses.

TABLE 5.1

Total Annual Distribution Cost

	6 WAREHOUSES (*Present*)	5 WAREHOUSES (*Proposed*)
Transportation	$1,500,000	$1,550,000
Inventory	30,000	25,000
Storage	60,000	50,000
Labor and Materials Handling	60,000	50,000
Other	12,000	10,000
TOTAL COST	$1,662,000	$1,685,000

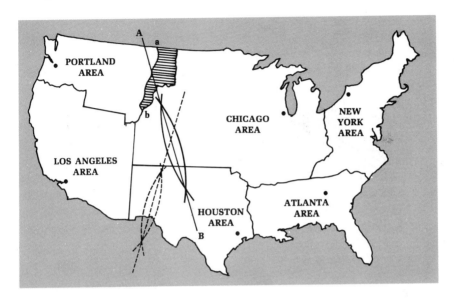

FIGURE 5.1

Illustration of the compass method

Decision: To reduce the number of warehouses and warehouse service areas from six to five by eliminating the Portland warehouse and the Portland area which it serves.

Problem: To subdivide the Portland area for the most economical and efficient service from adjacent or nearby warehouse areas.

Solution: (1) Consider Los Angeles and Chicago as sources for service to the Portland area. (2) Using a compass, draw a semicircle from Chicago in such a way that it will be intersected by a semicircle drawn, with the same compass setting, from Los Angeles. (3) Draw line AB through the tangent points of the semicircles so that it passes through the Portland area. The portion of line AB which passes through the Portland area is the theoretical dividing line between service from Chicago and service from Los Angeles. (4) Adjust the theoretical dividing line on the basis of local conditions, such as geographical features or rate variations. This will result in line AB which marks the actual dividing line between service from Chicago and service from Los Angeles. (5) The shaded portion of the Portland area now becomes part of the Chicago area. The unshaded portion of the Portland area now becomes part of the Los Angeles area. (6) The dotted lines illustrate that Houston will not be a source of service to the Portland area.

Total distribution cost. Since the total distribution cost for five warehouses is greater than the distribution cost for six warehouses, we should proceed to determine whether more than the present number of warehouses is the best solution.

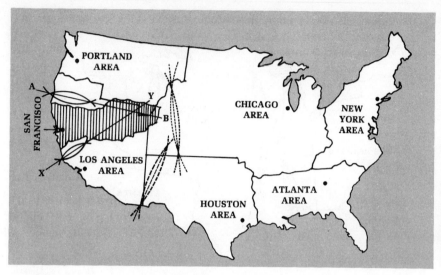

FIGURE 5.2

Illustration of the compass method

Decision: To increase the number of warehouses and warehouse service areas from six to seven.

Problem: To establish the seventh area, in this case the San Francisco area, since San Francisco is the nonwarehouse city with the largest annual weight volume.

Solution: (1) Using a compass, draw a semicircle from San Francisco in such a way that it will be intersected by a semicircle drawn, with the same compass setting, from Los Angeles. Repeat the process for any other city which must or possibly might have its supply area affected by the establishment of the new San Francisco area (Portland, Chicago, Houston). (2) Draw line AB through the tangent points of the San Francisco/Portland semicircles, and draw line XY through the tangent points of the San Francisco/Los Angeles semicircles. The triangle formed by the coast line and the two sides, AB and XY to their point of intersection, represents the theoretical San Francisco area. (3) Adjust the theoretical area boundaries on the basis of local conditions, such as geographical features or rate variations. This will result in the actual San Francisco area, as indicated by the shaded portion. (4) The dotted lines illustrate that the warehouse cities of Chicago and Houston do not affect the boundaries of either the theoretical or the actual San Francisco area.

It should be pointed out that if the cost of five warehouses had been less than the total distribution cost for six warehouses, our next step would be to determine whether the total distribution cost for four warehouses (eliminating the Houston warehouse) would be less than the cost for five warehouses, etc.

TABLE 5.2

Total Annual Distribution Cost

	6 WAREHOUSES	7 WAREHOUSES
Transportation	$1,500,000	$1,480,000
Inventory	30,000	35,000
Storage	60,000	70,000
Labor and Materials Handling	60,000	70,000
Other	12,000	14,000
TOTAL COST	$1,662,000	$1,669,000

Determining Whether More Warehouses Are Needed

1. List all nonwarehouse cities in order of total annual weight volume.

2. Simulate the new total distribution cost by placing a warehouse in the nonwarehouse city with the largest annual weight volume (for example, San Francisco). Carve out a new distribution territory for this city by using the compass method (Figure 5.2).

3. Determine the total annual distribution cost of using seven, instead of six, warehouses (Table 5.2).

The total annual distribution cost for more than the present number of warehouses is greater than the cost for the present number of warehouses. Thus, our solution shows that six is the optimum number of warehouses.

If the total annual distribution cost for seven warehouses had been less than for six warehouses, we would have proceeded to determine whether eight could be the optimum number of warehouses.

STEP III

Having determined the optimum *number* of warehouses, determine whether these warehouses are in the optimum *location(s)*. Using the weighted center formula approach, we determine the optimum location for warehouses in each distribution territory.

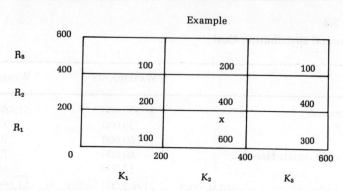

FIGURE 5.3

First Step

1. Divide each territory into grids.

2. Let the distance between each grid line represent a numerical value; for example, 200.

3. Insert into each grid the total tonnage distributed within the grid.

4. Use the following formulas:

$$Ah = \frac{D\sum TR_1 + D\sum TR_2 + \ldots + D\sum TR_n}{\sum TR_1 + \sum TR_2 + \ldots + \sum TR_n}$$

$$Av = \frac{D\sum TK_1 + D\sum TK_2 + \ldots + D\sum TK_n}{\sum TK_1 + \sum TK_2 + \ldots + \sum TK_n}$$

where Ah = Optimum horizontal grid location,
D = Distance (midpoint between grid lines),
T = Tonnage,
R_n = Row number,
Av = Optimum vertical grid location,
$T_{r,k}$ = Tonnage in rows and columns, and
K_n = Column number.

$$Ah = \frac{100(1,000) + 300(1,000) + 500(400)}{1,000 + 1,000 + 400}$$

$$Ah = \frac{100,000 + 300,000 + 200,000}{3,400}$$

$$Ah = \frac{600,000}{3,400}$$

$$Ah = 177 \text{ miles}$$

$$Av = \frac{100(400) + 300(1{,}200) + 500(800)}{2{,}400}$$

$$Av = \frac{800{,}000}{2{,}400}$$

$$Av = 333 \text{ miles}$$

Thus, the optimum warehouse location (x) is 177 miles on the horizontal grid (R) and 333 miles on the vertical grid (K).

Second Step

Determine the total annual distribution cost for the location selected and compare it to the present cost by using the cost table (Table 5.1).

The same procedures should be followed to determine the optimum warehouse location for each warehouse.

SUMMARY

Procedures, tools, and techniques are presented in this chapter to solve critical location problems without complex mathematics. The optimum solutions attained through the application of these procedures, tools, and techniques result in lowest-cost solutions for given location problems, but customer service requirements must also be considered in choosing locations of warehouses, plants, etc. If the optimum-cost answer does not correspond to a satisfactory level of customer service, then the second-lowest-cost solution may be the most feasible.

A THIRD and important function of logistics in marketing is inventory control. The next two chapters cover two critical areas of this function. Chapter 6 deals with the metholodogy for forecasting inventory requirements through the exponential smoothing technique; Chapter 7 introduces mathematical techniques for determining optimum levels of both cycle and safety stocks. (The reader is reminded that warehouse stocks represent only one aspect of the inventory control problem; goods are also stored at plants and branches, and on carriers in each step of the transportation cycle.)

The subject concerns an extremely important phase of inventory costing—opportunity costs, i.e., an opportunity to earn a return on invested capital as opposed to tying up a given quantity of capital. (It has been estimated that in some industries the opportunity cost of each pound of inventory is equal to 25 per cent of the wholesale value of the stock.)

6

Allan Vesley

Forecasting and
Inventory Control

INVENTORY CONCEPTS

A recent publication defines inventory as "an aggregate or total mass of goods. . . . Inventory serves the function of making a company's internal operation relatively stable while providing services to customers."[1]

While this is a traditional and partially correct definition, it is not as all-inclusive as it might be. An alternative definition describes inventory as "an idle resource of any kind provided that such resource has economic value."[2] The advantage of this definition is that it is broad enough to include such things as plant capacity to meet future demands, toll stations to meet varying traffic demand patterns, airline seats, and any other item or capability that must be provided to meet future requirements.

An expanded view of the nature of inventory is useful in two ways:

It enables us to apply the valuable theoretical concepts that have been developed for the control of goods to a much wider range of problems.

It broadens our horizons by inviting us to apply techniques from other types of decision problems to the management of commodity-type inventories.

Miller and Starr, in their book on inventory theory, structure the analysis of inventory problems in terms of opposing costs. Inventory policy is optimized by balancing the cost of carrying inventory against the cost of

---

[1]IBM Corporation, *General Information Manual, Impact-Inventory Management Program and Control Techniques*, 1962.
[2]Martin K. Starr and David W. Miller, *Inventory Control: Theory and Practice*, Prentice-Hall, 1962.

ordering it into stock. An optimum policy can be found when future demand is known and when a policy regarding a desired level of service is given. The setting of this desired level of service is determined by balancing the costs of being out of stock with the cost of carrying additional inventory to reduce the out-of-stock probability.

FORETELLING THE FUTURE

The application of inventory theory is one of the oldest examples of the use of management science or operations research techniques. However, traditional discussions on the subject of inventory control have dwelt on the determination of an optimum order strategy under the assumption that future demand is either known or can be estimated with some determinable degree of accuracy. There has therefore been recognition of the great importance of forecasting future demand in applying inventory theory. However, the problem of how to forecast future requirements has been set aside as an entirely separate subject. In past years this has led to the development of a large number of reasonably scientific inventory control applications utilizing demand forecasts that represented "seat-of-the-pants" guesswork or projections from past history, done in an informal or intuitive fashion. In the meantime, considerable progress in the application of quantitative techniques to the task of forecasting was being made in non-inventory problem areas. It is the combining of these improved forecasting techniques with traditional inventory control procedures that is now producing major breakthroughs in inventory management.

The task of foretelling the uncertain future is the common denominator in a vast array of human decision-making problems. Robert Brown[3] sheds considerable light on the nature of this activity by distinguishing between "forecasts" and "predictions": "I shall use the term 'forecast' to mean the projection of the past into the future. Literally, the word means to 'throw ahead,' to continue what has been happening. 'Prediction' or 'saying beforehand,' will be reserved for management's anticipation of changes and of new factors affecting demand."

Prediction does not readily lend itself to statistical or mathematical techniques. Unlike forecasting, it is not an extrapolation of the past into the future but rather an attempt to say something about an action or event that is not a continuation of the past. This does not mean that prediction can only be done with a crystal ball or by unfounded guesswork. It does, however, mean that human judgment must be applied to find the assumed

---

[3] Robert G. Brown, *Statistical Forecasting for Inventory Control*, McGraw-Hill, 1959.

similarities and correlations between the entity being predicted and other entities recalled from the past experience of the person doing the predicting.

METHODS OF FORECASTING

Forecasting is often thought of as a more exact means of foretelling the future. We must remember, however, that it is based on the grand assumption that the future is in some way related to what has gone before. Forecasting can be done in one of two basic ways:

> By assuming a relationship between an external event and the thing being forecast. This is known as *extrinsic* forecasting and is usually done by correlating a figure such as birth rates, freight car loadings, or housing starts with the entity being forecast on the theory that its behavior will lag that of the statistic being used but will be directly related to it.

> Forecasting the demand for individual inventory items is more likely to be done by extrapolating the past demand behavior for that particular item into the future. This is called *intrinsic* forecasting in that the correlation assumed is the correlation of the future behavior of an item with its own past behavior.

Numerous methods exist for forecasting from historical data. Five of these are illustrated in the Appendix to this chapter. The simplest approach involves averaging the past data and using that value as an estimate of the future. A refinement on this approach is to develop a moving average in recognition of the fact that it is the most recent period of history that is most meaningful. An extension of this idea involves the use of a weighted moving average in order to emphasize the most recent history even further. All of these approaches give a forecast that is somewhere within the bounds set by the values contained in the past history. Even if a weight of 100 per cent is assigned to the highest observation from past history, the forecast for the future will be equal to the value of that observation but no higher. In order to recognize the existence of a trend in historical data and account for this trend in the forecast, it is necessary to develop a line of best fit for the past history so that the slope of the line as well as its level may be extended into the future. The development of any sort of a simple or a weighted average can only give a horizontal or trendless forecast of future demand.

When the past data reveal that cycles or patterns rather than a linear function best describe the history, it is necessary to employ higher-order curve-fitting techniques and then to extrapolate the best-fitting curve into the future in order to make a forecast.

EXPONENTIAL SMOOTHING

Robert Brown describes a method of forecasting that is especially suited to inventory problems. This method is called "exponential smoothing" and has the advantage of reducing the amount of historical data that must be carried and making it possible to control the weight given to current data. Exponential smoothing is a form of weighted moving average. (An example is given in the Appendix to this chapter.) A publication by the IBM Corporation describes this method as follows:

> Consider an item for which the pattern of demand can be classed as constant, and for which data has been accumulated in monthly increments. One month ago the average of demand was computed to be 19 units per month. This month the demand was, in fact, 21. We want to take advantage of this new information to revise the estimate of the average. Assume that the old records which yielded the average of 19 have been inadvertently destroyed, so that the new estimate must be worked out using just the two numbers, 19 and 21. Two things seem immediately apparent:
>
> 1. Because 21 is larger than 19, the new estimate of average should also be larger than 19.
> 2. The amount of change from 19 should be proportional to the difference $(21 - 19)$.
>
> While these two statements explain exponential smoothing verbally, the following formula says the same thing:
>
> New average = old average + α(new demand − old average)
>
> (The Greek letter alpha α is commonly used to designate a smoothing constant between 0 and 1 which determines the influence of the new demand on the new average.) By controlling the weight of the most recent data, alpha simultaneously determines the average age of the data included in the estimate of [the] average. The value chosen for the smoothing constant can be such that the estimate is very stable (low value) or reacts very quickly (high value).
>
> If you use $\alpha = .1$, and work through the formula, you should get a new average of 19.2:
>
> New average $= 19 + .1(21 - 19)$
>
> $= 19 + .1(2) = 19.2$
>
> With a higher $\alpha = .5$, there is a greater response to the new information.

New average = $19 + .5(21 - 19)$

$$= 19 + .5(2) = 20.0$$

If the figures have been reversed so that the old average was 21 and the new demand 19, we would intuitively think that the new average should be less than 21 (the corollary of statement 1).

Solving the formula with $\alpha = .1$:

New average = $21 + .1(19 - 21)$

$$= 21 + .1(-2) = 20.8$$

When $\alpha = .5$,

New average = $21 + .5(19 - 21)$

$$= 21 + .5(-2) = 20.0$$

Obviously, a lower value of the smoothing constant introduces less effect from the new data. Correspondingly, the effect of older data persists for a longer period of time, though to an ever-decreasing extent. With a value of $\alpha = 0.1$, the newest data available make up 10% of the new average. One period later, its contribution is reduced to 9%, two periods later to 8.1% and so on until 20 periods later when the contribution of the data is reduced to about 1%. With a high α such as .5, however, the contribution of a given piece of data is reduced much more quickly. Regardless of the value of α, the weighting of data follows what is called an "exponential" curve—hence the name exponential smoothing.[4]

Exponential smoothing does more than calculate the weighted average of past history alone. For example, it is possible to develop an exponentially smoothed average of the difference between each old average and its succeeding value. If there is a true trend in the data, that trend will be revealed in this fashion. It is also possible to develop an exponentially smoothed average of the differences between forecasts made and the actual demand experienced during the period forecast. Such a measure can be used as a tracking signal to determine whether or not the system is indeed forecasting future demand with acceptable accuracy.

JUDGMENT AND PREDICTION

There are many inventory control situations where forecasting from history alone produces inadequate results. This is true in the following cases.

---

[4]IBM Corporation, *op. cit.*

1. Seasonal variations are an important determinant of future demand history;

2. The item being forecast does not have any previous demand history;

3. The numbers comprising the demand history for an item are too small to permit meaningful extrapolation;

4. There are external factors (e.g., a promotional campaign) which it is believed will have a greater effect on future demand than would the past history of the item.

The above characteristics are common to a great many inventory situations. In these cases, it is possible to combine the advantages of forecasting from past history with the advantages of making predictions based upon factors other than past history. This can be done by translating our prediction for the item into a pattern or profile. Brown refers to this approach in discussing seasonal forecasting; he refers to a seasonal item profile as a "base series."

A profile or "base series" is used to represent the expected or predicted pattern of demand. It does not attempt to indicate the quantity of demand at any point in the future but only the expected shape of the demand curve over a period of time. For example, where expected demand is known to be seasonal, its profile might be expressed in terms of a series of numbers representing the percentage of total annual demand expected in each of the weeks in a year. In this case, the sum of the numbers in the profile would be equal to one. In the case of a brand-new product, we might expect that demand will increase steadily and sharply for some period of time and then level off. In this case we could develop a profile representing this function even though we are not yet prepared to estimate what the level of demand will be. In effect, predict the shape or direction of the curve representing our prediction of future demand rather than try to give a quantitative estimate of what that demand will be during any given period of time in the future. The actual level of future demand remains to be determined by combining forecasting from past history with the prediction represented by a profile. The method for achieving this is to determine the ratio between actual demand and its appropriate profile point. The calculation of the average of these demand ratios can be handled by using a weighted moving average or, more likely, an exponentially smoothed figure. This is done in exactly the same fashion that would be employed in using exponential smoothing to track actual past history rather than the history of demand ratios. By the same token, we could apply a trend to our history of demand ratios and also measure our average error in order to determine whether or not the system is in control. The exponentially smoothed estimate of the demand ratio is then applied to future profile points covering the period for which a forecast is being made.

The forecast of future demand is therefore the joint result of a *prediction* about the expected future requirements and a *forecast* based upon the historical data available. A system such as this can be applied to inventory forecasting problems of any type. Obviously, if there is no past demand history whatsoever for an item, an initial order amount must be set so that demand can begin to be experienced and forecasting begun from it. The use of profiles in conjunction with forecasting from past demand data can be useful in cases other than those involving new or seasonal items. For example, an established product without any seasonality might best be described by a profile that is a straight horizontal line. However, if a major promotion were to be run for that item, it might be desirable to change the profile temporarily into one that represents an upward slope.

SUMMARY

Good inventory control theory and practice has been known for a long time. Electronic data processing increased the feasibility of applying inventory theory in a more complete fashion to the day-in–day-out control of individual items. In the same fashion, we may expect that computer technology will continue to foster the use of mathematical and statistical techniques for forecasting inventory demand.

The existence of uncertainty characterizes most business decision problems including those related to inventory management. Inventory theory does not eliminate that uncertainty but does enable us to take its existence into account and still work toward the achievement of optimum solutions. Better forecasting strikes directly at the problem of uncertainty itself and thereby makes its contribution to the economic management of inventories.

APPENDIX

EXAMPLE OF THE USE OF EXPONENTIAL SMOOTHING FOR FORECASTING

Figure 6A.1 and Table 6A.1 show an example of a demand forecast made by using both a seasonal profile and a tracking of previous demand history.

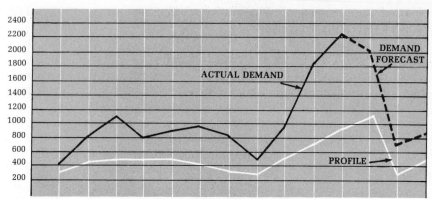

FIGURE 6A.1

Forecast of demand obtained by applying exponentially smoothed demand ratio to the profile for a future time period

TABLE 6A.1

TIME PERIOD	PROFILE	ACTUAL DEMAND	DEMAND RATIO	SMOOTH RATIO
				1.50
January	310	405	1.30	1.48
February	450	810	1.80	1.51
March	500	1,100	2.20	1.58
April	500	800	1.60	1.58
May	500	900	1.80	1.60
June	440	925	2.10	1.65
July	280	835	2.20	1.70
August	320	510	1.60	1.69
September	525	945	1.90	1.70
October	730	1,825	2.50	1.78
November	935	2,240	2.40	1.84
		Forecast		
December	1,140	2,095		
January	310	570		
February	450	830		

The points in the profile indicate the expected seasonal variation in demand for the items. It should be noted that these points repeat themselves every twelve months. The ratio of actual demand to the corresponding profile point provides us with the demand ratio. It is this demand ratio that is averaged by means of exponential smoothing to obtain a smoothed ratio. Since we are using an alpha value of .1, the formula is:

New smoothed ratio = .9(Previous smoothed ratio)
+ .1(New current-period demand ratio)

In the illustration above, an initial value of 1.50 is used for the average demand ratio. This gradually increases to a value of 1.84 at the end of November. It is this ratio of 1.84 that is applied to the profile points for December–January and February in order to obtain a forecast demand during that period.

If we examine the data in the illustration, we note a minor upward trend in the exponentially smoothed demand ratio. This would indicate that our forecasting could probably be improved by adjusting that ratio for the trend or by increasing the value of alpha so that the changes in the exponentially smoothed average ratio would be tracked more rapidly by giving greater weight to the most current time period.

EXAMPLES OF OTHER METHODS OF FORECASTING

Figures 6A.2–6A.6 show the results obtained from the use of various forecasting techniques other than exponential smoothing.

These techniques include:

A. Projection of simple average (Fig. 6A.2).

$$x = \frac{a + b + c + \ldots + n}{N}$$

B. Projection of four-point moving average (Fig. 6A.3).

$$X = [(a + b + c + d) + (b + c + d + e) + \ldots$$
$$+ (n_{-3} + n_{-2} + n_{-1} + n)]/4(N - 4)$$

C. Projection of weighted moving average (Fig. 6A.4).

$$X = [\alpha(a + b + c + d) + \beta(b + c + d + e) + \ldots$$
$$+ \gamma(n_{-3} + n_{-2} + n_{-1} + n)]/4(N - 4)$$

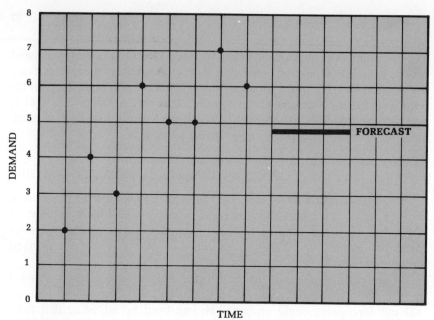

FIGURE 6A.2

Projection of simple average

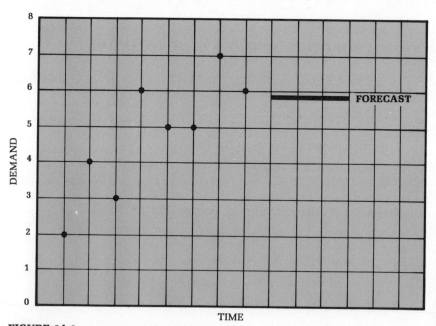

FIGURE 6A.3

Projection of four-point moving average

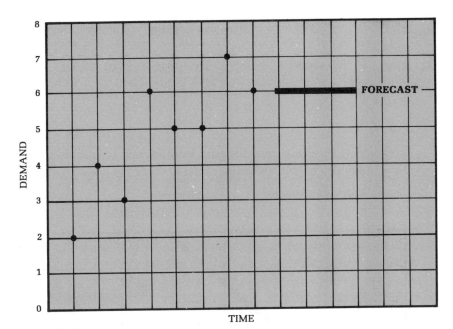

FIGURE 6A.4

Projection of weighted moving average

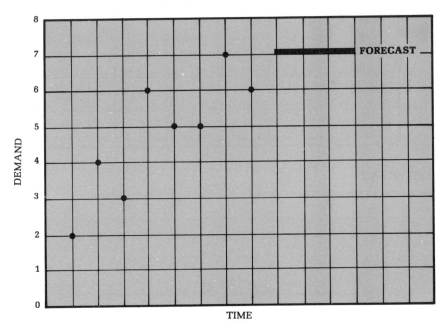

FIGURE 6A.5

Projection by assigning 100 per cent weight to the highest point

D. Projection by assigning 100 per cent weight to the highest point (Fig. 6A.5).

$X = Y$

$Y > A, B, C, \ldots, n$

E. Projection by fitting a trend line and extrapolating it into the future (visual technique) (Fig. 6A.6).

Use of "eyeball technique"

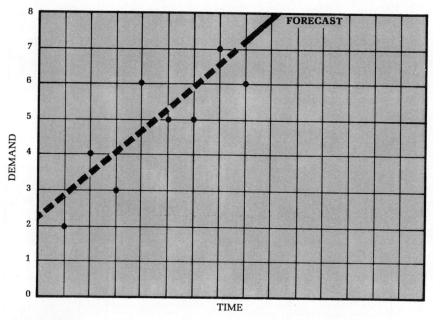

FIGURE 6A.6

Projection by fitting a trend line and extrapolating it into the future

7

Granville R. Gargiulo

Aggregative Inventory Standards for Management Decision

The management of most companies today considers it axiomatic that the business needs inventories of raw materials, work in process, and finished goods to permit a smooth, economical operation and to maintain a highly competitive level of customer service. Yet there is the concomitant concern with the return being earned on the capital invested in these inventories. The result has been an ever-increasing desire to exercise adequate control over this investment through the implementation of an inventory management system.

All too often, however, the design and implementation of the system put the sole emphasis on the rules for controlling the stocking and replenishing of an item or a class of items. This approach shortchanges management in that no aggregate standard of performance is readily available to them for an evaluation of the control system as it relates to their objectives in inventory investment. Further, there is no means for determining, on a broad basis, the investment consequences of alternative decisions regarding expanded customer service or product lines.

This chapter describes the development and use of a sensitive performance standard directly related to the inventory management goals of a wholesale distributor (hereafter referred to as ALDO Inc.), as reflected in their new reorder-point–economic-order quantity system of control. While the number of finished-goods items centrally warehoused and controlled (commonly referred to as stock-keeping units) by this distributor is in the thousands, standards of inventory investment are based on the study of the total inventory as an entity in itself, thereby eliminating any need to investigate each stock-keeping unit in detail.

THE INVENTORY MANAGEMENT SYSTEM

ALDO Inc. had formalized its control over stock replenishment in its central distribution facility by using various statistical inventory control techniques. During the past year purchase decisions were governed by an order point and purchases were made in economic-order quantities. A brief review of the underlying concepts of their present control system will be helpful in evaluating alternative approaches to determining the total inventory invest-ment required.

The systems department at ALDO Inc. conducted a formal investigation into the areas of ordering costs, inventory costs, order-processing lead times, vendor delivery performance, inventory stockouts, customer back orders, and forecasting procedures. The decision to use economic-order quantities was based on management's desire to maintain a minimum cost operation composed of (1) costs that increase as stocks increase, such as interest on investment, obsolescence, depreciation, storage, etc.; and (2) costs that decrease as inventories increase, which, in this case, was limited to the costs of preparing and processing orders.

For each item stocked in the warehouse, a purchase order quantity Q that would minimize total costs (as represented in Figure 7.1) was determined using the following formula:

$$Q = \sqrt{\frac{2SP}{I}} \tag{1}$$

where S is the expected annual sales (in dollars), P is the cost of processing a single order, and I is the annual cost of holding the inventory (expressed as a fraction of the investment).

Order points were also established for every item as a basis for the decision to replenish warehouse stocks. Figure 7.2 shows the concepts concerning reorder points. At time t_0 the available inventory, defined as the net amount still uncommitted for specific deliveries (stock on hand plus stock on order less any unfilled customer orders), may be at level A. Line AB then represents the expected rate of stock depletion based on a forecast of average demand for the item. If sales went according to forecast and stocks could be replenished instantaneously, ALDO Inc. could allow inventories to fall to zero at point B, whereupon they would place a new order.

The company recognized, however, that a certain amount of time elapsed (t_1 to t_2) between the release of an order and the receipt of material at the warehouse. In fact, groups of items had different delivery times because of the varied locations of vendors. Consequently, if the available stock were insufficient to meet the forecast of average demand during the

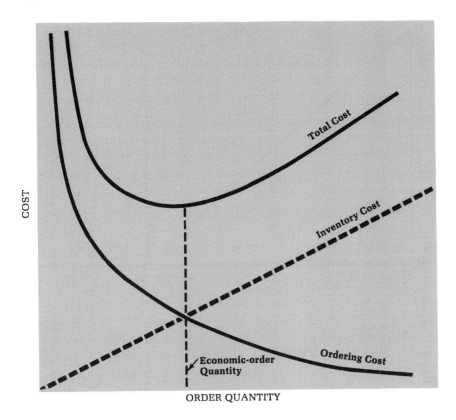

COST

ORDER QUANTITY

FIGURE 7.1

Relationship of inventory costs to ordering costs

lead time (t_1 to t_2), more material should be ordered. In the top half of Figure 7.2, an order would be placed at t_1 when the inventory level reached C.

ALDO Inc. used a simple moving average (described in the Appendix to the previous chapter) in developing short-term forecasts of demand for individual items. Since these forecasts represented estimates of average demand, it was no surprise to find that actual demand exceeded the forecasts 50 per cent of the time. Setting the new order points to cover forecasts of average demand would thus represent a 50 per cent chance that a stock shortage would occur before a replenishment order was received. To eliminate the difficulties resulting from a stockout situation, the company provided for additional inventory to be kept on hand to draw upon in those instances when demand might be expected to exceed the forecast. The specific amount of this safety stock for each item was based upon (1) a

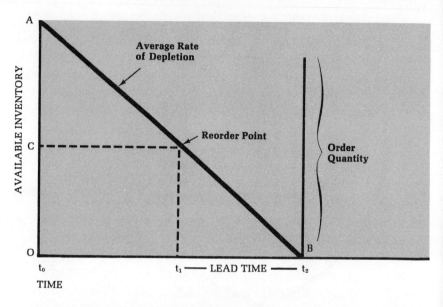

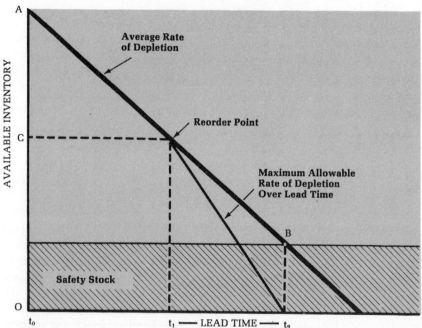

FIGURE 7.2
Reorder-point concepts

measure of forecast errors, i.e., how close actual demand during the lead time came to the forecast over the long run, and (2) the customer services requirements defined by management in terms of an acceptable frequency of stock shortages and the resulting backorder situation.

Based on these considerations, reorder points were set as depicted in the bottom half of Figure 7.2, that is, a replenishment order was to be released whenever the available stock equaled the expected or forecasted demand during a lead time, plus the safety stock. This may be restated as

Reorder point = Average lead time demand + Safety stock

where the safety stock is the product of a constant (representing the number of standard measures of variation between actual and forecast demand that will provide a defined degree of protection against possible excess demand over forecast) times the measure of variation itself (known as σ, the standard deviation of the distribution of forecast errors, which, in most inventories, has an approximate relationship to the sales rate of the item).

ANNUAL INVENTORY INVESTMENT

The inventory investment for an item controlled on the basis of reorder points and economic-order quantities is the safety stock plus one-half the economic-order quantity (cycle stock). Since both elements are related to the sales rate for an item, the total investment for an item becomes a function of its annual dollar sales, as shown in Figure 7.3.

It would thus be possible to determine what the company's total inventory investment should be under their new control system by determining the investment for each item based on its forecast of annual demand, and total the results over all items. The alternative approach is to select a representative sample of items, determine the average relationship of sales of these selected items to the cycle and safety stocks required, and then extrapolate these relationships to the total number of inventoried items. The key to a meaningful and valid extrapolation is the "standard ratio" (described in the following section of this chapter) which characterizes the sales relationships of individual items in the total inventory.

As a practical matter, ALDO Inc. wanted to establish standards of investment based on actual demand during the year in which their new procedures were in operation. Management would then be in a position to evaluate the system performance and effectiveness of the control rules inherent in the system by comparing such standards to the actual inventory investment. This evaluation would highlight those areas where the routine

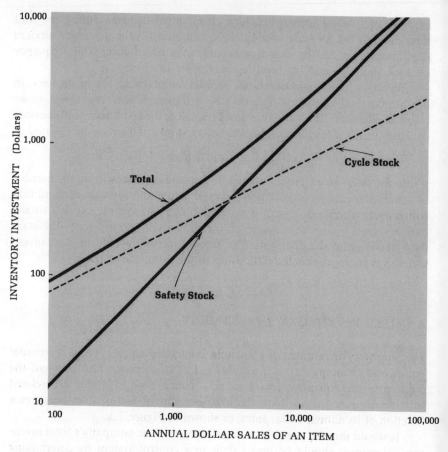

FIGURE 7.3

Inventory investment by item movement

decisions of stock replenishment were not being made in accordance with
management policies regarding costs and customer service, which in essence
determined the control criteria of when and how much to order of each
item.

Initially, one well-defined product line was selected to test this alternative
approach for determining aggregate inventory investment standards and to
serve as a basis for recommending a comprehensive evaluation of all finished
goods stored in the ALDO Inc. central distribution facility. The 850
individual items constituting this product line had a relatively stable sales
pattern and were particularly susceptible to routine stock replenishment
under a reorder-point–economic-order quantity system of control.

THE CONCEPT OF THE STANDARD RATIO

A random sample of 50 items was selected from the 850 items as a basis for describing the characteristics of demand for this product line. Table 7.1 gives the annual dollar sales for the 50 sample items ranked in descending order of sales. A few key items can be picked to describe the entire sample.[1]

15.9 per cent of 50 items = 7.95 (item 8 on Table 7.1)

50.0 per cent of 50 items = 25.00 (item 25 on Table 7.1)

84.1 per cent of 50 items = 42.05 (item 42 on Table 7.1)

Looking at items 8, 25, and 42 we note that the sales volume of the first ($6,747) is 3.2 times the volume for the second ($2,054), which is 3.2 times the sales volume for the third ($637). In other words, the annual sales rates of these items are related by a factor of 3.2.

Recognizing that the consistent and predictable relationships between sales rates for the 850 items would not normally be reflected in the sales rates for just three items, the general characteristics of the 50 items were established by plotting the information given in Table 7.1 on a log-normal graph as shown in Figure 7.4. For the sales of each of the 50 items a point was plotted (1) to indicate the percentage of items with sales in excess of that item and (2) to indicate the percentage of total sales derived from items with sales in excess of that item.

A straight line was inserted for each series of points which provided a good "fit" to the individual points plotted.[2] The standard ratio of 3.3 ($6,600 ÷ $2,000; $19,000 ÷ $5,800) was inferred from either line (average relationship) by dividing the sales rate where the line crosses the 15.9 percentile ($6,600 — items line; $19,000 — income line) by the sales rate where it crosses the 50.0 percentile ($2,000 — items line; $5,800 — income line). This simple description of the sales of items in the product line enabled ALDO Inc. to estimate what the inventory investment should have been during the past year on the 850 items in the selected product line controlled under their reorder-point–economic-order quantity replenishment rules.

---

[1]These percentiles were chosen because they represent the arithmetic average (mean) and one standard deviation on either side of it for a normal distribution. Widespread experience in industry shows that this distribution, or approximations of it, has particular importance in the description of almost any inventory.

[2]When the points on a log-normal graph fall—with limited scatter—near a straight line, the demand of the items can be described by the log-normal distribution. The standard ratio will then be the same whether we deal with percentiles of items or percentiles of total sales dollars.

TABLE 7.1

Ranked Distribution of Annual Dollar Sales, 50 Sample Items

Item No.	Annual Dollar Sales	Cumulative Dollar Sales	Per Cent of	
			Items with Greater Sales	Total Sales from Items with Greater Sales
1	17,030	17,030	0	0.0
2	12,649	29,679	2	10.4
3	8,723	38,402	4	18.1
4	7,345	45,747	6	23.5
5	7,202	52,949	8	28.0
6	6,955	59,904	10	32.4
7	6,760	66,664	12	36.7
8	6,747	73,411	14	40.8
9	6,136	79,547	16	44.9
10	5,733	85,280	18	48.7
11	5,551	90,831	20	52.2
12	5,463	96,294	22	55.6
13	5,005	101,299	24	59.0
14	4,576	105,875	26	62.0
15	4,303	110,178	28	64.8
16	3,744	113,922	30	67.5
17	3,419	117,341	32	69.8
18	3,185	120,526	34	71.9
19	3,107	123,633	36	73.8
20	3,003	126,636	38	75.7
21	2,899	129,435	40	77.6
22	2,405	131,840	42	79.3
23	2,288	134,228	44	80.7
24	2,249	136,377	46	82.2
25	2,054	138,531	48	83.5
26	1,872	140,403	50	84.8
27	1,807	142,210	52	86.0
28	1,775	143,965	54	87.1
29	1,729	145,694	56	88.2
30	1,638	147,332	58	89.2
31	1,612	148,944	60	90.2
32	1,287	150,231	62	91.2
33	1,222	151,453	64	92.0
34	1,196	152,649	66	92.8
35	1,183	153,832	68	93.5
36	1,079	155,011	70	94.2
37	897	155,808	72	94.9
38	767	156,675	74	95.4
39	728	157,303	76	96.0
40	728	158,031	78	96.3
41	676	158,707	80	96.8
42	637	159,344	82	97.2
43	611	159,955	84	97.6
44	598	160,553	86	98.0
45	520	161,073	88	98.3
46	481	161,554	90	98.7
47	468	162,022	92	99.0
48	429	162,451	94	99.2
49	403	162,854	96	99.5
50	312	163,166	98	99.7

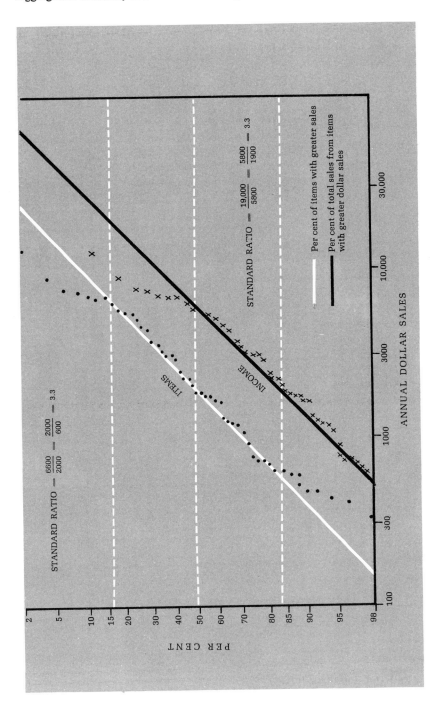

FIGURE 7.4
Ranked distribution of annual dollar sales, 50 sample items

ESTABLISHING INVESTMENT STANDARDS

At the beginning of the previous year, management decided to establish an across-the-board policy on service, namely, to provide a safety stock level to assure a potential shortage in only 5 out of 100 replenishment cycles (0.0500; or 5 per cent). Consequently, the safety stock on each item was set at 1.65 (one-half of the standard ratio) times the standard deviation of forecast errors.

The first step was to establish the specific relationship of the safety stock of an item under the order point pressure to its annual sales rate. In essence, it is the standard deviation that has an approximate relationship to the sales of an item. To obtain this relationship, the standard deviation of forecast errors was determined for each of the 50 sample items (comparing forecasts against actual sales during the past year). The 50 standard deviations were plotted against the annual dollar sales of each item, as shown in Figure 7.5.

While the points scatter somewhat, they fit a straight line reasonably well (when plotted on log-log scale paper). This line can be used as an average relationship. The slope of the line is 0.9; that is, for each unit one moves to the right, the line rises by 0.9 unit. The interpretation of this line is that the standard deviation of forecast errors is proportional (on the average) to the annual sales (S) raised to the 0.9 power, or

$$\sigma = 0.05S^{0.9} \tag{2}$$

For any item with annual sales of S dollars, the safety stock may be estimated:

$$\text{Safety stock} = (1.65)(0.05S^{0.9}) \tag{3}$$

For the 850 items, the total value would be the sum of the separate safety stocks. Another method is to multiply the average safety stock by 850, where the average safety stock is simply 1.65 times the average value of $0.05S^{0.9}$. The average of $S^{0.9}$ is a factor times the average S to the 0.9 power, where the factor is dependent upon the standard ratio.[3]

The average S for the sample of 50 items is $3,263.00 or $163,166 ÷ 50. The total safety stock (SS) investment was estimated by:

$$\text{Total } SS = (850)(1.65)(0.05)(3,263)^{0.9}F(3.3, 0.9) \tag{4}$$

The factor F in the above equation is a function of the power of the general equation (0.9 from the graph) and the standard ratio (3.3 from

---

[3]The theory and proofs of these relationships in the log-normal distribution are covered in J. Attchison and J. A. C. Brown, *The Lognormal Distribution*, Monograph No. 5, Cambridge University Press, 1957.

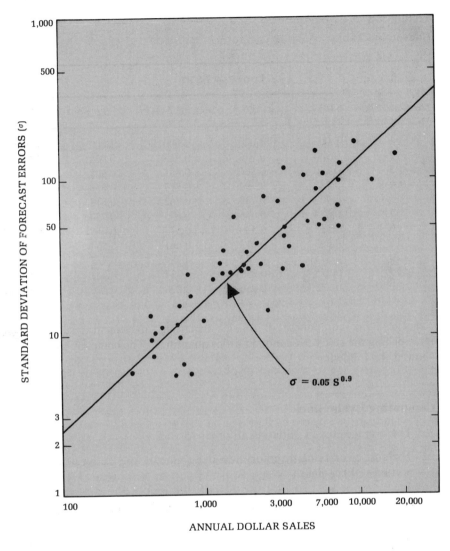

FIGURE 7.5

Relationship of standard deviation of forecast errors to annual dollar sales, 50 sample items

the earlier analysis). Table 7.2 can be developed for combinations of different slopes or powers and standard ratios. In this case the factor F is equal to approximately 0.938. The total safety stock investment during the past year should have amounted to about $95,500.

TABLE 7.2
Conversion Table

	POWER OR SLOPE				
Standard Ratio	0.5	0.6	0.7	0.8	0.9
1	1.000	1.000	1.000	1.000	1.000
2	0.944	0.946	0.953	0.964	0.980
3	0.860	0.866	0.881	0.908	0.947
4	0.786	0.794	0.817	0.858	0.938
5	0.723	0.733	0.762	0.813	0.890
7	0.624	0.636	0.673	0.750	0.844
10	0.515	0.530	0.573	0.655	0.788
15	0.398	0.413	0.461	0.554	0.718
20	0.325	0.340	0.389	0.487	0.668
25	0.275	0.289	0.337	0.437	0.628
30	0.235	0.250	0.296	0.396	0.594

The other component of regular inventory investment results from replenishing the stock in economic-order quantities. The company's analysis showed the following:

Computing Cycle Stock

1. The average cost of initiating an order was $2.50.
2. The cost of carrying inventory was determined to be 25 per cent of the unit cost of the item.

From the economic-order quantity formula, the value of any quantity ordered at one time is

$$4.4 \sqrt{S} \text{ (annual dollar sales)} \tag{5}$$

where the factor (or standard ratio) 4.4 was determined on the basis of the above costs. The average inventory (cycle stock) is half of this quantity. Therefore, the total inventory is the sum of these half-purchase quantities or, for the product line being investigated, 850 times the average value of half an economic-order quantity.

As we had reasoned for the safety stock, the average value of half an order quantity is

$$\frac{4.4}{2} \text{(average } S) \tag{6}$$

or

$$\frac{4.4}{2} \text{(average } S)^{0.5}F(3.3, 0.5), \tag{7}$$

where the factor F has the same interpretation as previously outlined; for the power of 0.5 we can determine the conversion factor from Table 7.2 to be about 0.838. Thus, the total value of the cycle stock should have been:

$$\text{Cycle stock} = 8 \frac{(4.4)}{2} (3,263)^{0.5}(0.838) = \$93,500 \tag{8}$$

The estimated total investment under ALDO Inc.'s reorder-point-economic-order quantity system should have been the sum of the cycle plus safety stock investment, or $189,000.

MANAGEMENT EVALUATION

For the previous year, actual investment in the stock of this product line averaged $317,100, or $128,100 in excess of the investment that should have resulted from ALDO Inc.'s control procedures and the actual sales volume attained. To evaluate the components of this investment, copies of all purchase orders for the 850 items involved were pulled from the files to estimate the average dollar value of an order placed during the year. This was determined to be about $248.

Total annual sales for this product line amounted to $2,774,000, or an average of $62 per item per week. Consequently, the average order placed represented a four weeks' supply and the average cycle stock amounted to $124 per item (850 items), $105,400 for the product line. The investment in safety stock was the difference between $317,000 and $105,400, or $211,700. A comparison of actual investment versus the standard is in Table 7.3.

Upon further discussions with the personnel responsible for inventory control and replenishment, management noted the following conditions:

1. The purchasing department had adhered to the economic-order quantities established at the beginning of the year. Several had been modified, because of significant revisions in the annual sales estimates. The higher-than-standard investment in cycle stock was justified on the basis of purchases of larger quantities at special prices that would result in higher-than-average unit margin when subsequently sold.

TABLE 7.3

**Comparison of Actual Inventory Investment
Against Standard Under Control System**

	Cycle Stock	Safety Stock	Total
	INVENTORY INVESTMENT		
Actual last year	$105,400	$211,700	$317,100
Standard	93,500	95,500	189,000
Difference	$ 11,900	$116,200	$128,100

2. The inventory control department monitored stock status in accordance with the procedures for the reorder-point method of control. However, they tended to "second guess" the pre-established reorder points following a backorder situation. This, of course, resulted in the gradual accumulation of safety stocks beyond the point set to take account of stock shortages and back orders.

Management was satisfied that the use of a representative sample provided meaningful aggregate inventory investment standards where the concept of the standard ratio was applied. They were able to pinpoint problem areas in the past operation of their newly developed control procedures. Having satisfied themselves that appropriate corrective action would now be taken to control the 850 items initially studied by approved procedures, the management of ALDO Inc. wanted to use the information to consider future investment standards for this product line under alternative conditions and/or policies. In particular they wanted to investigate:

1. The turnover resulting from the operation of their reorder-point–economic-order quantity system as a function of sales volume change.

2. The change in investment required to meet a change in management policy with regard to customer service.

3. The effect on total investment of the addition of items to the product line.

The annual inventory turnover is obtained by dividing annual sales by the average inventory investment. It will be affected by a change in sales volume and any resultant change in inventory investment. In ALDO Inc.'s inventory control system we note, from investment formulas (4) and (8), that only the average sales per item would change with a change in total

TABLE 7.4

Effect of Change in Sales Volume on Turnover

Sales Volume (millions)	Average Sales per Item (850 items)	Cycle Stock Investment	Safety Stock Investment	Total Investment	Annual Turnover
$1	$1,176	$ 55,500	$ 38,100	$ 93,600	10.7
2.7	3,263	93,500	95,500	189,000	14.7
4	4,706	112,300	135,400	247,700	16.1
5	5,882	125,600	165,600	291,200	17.2
6	7,058	137,600	195,100	332,700	18.0

sales. These relationships make it easy to estimate the impact on investment and, consequently, turnover, of changes in sales volume. Table 7.4 presents an evaluation of turnover for sales volume change from ALDO Inc.'s present $2,774,000 (on the product line studied) to any of several levels ranging from $1 million to $6 million (Figure 7.6).

Management had established a level of customer service by selecting a safety factor of 1.65 for a 5 per cent chance of a stock shortage in any

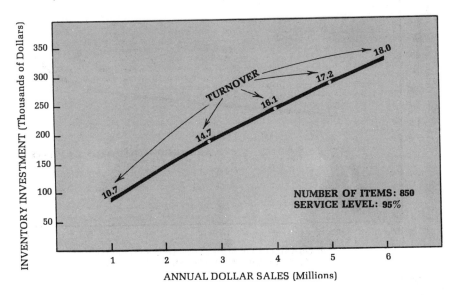

FIGURE 7.6

Effect of sales volume on investment and turnover

TABLE 7.5

Effect of Change in Customer Service on Aggregate Inventory Investment

Change of Stockout	Safety Factor	Safety Stock Investment	Total Investment
0.01	2.33	$134,900	$227,400
0.02	2.05	118,700	212,200
0.05	**1.65**	**95,500**	**189,000**
0.08	1.41	81,600	175,100
0.10	1.28	74,100	167,600

replenishment cycle. With sales at $2,774,000, the cycle stock component of total investment remains at $93,500. Table 7.5 indicates the additional investment in safety stock and total investment required to meet changes in routine customer service. Management must, of course, evaluate the additional investment needed to improve customer service (Figure 7.7).

Marketing management generally agrees that an expanded product line is the key to increased sales volume and a greater market share. Consequently,

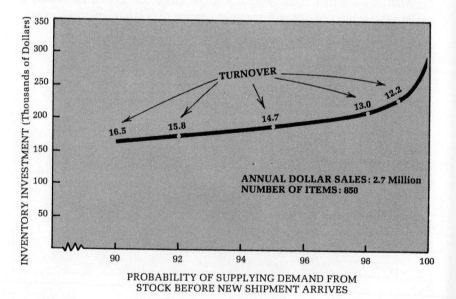

FIGURE 7.7

Effect of service policy on inventory investment and turnover

TABLE 7.6

Effect of Changing the Number of Items in the Line

Number of Items	Sales Volume (millions)	Average Sales per Item	Cycle Stock Investment	Safety Stock Investment	Total Investment
850	$2.7	$3,263	$ 93,500	$ 95,500	$189,000
900	2.7	3,082	96,300	96,100	192,400
900	3.0	3,333	100,100	103,100	203,200
1,000	2.7	2,774	101,500	97,200	198,700
1,000	4.0	4,000	121,900	135,000	256,900

it is important to be able to estimate the added investment required. If an increase of 20 per cent in the number of items resulted in a similar increase in total sales, then the investment required would also increase 20 per cent. However, the effect on inventory investment of supporting a broader product line is somewhat more complex, since both the number of items and the average sales per item would change.

Table 7.6 shows an evaluation of a contemplated expansion of the product line studied in this case under different assumptions of sales volume attained, namely, no charge from the current $2,774,000 to an increase of 10 per cent with 900 items and 15 per cent with 1,000 items.

This table is based on the single distribution facility used by ALDO Inc. In any consideration of additional warehouses the number of items and resulting investment would have to be increased by the number of different stocking points.

SUMMARY

The inventory tools and techniques in this chapter demonstrate an approach to determining aggregate inventory investment standards that are directly related to the methods of control employed by a company. The concepts used permit the development of these standards from a sample of representative items which can then be extrapolated to the total number of inventoried items. Once established, these relationships—extremely sensitive to changes in total sales volume and/or the number of items stocked—enable management to (1) evaluate the past performance of their control system, (2) evaluate alternative methods of stock replenishment, (3) establish standards of performance for future inventory management reporting, and (4) effectively consider alternative operating policies that will affect inventory investment.

AS IS self-evident, the functional flows within and between the three logistical activities of moving, positioning, and balancing stocks (the theme of the five preceding chapters) entail a staggering amount of paper work. Hence the importance of the next chapter, which explores the area of order processing: its cycles, problem areas, and the use of electronic data processing to speed orders to their destination in ways that minimize costs.

Paul R. Saunders

8

Marketing Logistics, the Order-Processing Cycle, and Computerization

Any discussion of merchandise movement from factory to customer must emphasize the application of data processing machines to order processing.

Order processing is a broad term used to describe the flow of paper work from a customer's purchase to the physical delivery of the products to the purchaser. At some point in time an order form, invoice, bill of lading, factory order, and other necessary papers are prepared. These papers must be processed in order to complete the delivery to the customer and also to account for the sale. The importance to a company of the proper handling of its paper work cannot be overemphasized. For example, communication between the purchasing, manufacturing, sales, distribution, accounting, and planning functions is accomplished by means of paper and data processing.

ORDER PROCESSING

The order-processing cycle is broadly separated into six areas: order entry, order writing, order analysis, invoicing, accounts receivable, and sales analysis.

Order entry includes receiving or transmitting the order, editing the order for correctness and completeness, adding any necessary codes to the order or verifying previous coding, checking the credit of the customer, controlling totals, checking prices, determining stock (product) availability, key punching of cards or tub file card pulling, and other operations necessary to place the order into the system.

Order writing is the physical preparation of the order on an order form by either handwriting, typing, electric accounting machines, or computers. Depending upon the size of company and the industry, a separate order other than the original sales order form may or may not be prepared. Shipment is usually not accomplished by using the original sales order, the customer's purchase order or letter, nor by verbal instructions. The order-writing operation will also normally prepare other copies for use as bills of lading, factory production orders, or acknowledgments of orders. Under a pre-billing system the invoices would also be prepared during the order-writing operation; prebilling and postbilling will be discussed later in this chapter.

Order analysis covers all the reports generated as a result of the receipt of an order. The reports may be elaborate and involve detailed statistics by individual products, sizes, colors, shapes, packaging, etc., within selling, manufacturing, or distributing regions and may include comparisons with last month, same month or period of prior year, moving average of past three months, quotas, or budgets. There are infinite combinations of data that can be reported. In contrast, a company may only maintain a running total of orders received to date by total dollar amount. Quite often, however, the order analysis reports will be utilized for sales forecasting and production scheduling and must contain sufficient detail for those purposes.

Invoicing is billing the customer for merchandise shipped. After invoicing an accounts receivable account is set up for the customer, sometimes as part of the same operation.

Accounts receivable work includes the paying (cash receipts) cycle, preparing trial balances, sending out statements and/or dunning notices, and notifying past-due accounts.

Sales analysis is similar to order analysis, but its statistics are based on shipments rather than orders. Sales and orders may be significantly different if (1) items are unavailable for shipment, (2) there are many returns of unsold merchandise, or (3) orders are booked for advance shipments.

CUSTOMER SERVICE

The type of organization, volume of sales, type of sale, and industry practice determine the complexity of the paper work and order-processing cycle. The smoothness and efficiency of order processing is one element in what is termed "customer service." Customer service, of course, relates to the company as a whole and is not limited to handling paper work. Assuming an average-quality product at an average price, the company which supplies the better customer service will gain the upper hand. A company may even sell at lower prices, but if it does not process orders in a reasonable time and does not accurately ship the desired products, it will lose substantial business. Many companies have developed customer service sections within their order-processing operations to handle customer inquiries. Questions frequently arise in tracing orders as to date of shipment, expected shipment dates, carrier identification, billing information, and adjustments. Answers to these questions should be readily available in a well-run data processing installation.

ORDER-PROCESSING CYCLE

The sequence of events in the processing of an order is approximately the same for all companies. A complete list of these steps is presented below for a company in the packaged consumer goods field. The order-processing system illustrated is a postbilling operation that could be mechanized in part or in total.

1. The customer is called upon by the salesman, and an order is taken. A preprinted order form with several carbon copies is normally used, which lists the majority of products sold by the company. The salesman fills in customer identification information, such as name, store number, address, account number, etc. He then fills in the quantities for each item ordered. The salesman also is responsible for special notes such as "ship by a set date," "deliver only on Tuesdays or Thursdays," "a special packing (sizes)," or "use specified carrier." The special notes plus the names and addresses, store numbers, codes, shipping instructions, prices, and other semifixed customer data are usually contained in the salesman's call book. A copy of the order will be left with the customer, one or more copies will be forwarded to the order-processing point, and a copy may be retained by the salesman.

    The order is sent to a sales office, a warehouse or other distribution point, the home office, or a manufacturing facility. The order may be written by the salesman in the evening, then placed in the mail that night. This saves the salesman time during the day to concentrate on selling activities. Orders for large orders or rush orders may be telephoned in by the salesman. In addition, the customer can send an order directly (independently) to the factory. If the order is telephoned to the factory (or order-processing point), the order form is prepared by the factory as it is being received over the telephone. (In the wholesale drug industry, for example, almost all orders are telephone orders. A battery of clerks equipped with telephone headsets and typewriters, write the majority of orders.)

2. The order is received at the point where it is to be processed. There, the incoming mail is opened and the orders are separated by sales area, product division, or location of shipment. Rush orders and large orders (carloads or truckloads) are given special handling. Orders are then edited.

3. The editors review the orders, checking the important items:
   a. Customer, billing, and shipping addresses are superficially checked for legibility and completeness, or are thoroughly checked against the customer's file. The customer account number (code) is checked or added to the form, if it is not already coded. Special instructions for this particular customer or for the shipping location are also added to the order form at this time.
   b. Special instructions on the order form are reviewed to determine if they are understandable and conform to company policy.
   c. Routing instructions may be assigned if the method of shipment and name of carrier for the customer have been previously established. Normally the traffic department will have approved specific routing for regular customers.
   d. All other codes necessary are added to the order form or verified if it has been coded. These codes identify salesman, sales region and territory, state, class of customer, type of sale, etc.
   e. The order date and shipping date are established. The customer may have specified the delivery date. The order editor should know the normal shipping time to that customer. In order to do this he must consider the elapsed time for order processing, assembly, and loading of goods, transportation, and final delivery. The transportation portion may include multiple carriers and temporary warehousing.
   f. The products ordered are reviewed item by item for stock availability, minimum-order quantities, and price. The order editor scratches items off the order, reduces the order quantity, or makes up a back order for out-of-stock items. It may be the practice in the industry to cancel all items not available for immediate shipment and have the customer reorder rather than prepare back orders.

4. Edited orders now move to a control point where quantity, price, extended amounts, or combinations of these, are added for each order

The object of adding (or totaling on a comptometer) combinations of quantities and stock number or price is to obtain a "hash total" which can be verified (totaled) later by accounting machine or computer. This is to insure that the correct quantities of the proper products have been pulled and invoiced. Control by quantity alone does not catch errors where the correct quantity of the wrong product was selected. The orders may be added and controlled by groups or batches, although normally the emphasis is placed on the control of each order.

A control number, called an order number or invoice number, is assigned (stamped on) each individual salesman's order. This sequential number identifies that order through all future processing steps. All orders entered into the system may be listed by this sequential "invoice" number in the form of a register. (This is more common under a manual system than in a machine system.) The register usually shows invoice number, date of order, customer name, location, and amount of order. The register is for tracing orders and for control; it also indicates order volume.

5. The salesman's orders have been received, edited, and controlled. Up to this point the processing has been in handling the original order prepared by the salesman (or a telephone order). Work toward the machine preparation of an order form or shipping papers now begins. For example, assume a punched card system of order writing using tub card files.[1] This is typical of the consumer packaged goods industry and other industries with similar selling and distribution operations.

The salesman's order forms are taken in batches to a key punch machine where an invoice control card is punched for each order. The information punched in the control card relates to the order as a whole. The invoice number (assigned at the control station), order date, shipment date, and codes for account (customer), salesman, sales region, class of sale, etc., are punched. The batched orders with their invoice control cards are taken to the tub files.

Normally there are separate tub files for name and address, product items, special instructions, routing, notation, and other classes of cards.

---

[1] If a company does not have conventional punched card equipment, the order may be prepared on a typewriter or some type of an electric calculating typewriter. A company can also ship by using the salesman's order as the shipping authority. In the latter case, bills of lading and other by-products of the order form must be prepared separately. Companies utilizing computers for order processing generally follow the same procedure as for punched card equipment. Computer and punched card equipment order-processing systems will be discussed in detail later.

The proper cards are pulled from the different tubs for all orders and the cards and orders are taken to the accounting machine section.

6. The punched cards are used by the electric accounting machine (tabulator) to print and total the shipping papers (orders). The machine prints names, addresses, routing, special instructions, product descriptions, weight, quantities, and all other information contained in the cards. It also totals each product line by quantity and amount and accumulates order totals. Weight accumulation by freight classification is also calculated by the machine. (It should be remembered that the punched card accounting system is only used as an example.) The shipping papers can be prepared by typewriter or computer, or the salesman's order can serve as the shipping paper. The order form printed on the accounting machine is a multiple copy form. Typically it has eight or nine parts, three copies for bills of lading, a packing list, a file copy, the original copy (used to trigger the billing), and two or three duplicate copies for order picking, loading tally sheets, and assembly processes. Labels may also be prepared at the time of machine order writing. These may be individual labels, one for every carton indicated on the order, or a stencil type.

A summary card is then punched as a by-product of the printing of orders on the accounting machine. In addition, summary cards for each line item may be punched if the product tub file cards are the denominated type, i.e., more than one card needed for the quantities ordered. Cards may also be punched for products to be assembled by an automatic warehouse or picking device. The line item and order summary cards are held for later use in order analysis work. The automatic picker cards would accompany the order to the warehouse. The original salesman's order, the machine-prepared order, and the cards used to prepare the machine order are passed to a review or balancing station.

7. At the order review station the orders are scanned and compared with the original sales order to see that the names and addresses, both "bill to" and "ship to," are correct. The hash total figures are checked for a zero balance to verify the product quantities. The order is reviewed for general accuracy and completeness. Errors are corrected, and erroneous orders are rerun. Care must be taken to correct all cards, including those from the first incorrect printing of orders. The cards are returned to the machine accounting section to set up a "pending file" (awaiting shipping and invoicing) and to be reproduced for order analysis. The orders themselves are burst, stripped of carbon paper, and passed to the credit department for credit approval.

8. The approval of orders from a credit standpoint is usually routine. Total order value standards can be established by class of customer. All orders with a dollar amount less than the standard can then be passed without futher review. Customers with past-due accounts have their name and address card in the tub file "blocked" so that orders from these accounts are flagged when the machine order is printed. The blocking of the name and address file is initiated by the accounts receivable section. Orders not approved for credit are placed in a hold file until they can be released. Release of these orders would normally be the result of the customer paying a past-due amount. All approved orders then move to the traffic department.

9. The traffic department has two major functions in the handling of orders. The first is to review the routings which have been assigned previously (from the tub files). These routings may have changed as a result of difficulty with a particular carrier or as a result of a customer's request. Any revised standard routings must be reflected in the tub files so that future orders for those customers will show the proper routing. There may be different selections of carriers for a customer, the choice depending upon the size of the order, e.g., truckload versus carload.

    The second major function of the traffic department is to combine individual customer orders into pool-truck shipments, dropoff shipments, and other combinations of loads. Orders are accumulated in traffic until the minimum weight is attained for a pool-car or truck shipment. The length of time the orders are held for weight accumulation will depend upon the degree of customer service desired. Some companies make it a rule that no orders are held beyond three days. Orders also may be held for a regularly scheduled pool car. An example of the latter would be a truck going to Cincinnati every Monday regardless of the size of the load.

    If a pool-car or combined shipment is performed, a master bill of lading must be prepared by summarizing the individual bills of lading from the machine-prepared order form. This can be done by accounting machines or by typing.

    Orders for future shipments less than thirty days in advance are normally held in the traffic department for release at the most opportune time with regard to freight costs. Future orders not to be shipped for thirty days or more are usually held aside at the order balancing and review station. In this way, they pass through the credit department before being released for shipment. They are also more readily available in case of change.

10. Orders flow to the shipping department (warehouse) from the traffic department. The functions performed by these two departments are sometimes combined in one operation since they are closely related. In this illustration, their functions are separated, and the assumption is made that the shipping department is physically located at the warehousing site while the traffic department is located at the order-processing location.

Orders may be received in shipping intermittently during the day or all at one time. Orders for shipment on a given day normally must be received before noon the previous day. Time must be allowed for the orders to be reviewed, for cars and trucks to be ordered, and for the products to be assembled. This time cycle varies depending upon the industry and company.

When the orders for the day are received by the shipping department, they are first reviewed for full truck or car loads, possible further pooling or combination shipments, and rush orders. A summary of orders is prepared by total quantity to ascertain total shipping requirements for the day. The number of loads and sequence of loading are determined. All goods are shipped, assuming that the warehouse has sufficient labor, assembly area, and equipment to handle all orders. During the process the multiple-part order form is separated, each part serving a specific purpose.

Shipping order form copies are used by several separate operations within the shipping organization itself. It is not unusual to have a reproduction machine in the warehouse to make additional copies of the shipping order. Copies may be required by the manual assembly area, automatic assembly machine operators, pallet loaders (forklift operators), door checkers or loaders, and others. A copy will normally be retained in the warehouse office.

After the order is shipped, the copies of the machine-prepared order form will have been distributed as follows: (1) original copy to accounting or data processing section for billing; (2) copy to warehouse file; (3) bill-of-lading copy for carrier use; (4) bill-of-lading copy for carrier to leave with the customer or forwarding carrier; (5) bill-of-lading copy signed by carrier as receipt of goods, then forwarded to the traffic department for checking of freight bills and claims; (6) packing list copy for the customer, either included with shipment or mailed direct; and (7) copies for tally sheets (8) or copies used for assembly of the order (these are later destroyed).

For the order-processing cycle only the original copy will be followed after the shipment of goods. This is the copy that is forwarded to the accounting group to initiate invoicing.

Time Cycle

The sequence of steps in the flow of the order, from the receipt of the order through the shipping of the products, is now complete. Here is the approximate time cycle of these steps:

Day 1 Salesman calls on customer and obtains order. Order is written up and placed in mail that night.

Day 2 Order in transit in mail.

Day 3 A.M.—Order received at order-processing section. Order edited and machine written. P.M.—Order sent to shipping department by end of day.

Day 4 Order received in shipping. Goods picked, and order assembled.

Day 5 Order loaded on carrier vehicle, and local area deliveries made.

Days 5–15 Delivery time to customer outside local area.

The major portion of time to move goods to the customer is the delivery time by the carrier. This is typical of packaged consumer goods, and to reduce this time cycle is quite difficult. The wholesale drug industry, however, often gives same-day or overnight service. Orders are received by telephone in the morning, assembled and loaded that afternoon or night, and delivered that day or next day.

ORDER-PROCESSING PROBLEM AREAS

Order processing is an integral part of logistics. It is also a cost to a company but does not show a direct dollar return. For maximum profit a company must keep its order-processing costs as low as possible but still consistent with good customer service. Development of an efficient order-processing system therefore is important. The details of the type of system used, whether it is a manual system, conventional punched cards, or a large-scale electronic computer, varies from company to company according to the size of its operation, the volume of its transactions, type of industry, and organization structure. But all systems have in common many problem situations—difficulties that are not related to the mechanics of a particular system but are outside the system. As the situations are outlined it will become apparent that policy decisions and good management control can, to a great extent, overcome these problems. The assumed objective in all instances is to operate at the lowest cost, solving the problems rather than living with them. The problems will be discussed by functional area—first, that of the general processing of orders and the order entry operations performed by the salesman.

[1]   Order-Processing Department

Any data processing system is only as good as its input. Orders comprise the order-processing input. The order form filled out by the salesman is very important. Coding on the order form, which is essential to a mechanized system, should be accurate and legible. If not, the order editors must verify the coding. Extra work means the hiring of extra personnel. Legibility is a sore point in many companies. Sales management may adopt the attitude that their people are salesmen and not clerks. The sales force should be made to realize that the more accurate the order is, the less chance of error on the part of the order-processing group. Mistakes in handling orders reflect on the entire company, including the salesman. Very often the customer's most frequent contact with the company is the salesman. It is to the salesman's best interest to write up his orders properly. The salesman can also help order processing (and the company) by restricting the number of rush orders. If each salesman turns in many rush orders, the rush order identification becomes meaningless.

The order-processing cycle should be working at optimum efficiency. The salesman can assist by submitting his orders promptly. However, on the other hand, there are instances where salesmen send in their orders too soon. If a new product or special deal is being introduced on a given date, orders for these products combined with the customer's regular order and submitted prior to the release date will create extra clerical work, since a back order must be prepared for each new product or special deal order.

Obviously, the informed salesman is a key to optimization. For example, the salesman helps the shipping department by selling products in even-pallet quantities or other standard shipping lots. If a customer refuses a few additional cases to make a common shipping quantity, it might even be more profitable to reduce the order to standard shipping quantity. The salesmen should be advised of the most economic shipping quantities for each product. Conducted tours through the order-processing, shipping, and production departments give the salesmen a better understanding of the company's method of operations.

A common problem among companies that receive orders by mail is the peaking of work. In addition to a regular Monday peak, there will normally be peaks at the end of each month, at the close of each quarter, and at the end of sales campaigns. The question arises, Do you staff for the average day's work or for the peak days? One solution is to have the office force cross-trained, so that personnel can be switched from job to job as the need arises. Overtime and part-time help may be less expensive than staffing for peak periods.

Another problem is the balance of inventory to orders. Companies generally want to maintain a relatively low inventory investment. This creates a potential out-of-stock condition which may turn into back orders. Back orders mean additional work in paper handling, changing control figures, and future checking for items now unavailable. In addition, the cost of handling back orders may be more than the profit on the items eventually shipped. Substitution of products which are temporarily out of stock may be possible, especially where only a change of packaging is involved; for example, two six-packs in place of one twelve-pack. The company can also set a minimum dollar value on back order shipments. A good stock availability or a good inventory control system minimizes back order problems. A clearly written management policy on substitutions also helps. Substitution rules often become complex, since they generally must be defined product by product and customer by customer. Some customers will accept substitute products, some will not.

Within the general framework of order-processing problem areas are those orders which require special handling:

> *Government orders* often require special pricing. Rather than case or dozen price the government demands a single-unit price. In addition the information required on the invoice is far more than for regular customers.

> *Overseas sales* need special forms, packing, identification, and perhaps special licenses.

> *Contract sales* may be uncommon for the company and may require additional effort in that contract prices vary.

These are illustrations of orders that may well fall outside the regular data processing system. Every order that must be treated as an exception adds to the cost of doing business. There are other types of orders that create extra work: *Bill separate orders*, where some products are invoiced separately. *Future* shipments, which must be held aside and released at a stipulated time outside the normal shipping cycle; seasonal orders for shipment at a set date, such as Christmas, are an example of a future order. *Split orders* contain products which are to be shipped from separate plants or warehouses; this means that two pieces of paper must be handled for one order. *Direct shipments* to customers, by-passing the normal distribution channels, may cause invoicing and inventory control problems.

[2] Use of Codes

The order-processing group is probably the largest user of codes within a company. The codes for products, product grouping or classes, salesmen, sales regions, territories, districts, divisions, customer accounts, stores, drop ship locations, billing locations, part numbers, manufacturing or production components, general ledger accounts, expense accounts, all have to be maintained. The responsibility for establishing codes, assigning new code numbers, making changes, and general control of the code structure involve considerable clerical work. Communication between different sections of one plant and between plants is necessary to advise all users of code revisions. The purpose of codes is to reduce the burden of identifying items by their full alphabetical description. Under a mechanized system, the use of codes is practically mandatory. The future uses of code patterns should be carefully analyzed before the codes are installed. They should be capable of expansion to cover a wider range of items than exists at the time of installation. If an account provides only four digits, what happens when the number of customers reaches 10,000 for the first time? If there are frequent re-arrangements of codes, reports which compare one period of time to another may be worthless. For example, a sales report by territory, comparing sales for the month with prior year's sales for the same month, would not be valid if the territories and codes had been changed. To bring the prior year's figures into an altered coding pattern may be difficult. A change in a major code such as product or customer account could mean that pre-printed forms, addressograph plates, IBM cards, ledger cards, file folders, price lists, or salesmen's call books have to be revised.

These are some of the potential problem areas within the general order-processing function. The manner in which salesmen complete the order form, the peaking of work in the office, the substitution policy, the number of back orders and orders requiring special handling, the maintenance of codes and files—all contribute to the order-processing work load.

[3] Traffic and Shipping Departments

Order processing and paperwork problems within the traffic and shipping areas are not numerous. One problem will be the length of time that orders are to be held pending weight accumulation for pool cars or other combination loads. In order to achieve freight savings, traffic will want to wait until the maximum weight has accumulated before releasing pool shipments. Sales management will want immediate shipping of all orders to give fast customer delivery. This question should be decided by marketing management. The preparation of the master bills of lading for combination loads may present a problem of clerical effort in that the workload is uneven and outside the normal procedure. Under a mechanized system this clerical effort can be minimized.

The shipping department has two paperwork problems. The first is that the number of copies may be insufficient and that orders may be hard to read because of poor penmanship or smudged carbon copies. Poor penmanship is overcome by educating salesmen and others concerning the importance of legible writing. Smudging is a technical problem. There is a limit to the number of copies that can be effectively written or typed by any given office machine. If this limit is exceeded, a new method of preparing the orders should be considered. It is better to go to the expense of reproducing readable copies of the order form than having mistakes made through the use of illegible documents. A method for doing this, and making available as many duplicate copies as are required, is to have one part of the order made from a special reproducing paper stock. There are numerous inexpensive office copying machines which could be physically located on the shipping department premises and used to reproduce the necessary copies.

The second and more significant order-processing problem for the shipping department is inaccurate stock availability status reports. Orders that have items lined off erroneously, supposedly nonavailable, but are in stock in the warehouse, create a dual problem. The question arises whether the order-processing people have deliberately canceled items due to other commitments for the stock on hand or whether they are misinformed about the stock's status. The tendency is for the shipping department to change the order and ship as many of the products originally ordered by the customer as possible. Inaccuracy in stock availability causes additional work, since the order must be changed because either the stock was located or time was spent fruitlessly attempting to locate nonexistent products. The obvious solution is to improve the stock availability procedure so that more accurate and up-to-the-minute data are available to the order-processing people. A special effort may have to be made to insure that new production and outside purchases (receipts) are recorded promptly, that transfers of products to and from other warehouses and plants are reflected in stock availability records, and that returned merchandise is also included.

It should be realized that not all companies maintain a perpetual inventory, nor do all companies check for stock availability before sending orders to the shipping department. Depending upon the particular circumstances of the organization it may be better to use a physical minimum reorder point rather than maintain a perpetual inventory. Under this system, the office is notified when a product in the warehouse or bin is reduced to a certain level.

[4]   Forms

A problem area often overlooked is that of forms. In order processing, forms that are properly designed and constructed reduce clerical work. The people who have to separate the order or invoice forms into the copies that go to the customer, factory, salesman, etc., appreciate a good snapout form which comes apart easily at the proper places. This is an operation performed many times every day. If by improving the form, twenty seconds can be saved in the separation of the form, and 360 invoices are handled per day, this represents two hours less work each and every day. The problems that a bad form can create are too numerous to elaborate. Size of the form is important. A small form, although adequate for the information, may be easily lost or overlooked. It may pay to use a larger, more uniform size of paper. On the other hand, a large or odd size of paper may not fit easily into existing file cabinets.

The number of copies of a form is a part of form design. If the number of copies can be reduced, there is a decided form saving. A more significant saving, however, is that of the clerk's time who no longer has to handle, separate, file, or throw away this piece of paper. For a form which has few copies and for which extra copies are often made on copying machines, it may be cheaper to increase the number of copies in the form and throw away the extras in cases where they are not needed.

There may be an outside requirement which creates a form problem. An example of this would be a company address change or a new freight classification added to the bill-of-lading copy of the invoice form set. A several months supply of the form is usually on hand. Is it better to have a clerk type or hand stamp the old forms with the correct information, or should the old forms be thrown out and replaced by new forms? Either procedure is expensive. If at all possible, changes in forms should be correlated with existing supplies of the forms.

The front-line supervisors should be aware of the desirability of improving the day-to-day operations and of bringing to the attention of the systems analyst many of the problems inherent in using forms. In addition, there should be at least an annual review of each company form to answer these questions: Who uses the form? For what purpose? Is it really needed? Will another form or report do just as well? Can the form or report be improved? Can the number of copies be reduced? Tracking down the need for each copy of every company form or report generated can be a full-time job. In large companies, there may be a separate forms control section to deal with the review, design, approval, and ordering of forms. In other companies the systems department or the controller may do this on a less formal basis. Regardless of who does it, forms control is an area in which many opportunities exist both to improve the operations and to decrease the cost of doing business.

Summary of Problems

The problem areas discussed above concerned, for the most part, day-to-day operations. A good data processing system or computer installation may help to eliminate some of the difficulties. Written procedures and progressive management practices also go a long way toward making a smooth operation. Many companies do not realize the problems they have until they attempt to install a computer or make some other major change in their order-processing system. The benefits of installing a computer are often realized in establishing good procedures in both the nonmechanized and mechanized operations.

APPLICATIONS OF EDP TO ORDER PROCESSING

The application of machines to clerical work is commonplace in business today. Mechanization of the repetitious, routine functions involved in handling office paperwork has many advantages. One of the best applications for mechanization is in the processing of orders. In the preceding sections the order-processing cycle was described in detail. The illustration selected was basically a punched card system of order processing. In this section punched card equipment is discussed briefly and then computers and computer (EDP) systems are outlined in more detail.

[1]   Punched Card Systems

A company using conventional tabulating machines is said to have a punched card system. The machines are called punched card, conventional, unit record, or EAM (electric accounting machines) equipment. The majority of EAM equipment used in the United States is manufactured by the International Business Machines Corporation and the Univac Division of the Sperry Rand Corporation. The IBM machines use an 80-column card and Univac EAM machines use a 90-column card. Although there are some differences between the two manufacturers' equipment, the data processing principles and procedures they employ are very much alike.

The type of information storage for EAM systems is the punched card itself. The card (or data) is grouped with other cards and sorted, collated, gangpunched, tabulated, etc., to produce a given report. In order to process the cards, at least one of each type of machine is needed. Here are the most common types of machines and their uses: a card (key) punch initially prepares the cards; a card verifier checks that the cards are punched correctly; a sorter arranges (sorts) the cards into sequence; a collator merges two groups of cards; a reproducer makes cards over or reproduces selected portions into another card format; an interpreter prints on the card (interprets the holes in the cards); a calculator performs multiplication and division functions with the data in the cards; and an accounting machine (tabulator) adds figures and prints reports. There are, of course, many models of each type of equipment, with varying speeds, capacities, and special devices.

The order-processing cycle utilizing punched card equipment was described in detail previously. A brief review of the same general cycle from the machine aspect follows:

1. After the salesman's order is received, reviewed, and entered into the system, it is key punched. One card is prepared for each line item ordered. The same cards are key verified to insure that they are correct. The cards are punched with the invoice number and customer account code as well as the product codes and quantities ordered.

2. Cards for many orders are accumulated for processing at one time. (This is batch processing; it would be uneconomical to put only one order at a time through the cycle.) The cards are then all sorted together by product code. A master product price deck is obtained from the file and matched (also merged) against the sorted product detail (line item) cards on the collator. This also verifies that no products have been ordered for which a master price card has not been previously prepared.

3. The matched and merged cards are processed on a reproducer to gangpunch the unit product price and description from the master cards into the detail cards. On the sorter the cards are separated, and the master price cards returned to their file.

4. The product detail cards are processed on the calculator to extend (multiply) the unit price by the quantity ordered. Next the figures or

letters represented by the holes may be printed out by the interpreter, so that people as well as machines can read the cards. Then the cards are sorted by invoice number and customer account code to place them in customer sequence.

5. The master (customer) name and address file is obtained and the product detail cards are used to select their machine name and address cards on the collator. The selected cards, both product and name and address, are now ready to be used to print shipping orders on the accounting machine. (Invoices would be printed under a prebilling system.)

The EAM order-writing cycle described above differs from the previously described punched card system of order processing in that tub files were not used. Tub files both for product cards and for the names and addresses would materially cut down on the number of machine steps necessary to prepare a shipping order. The use of tub files, however, requires clerks ("card pullers") who are no longer needed after key punching is completed. The number of orders processed per day, peaking of orders, size of master files, need to process orders currently, and other factors will influence the choice between the tub file or key punch approach in a punched card order-processing system.

A company normally will install EAM equipment when it becomes too expensive to process the paper work purely on a manual basis. The cost of paper work includes the gathering of statistics as well as preparing invoices. The rental cost of EAM equipment ranges from hundreds to thousands of dollars per month. For approximately $2,000 per month (1965 dollars) one can rent a card punch ($40), verifier ($50), sorter ($110), reproducer ($125), collator ($125), interpreter ($100), accounting machine ($800), and calculator ($550).

Depending on volume and time requirements, it may be necessary to have more than one of each type of machine. In addition to the equipment cost, there must be qualified people to operate the machines. One major advantage of an EAM data processing system is its ability to absorb additional work, especially increased volume, with only a small increase in cost. Another principal advantage is that interrelated work often can be accomplished easily, since the output of one is an input to the other. The order-processing cycle is a prime example of this advantage.

[2] Small Computer Systems

The first step up in data processing power from an EAM installation is to a small computer. The computer takes the place of both the accounting machines and the calculator. The difference between a calculator and a computer is that the computer has an internally stored program which directs its operation. This is in contrast to the externally wired control panel of the calculator. The stored program is the step-by-step sequence that the systems designer wants the computer to go through to produce a report or a given result. The number of individual program steps for a complete computer program will vary from several hundred to several thousand. The application to be placed on the computer must first be defined in exact terms (problem definition), a computer approach designed (flow charting and block diagraming), the computer program developed (programing and coding), the program tested (debugged), and finally put into operation (parallel operation and conversion). Once a computer program is tested it is used over and over again. The stored program is punched into cards as a program deck and read into the computer before each job is processed.

The majority of small computers are card oriented. Even though they have some storage or memory capacity these computers still rely on punched cards being read in as their principal information storage. In contrast to the EAM system, which requires several passes on different machines in order to generate a report, the computer encompasses the card-reading, punching, calculating, and printing functions in one machine complex. There are separate machine units for card reading, printing, and card punching. The units that feed data into or out of computers are called input-output (I/O) devices. Although these I/O devices are separate units, they are all cable connected to the power unit and the central processing unit (CPU) so that data read by the card reader can be calculated upon, printed, or punched. Numerous computer configurations are possible, since the types of I/O devices are many. They also come in high-, medium-, and low-speed models. Multiple readers, printers, etc., can be added or "hung on" to the main frame (CPU). The I/O devices presently available are practically unlimited and include types of card readers, card punches, paper tape readers and punches, optical scanners, magnetic ink character readers, magnetic tape drives, drum memory units, disk storage units, magnetic card memory units, thin-film memory units, core storage, printers, visual display units, remote inquiry stations, console typewriters, audio response units, and many communications devices. The list of possible equipment is constantly growing. With a small computer the number and types of devices are limited, often including only a card reader, card punch, and printer. Large-scale computer systems which use some of the other I/O devices are discussed later.

The order-processing cycle using a small, card-oriented computer does not differ greatly in procedure from a good EAM system. Cards still must be punched or pulled from tub files, sorted to proper sequences, and merged with balance forward or master cards prior to being run through the computer. However, the processing can be accomplished faster and many individual machine operations can be combined with a computer. For instance, the extension of amount on the invoices can be made as the invoices are being printed. In addition, the calculation of taxes and discounts can be done at this time. In an EAM system the calculations would have been separate machine operations. With a card computer certain checks and controls which were not possible with conventional EAM equipment can be performed internally. Examples of the types of things that can be programed are the comparison of products ordered with the "short list" (items out of stock) and the comparison by dollar amount of the total value of the order to the customer's credit limit. In the former example the number of products not available should be fairly small, and it is only necessary to store the code numbers for these products in the computer memory. As the line items of the orders are processed, the computer compares the product codes ordered with those products not available and deletes the latter from the order. A separate back order would still have to be prepared by some other means. In the other example, the computer can translate a credit code contained in the customer's name and address card into a dollar amount, compare the total amount of the order with the credit limit, and signal if the order is more than 5 per cent (or any percentage) over the credit limit. In both examples the core storage (memory) requirement is small and does not require that other files or data be referred to in order to continue processing.

The small computer will frequently displace enough EAM equipment (accounting machines, calculators, reproducers) and tabulating operators to make its installation economically sound. The monthly lease price of a small card-oriented computer ranges approximately from $2,500 to $4,000. Other advantages of the computer are faster reports, possibly types of reports that were not feasible with the conventional EAM equipment, and a start in the EDP field without a major risk.

[3]   Large Computer Systems

Computer systems can be described or classified several ways. The principal type of input-output—card, disk, magnetic tape—can be used as a classification. The monthly rental (1965 prices) could be used to separate computers into classes: small ($2,500–$5,000), medium ($6,000–$10,000), intermediate ($12,000–$20,000), large ($25,000–$70,000) and super ($135,000 per month and up). A computer can also be described as a satellite system if its function is to feed a larger EDP system. It might be called a special-purpose or a real-time computer if performing a job such as airlines reservations where it is instantly updating all changes. The typical EDP system of a company doing order-processing work, and having sufficient volume to warrant more than a small card machine, will be a medium-sized tape computer. The exact configuration depends upon the company. The computer used as an example in the order-processing cycle will have a card reader (800 cards per minute), a card punch (250 cards per minute), a printer (600 lines per minute), a console typewriter (40,000 characters of memory), and seven magnetic tape units (transfer rate: 45,000 characters per second). This computer complex will cost approximately $10,000 per month on a single-shift basis.

The economics of paying $10,000 per month for a computer is often based upon replacing a smaller computer plus peripheral punched card equipment and clerical personnel. The card computer discussed earlier needed EAM machines to sort and collate the cards used with it. A tape computer would eliminate this EAM equipment—the fewer machines, the fewer machine operators required. Initial input to the majority of computers remains the key punched card; so key punch machines and operators are still required.

The small card computer has limited internal storage capacity and depends upon cards as its principal storage. Larger EDP systems use magnetic tape as their storage media. A comparison of the two kinds of storage, cards versus magnetic tape, illustrates the vast amount of information that can be stored on tape. A card has 80 columns of data while a magnetic tape reel (2,400 feet) can hold 15 million characters of data. Characters (actually magnetized bits) are stored on tape at densities of either 200 characters per inch (CPI), 556 CPI, or 800 CPI, with 556 being the general mode. The transfer rate of the magnetic tape units used in the example was 45,000 characters per second. This means that the computer can read into its central memory from magnetic tape or write out of memory to magnetic tape at a speed of 45,000 characters per second. The ability to store and manipulate large amounts of information in a computer changes the order-processing cycle and operation significantly.

The order-processing operation utilizing a medium-sized tape computer might look like this:

1. The salesman's order is reviewed for accuracy and completeness of information, especially codes. Controls of products ordered (hash totals) also must be established. The orders are forwarded to key punching, where a card is punched for each order containing the information concerning that particular order. Product spread cards are also punched (product code and quantity) for each item ordered. In a spread card, as many quantities and their codes would be punched as

there is room in the card. Punching a spread card rather than individual detail cards for each product ordered reduces the number of cards used and increases the speed of getting the data into the computer. Up to this point a tape computer order-processing operation is very similar to the order-processing cycles where EAM equipment or a small computer was used. The differences between the three systems would be in the amount of editing or review done initially. The tape computer system would allow the least manual editing, i.e., it would be able to do the most editing within the computer.

In addition, the computer would have the salesman's code, territory codes, class of customer code, etc., stored on tape in conjunction with this particular customer and shipping location. These miscellaneous codes would not have to be entered into the system from the salesman's order. The customer account code and shipping location codes would come from the salesman's order form and assume much greater responsibility under this type of operation. Because of its importance, a self-checking digit might be added to the customer number. This is a suffix number which is a mathematical combination of the other digits in the customer code number. The suffix would be calculated for each customer and then added as a permanent part of that customer's number. This self-check digit can be used to catch the great majority of errors that occur in manually transcribing numbers. It is highly unlikely that a salesman in making out an order form would make both an error in the customer code number and another error in the self-check digit which would result in an over-all correct code.

2. The key punched cards are processed on the computer (they need not be sorted in any sequence) in a card-to-magnetic-tape operation. At the same time some checking is done of the data placed on tape. The hash totals or other controls are verified, customer account code self-check digit calculated and verified, and any other editing done, such as minimum order quantities, that can be accomplished at this time. From this point forward all processing is done on the computer and under the control of the stored program.

3. After the day's orders have been accumulated on tape (the cycle could be more frequent than once a day if desired), the items ordered are tape sorted to product sequence. After sorting, a master price and inventory tape is read in and the products priced. This pricing pass could accomplish several things at once since the computer configuration used as the example had seven magnetic tape units. In the pricing run, all seven would be used, four as input and three as output. The inputs would be (a) master program tape containing the program to tell the

computer what to do, (b) orders for the day in product sequence, (c) master price and stock availability tape, and (d) new production, returned merchandise, or other goods which are to be added to available stock. The outputs would be (a) priced orders, (b) master price and updated stock availability tape, and (c) daily order statistics or exceptions. The printer, card punch, and console typewriter are also available for signaling errors or exceptions. Normally the console typewriter would be reserved for printing the operations log. The operations log is the detailed listing of all work run on the computer. It might show job or program number, time started, all stops or halts that occurred during the run and their reason, the action taken on the halts, constants entered, and all other items which reflect what was done during the processing day.

Substitutions would also be made during the pricing run. If the product ordered was out of stock, the computer would attempt to substitute the same product packaged differently. If not able to do that, it might substitute a regular item for "deal" merchandise at the deal price, or do any other substituting that had been previously defined in the computer program. In all the substitution procedures the computer must remember what customer it is working with and what types of substitution that particular customer will allow.

As indicated by the output tapes the pricing run would also update the stock availability or inventory records and maintain daily order statistics.

4. The priced orders on tape are next sorted to customer account sequence. After sorting they are processed against the master name and address tape file. Again the computer run accomplishes several functions at the same time. The four input tapes in this pass would be (a) master program tape, (b) orders in customer account sequence, (c) master name and address file, and (d) accounts receivable and orders pending file. The three output tapes would be (a) orders with name and address information included, (b) updated accounts receivable and orders pending file, and (c) exceptions. It should be remembered that the tape drives can be used either as inputs or outputs and that there is no one best system. For example, in the illustration above, the accounts receivable file could be included with the name and address file or a running total only of the outstanding accounts receivable could be maintained on the name and address file.

In the name and address run the shipping and billing addresses, routing data, special instructions for this customer, and other customer information are pulled off the name and address file and added to the order. At the same time the customer's credit is checked in relation not only to this order but also to other orders he may have in the house unshipped and to his outstanding accounts receivable plus his past history of payment.

5. The orders, priced and with all customer information (name and address) included, are sorted by shipping dates and shipping areas. In the operations so far there has been no printing of orders, and all processing has been within the computer. The only external activity has been the changing of tape reels by the computer console operator to obtain the proper files. One file may require several reels of tape.

6. The next program to be run in the order-processing cycle combines today's orders, in shipping date and shipping area sequence, with the pending order file from the previous day's orders. In this pass the three inputs are (a) master program tape, (b) today's orders, and (c) prior orders on pending file. The tape outputs would be an updated pending file and any exceptions. The computer would print a summary of the orders contained in the pending file, indicate which orders should be shipped, and punch a card for each order which should be shipped. The listing and the cards are forwarded to the traffic department (shipping department or other supervisory person). The listing shows the backlog of orders and allows management to make the final decision as to what will be shipped today. The listing would only have to show customer name, destination, routing information, date order received, total quantity and dollar amount of the order, total weight and cubic area of the products, and date the order has to be shipped to reach its destination on time. The punched cards would contain much the same data as on the listing and would be used merely as a means of approval by management and a feedback to the computer that the orders represented by the cards should be processed and shipped. The listing of orders can also be used by the traffic department to order out the trucks and rail cars necessary to load and ship the products.

7. When the cards representing the orders to be released are forwarded to data processing from the traffic department they are fed into the computer.

In this program, the "order-writing run," the three inputs would be (a) master program tape, (b) pending order file, and (c) trigger cards (in the card reader). The outputs would be (a) pending file, (b) pool or other combination load orders, and (c) backorder items, (d) printed orders themselves, from the printer, and (e) punched cards, if required for an automatic stock picker device.

Internally the computer could rearrange the sequence of products as they are being printed to print them on the order form in the sequence that they should be picked in the warehouse. The printed orders and cards for the stock picker are forwarded to the clerical order processing group for review, separation of the order forms, and distribution of the copies. The orders to be shipped in pool trucks or other combination loads would have the routing indicated on the order form so that they could be held aside until master bills of lading are prepared.

8. The tape output from the order-writing program for the combination loads would be sorted by product and master bills of lading prepared.

At this point the order-writing procedure is complete. The orders have been printed, stock availability records updated, and order statistics accumulated. The next day, after the products have been shipped, a copy of the shipping order form would be returned to the data processing section.

A card would be key punched for every order shipped. The card would contain the customer account number, invoice number, total quantity and dollar amount, plus the detail of any changes in the order that occurred in the shipping operation. These cards are used in the next step to initiate the invoicing for the orders shipped.

9. The cards representing orders shipped are read into the computer for the invoicing program. Along with the cards are these tape inputs: (a) master program tape, (b) pending file of orders, and (c) accounts receivable file. The outputs would be: (a) invoices, prepared on the printer, (b) updated accounts receivable file, (c) updated pending file (orders shipped have to be removed from the pending file), (d) sales statistics, and (e) controls for balancing or exceptions. This run prepares the invoices, updates the accounts receivable file, and accumulates sales statistics.

The order-processing cycle steps not yet outlined are the order analysis reports, sales analysis reports, and the cash receipts for accounts receivable. The accounts receivable cash receipts procedure would be to key punch a card for the monies received and process the cards against the tape file of outstanding receivables. The analysis reports involve tape sorting to the desired sequences, adding prior-period figures from a tape record, and printing reports.

Summary of Differences Between EDP Systems

The order-processing cycle has been described in detail, and systems for an EAM punched card, card computer, and tape computer order-processing operation have been outlined. The major difference between a manual system and an EAM system is that the punched cards prepared for the latter can be further used for order and sales analysis reports. Manually to accumulate order or sales data by product, salesman, and customer, compare it with prior-period data, and prepare accurate reports within a short space of time is almost impossible. A punched card system may not save money in printing invoices, when compared to the cost of several clerk-typists, but it provides the management reports which are vital to the business.

The major difference between an EAM system and a card computer system is in the machine processing steps. The same clerical operations are required, and the same outputs are generated. The justification for a card computer normally is that more data processing capability is obtained for less cost as measured by data processing equipment and personnel.

A card computer system and a tape computer system for order processing can be much the same if the design of the system for the larger EDP equipment merely copies the existing procedures. This does not take full advantage of the capabilities of the more powerful computer. The tape EDP system should integrate as many functions as possible. For example, the orders should be processed against a stock availability or inventory file before they are printed. The results of checking orders against availability should be used for production scheduling. The tape computer system should also reduce clerical work to a minimum. Such things as checking of the customer's credit, assignment of routes, and preparation of master bills of lading for combination loads should be handled by the EDP system. It is not every company that can afford a tape computer system. The volume of orders, size of orders, type of distribution pattern, selling policies, etc., will influence the choice of EDP equipment.

The tape computer approach of the order-processing cycle example is that of batch processing. This means that orders are accumulated and processed in batches. The larger the batches the more efficient the operation from purely a machine standpoint. Batch processing is also sequential in nature. The orders are processed in a given sequence. They are sorted for pricing, priced, sorted for name and address, name and address located, etc. In contrast to the batch-processing approach there is the random access approach. The most common random access equipment are magnetic disk files. Information stored on disks is located at a particular position or address so that it can be obtained without searching the entire file. With tape it is necessary to search the file sequentially until the item is located. Orders processed on a random basis would be read into the computer, the customer account code would tell the computer where to find the name and address data and other customer information on the disks, the product codes would determine the proper disk address for those products so that pricing and stock availability could be accomplished. In a single pass the orders could be completed with all records updated.

Although the random access approach appears satisfactory, it has some drawbacks. First, there is the question of whether the company requires that all records be current at all times. In the majority of companies the requirement for information is seldom even as short as daily. If the stock status is known every day this is sufficient for production planning. Weekly reports of sales by product, salesman, and territory are often all that management can absorb. Generally, orders are processed one day for shipment the following day. If the orders are ready a few hours earlier, the merchandise would still not be shipped any earlier. Second, the amount of random access storage required for an application can be extremely large. A customer master name and address file for 10,000 customers using 500 characters per account would consume 5 million storage positions. It may not be possible to allocate this much storage to one file. Many times this total could be required for the entire order-processing application. In comparison to magnetic tape storage, random access storage is expensive.

Random access in an order-processing system may not be justified. There are special applications, however, that require random access. Some of the better known of these are the airlines reservation system, savings accounts in banking, and the stock market quotation system.

Advantages of a Computer

The value and use of a computer to a company can reach into almost every facet of the business. The advantages outlined here are limited to those of an order-processing system. There are four basic areas where the use of a computer has advantages. These are mangement reporting, administrative and operating costs, customer service, and information for other departments.

Management reports may be prepared in various ways. The advantages of an EDP system are that it is generally faster in producing reports, can generate a great amount of detail data quickly if desired, and makes exception reporting a practical procedure. Previously, it was cumbersome to make comparisons of sales with prior-period sales or quotas and print only those figures that deviated from the expected answers by any given percentage. Under a computer system it is very easy to prepare this type of report. The most difficult part of developing exception reports is the education of management personnel to accept them.

An EDP system installed after a proper feasibility study should result in lower operating costs. Normally, there should be savings in clerical personnel, data processing personnel, supervisory personnel, and data processing equipment. The personnel reductions will be in the areas of order processing, shipping, traffic, credit, accounts receivable, accounting, analysis, inventory control, production control, production scheduling, and other sections that touch on order processing. Intangible savings from better internal control should also result with a computer installation. Lower inventory should be possible from a computer-processed scientific inventory management system. Reductions in the amount of office space and number of forms are other advantages of a computer. While a company should realize operating economies from an EDP system, the truth is that a great many companies that have installed computers, especially large-scale machines, have not reduced clerical costs. To a degree this is due to the newness of this type of equipment and the lack of experienced people in the field. While companies may not have reduced costs, they may have restricted a rise in costs. An advantage of a computer is that it can process additional volume with almost no increase in cost.

The third major area where a computer system has an advantage over other types of data processing systems is customer service. Less stockouts and fewer back orders give the customer the merchandise he ordered originally. This comes from an efficient stock availability system. Knowledge of the status of each customer's order helps in dealing with an inquiry about the order. Computer-generated shipping orders timed to meet shipping schedules improve the movement of the products to the customer. Fewer errors are another computer system advantage. While customer service can be considered an intangible benefit, an EDP system can improve it without much, if any, additional cost.

The other major area of order processing in which a computer system has an advantage is in supplying information to all departments of the company. The order analysis figures will probably be used by production scheduling. The computer may even do the production scheduling as a by-product of stock status information and order processing. The market research department will use the order and sales analysis data available from the computer in their work. The design of the EDP system should include provision to generate market research information. Product costing is another part of order processing which the computer is able to produce easily. The product costs may be used by both accounting and industrial engineering. Sales forecasting also can benefit greatly from the information available from an EDP order-processing system.

ORDER PROCESSING IN THE FUTURE

Order-processing methods have changed greatly with the use of computers, and additional changes can be expected in the future. There are several trends apparent at this time. The first trend is toward the increased use of computers for all sizes of companies. The cost of EDP equipment is constantly declining, and as more experience is gained with computers, companies, including small ones, will find it profitable to install a computer. This same trend is reflected in large companies by centralization of EDP operations. Communications devices are becoming more flexible as well as lower priced, which makes it more practical to tie outlying plants into a central computer complex.

The order-processing operation for a medium-sized to large company in the near future might be as follows:

The company would have a central computer complex at the main (executive) office with magnetic tape and random access capabilities. Communications devices including both voice grade lines and conventional teletype would be coupled with the computer. The equipment would be able to generate paper tape (teletype) from magnetic tape and vice versa. All communications would be handled through a message-switching center which would be computer operated. The manufacturing plants would have small card computers with communications devices to enable them to communicate directly with the large central computer. This would require voice grade communications lines either by direct leased lines or regular long distance. The plants would also have regular teletype machines for executive messages. Distribution points, warehouses, and major sales offices would have teletype equipment but not computers.

The actual order-processing procedure would start with the salesman's order telephoned or mailed to either a sales office, warehouse, plant, or main office. If the order was handled at the sales office or warehouse it would be teletyped to the EDP center. Only the customer account code, order number, product codes, and quantities would have to be transmitted. In this way the preparation and transmission of the orders would be rapid. The order data would be received at the EDP center in paper tape, converted to magnetic tape, processed, and all the completed order information punched back into paper tape for transmission to, and printing of, the shipping papers at the proper warehouse. If the salesman's order was sent to a plant location, the procedure would vary only in that the transmission to and from the EDP center would be via computer and received on magnetic tape. The logic of having a small computer at the plants, and the assumption that the plants are major distribution points while the warehouses are not, has two aspects. The first is that the plant has available its own computer to perform those jobs which are local in nature or too small to involve the larger central computer. The second aspect is the possibility of a breakdown of the central computer or the communications link. With computers at the plants (major distribution points), the shipping papers can always be prepared regardless of a breakdown at the EDP center. The order processing at the EDP center would cover the complete cycle, including credit checking, stock availability, routing, assignment of shipping point, generation of all shipping paper data including calculation of freight charges, and the updating of all order analysis statistics. Invoicing, accounts receivable, and sales analysis would, of course, be on a centralized basis.

There are several advantages to the central and satellite computer arrangement. It minimizes the cost of computers at every plant while providing the plants with the means to communicate with (and use) a large computer. Another management advantage is the centralization of information and the control it affords.

The second trend in order processing for the future is the advance in order input techniques. For many years the input to all data processing systems were punched cards, either key punched or pulled from a tub file. This means of computer entry is slowly being replaced. One method presently available is optic scanning. Widely used for several years by the petroleum industry for retail credit card purchases, optic scanning of full $8\frac{1}{2} \times 11$ pages is now practical. It is also possible to have the computer give the inventory status verbally, via telephone. It is not too difficult to visualize a salesman taking the customer's order via a portable tape recorder. After completing the day's orders he would use the telephone to dial the computer, plug in his tape recorder, and transmit the orders.

The third trend in data processing is toward a master file. This approach places all information within the company in one large computer memory. The master file (or one-file) approach goes beyond the integrated information systems concept. The integrated information systems concept is that one computer program's output becomes the next program's input. An example of this is the invoicing operation which generates the new sales input to the accounts receivable program. The integrated information systems concept is a sequential process, although the time delay may be very brief. In contrast the master file approach utilizes a large mass memory, and all updating is done at once. This means that the entry of an order into the system not only sets off all the order-writing functions but also updates the order analysis reports, adjusts the production control schedules, issues purchase orders for new materials if required, and influences sales forecasting. All this work is performed almost simultaneously. A computer printout is not made as a result of every order entered (the shipping papers would still be printed), but the information is updated and available. For example, the orders processed would be summarized and compared to the already established manufacturing production schedules. If the orders received indicated that the production schedule should be adjusted, a new production schedule would be printed. The master file concept requires a large-scale computer with the ability to process several programs at the same time. This concept may not be practical for smaller companies, since large random access capability is required. The advantage of the master file concept to a company is that all information is available in all areas at any time. If a company can establish a master file data processing system it has achieved simulation on a complete basis. In effect it can play games with varying business conditions and see what the results would be.

THE potential of packaging in minimizing the costs of physical distribution went largely unrecognized until the 1960's. Hence the special economic significance of the two subject areas covered by Chapters 9 and 10—packaging and containerization.

Apart from its generic function of protecting the product, the opportunities to optimize packaging solutions have really come into their own because of the emergence and acceptance (by business) of the pipeline flow concept of physical distribution. The rationale is (perhaps deceptively) quite obvious: The package, as a part of total weight, is of course included in transport charges. Also, the less appropriate the package, the higher the cost of packaging itself, materials handling, warehousing, etc.

The next chapter explores the relationship of packaging and package design to the total physical distribution system. It is followed by a chapter on containerization—an increasingly common means of reducing packaging and handling costs.

Throughout, it is well to note that materials handling is a vital element in the cost control of both packaging and containerization. Appendix B reviews the pervasive elements of materials handling, which recur throughout the pipeline flow of commodities from origin to destination.

9

Nelson R. Jantzen / Milton Alexander

A Logistical View
of Packaging

In a text on marketing *logistics*, it is necessary first to qualify the treatment to be given to packaging. We are not directly concerned here with identification of packaging factors that influence the company or product image, although these may be equally important considerations. Nor are we concerned with the specifics of packaging technology. But, since we are concerned with product movement, we are interested in the *utility factors* that influence package design. In short, we are dealing more with functional utility than with esthetic considerations.

It therefore follows that this perspective must take in what has sometimes been termed a "total" or "multiple packaging" system. The elements of such a system may include a customer unit package (consumer, retail, wholesale, and/or industrial package), a handling unit (tote container, shipping package, shipping container, or unit load), special bulk product treatment in storage or transit, plus interior packing components, identification, closing or sealing components and modes, etc., related to each type of package. When speaking of packaging or package design, we are referring to any one or all of these components.

The relationships within a multiple packaging system are too extensive to deal with in this text. Our concern, therefore, will be the relationships of a package or packaging system to other systems.

HISTORICAL BACKGROUND OF THE PROBLEM

It has not been uncommon to hear executives urge attention to cost reduction, stating in effect that costs of packaging are rising faster than the value of products contained within the package. They suggest that a major goal of distribution management should be to reduce the materials costs and the number of steps needed to package products. This is a prevailing thought, but it is not necessarily valid. It has also been alleged that a proper approach to industrial packaging could parallel that employed in consumer packaging. This is difficult to accept, for the parameters are entirely different, since the former is mainly concerned with meeting the requirements of internal handling and shipping, and the latter with consumer appeal. Most of these timeworn criticisms point up the merits of cost reduction, damage claims reduction, more adequate testing, etc., but they do not go far enough toward the need for a comprehensive *integrated system* of packaging and handling, storage, transportation, and so on.

The old approaches to package planning lead to a piecemeal treatment that places total or undue stress on one or two facets at the expense of all others, and at best treats the packaging system as a separate entity. For instance, new packaging materials and equipment development have enjoyed a pre-eminence in market planning in recent years—very probably under the promotional impetus of suppliers. By comparison, however, relatively minor progress has been made in developing valid techniques for evaluating the operational effectiveness of a package component when the package actually becomes part of a physical distribution system. Trial and error still dominate; there are a few laboratory testing techniques, but usually they give only a general indication of probable performance under certain stresses and strains. Two additional examples will bring us closer to the point:

1. The merchandising potentials of packages have been greatly enhanced through concentrated attention to consumer package closures, graphics, and, to some degree, consumer utilitarian factors. This development is now even penetrating the industrial product packaging field. By comparison, development of functional potentials of package designs in relation to the physical distribution area is still in its infancy.

2. Within the physical distribution area, emphasis in package planning has been disparate. There has undoubtedly been a preoccupation with damage and loss facets, with only secondary attention to such facets as materials handling efficiency, order-picking facility, or ease of inventory control. Most companies, for example, use damage claims as an index to determine how much they should spend on package quality, figuring that a near-perfect damage claim record is indicative of overpackaging; while high damage claims induce an examination first of handling, then, perhaps, of better packaging. This is actually a hopeful sign, because at least packaging costs are being related to one element of distribution costs, rather than being considered as an entity in itself. But this does not go far enough. Increased packaging expenditure often

can have a notable effect on distribution costs in many ways other than in reducing damage or loss claims.

Historically, therefore, the attention of package planning has been focused mainly on the package system cost elements, and secondarily on a few isolated distribution system results, notably, (1) losses and damage and (2) product and corporate image enhancement. Logistically, this is inadequate, even though great strides have been made in packaging technology.

SYSTEMS APPROACH PHILOSOPHY

The philosophy generally called for now is a *systems approach* to packaging design. What do we mean by that? Since "system" is an overworked word, it is necessary to redefine the concept. The statement does not mean that the package components must be integrated into a packaging system, nor that the steps in packing must be systematized (as in the packaging system concept previously mentioned), for that is only part of the story. Packaging technology is too narrow a concept for design. The original and often stated basic purpose of packaging is to contain and protect the product at an optimum cost consistent with its value, so that it can be transferred from production line to customer unadulterated, intact, and on time. But it is not the package alone that accomplishes this. We must therefore recognize that (1) packaging is but one element of a total system we can call physical distribution; (2) all of the elements of the physical distribution system interact on each other; and (3) optimization of the total system provides a better basis for improving profitability and service than optimization of its elements.

The old objective of optimizing a package or packaging system by minimizing cost consistent with providing adequate protection is no longer acceptable. We need not optimize gains nor even necessarily gain at all when we set out to save money on the package or on the cost of the packaging system. The purpose here is to suggest other bases for the relationship in package planning in order to enhance the over-all profitability of the company.

A Distribution System: Packaging— Nature and Relationship

Properly to relate packaging planning to physical distribution, we must start with the assumption not that physical distribution is one facet of the packaging problem, but that packaging is one element in analyzing an optimum distribution system—it is a part of the system. The system is not packaging; the system is distribution. Only through this approach can the optimum requirements for distribution packaging be determined, and then ultimately these can be compromised in packaging decisions to the extent that other facets like merchandising and production require it.

A distribution system starts with the dispatch of a finished or partly finished product from the production or manufacturing process, and ends with its delivery to the industrial user or consumer. It may or may not be interrupted by a secondary fabricating, assembling, or production process. It usually involves storage of the product; and it always includes some sort of man–equipment subsystems of product handling, internal and external transport, counting or tallying, inventory, order assembly, and packaging in its broadest interpretation. We say "broadest interpretation," for sometimes packaging is achieved by the mere selection of a transport mode, as in the case of phases of bulk products distribution systems. Cycles of storage, issuance, transport, receipt, and packaging may repeat themselves several times in a given system, and in each phase the requirements of the system, including packaging requirements, may be altered. These requirements are influenced not only by the system itself but also by the system's environment. With a systems approach to packaging design, all functional elements are given commensurate attention along with protective packaging elements.

SYSTEM ELEMENTS THAT ESTABLISH PACKAGE DESIGN PARAMETERS

Package planning (i.e., design) is a multifaceted problem. No two situations are alike, and no single situation remains static. While we are faced with the problem of compromising between a number of influential factors to arrive at a so-called optimum contributory design, and while in each packaging problem these factors will so vary in character and intensity that it will be difficult even to identify them (much less evaluate their relative importance), it is encouraging to know that the parameters appear to be rather standard.

The principal elements worth enumerating here may be found in one or more of these functional areas. Packing and marking activities may take place in production, again through one or more warehousing stages, even in-transit, and finally at the customer level. Each area may impose constraints based on packaging ease or utility of the package. The following elements are to be considered.

Facility in packing or repacking at production line, warehouse, and customer shipping departments;

Facility in closing or reclosing at above locations or in other storage areas;

Adaptability to product structure and configuration;

Adaptability to product unitization (i.e., accommodation of proper number of units, separate heterogeneous product parts, etc.);

Adaptability to existing or obtainable equipment at packing stations in production or at warehouse;

Protection, support, and containerization to withstand adequately the forces of internal mechanical movement, and adaptability to related handling equipment;

Provision for manual handling without imposing undue physical strain (e.g., weight distribution constraints), and to permit easy grabbing and holding in various operative positions;

Protective strength, configuration, and surface properties to permit stacking in storage at plant, warehouses, customer locations, and in-transit vehicles; protection against environmental influences that would affect the product and the packaging materials;

Protection, support, and containerization adequate to withstand forces encountered in external movement;

Accessibility for order picking from package at warehouses and customers or to permit inspection of contents as required in the system;

Provision for marking identification effective in order picking and in taking inventory at plant and warehouses and by customers, and adaptability to marking equipment;

Facility for marking and labeling for shipment and adaptability to related equipment;

Provision for special marking, e.g., with corporate image identification;

Facility for storage of empty packages and components and return or disposal of used packages and components;

Vendor capabilities: package material characteristics and functional effectiveness; structural design characteristics and functional effectiveness; close characteristics and functional effectiveness; internal packaging components characteristics and functional effectiveness; labeling and graphics materials and application equipment suitability; packaging equipment features and capabilities; delivery conditions;

Incremental cost effects in distribution operation that can be expected from packaging alternates; and

Incremental direct costs of alternate packaging materials, equipment, and packing modes.

Probably the most significant item in this list, from the systems approach standpoint, are distribution cost effects of alternate packaging. These pinpoint the relative *contribution* each packaging alternate would make toward deriving an ideal distribution system. Too often, the tendency is to concentrate on the direct costs of packaging alternates.

GENERAL APPLICATIONS OF SYSTEMS APPROACH PHILOSOPHY

Take a simple hypothetical case of a company producing a product like small plastic pellets. Let us assume these are packaged in lined bags, put on pallets for storage in the company warehouse, and shipped by truck to customers in small lots. The bags must be removed one by one from the pallets before shipment, and freight and handling charges are therefore relatively high per unit. The package may be satisfactory in all respects, considering the nature of the handling it receives and the nature of the product.

Now let us change the system and insert distributor warehouses that can accommodate larger shipments. From the company's shipping standpoint, its "package" may now be a palletized and strapped unit load, or some sort of container for bags. The original bag package remains as a component, but a shipping pallet or container is incorporated to facilitate external movement. (A change in bag size or standardization of sizes might be required to permit standardization of pallet or container sizes.) In any case, the packaging problem will be different, either more or less complicated or costly, and other factors (e.g., container service) will also be adjusted. But this too may not be the ultimate step to optimize distribution. Now perhaps a package-filling operation can be introduced at the distributor level, and shipment from the key plant might be in bulk by hopper rail car, direct from the production line, with silo-type storage provided by or for distributors to permit bulk discharging and storage there. Now the shipping "package" is the rail car itself. One can readily see that the costs and methods of packaging materials, packing, handling, storage, and transportation would be realigned, presumably to provide a better distribution system. The optimization of the package within this system becomes a different solution at each stage. Packaging costs more or less than before, but that is secondary. More important is the over-all profitability and/or customer service improvement.

The Special Problem of
External Influences

Changes of the sort just described need not be initiated by the manufacturer. Distribution system changes may originate with the customer, with vendors, or with the transportation companies. From the standpoint of the customer, when the package finally reaches him, there is always the question of its further transfer, use, or disposal. For instance, if the "customer" happens to be a manufacturer and if the product is one of his ingredients, changes in his product mix volumes or in his handling methods may well open up opportunities for improvement in the vendor's distribution system and changes in his packaging. With vendors, it is primarily a question of their improved capabilities for provision of materials, equipment, or service that causes changes in the distribution system and/or the packaging subsystem.

As for transportation companies, there is no question that the demand for faster service, the increasing volumes handled, and the requirement to reduce or hold the line on costs will continue to spark developments toward faster, more mechanized, and more sophisticated handling systems at and between terminals. This will mean that packaging requirements will be changing as opportunities arise to improve company distribution systems by taking advantage of these developments.

Failure to consider packaging in the context of these opportunities can place companies at a serious competitive disadvantage. Yet, in dealing with packaging via the total systems approach, there is strong evidence that information available in shipping companies on external handling is usually fuzzy. It is a shattering experience to observe the losses that occur due to the inability of packaging to cope with some of the problems of mechanized handling encountered in truck, airline, and rail systems. But often the shipper has little understanding of the packaging stresses imposed by speedy handling both in its mechanized aspects and in the manual transfers that attempt to keep pace with mechanized equipment. Information about the effects on packages of actual transport in "the vehicle" is somewhat better, but still far from adequate.

One major motor carrier with no primary responsibility for packaging has taken the interesting step of upgrading the packaging knowledge of its customer service personnel. Why? Because by doing so, it hopes to be able to provide a packaging appraisal that its customers cannot provide themselves; an appraisal of the adequacy of packaging for processing through its high-speed system. Other common carriers are taking similar steps. The machinery is being provided, therefore, for cooperation between companies that ship by common carrier and transportation companies that serve them in broadening packaging development perspectives. This is a hopeful sign, but only a beginning. Many companies are reluctant at first to accept outside help or suggestions. The fact remains, however, that it points the way toward a systems approach to packaging.

Packaging Changes Improve the Distribution System

In many actual physical distribution system studies there have been cases where improvement of the profitability of the system has largely depended on packaging innovations. This has been true of highly sophisticated systems employing considerable mechanized handling and automatic controls and also of more simple operations. In one complex system developed for a large mail order warehouse a modular carton was designed that made significant contributions. It was found that approximately 80 per cent of the products handled could be packaged in a four-sized modular arrangement with size ratios of $\frac{1}{4}, \frac{1}{2}$, 1, and 2, where formerly an almost unlimited number of sizes had been used by vendors to ship to the company distribution center. One of the four modules was selected for each product, depending on cube and weight constraints imposed. This permitted uniform palletization into unit loads with a single over-all configuration. Standardization of sizes also permitted a considerably denser utilization of space in storage racks in the forward order-picking areas. Both the internal handling system and storage racks were designed around the modular container and resulting unit loads, and the containers served as the bin in the forward area, since they were designed as end-openers. Handling and flow, storage, order picking, and stock replenishment all benefited from the container design. This case illustrates a special situation requiring external cooperation. Packaging adjustments had to be arranged with the compliance of many vendors (approximately 85 per cent compliance was achieved). While the internal handling, scheduling, picking, and replenishment problems to be resolved were quite complex, packaging played a major role in the solution.

A Specific Case in Detail

Perhaps the detailing of a relatively simple case will better illustrate the relationships and interdependence of packaging and the distribution system and the gains that can be achieved by a systems approach to packaging.

A consultant was engaged to review the physical distribution operations of the women's sportswear division of a major company. The company distributes its line nationally from one modern distribution center. The line includes blouses, shirts, sweaters, skirts, pants, and shorts. They are transferred to the center from a number of manufacturing plants, including one adjacent to the center. Items might be received and stored as hanging or boxed goods, and the ratio changes constantly (although boxed items predominate). All shipments to customers are boxed.

Management was concerned mainly with the center's capability to handle a flow of goods double the present volumes, which indicators showed would be necessary in the not too distant future. Its only current problem was a familiar one to the garment industry: to ship more merchandise sooner in the three peak shipping seasons and, it was hoped, to level off labor requirements. It had identified no particular packaging problem.

A complete analysis of all pertinent data pertaining to the distribution system, both current and long range (e.g., receiving patterns, order characteristics, production batching, inventory requirements, style changes, shipping modes, returned goods performance, backordering performance, and sales and production volumes), led to a number of systems changes of varying importance. One fundamental change was in packaging through the total systems approach.

Early in the systems analysis it became obvious that order picking was a key function in which improvement would level off fluctuations in labor requirements between seasons and increase output per man-hour. Statistical analysis of orders and time and motion studies showed that considerable effort could be saved by substituting prepackaged size assortments and solid sizes in half-dozen quantities for the existing one-dozen quantity packages. The incidence of special make-up of orders could be reduced by as much as 52 per cent by using this formula. And it would practically eliminate the incidence of stock disorganization under the old arrangement. This focused attention on the package itself, for one of the requirements was that the change be accomplished with little or no increase in packaging costs.

The old method utilized expensive corrugated boxes with full telescopic lids, stocked in approximately ten different sizes. The next step, prior to actual design of a new package, involved determining its function in the distribution system. Essentially, the elements listed earlier in this chapter that establish parameters for design were reviewed, one by one; and specific questions were formulated about the package in relation to the existing system and alternates being considered for adoption. For instance, in receiving goods at the distribution center and placing them in storage, was palletization or mechanized flow line handling contemplated? What would the modes contemplated require of packaging? Would the half-dozen unit package require further containerization? Could it be accomplished within the limits placed on packaging costs? Also important: How can item identification best be provided for taking inventory and order picking? Where should it appear on the package? Or, in internal movement from stock to shipping, to what degree must the half-dozen unit package be self-containing?

In this process, a whole series of requirements were listed, weighed, retained, or compromised until eventually the fixed parameters were identified and supplemented by "desirable but not necessary" ones. In this particular situation, the principal parameters (ultimately established) are specified below: The terms "unit package," "tote container," and "shipping container" refer to three major components of the total packaging system contemplated, the first dealing with the half-dozen unit and the others with multiples of it. The decision to design three components rather than one or two was itself arrived at only by visualizing the total system.

Unit packages must accommodate a uniformly fixed quantity of many varieties and sizes of garments; must provide support for manually handling and carrying six folded garments; should permit stacking of five to eight packages without other support; need provide only minimum protection against spilling garments when carried on a reasonably level plane; must provide item identification on ends that can be readily seen when stacked in storage; could possibly provide means for corporate identity; must be easy to pack manually; must be usable also for shipments to customer and handling by him; must be reasonably attractive.

Tote containers must permit top loading manually in packaging; must permit end discharge in picking; should be suitable for closing by semi-automatic strapping equipment; along with unit package, must protect adequately in shipping by truck from plants to distribution center; must knock down for storage and return to plants for reuse; must be easy to set up manually; should provide for some compression in closing and permit at least 2-inch adjustability in interior depth contents (not to exceed 40 pounds); must permit identification of contents on ends and shipping information on top surface; must permit safe stacking of eight or nine units high in trucks, and three high in storage for up to eight months; must survive at least four cycles of use if not shipped to customer.

Shipping containers must permit top loading manually in packing; should be suitable for closing by semi-automatic strapping equipment; along with unit package, must provide adequate protection in shipping by truck or rail car and in intermediate handling at terminals; must knock down for storage; must be easy to set up manually; should provide for some compression in closing and permit depth adjustability of at least 2 inches for smaller sizes, 5 inches for larger; must permit application of shipping information, and possibly of corporate identity on top and/or side surfaces; weight of contents of smaller sizes limited to 60 pounds, of larger sizes, up to 150 pounds.

All packages must have as few surfaces as possible, construction joints, and set-up and closure modes to minimize possibility of snagging garments.

The foregoing is not an exhaustive list, but covers the main parameters. It was ultimately possible to reduce the number of unit package and tote container sizes to two, which varied only in length. Shipping container sizes were reduced to five, including one special size.

The half-dozen unit package became a simple corrugated pad on which garments were packed and taped in position. Identification of items was accomplished on the tape itself, for standard assortments, and on the pads for solid sizes, where the tape would be discarded during the picking of individual garments. Special-order quantities were made up by the picker on spare pads, and identified with a differently colored tape applied on the spot.

Usually this package, in the case of standard assortments, moved first to the distribution center and then to the customers, first in tote containers and then in shipping containers. For internal movement in the distribution center, monorail carriers were designed to accommodate and support stacks of these unit packages.

The tote containers were packed in the various production units and contained specific quantities of the unit package, varying by style and type of garment, but always the same number for a specific item. Totes were reusable after they were emptied by order picking. In some few cases they would be used intact as a shipping container, where the quantities ordered made it feasible. Shipping containers were also designed to fit varying quantities of unit packs so as to minimize the number of containers per shipment.

What have these package designs contributed to the system? Most directly, a half-dozen unit package was derived that satisfies customers' ordering demands and distribution system functional requirements right through to and including the customers' use of the package. The total packaging costs (material and labor) were reduced by 25 per cent. A more efficient packaging operation became possible at all plants. Indirectly, but even more significantly, the distribution center is enjoying a 32 per cent saving in labor costs, to which packaging has made its contribution mainly in the following ways:

Some gains were made in receiving and putting away stock, due to expansion of handling unit (four to twelve times larger quantities).

The transfer of prepackaged garments from plants to distribution center was facilitated for the same reason.

Reorganization of stock into a double-depth as opposed to single-depth bin storage was facilitated, as the tote container permitted pulling forward from four to twelve dozen garments at a time, using the strapping as hand grip.

The open-end feature of the tote box, and the use of pads as a unit package, greatly improved order-picking operations; also pads have proved easy to handle in special-order assembly.

Stock organization planning was improved. Dealing with tote container units of uniform size instead of a variety of box styles made space allocation simpler; and spot-checking stock status was facilitated because part-empty totes could be easily identified on the shelves (since the end components are removed when the tote is first broken).

Taking physical inventory was greatly eased. To arrive at dozens one had only to count full totes and multiply by a packaging factor, and then count visible pads in partly empty totes and multiply by two. In the old system many boxes had to be opened to permit counting the contents, and each dozen had to be identified and counted individually.

Checking of orders and subsequent billing were simplified by making all garments visible on pads, as they passed along the flow line. It also facilitated adoption of an in-line billing procedure.

The new shipping containers were somewhat easier to pack with unit packages and the garments were kept in better condition because they were more compressed.

The case cited demonstrates that substantial gains may be achieved through better packaging; and that simple adjustments in package design often facilitate operations of the total system.

ORGANIZATIONAL EFFECTIVENESS

It is not too difficult to "sell" businessmen "on" the systems approach to packaging or to distribution management. The main problems usually come from the organization structure and from communications shortcomings. The form of business organization popularized in the 1940's and 1950's, embodying specialization, a segmented functionalized staff, and decentralization of line responsibility, creates very serious roadblocks to a systems approach—roadblocks which must eventually be circumvented. For instance, the question might very likely arise as to who can initiate or authorize a systems analysis in the first place, or who can explore the scope of a problem in packaging in a total systems approach.

The beauty of a package is in the eye of the beholder. A bit of oversimplification will illustrate the point: To the public relations–advertising executive it is a medium for carrying the corporate image and sundry promotional slogans; to the merchandiser–salesman–customer-service man it is a protective device (to get the product safely to the customer) and a display, an eye-catching medium; to the traffic manager it is a cube–girth–weight relationship; to the warehouseman it is a storage device and a unit count; to the truck driver it identifies contents and destinations; to the package designer it is material structure and form; to the purchasing agent it is a specific cost; to all handlers along the chain of distribution it is a handling device; and to the packer it is a challenge. An oversimplification to be sure; but who in our specialized organizations will have the perspective and training of a generalist to analyze the package as part of a total system? Who can coordinate the data about the system and make a decision about how it shall operate, and in so doing evaluate the total contribution of a package? This is the problem. Organization segregates interests, whereas a systems approach demands integration.

Of course, anyone with personal charm, influence, authority, broad knowledge and perspective, vision, interest, and energy can bring together the interested parties so that a systems approach of sorts might be employed. It could be the packaging manager or engineer, the traffic manager, the warehouse superintendent, the marketing or manufacturing vice-president, the president, or a host of others; and he could do it within the structure of present organizations. In some companies it might be advisable to try committees, to ease the communications problem; but very often one finds the wrong people either appointed or excluded. In some companies, for varying reasons—ranging from political to organizational, from lack of know-how to lack of time for planning—consultants can do an effective job of synthesizing, coordinating, and creating to achieve a systems approach, provided they work with the people concerned and not just for them.

All of the foregoing are possible approaches to get around the problem of organizational specialization. For maximum effectiveness, the systems approach to anything (packaging or data processing, distribution or production) should be a continuous planning process. Ultimately, what is needed is organizational realignment and redefinition of relationships for a systems approach (first understanding how it can be applied to a company's particular situation). Very likely, however, the organizational solutions will involve a special emphasis on restructuring staff, separating planning into some form of project-system structure, and retaining purely service functions in more or less the conventional form. The relationships between staff and line would also undergo change.

Until more experience is gained with reorganizing for a systems approach to planning, companies will doubtless prefer to rely heavily on internal communications arrangements, both formal and informal, on a more or less idealistic concept called "self-coordination," and on-spot internal task forces or assignments to consultants. Those companies that devise or seek help in devising a more permanent arrangement will no doubt arrive at a better packaging and better total physical distribution effectiveness that much sooner.

WHAT TO EXPECT FROM A SYSTEMS APPROACH

The potential of the packaging function for making a significant contribution to corporate profits can be increased by applying a "total systems approach" to packaging planning.

First, none of the isolated problemsolving potential is lost, while a distinct measure of insurance is added that solution of one problem will not create others more consequential. This is due to the broadening perspective of the systems approach.

Second, conscious efforts may be made to alter the handling, promotional, or service elements of the distribution system to simplify packaging (a major cost factor). For instance, altering distribution channels, storage time cycles, handling methods, or transportation modes can have an appreciable effect on packaging materials and modes.

Third, an awareness at the packaging planning center of total systems requirements and problems can make possible improvements in the utility of the package itself and in the effectiveness of total system performance

APPENDIX

SEVEN BASIC STEPS TO SUCCESSFUL PACKAGING

The questionnaire[1] shown below represents a wide cross section of opinion and experience among packagers. The points listed will not all be applicable to any one product, but consideration of each question can eliminate oversight of important items. Many packagers develop a short-form checklist tailored to individual circumstances and streamlined to cover only those points that are pertinent to a specific product and its packaging parameters.

Steps 1, 2, and 3 of the questionnaire deal with the planning phases of a package development program. The remaining steps pertain to selection and design. There is necessarily some overlapping. In general, the arrangement is sequential; but in numerous cases the items are interrelated. For example, certain aspects of container selection will depend on packaging-like considerations or vice versa. Balanced planning and numerous compromises or adjustments are essential elements of a successful package development program.

STEP 1: Piloting the Program

Package designation ⸻⸻⸻⸻⸻⸻⸻
Project or code number ⸻⸻⸻⸻⸻⸻
Product ⸻⸻⸻⸻⸻⸻⸻⸻⸻
    new ⸻⸻ repeated ⸻⸻ modified ⸻⸻
Package is new ⸻⸻ revised ⸻⸻ member of family design ⸻⸻
    sizes and variations needed will be ⸻⸻⸻⸻⸻

Who will be responsible for coordinating package planning ⸻⸻⸻

---

[1]Adapted from *Modern Packaging Encyclopedia.* McGraw-Hill, 1965. By Permission.

Departments participating in planning and steps assigned:

Executive _____

 steps _____

Product development _____

 steps _____

Market research _____

 steps ___ _____

Advertising _____

 steps _____

Sales _____

 steps _____

Art _____

 steps _____

Legal _____

 steps _____

Traffic _____

 steps _____

Production _____

 steps _____

Purchasing _____

 steps _____

Packaging _____

 steps _____

Other _____

 steps _____

What schedule of meetings will be needed _____

Outside services that may be required:

research and development _____

packaging materials and constructions _____

package design _____

package production _____

machinery development _____

market research _____

package testing _____

other _____

Lead time for package development will be _____

Final deadline date will be _____

Records for this project will include _____

STEP 2: Determining Product Needs

Product name or designation _____

Product end-use _____

How merchandised and distributed _____

Quantity and size of packaged unit:
    unit quantity packed ____ dimensions (or cube) ____ net weight ____
    standard shipping quantity _____ cube _____ net weight _____
Physical form:
    powder _____   viscous _____
    granular _____   liquid _____
    tablet or capsule _____ gaseous _____
    solid _____   combination _____
    other _____
General characteristics:
    particle size _____   volatile _____
    density _____   perishable _____
    lumpy or sticky _____ flowable _____
    viscosity _____   abrasive _____
    corrosive _____   chemically active _____
    toxic _____   fragile _____
    other _____
Approximate value of unit quantity:
    after processing _____ at retail _____
Essential protective needs: index of failure
    temperature extremes _____   _____
    moisture retention _____   _____
    protection against moisture _____   _____
    retention of volatiles, flavors _____   _____
    protection against gases _____   _____
    protection against light _____   _____
Product requires protection from or against:
    bacteria _____   soilage _____
    mold _____   staining _____
    rodents _____   breakage _____
    insects _____   pilferage _____
    odors _____   grease or oil _____
    corrosion _____ loss of purity or strength _____
    sifting _____   chemical interaction _____
    leakage _____
    other _____
What special protection is needed for delicate parts or fine surfaces ____
_____
Must the product be able to breathe _____ have access to light _____
    other special environmental conditions _____
_____
Must seals on package give same protection as the materials _____
Is reclosure needed to protect unused portion _____
Will product and package be compatible during all conditions of distribu-
    tion and use _____

Will product be processed in package:

    sterilization _____   gassing _____

    forming _____   cooking _____

    freezing _____   refrigeration _____

    vacuumizing _____   other _____

Average shelf-life needed is _____ use-life needed is _____

Product requires these special package features to protect against injury
    or hazards to handlers and users _____
_____

Product requires these special package features to assure:

    ease of handling _____

    ease of shipment _____

    ease of stocking _____

    ease of use _____

STEP 3: Selecting the Target

THE PRODUCT

Special features are _____

Relative competitive quality is _____

Packages most widely used for this type of product are _____
_____

THE MARKET

Ultimate consumer:

    age _____   income _____

    geographical location _____

    socio-cultural level _____ export markets _____

Special markets are:

    juvenile _____ senior _____ homemaker _____

    do-it-yourself _____ hobby _____ industrial _____

    special diet _____ gift or special occasion _____

    other _____

Packages that might best serve these markets are _____
_____

Can new outlets or greater market penetration be obtained with:

    unit-of-use packs _____

    bulk sizes _____

    fractional packs _____

    one-way packs _____

    bantam sizes _____

    table-service packs _____

    multiple or carry packs _____

strip packs _____
aerosols _____
second-use or reuse packs _____
cook-in-packs _____
dispensing packs _____
gift or novelty packs _____
easy-opening packs _____
other _____
Regular channels will be:
    independents _____   discount _____
    self-service _____   food _____
    chains _____   drug _____
    mail order _____   department stores _____
    house-to-house _____   variety _____
    other _____

BUYING HABITS

Standard units of purchase are _____
Storage procedures prior to sale are _____
Should design be for:
    shelf _____ window _____ checkout _____
    rack _____ counter _____ other _____
Will package most often be seen:
    at eye level _____ above _____ below _____
What panel will be displayed _____
What are problems of:
    facing _____ stacking _____
    racking _____
What point-of-sale support will be given _____
Can shipping package be adapted for display _____
    how _____
How should package size be adapted:
    distribution methods _____ consumer habits _____
How might changes in size affect consumer convenience in regard to:
    economy _____ frequency of repurchase _____
    storing _____ ease of carrying _____
    ease of use _____

RETAIL CONSIDERATIONS

What sizes, shapes, will be most convenient for:
    distributors _____ retailers _____
Must package expedite:
    self-service _____ quick turnover _____
    self-selection _____ repeat purchase _____

Must package be specially designed to meet problems of:

pilferage _____	reduction of waste _____
soilage _____	elimination of returns _____
breakage _____	seasonal turnover _____
tie-ins _____	special promotions _____
adequate shelf life _____	quantity of purchase _____

USE FACTORS

Unit sizes most needed by customers are _____

Is inspection prior to sale desired _____ practical _____
   how best achieved _____

Will package handling or use present special safety problems _____

Must package be opened easily _____ be reclosed readily _____
   is captive cap needed _____

Must consumer measure out quantity easily, accurately _____

Can a dispensing device be provided _____

Will package disposal be a problem _____

What reuse or second-use feature might be desirable _____
_____

What features, such as hand-grip design, handles, etc., are desirable
_____

What package sizes are most appropriate for consumer storage _____
_____

How long must packages protect contents to assure normal use-life ___
_____

What working packages might be used:

aerosol _____	roll-on dispenser _____
cook-in pack _____	squeeze-to-use _____
water-soluble _____	dust gun _____
table-service _____	metering dispenser _____
unit-of-use _____	other _____

STEP 4: Selecting the Package

Package will be:

regular _____	luxury _____
gift _____	seasonal _____
other _____	

Special characteristics (feeling of thrift, purity, tradition, etc.) _____
_____

Quantity:
   initial order _____ annual _____ potential _____
Specifications required _____
   blueprints _____ samples to be submitted _____

Structural design will be by:

    company _____ independent _____

    supplier _____ jointly _____

Surface design will be by _____

Primary pack will be:

    bag _____   wrap _____

    glass _____   set-up box _____

    envelope or pouch _____   metal _____

    folding carton _____   plastics _____

    card-pack _____   corrugated _____

    capsule _____   molded pulp _____

    style or construction _____ paper can or tube _____

    other _____

Dealer pack will be _____ number of units packed _____

Shipping package:

    corrugated _____   fiber drum _____

    shipping sack _____ plastics _____

    carboy _____   wooden _____

    solid fiber _____   metal pail or drum _____

    other _____

Material and style of construction _____

Interior packing or cushioning _____

Is pallet load, unitized load, or containerization desired _____

    type _____ size _____

What package modifications will be needed for distribution in:

    cold temperature _____ low humidity _____

    warm temperature _____ high humidity _____

    air shipment _____ export _____

    other _____

CLOSURES

Lid or cap will be:

    screw-type _____ tamperproof or safety _____

    friction _____   dispenser-applicator _____

    pry-off _____   roll-on _____

    lug _____   vacuum _____

    other _____

Material will be:

    metal _____ plastic _____ paper _____ cork _____

    rubber _____ other _____

Seal or gasket will be _____

Heat seal will be:

    direct _____   thumb notch _____

    shear-cut _____ ultrasonic _____

    impulse _____   elliptical lip _____

    serrated _____   high-frequency _____

Adhesive seal will be:
 dextrin _____ animal _____ synthetic _____
Mechanical seal or fastening will be:
 staples _____ strapping _____ cord _____
 other _____

STRUCTURAL CONSIDERATIONS

Will strength be adequate for intended use _____
Will package lend itself readily to processes of fabricating _____
 graphic arts _____
Will package stand up under handling
 in transportation, in warehouses, and in retail stores _____
Will package
 permit mechanized handling _____ high-speed filling _____
 economical filling _____

PERFORMANCE CHECKS

Will package meet the processing, handling, and protective requirements
specified in Step 2:
  moisture _____   thermal _____
  light _____   mold or bacteria _____
  leaking _____   rodents or insects _____
  odor or flavor _____ breakage _____
  sifting _____   staining _____
  soilage _____   loss of strength or purity _____
  pilferage _____ corrosion _____
  grease or oil _____ protection of fragile or
          delicate parts _____
Will package meet the special requirements in Step 2 for:
  breathing _____ resealing _____
  compatibility _____ transparency _____
  safety _____   ease of handling _____
  processing _____ other _____

STEP 5: Design Considerations

DECORATION

How will container be decorated:
  direct imprint _____ applied label _____
  if applied type, will label be:
   spot _____   die-cut _____
   embossed _____   wrap-around _____
   pressure-sensitive _____ removable _____
   permanent _____ semipermanent _____
   other _____

Material will be:
    paper _____ foil _____ plastic _____
    metal _____ other _____
Printing will be:
    letterpress _____ lithography _____
    flexography _____ gravure _____
    screen process _____ other _____

IDENTITY

Is a brand name used _____ is it unmistakable in position _____
Is symbol or trademark used _____ is it adequately featured _____
Is manufacturer's name given due prominence _____
Is the address handled adequately _____
Is product name featured for quick identity _____
Are contents clearly and properly stated _____
Can color coding be used _____
Is shape distinctive _____

FOR INFORMATION AND ATTENTION

Must package carry:
    mandatory information _____ cautionary information _____
Are there other legal regulations to be observed _____
Is this information properly positioned _____ legible _____
Are instructions to be used _____ recipes _____ serving por-
    tions _____ illustrations _____ other _____
Are directions legible _____ easy to understand _____
Can directions be shortened _____ made more interesting _____
Is a price panel needed _____ where is it to be located _____
What colors are to be used _____
Are colors appropriate for product, retail outlet, consumer use _____

Does design reflect outstanding qualities of product (strength, dignity,
    reliability, economy, luxury, value, newness, work saving) _____
Is design truly appropriate _____
Does it reflect manufacturer's integrity, responsibility _____
Can it be adapted to upgrading product _____
Can it be adapted to special occasions _____ hobby or special
    interest _____ other _____
Does design make adequate use of all space available _____

CONSUMER ACCEPTANCE

Does package make a pleasing consumer impression:
    from a distance _____ from a closer view _____
    on shelf _____ on counter _____
    in window _____ as a gift _____

Is the package newsy _____ exciting _____ beautiful _____
    friendly _____ what should it be _____
Does it carry a self-selling story _____
Is remembrance value high _____
Is package a self-sufficient advertising unit _____
Is visibility desirable _____ opacity _____ both _____
What type of coding will be required _____
Has all package copy been prepared _____
Are legibility and emphasis satisfactory _____
Has package been checked for correctness and clarity _____
Have copyright and patentable features been checked for protection
    _____ risk of infringement _____
Will container lend itself to quality control _____ good standardiza-
    tion practice _____ adaptability to changes in size _____
    changes in surface design _____
Does container have "personality" _____
Is it promotable _____
Will frequent changes be needed _____ if so, how accommodated
_____

What steps must be taken to ascertain dealer attitudes _____
_____

Package pretesting—how and by whom _____
_____

STEP 6: Production and Handling Considerations

PACKAGING LINE

Will the package be filled on an existing line _____ new line _____
What line speeds are proposed _____ approximate annual output _____
Will output be continuous _____ intermittent _____ cyclical ___
Equipment required:
    filling machine _____ closing machine _____
    labeling machine _____ other _____
What machine modification will be needed _____
What new equipment _____
Will packaging be manual _____ semi-automatic _____ auto-
    matic _____ special _____
Will packaging require:
    temperature control _____
    humidity control _____
    special power facilities _____
    preconditioning of package materials _____
    air lines _____
    water lines _____
    static control _____
    other special conditions to provide for safety and/or performance __
_____

Can services of a contract packager be used advantageously _____
If existing equipment is to be used, will package form, fill, weigh, and close
    satisfactorily _____
Will change in package permit use of present equipment _____
If new equipment is needed, have specifications, sources, and delivery
    dates been arranged _____
What is the anticipated production schedule _____
Does this package lend itself to standardization _____
What will be involved in adapting package to changes in volume _____

How many operators will be required per shift _____
What skills will be needed _____
Will package impose unusual difficulties of:
    breakage _____ inspection _____ control _____
What occupational hazards may be involved _____

DESIGN AND STRUCTURE

Is container of size and shape to move through packaging line at right
    speed _____
Is closure suited to efficient line operations _____
Are openings adapted to filling devices _____
Are there suitable label spaces or surfaces _____
Will label application present unusual problems _____
Is design engineered for greatest shock resistance in machine handling

_____
Does design permit:
    easy storage _____ handling _____
    selection _____ stacking _____

PREPRODUCTION FACTORS

Does fabrication involve standard, usual methods and equipment

_____
Can packages be shipped and stored readily before delivery to production
    line _____
Are sources of service and supply conveniently near _____
What alternate sources are available _____
Are materials and containers properly packaged for automatic feed to the
    line _____
What problems exist in regard to:
    preconditioning _____
    quality control _____
    inventory control _____

PACKAGING AND SHIPPING

Can components of the packaging material be conveniently assembled

_____

Is package of proper weight in relation to bulk container _____
Can package be shipped in supplier's (income) container _____
Can package be shipped in a display or second-use container _____
Can an accepted method be used for packing product for shipment _____
Can package be adapted for group or bulk packaging _____ type
  _____ pallets _____ sizes _____
Have packages been cleared in relation to over-all plan of materials
  handling in your plant _____ in plant of principal customers
  _____

Are there any known developments in regard to materials or equipment
  that might soon make obsolete the proposed package or methods of
  filling and handling _____

STEP 7: Auditing the Package

Does package use minimum material _____
Does it comply with standardization practices _____
What is the ratio of container cost to product cost and price _____
Is ratio in balance for market _____ for class of product _____
Does price paid for materials assure:
  minimum defects _____ normal shelf-life plus margin of
    safety _____
In weight, size, structure, will package be an economical shipper _____

Have all sources of supply been checked and listed _____
Will prices fluctuate _____ if so, what special provisions will help
  offset this _____
What regulatory bodies—local, state, federal—have jurisdiction _____
  _____

Is compliance met for:
  contents _____   identity _____
  weight or measure _____   safety _____
  labeling _____   nondeception _____
  F&DA approval _____   other _____
What usable records are provided for:
  specifications _____   copyright or other legal aspects _____
  color identity _____   special fabrication _____
  instructions _____   package research _____
  costs _____   sources of supply _____
  other _____

FINAL EVALUATION

Have all vital areas in Steps 1 through 6 been considered _____
Have all conflicts in respect to package size, appearance, etc., been
  resolved _____

Has a final audit of the package (per cent of maximum or ideal) been made to rate its performance for:

protection _____   retailer convenience _____
productibility _____   consumer acceptance _____
distributability _____   nondeception _____
promotability _____   over-all rating _____
retailability (display, self-selling, etc.) _____
safety (elimination of known hazards) _____

COMPETITION

Compared with competition:

materials and construction are similar _____ different _____
colors are similar _____ different _____
sizes are smaller _____ same _____ larger _____
over-all appearance is superior _____ equal _____ inferior
_____

Is single unit attractive _____
What is mass effect _____
What is probable effect when displayed with competitive packages _____

10

Fred Muller, Jr.

A Logistical View of Containerization

"Containerization" (unitization) as the medium by which the various modes of transportation can be coordinated is a dynamic subject of nationwide interest to shippers, carriers, manufacturers, governmental bodies, financial institutions, and the general public.

A container may be defined as "a carrying unit in or on which goods may be loaded for a shipment, but which is neither a transportation vehicle nor an essential means for packing goods for shipment." A container is, in this context, a means by which goods can be transferred and through which coordinated, integrated shipments can be made using any or all transportation media: rail, highway, marine, or air.

The subject of containerization is confusing. And it has been further confused through the introduction of broad definitions as to use and application, optimistic appraisals of cost reduction potential, minimization of the problems associated with implementation of the use of containers on a large-scale nationwide basis, etc. One thing is certain—the use of containers and the diversity of their application are growing rapidly (see Figures 10.1[A–D]).

HISTORICAL BACKGROUND

The containerization story is not new, however. There are many recorded attempts to arrive at an optimum use of containerized freight handling dating back to the early 1900's and even before. Prolific and comprehensive systems have since been devised by the Pennsylvania Railroad, and many others. A profusion of highly sophisticated container systems is already in use in other countries, such as *Von Haus zu Haus* (from door-to-door) by the

FIGURE 10.1 (A)

Phase 1 of Unit-Haul 20 operation shows side loader drawing container from C-85 car toward chassis at right.

FIGURE 10.1 (B)

Close-up of phase 1 highlights alignment required of front and rear bolsters on car, side loader and chassis.

FIGURE 10.1 (C)

Phase 2 portrays container moving from side loader to chassis. Side loader can face in either direction for move.

FIGURE 10.1 (D)

Last phase shows container set firmly on chassis as driver inserts locking pins at four corners for safety.

German Federal Railway, and comparable systems in France, Sweden, and England.

The failure of earlier domestic United States container ventures has never been fully or clearly explained; several knowledgeable groups have advanced the opinion that nonacceptance on a large scale was directly attributable to lack of uniformity, inability to interchange between carriers and modes, and unfavorable tariff and rate structures.

WHY CONTAINERIZATION?

There appears to be a number of both unrelated and interrelated reasons for the rapidly growing interest and activity related to containers:

1. Many groups are impressed by the extent to which containerization can produce useful new services or increase the existing efficiency of the transportation function.

    Coordinated transportation could be of tremendous impact to the military as well as to the general shipping public through improvement of over-all efficiency and attendant economies in transportation, and by creating flexibility in operations, and eliminating redundant transportation functions.

    Applicable examples of a growing trend include (a) joint service by railroads and highway carriers in trailer-on-flat-car operations, where the flexibility of the trucking operation (from the standpoint of collection, pickup, and delivery of freight) is coupled with the low-cost, dependable, long-line haul capabilities of the railroads, and (b) the use of the marine operators' inherently low-cost water routes, through interchange of containers from rail or highway carriers.

    Containerization has already achieved a certain degree of acceptance and undergone (in several instances) appreciable expansion within captive and prototype operations: New York Central Railroad's "Flexi-Van" service; Matson Navigation Company's marine–highway–rail container service between Hawaii and West Coast ports as well as to inland points; States Marine, Pan Atlantic, Isthmian, Seatrain, Grace Line; and the introduction by REA Express of a multitude of container services.

    The military services, too, have shown much enthusiasm for containerization and coordinated transport because of their concern about the availability of a reservoir of flexible transportation capability in the event of national emergency. The military Conex system is probably the largest single-agency use of containers, with some 80,000 to 90,000 units being used throughout the world. Development of roll-on–roll-off concepts represents another approach to this idea.

Further, the container principle has, to a degree, encouraged certain carrier groups to diversify their operations to include other transport functions besides those they have been concerned with in the past.

Groups such as those previously mentioned as well as some major industrial corporations, notably in the chemical field, have invested large sums of capital in container equipment and programs, and there is every indication that much larger sums of capital are soon to be committed to this concept.

Certain of the carrier groups facing growing competitive problems have found that operating improvements of major magnitude can be realized by the unitization of cargo through containerization. This is particularly true of the marine carriers engaged in off-shore trade. The lower costs of transporting cargo enjoyed by many foreign-flag ships have placed the United States-flag ocean carriers at a competitive disadvantage; but this disadvantage has been greatly reduced by the economies permitted through use of containerized cargo.

2. The basic advantage of cargo unitization is in the reduction of labor requirements by the substitution of capital equipment. This advantage is, of course, also available to foreign-flag steamship lines. However, the factor which favors the United States ship operator vis-à-vis his foreign competition in the transition to containers is the availability of capital at lower interest rates than those prevailing in most foreign nations. This should permit the United States flagships to improve their competitive position vis-à-vis their foreign-flag competitors, who will probably be unable to complete the transition to unitization as rapidly. However, this United States advantage seems unlikely to be more than temporary. In perhaps five to ten years, the major foreign competitors can probably attain the same balance of capital investment costs to labor costs, as interest rates in overseas industrial areas approach equality with those in the United States.

3. Containerization makes possible coordinated carriage because the unit permits efficiencies in transport by rail, highway, air, and marine carriers without imposing major penalties on any of them (see Figures 10.2 and 10.3[A–D]).

4. The "turn-around" time for a ship can be materially decreased through use of unitized loads. This increases the profitability of the vessel

FIGURE 10.2

because it can then make several extra voyages per year. Where reductions in ship turn-around are great enough and sailing schedules are sufficiently flexible, it may be possible, alternatively, to reduce the number of ships in the fleet while maintaining the same frequency of service and the same annual cargo capability.

5.   Further proven advantages of unitized-container loading are (a) appreciable reduction of loss and damage claims, which now cost the transportation system as a whole hundreds of millions of dollars per year; (b) elimination of a great deal of paper work related to shipment; (c) expedited door-to-door pickup and delivery service; (d) elimination of multiple handling of cargo; (e) economies by consolidation of small loads into the unit load; (f) reduction of expensive railroad switching service. There are many other advantages that become more obvious as containerization becomes more diversified.

Containers can take many forms and characters in addition to those designed for handling dry cargo. For instance, containers of modular size are being used or developed for handling liquid products such as liquid latex, acids, petroleum products, edible oils, tetraethyl lead, liquefied gases, chemicals, etc. Containers are also being used to transport bulk food products such as malt from supplier to user, who may be located in an area without rail connection. Food products requiring refrigeration—for example,

FIGURE 10.3 (A)

Regardless of weather, one man can operate side loader from cab controls; novice can learn in hours.

FIGURE 10.3 (B)

Side loader's four hydraulic jacks can lift entire unit off ground to permit insertion of legs into built-in pockets.

FIGURE 10.3 (C)

Successive hook stations under both ends of container are engaged by side loader bails during transfer action.

FIGURE 10.3 (D)

Manually operated container locks built into C-85 car secure each container during line-haul rail transit.

processed meat—are being transported in specialized container units handled by multitransportation modes.

Interested members of transportation and industrial enterprises have banded together to appraise the implications of containerization and the problem areas to be considered, as well as to develop standards for compatibility of containers with the carrying or transporting media.

WHY RESEARCH NOW?

The basic problem in its application is to determine the optimum place for containerization in the transportation complex. The negative as well as the positive implications of container use and container systems must be intensively explored. Thus, there are still many unanswered questions about the ultimate position which containerization will occupy in the over-all transportation complex. Certain hardware aspects are currently being studied, and fairly acceptable solutions to operational problems of compatibility and interchangeability between carrier modes should be forthcoming soon.

However, it is not so much in the area of the hardware problems that study and research projects are needed as it is in the psychological, sociological, industrial, managerial, labor, and regulatory implications. If direction and definition are not provided in the near future, containerization may fail again; or else grow haphazardly in a way that will minimize its economic benefits. Continued accelerated use of containers without standardization in the foreseeable future bring with it acceptance of a philosophy which might be detrimental rather than beneficial to the over-all transportation function, and thus contribute to ultimate discredit of an otherwise valuable aid. This would be true, for example, if containers were to become primarily components of captive systems. Fortunately, there are already signs of an awareness on the part of various groups that focus and definition are needed to determine the validity, desirability, and methodology of the use of containers as the coordinating medium for transportation.

The full and complete understanding of the container, its potentials, and its limitations and applications needs to be developed at the earliest opportunity so that the governmental regulatory bodies will have valid data and the full understanding needed for their decisions. Arbitrary regulatory confusion about containers might be forestalled by adequate research now.

Containerization also has international implications, some of them needing immediate understanding. Among the most important issues is that of universal standardized dimensions so that containers may move freely in international trade.

STANDARDIZATION

In order to achieve the goals of complete integration and coordination of transportation by use of container-type systems, standardization and compatibility of the various pieces of equipment involved is mandatory. Standardization of the exterior size and shape is necessary and must provide for compatibility in the methods of handling, tie-down, and transfer of containers from one transportation system to another.

A statement on standardization from the 1933 Eastman Report issued by the Interstate Commerce Commission is apropos today:

> We take this occasion to point out to the carriers the absolute necessity for uniformity in container equipment and the urgent desirability of obtaining such uniformity before the present lack of it spreads to serious proportions and threatens to neutralize to a considerable extent the economic benefits inherent in the container.

Several groups are now earnestly at work trying to reach agreements about standardizing physical dimension, design characteristics, methods of handling, methods of tie-down, and over-all problems of physically integrating containers into the various systems and modes of transportation for optimum interchange. The end purpose is to make available to the shipper, the transportation agencies, the military, and the general public the economies of this efficient type of distribution.

One of the largest and most active of these standardization groups has been the American Standards Association, MH-5, "Committee for Standardization of Freight Containers for Optimum Interchange with All Transportation Media." Other groups that have conducted standardization studies and made the results of their committee action available to the ASA committee include the Maritime Administration and the National Defense Transportation Association Committee for Standardization of Containers.

The degree to which standardization should be applied to containers has still to be determined. Concern has been expressed by many groups, carriers, and shippers regarding the scope of standardization—in particular, the danger of overstandardization, which possibily could, in time, stifle or minimize the benefits of technological advances.

In certain areas of container design and usage, standards are of negligible value. Some of these are in the actual design characteristics beyond dimensional standards, use of materials, and handling equipment; and the use of special attachments for other than basic purposes.

RESEARCH ON CONTAINERIZATION

The premise that "containerization," "coordinated transportation," etc., are panaceas for the ills of the transportation function has been advanced in many instances through promotional types of presentation, unsupported by factual data or research. Operating and economic advantages, beyond the obvious gains, have been claimed to accompany the large-scale acceptance of containerization; and these claims have served as inducements to accelerate the use of containers in the transportation complex.

Study is necessary to close certain gaps in knowledge about containerization principles presently being discussed, for example:

1. Should containerization be thought of as the "link," the coordinating medium, between methods of transport, or should the premise be expanded beyond the "link" to occupy a greater over-all position in the transportation function? The development of the optimum role or justification for containerization should be based on factual research data.

2. The origins and destinations of freight movements "across the face of North America" is another area about which little is known. Information about the flow of key commodities is needed in order to determine the most efficient use of transportation capability by increasing load factor and equipment utilization.

3. Ownership of the containers is an issue of great concern to both shippers and carriers. The huge sums necessary to provide the needed quantities of containers, related handling equipment, and terminal facilities are a strong deterrent to the growth or acceptance of containerization. The formation and organization of a national container pool through which a single agency, on some equitable basis, could make available the equipment and facilities necessary to implement the program have been suggested by many groups. Leasing plans have received some considerations and may offer a solution. Interchange agreements among multiple owners with railroad freight cars is yet another alternative. Other related questions pertain to the need for logistical control of containers, maintenance of regional or area pool balance, central accounting for service charges, and maintenance and repair responsibilities.

4. The subject of rates suggests an almost unlimited number of research projects, some of which may be subject to rationalization. One in particular which is causing much controversy is related to the classifica-

tion versus all-commodity rate structure. Certain groups fear that adoption of the all-commodity rate will doom the historical commodity classification rate structure. The complete story of containerization must be developed, so that the affected groups can see the premise in its true light and eliminate some of the arbitrary regulatory confusion.

5. The psychological and sociological implications of large-scale adoption of containerization on the labor force and labor practices should be investigated to determine the positive and negative effects on the value of containers as well as to reconcile equitably conflicting owner, management, and labor requirements.

6. The impacts of containerization on the various management functions of transportation users would be worth investigating, including its effect on (a) traffic management, (b) location of plants, (c) competitive implications, (d) effect on private carriage, (e) implications as to financing of container-related equipment, and (f) impact on production plant layout, for example, the use of containers for in-plant materials handling and in-process inventory storage.

7. The impact of containerization on internal management of transportation enterprises is another area for business administration-oriented research, including its impact on (a) organizational structure for optimum effectivensss, (b) rate-setting implications, (c) marketing implications, (d) management of coordination between separate companies operating different modes of transport, (e) accounting and control consideration, (f) financing of containers and container-handling equipment, (g) labor relations implications, and (h) disposal of existing physical plants made obsolete by containerization.

8. Containerization will probably have an impact on urban planning and growth. Areas to be studied include (a) contribution of containerization to industrial diversification within a community, (b) effect on railroad lines and terminal location, (c) extent of obsolescence created in the existing railroad plant, (d) effect on highway traffic volumes and flow characteristics, (e) effect on location of industrial areas, and (f) effect on terminal planning, construction, and location.

9. The impact of containerization on architectural layout and design of buildings and other structures—including retail stores, warehouses, factories, wholesale plants, docks, shipping and receiving facilities, etc.—needs investigation.

Part

Three

LOGISTICS: THE COMPOSITE PICTURE

The entire concept of logistics revolves around the premise that all physical distribution functions are just integrated parts of a logistical system. As such, the tradeoff possibilities of functional costing must simultaneously be considered as part of the total cost approach for the firm as a whole. (A typical illustration: A rise in transport cost may yield substantially lower costs in warehousing, inventory holdings, and order processing, therefore resulting in a lower total cost.)

Chapter 11 enlarges on this idea by means of a "Profit Improvement Approach to Marketing Logistics." This discussion is followed by an analysis of the role of communications in logistics, which not only helps organize the order-processing cycle, but also serves as the connective tissue between the various segments of logistics previously discussed.

Chapter 13 relates systems analysis to logistical (and therefore, marketing) planning.

11

Marvin Flaks

Profit Improvement Approach to Marketing Logistics

The preceding chapters discuss the progress of distribution technology and of the specific techniques used to organize and manage the distribution function. Each of the techniques can be useful in improving distribution efficiency in one or more distribution functions. Most promising, however, is a systems approach, which recognizes that virtually all segments of the business are affected by distribution decisions, and therefore seeks to base decisions on the impact on total profit. Such an approach is presented in this chapter.

Steps toward development of a profit improvement approach can be seen in recent changes in distribution organization. In the older form of organization, different activities were regarded as distinct segments, each requiring the abilities of a specialist: Warehouse, traffic, and customer-service activities were located at different points in the organization table. But recently it has been recognized that, to achieve maximum effectiveness in distribution, quite often these activities should be organized as a single integrated function. This acknowledges that the relations between specific distribution activities are more intimate than we used to realize.

Yet integrating all of the distribution activities under one responsibility does not in itself solve the problems involved in distribution decision-making. However, it does put the company in a position to profit from a well-run distribution operation.

Some of the problems that result from failure to recognize the relationships between specific distribution activities can be seen in the following examples.

1. A company with a wide range of products and a number of plants across the country had developed an advanced approach to warehouse

management. As a result, it cut warehouse costs significantly. However, when its distribution operations were examined, it was found that in order to achieve an over-all improvement in profits it was necessary to improve the level of customer service, which required an increase in the money spent for warehousing.

2. A company with markets in Europe had built a plant on the continent to manufacture products for distribution there in order to reduce trans-Atlantic transportation costs and to eliminate tariff problems. Upon investigation it was found that the European plant was too small to match the efficiency of competing plants there. The company was advised to manufacture its product in the United States, where the scale of production was sufficiently large to more than offset the transportation and tariff charges.

3. A West Coast drug distributor, in an effort to cut distribution costs, developed a very sophisticated electronically controlled warehouse facility in which a computer automatically analyzed and controlled the filling of orders. Studies had shown that, when operating at what was considered a reasonable capacity, this warehouse would be one of the lowest-cost warehouses in the industry. Within a few months after opening the warehouse, the company found that although it could process orders very rapidly and at very low cost, it had to serve the outlying suburbs of the city from this central warehouse, which involved time delays. This made it impossible to match the service rendered by competitors who had located subsidiary warehouses in these suburbs, from which they were able to render better customer service.

What do these actual corporate experiences illustrate? They show that, if maximum profits are to result, consideration cannot be confined to only one or two distribution activities. All of the pertinent distribution activities must be considered, as well as production and marketing alternatives. The latter may turn out to be the key factors. In addition, customer service is a critical variable in many distribution analyses; customer service has to be quantified in order to determine the optimum balance between the *cost* of service and the *value* of service.

The above relationships led to the development of the *profit improvement approach* to analysis and solution of distribution problems. This approach insists that distribution decisions be made in the light of their impact on total profitability.

The approach can be simply stated: (1) identify the cost and service elements and trace their relationships; (2) develop the information needed to measure the impact of each alternative distribution decision on profitability; and (3) determine which distribution decision will result in maximum profit.

This is the approach discussed in the remainder of this chapter.

COST ELEMENTS

In every business most costs are affected by distribution. The same costs are present in most distribution problems, although the relative importance of each will vary from one company to another.

The analysis of distribution problems is complicated by the interdependence of most cost elements; that is, a change in one element is likely to produce a change in all the others, thus resulting in both positive and negative trade offs. Let us examine the major cost elements and some of the ways in which they interact.

Production or Supply Alternatives

Figure 11.1 shows, for a typical case, the cost significance of the production alternatives for a manufacturer who operates three plants, producing the

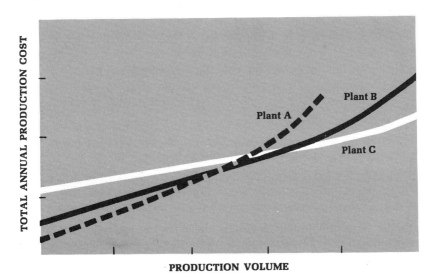

FIGURE 11.1

Interdependence of distribution cost elements: production or supply alternatives

same products. For a given product, fixed cost varies among plants and production cost varies with the volume of each plant. Each plant has a different fixed cost and a different unit cost as volume is increased. Plant A is a small plant, not highly mechanized, and thus has a relatively low fixed cost. However, for the same reason, this plant has a high variable cost. Plant C, on the other hand, is a large automated plant with a high fixed cost but a much lower variable cost and, consequently, a lower unit cost as volume is increased. Plant B illustrates the in-between situation.

Other factors which produce different cost curves for local plants include labor rates; taxes; landed cost of raw materials; and utilities.

Figure 11.1 makes it clear that the decision regarding "which plant should service which customers" must give weight not only to transportation and warehousing costs, but also to *total production costs*, because it will vary with the volume allocated to each plant.

Warehousing

Size is an important factor affecting the cost of warehousing. Each warehouse has certain fixed expenses. Thus, for a given volume of business, a smaller number of large warehouses will involve a lower total of fixed expenses. This is illustrated in Figure 11.2 by the curve marked "fixed and semi-variable costs."

In larger warehouses, automatic handling devices can be justified by the resulting reduction in operating costs. Thus, cost reductions have been quite significant in highly automated warehouses. For example, devices are now available that make possible the following functions:

Incoming merchandise can be directed automatically by a receiver to an assigned storage area.

Customer orders can be converted to punched cards or magnetic tape to activate a mechanism for automatic order picking.

Outbound customer orders can be automatically sorted and routed to preselected truck or freight car loading docks.

The effect of mechanization is demonstrated by the "direct costs" curve in Figure 11.2. Direct costs, by definition, are those which vary directly with the quantity of merchandise handled. However, on a unit basis, these direct costs are less in a large (high-volume) warehouse than in a small (low-volume) one, since additional automatic, laborsaving devices can be justified in the larger warehouse.

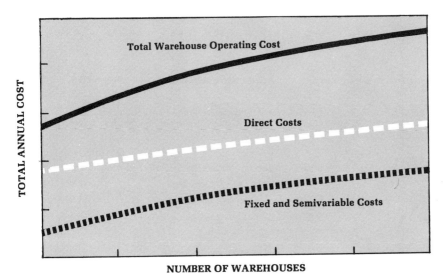

FIGURE 11.2

Interdependence of distribution cost elements: warehousing

Transportation

Transportation cost, a major expense in most distribution systems, is related directly to the number and location of warehouses, as well as to the mode of transportation. For the manufacturer whose products are shipped via field warehouses, additional warehouses will generally reduce the distance goods must travel between factories and customers. In general, cost is lowered as distance is reduced.

However, as the number of warehouses increases, the total business is divided among them, and the volume handled by each decreases. Hence, the manufacturer finds that where he could previously ship carload or truckload lots from his factories to a small number of warehouses, he is no longer able to do this. Consequently, his transportation cost increases. Figure 11.3 illustrates this, as shown by the curve labeled "transportation cost: factories to warehouses." In many cases, as the number of warehouses increases, the inbound transportation cost decreases to a minimum, then begins to increase as the number of carload movements decrease.

As shown in Figure 11.3, the transportation cost outbound from warehouses decreases continuously as warehouses are added. Theoretically, this cost is minimized when every city has its own warehouse.

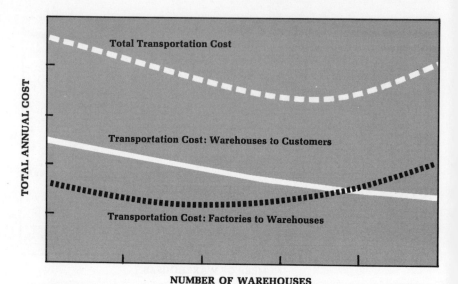

FIGURE 11.3

Interdependence of distribution cost elements: transportation

The chain retailer faces much the same dilemma as the manufacturer. However, the retailer generally has more flexibility than the manufacturer. Thus, when the retailer establishes a new warehouse in an area of retail store concentration, some new suppliers may be located in the vicinity of that warehouse, thereby reducing the distance the merchandise must move and, consequently, the cost of transportation.

Service level is another factor. For example, the chain retailer may feel that he requires daily shipments from his warehouse to his stores. Yet this cuts down the amount of merchandise moved in each shipment; and, to the extent that bulk shipments are reduced, transportation costs are increased.

Also requiring analysis are the modes of transportation used. It is usually true that the most rapid service is also the most expensive. However, the cost relationship also varies as a function of the size of shipment, the distance moved, and the specific products involved.

Carrying Inventory

Carrying inventory is a major expense item. It can range from 10 per cent to 30 per cent of the cost of goods. The components of this cost are insurance, taxes, space costs (including heat, watchmen, and maintenance), spoilage, pilferage, and interest on investments.

As the number of warehouses increases, the turnover in each decreases. Thus, for a constant sales level, average inventory level increases with the number of warehouses, as shown in Figure 11.4.   This is true for the following two reasons:

1. As the number of customers served by each warehouse decreases, the beneficial "balancing" effect is reduced.   To illustrate, a warehouse serving a single customer must be prepared to meet that customer's peak demands.   However, if the warehouse serves two customers, it is unlikely that the peak demand of each for the same product would coincide. Hence, the warehouse need only be prepared for a peak demand somewhat lower than the sum of the peak demands of the customers.

2. The average warehouse inventory level for each stock-keeping unit can be reduced as the volume through a given warehouse decreases.   A practical limit is reached when the reorder quantity is reduced to the minimum factory pack or to a minimum economic order quantity. Thus, for some stock-keeping units, subsequent reductions in volume will *not* be accompanied by reductions in inventory.

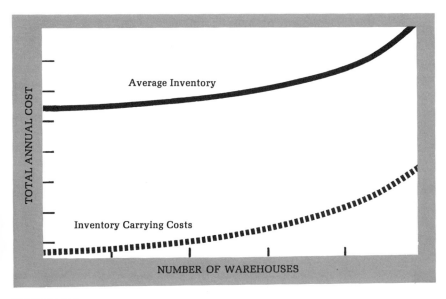

FIGURE 11.4

Interdependence of distribution cost elements: carrying inventory

The retail chain operator is also concerned with the stock levels which he must maintain. As the number of warehouses increases, transit time from warehouses to stores is reduced. This permits the stores to operate with lower stocks, which, in turn, produce significant benefits to be discussed later.

Inventory Obsolescence

If total system inventory is increased to provide better customer service (at a given level of sales), inventory turnover will decrease. This automatically exposes the owner to greater risks of obsolescence and inventory write-down. The relationship is shown in Figure 11.5. This is a particularly important factor for companies having frequent model changeovers, style changes, or product perishability. The greater the "pipeline fill" in the distribution system, the slower the inventory turnover. When turnover goes down, write-down costs go up.

Communications and Data Processing

The nature and degree of administrative controls frequently spell the difference between a mediocre distribution system and a highly efficient one.

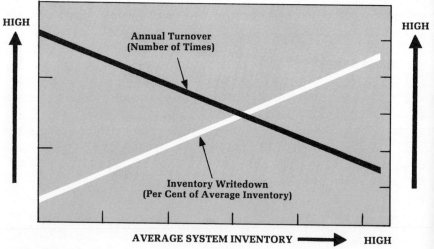

FIGURE 11.5

Interdependence of distribution cost elements: inventory obsolescence

Therefore, a comprehensive distribution study should consider the following costs related to data processing.

[1]   Receiving and Processing Orders

Many automated devices are available, and additional devices for the efficient processing of large quantities of orders are in advanced stages of development. These devices may yield economies, not only in the receipt of orders, but also in the physical handling operations. Warehouses can be planned to segregate case-lot picking from less-than-case-lot picking and to accommodate groups of items on the basis of their activity, with specialized treatment accorded each group.

Devices are also available to permit manufacturers to offer various forms of automatic replenishment to their customers. A typical example is the punched card which some manufacturers attach to each unit of merchandise shipped to a customer's sales outlets. When a unit of merchandise is sold, a punched card is returned to the manufacturer. This represents an order to replace the particular item, enabling the sales outlet to maintain preestablished stocks.

[2]   Handling Invoices

The preparation of invoices, shipping documents, and accounting inputs also lends itself to efficient electronic data processing. The costs and benefits of these operations must be considered an integral part of any distribution survey. (See Chapter 8.)

[3]   Controlling Inventory

The maintenance of appropriate inventory levels is a major consideration in operating a multiwarehouse network. An approach should be developed to assure that the desired merchandise is available when and where required, while at the same time holding inventory investment to a minimum. Recent data processing system developments permit a degree of sophistication not heretofore obtainable.

[4]   Communications

Consideration must be given to the manner in which information is transmitted. This generally includes the receipt of orders and the issuance of shipping instructions.

Normally, the faster the mode of communications, the more expensive the system will be. On the other hand, more rapid communications can shorten the replenishment cycle and, consequently, reduce required inventory levels as well as give better service.

CUSTOMER SERVICE FACTORS

In most distribution problems, the cost elements can be expressed in quantitative terms by use of straightforward industrial engineering techniques. However, the related service factors are not handled as readily. Yet they are every bit as important, since a given combination of cost factors produces a given service level, and service improvements normally will increase the sum of the cost factors. The value of service must be quantified so that the optimum balance between cost elements and service factors can be determined.

The usual measures of service are:

Time required to fill orders

Variability in time required to fill customer orders

Percentage of customer orders that can be filled (which determines back orders and cancellations).

The relationship between these service factors and cost elements is discussed below.

Time Required to Fill Customer Orders

A key measure of customer service is the elapsed time between the creation of a demand by a customer and delivery of the goods ordered. As a minimum, customers given an otherwise equal choice will order goods from the supplier offering quicker delivery.

The supplier has several courses open in order to reduce filling time. He can do any or all of the following:

Reduce the cycle time required (through use, say, of wire communications to receive orders faster or computers to process orders faster)

Increase his use of field warehouses

Use premium (high-speed) modes of transportation.

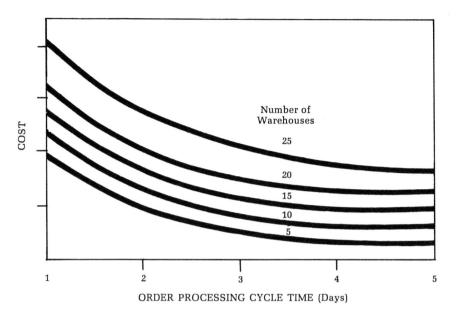

FIGURE 11.6

Typical relationship among number of warehouses, order-filling time, and operating cost

A typical relationship among number of warehouses, order-filling time, and operating cost is shown in Figure 11.6.

Variability in Time Required to Fill Customer Orders

Frequently, the *variations* in order-filling time are as important as the *absolute* order-filling time. For example, if the customer knows that a supplier requires two weeks to fill an order, he can plan his own inventory levels on a two-week lead time. On the other hand, if replenishment time *averages* one week, but frequently is three weeks, the customer usually is required to assume a lead time of *three* weeks and carry more inventory as a consequence. Therefore, we again find that customers, given an otherwise equal choice, will order goods from the supplier offering more dependable delivery.

The major factors affecting consistency of order-filling time are related to transportation. The first factor involves the delivery time itself. And this is the most frequent reason given by shippers for use of private carriage.

When the shipper controls the transportation facilities, he frequently is able to offer his customers more dependable service.

The other transportation-related factor involves policy decisions regarding the time period during which shipments will be accumulated in order to utilize bulk shipment rates (in carloads, truckloads, etc.).

Percentage of Customer Orders
Which Can Be Filled

Every time a customer's order cannot be filled, the supplier risks loss of a sale and, perhaps, loss of a customer. The out-of-stock item may be back-ordered, involving some added administrative expense; the customer may cancel his order, resulting in a lost sale and the related profit; or, the customer may satisfy his need by going to another supplier—and may never come back!

The percentage of customer orders which can be filled is related to the amount of merchandise the supplier carries in inventory (specifically, the size of his safety stock). However, increased safety stock, while it reduces stockouts, also increases inventory carrying costs.

CASE EXAMPLES

The previous sections described the usual cost and service factors. Maximum profits are obtained when all of the pertinent factors are treated in a manner which recognizes all of the interactions. Many distribution problems are sufficiently complex to require a computer to accomplish this. Basically, the required steps are (1) develop a model which describes the real situation and (2) manipulate the model to find that combination of elements which will produce maximum profits.

Described below are two studies which illustrate this approach and the application of the profit improvement concept. The first deals with a manufacturer and the second with a retail chain operator.

MANUFACTURING CASE

This illustration deals with a manufacturing company having a $45 million sales volume. This company ships from five manufacturing plants to over

3,000 customers located in every state. Distribution is primarily direct from plant warehouses to customers, via both rail and truck transportation. At the start of the study, this company was losing about $200,000 per year (pretax).

The principal question asked by management was: Can profits be increased by reallocating volume among the five plants and/or by altering the number or location of plants?

Answers to these questions were developed in these steps:

First, it was determined where customers are located and how they are served.

Next it was determined what costs are involved in the distribution system.

Next the benefits of improved service were quantified.

Finally, the profit improvement approach was applied to develop a unique solution for this company which maximizes profit, giving regard to all of the factors involved.

[1]   Where Customers Are Located and How They Are Served

Location of plants and customers. Figure 11.7 summarizes the geography of the company's distribution situation. The dots show the locations of the five manufacturing plants, the numbers show the percentage of total sales made in each sales area.

Customers' transportation preference. Figure 11.8 shows the rail versus truck delivery preference of customers in each area. The upper number is the percentage of total area sales shipped by rail, and the lower number is the truck percentage. A wide range of customer transportation preference is seen on this map. For example, the San Francisco area is 100 per cent truck movement while shipments to Florida are 100 per cent rail. As would be expected, rail shipments increase with distance of customers from the plants.

[2]   Costs Involved in the Distribution System

On the left in Figure 11.9 are shown the cost factors that were discussed earlier. On the right are shown the company accounts which contain these elements.

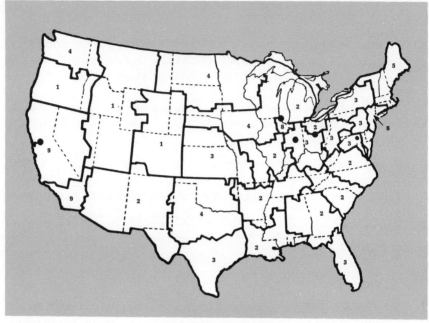

VOLUME OF SALES IN PER CENT

FIGURE 11.7

Manufacturing illustration: location of plants and customers

The production or supply element is expressed here as materials, direct labor, and overhead costs in the five plants and, in total, amount to $32.3 million. These costs vary considerably from plant to plant and with volume at each plant. Therefore, the decisions as to which plant serves each customer will have significant effect on over-all total production costs, since individual plant volumes will be affected.

Warehouse operating, inventory-carrying, and inventory obsolescence costs are grouped in the example under the single heading of warehousing costs and amount to $2.0 million. These costs vary from warehouse to warehouse, and with volume handled at each location—and thus are affected by distribution patterns.

The transportation element is made up of rail and truck freight costs outbound from plants to customers and amounts to $3.3 million. Freight rates, of course, vary considerably among plants for serving any given customer.

Communications and data processing amount to $0.5 million.

All other elements amount to $7.1 million. These elements were unaffected by changes in the distribution system.

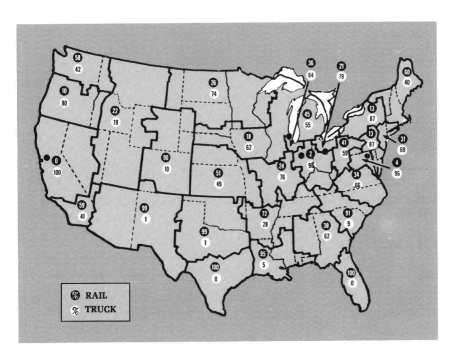

FIGURE 11.8

Manufacturing illustration: customers' transportation preference

Figure 11.10 shows total production and warehousing cost curves for all five plants in this system. Three relationships can be noted:

First, because fixed costs vary among plants, the curves begin at different levels.

Second, as volume increases, the rate of cost increase at each plant is different, because of the difference in costs of materials, labor, overhead, and warehousing.

Finally, because of different materials sources and local warehousing capacities, the volume at which total costs begin to increase more steeply varies at each of the plants.

Thus, total costs differ considerably among plants, and the relationships change at different volume levels.

The last major cost element, outbound transportation, is shown in Table 11.1, which lists the rail and truck rates from each plant to each sales area.

Distribution Elements	Costs as Treated in Company Accounts	
		Millions of Dollars
Production or Supply Alternatives	Materials	$25.8
	Direct Labor	2.0
	Overhead	4.5
Warehouse Operating Cost Inventory Carrying Cost Inventory Obsolescence	Warehousing	2.0
Transportation	Freight	3.3
Communications and Data Processing	Data Processing	0.5
	Total Costs Affected in this Problem	$38.1
All Other	....	$ 7.1
	Total Costs	$45.2

FIGURE 11.9

Manufacturing illustration: identification of cost elements

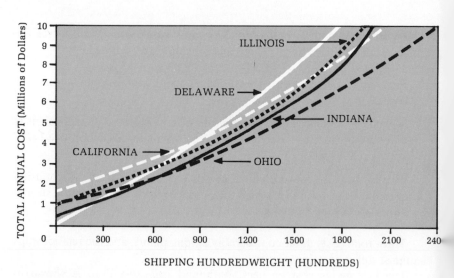

FIGURE 11.10

Manufacturing illustration: total plant and warehousing cost

[3] Value of Service

Early during the study, an examination was made of the level of service offered by the company, and its competitors, in various parts of the country. Comparative data were gathered on:

The time required to fill customers' orders (from the time an order is written until the ordered goods are received by the customer).

The variability in order-filling time.

The portion of ordered items which are shipped at once, rather than backordered or canceled.

TABLE 11.1

Manufacturing Illustration: Outbound Transportation Cost Matrix (Dollars per Hundredweight)

District	Illinois	Indiana	Ohio	Delaware	California
Baltimore	R .83 T 1.43	R .72 T 1.30	R .65 T 1.18	R .26 T .32	R 1.94 T ___
Washington	R .83 T 1.40	R .73 T 1.27	R .70 T 1.20	R .31 T .41	R 1.94 T ___
Hagerstown	R .78 T 1.31	R .68 T 1.18	R .59 T 1.05	R .35 T .52	R 1.94 T ___
Boston	R .95 T 1.62	R .93 T 1.58	R .85 T 1.33	R .50 T .73	R 1.94 T ___
Hartford	R .93 T 1.58	R .88 T 1.51	R .80 T 1.24	R .44 T .94	R 1.94 T ___
Butte	R 1.67 T 3.60	R 1.74 T 3.81	R 1.74 T 3.92	R 1.94 T 5.22	R 1.47 T 1.63
San Francisco	R ___ T 3.67	R ___ T 4.34	R ___ T 4.34	R ___ T 5.66	R ___ T .25

R = Rail   T = Truck

Four major conclusions resulted:

Customer service was on a par with competitition (as regards order-filling time).

Improvements in order-filling time, or the variability in order-filling time, would not have a measurable effect on sales volume.

Operating costs would not be reduced by increasing the order-filling time.

Sales volume was being lost as a result of stockouts; hence, an improvement in the in-stock position *would* increase sales.

The final conclusion led to a close examination of the consequences of stockout. It was determined that:

Some customers permit the desired item to be backordered, and the only consequence is an added administrative expense.

Some customers require automatic cancellation of unavailable items. Of this group, some customers subsequently reorder the desired item, but others never do. This latter group produces a loss of the gross profit on the given item.

The above relationships were quantified to determine the cost of each stockout. Next, a relationship was developed to quantify the reduction in the number of stockouts as the average warehouse inventory level is increased. The final relationship between the cost of carrying the additional inventory and the net profit change is shown in Figure 11.11.

[4]   Solution

To develop the required solution, it was necessary to construct a mathematical model which expressed the interrelationships among the various factors. A computer program was written to permit rapid manipulation of the model. This allowed simulation of a variety of alternatives and development of optimum solutions for each of these situations. The optimum solutions are presented below in terms of the major questions answered.

Can profit be increased without facilities changes? Figure 11.12 shows the assignment of territories to each plant that will result in maximum profits, as defined earlier. This is distinctly a different pattern from that which previously resulted from an analysis of cost factors alone.

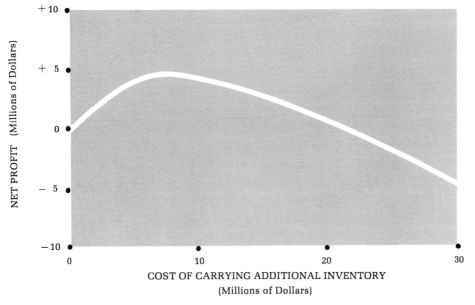

FIGURE 11.11

Manufacturing illustration: net profit attributable to increased inventory

Western territories would all be served by the California plant.

The South and Southwest would be served from Indiana, the Midwest from Illinois and Ohio, and the East from Ohio, with the exception of the high-population East Coast area, which would be served from Delaware.

This maximum profit distribution pattern required a shift in production volume—but one that could be made without moving any facilities. For example,

Volume at the Illinois plant would be decreased from 26.1 per cent of the total to 19.0 per cent.

Volume at Indiana would increase from 11.6 per cent to 17.8 per cent of total production.

As shown in Table 11.2, a pretax profit improvement of $1.7 million is achieved.

Can profits be increased further by transfers of equipment among plants? The production cost curves developed earlier reflect the then existing equipment and capacities of each plant. However, it was suspected that further

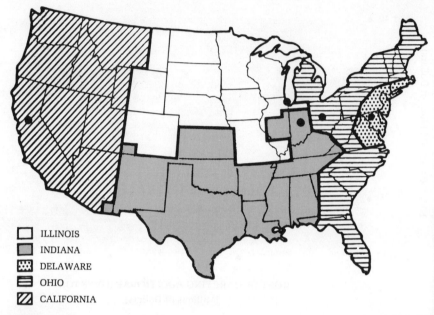

ILLINOIS
INDIANA
DELAWARE
OHIO
CALIFORNIA

FIGURE 11.12

Manufacturing illustration: maximum profit distribution pattern with current facilities

savings could be achieved by shifting equipment among plants. To test this new production cost curves were developed for several alternative equipment transfers—and the computer program was run to evaluate each of these. This showed that the equipment transfers would effect a further profit improvement of $200,000, and involve relatively minor costs for equipment transfer.

Should plants be relocated? A number of new plant locations were evaluated. They were included in various combinations with existing plants. For several combinations, it was determined that profit would be increased—but in each case the return on the capital required to build the new plant was too low to warrant the expenditure.

Should warehouse capacity be increased? The return on investment for a range of possible warehouse additions, at each plant, was determined by the computer, using input data reflecting warehousing costs for each increment of additional space. As changes in warehousing capacity were made, changes in distribution pattern and changes in total cost and profit occurred. It was found that a 45,000-square-foot addition at the Delaware plant was an attractive investment. This produced savings of $100,000 annually.

TABLE 11.2

Manufacturing Illustration: Profit Increase Without Facilities Changes

	OLD MODE OF DISTRIBUTION		NEW MODE OF DISTRIBUTION	
	Millions of Dollars	*Per Cent of Sales*	*Millions of Dollars*	*Per Cent of Sales*
Sales	45.0	100.0	45.0	100.0
Materials	25.8	57.3	25.8	57.3
Direct labor	2.0	4.4	1.4	3.2
Overhead	4.5	10.0	3.7	8.2
Warehousing	2.0	4.4	2.1	4.7
Freight	3.3	7.4	3.4	7.6
Data processing	0.5	1.1	0.5	1.1
All other	7.1	15.8	7.1	15.8
SUBTOTAL	45.2	100.4	44.0	97.9
Added net profit, from increased sales			0.5[a]	1.2
Pretax profit (or loss)	(0.2)	(0.4)	1.5[a]	3.3

[a]An added $0.5 million in net profit is indicated. This is based on increased sales which result from reduced stockouts because of the new mode of distribution. Thus, the pretax profit figure of $1.5 million includes $1.0 million in cost of sales and an added $0.5 million net profit from a $5 million increase in sales.

Summary of Benefits   The total near-term profit improvement is summarized below. Near-term benefits were defined as those that could be implemented within twelve months.

	Millions of Dollars
Profit from the change in distribution pattern without facilities changes	1.7
Profit from relatively minor shifts in production equipment	0.2
Profit from a change in warehouse capacity at the Delaware plant	0.1
TOTAL	2.0

This profit improvement changed a $200,000 annual loss to a $1.8 million annual profit (pretax).

RETAIL CASE

At the time of the study, this large retail chain had sales of over $1 billion in a wide variety of general merchandise lines. There were over 1,000 stores in the chain, located in every state. Distribution was direct to each store from 5,000 suppliers. No one store ordered from every supplier. Vendors and public warehouses provided some limited warehousing. The inventory was enormously complex: There were about 700 categories of merchandise, which embraced about 16,000 style numbers; taking into consideration size and color, there were over 100,000 stock-keeping units in the system; they represented over 200 commodity classifications for transportation analysis.

The company had plans to replace many older small stores, often in different locations, with new large stores. Significant new lines of merchandise were being added, increasing assortments and sources of supply. Space was needed within the stores to display many of the newly added merchandise lines.

A study was undertaken to design an optimum distribution network. The task was to determine *how many* warehouses, located *where*, handling *what lines*, would yield *maximum profit* improvements. The basic steps in the approach were:

Identify the variables in the problem.

Quantify the variables.

Trace the interactions of the key variables.

Determine the best solution.

Each of these steps is discussed below.

[1]   Identify the Variables

The major variables are:

Transportation cost   the cost of moving merchandise from vendors to stores, either directly or via warehouses.

Warehouse cost   the total cost of operating warehouses, including all fixed and variable elements.

Inventory-carrying cost   the cost of carrying all inventory in the system (in-transit, warehouses, and stores) includes cost of money, taxes, and insurance.

Inventory obsolescence cost   the cost of markdowns, both in stores and warehouses.

Supply alternatives   refers to deductions in the price paid for goods when vendors can make bulk shipments to the retailers' warehouses, rather than many small shipments to individual stores.

Value of space released   when store inventory is reduced, some store stockroom space can be converted into selling space; the factor refers to the profits such space will produce.

Value of reduction in out-of-stocks   reduction in the time required to replenish store stocks will result in fewer stockouts in the stores; hence fewer lost sales.

[2]   Quantify the Variables

For each variable, it was necessary to develop expressions which described how that variable changed as a function of all the other variables which affected it. The major relationships are shown in Figures 11.13–11.19.

Warehousing Costs (Figure 11.13)

The fixed cost component of warehousing rises at a decreasing rate as the number of warehouses increases.

The variable-cost component rises slowly at first (few, large warehouses), then accelerates rapidly as an increased number of smaller warehouses lose large-scale efficiency.

Total warehousing cost is essentially linear through the first portion of the curve, but as average warehouse size drops, costs accelerate.

Transportation Costs (Figure 11.14)

Inbound transportation cost, from vendors to warehouses, increases as the number of warehouses is increased, because more shipments fall short of carload or truckload size.

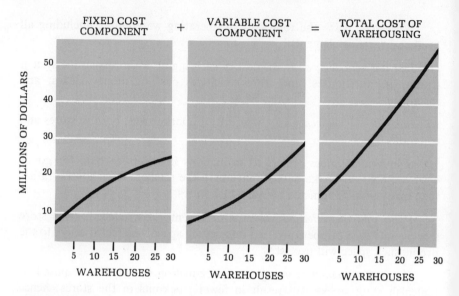

FIGURE 11.13
Retail illustration: warehousing costs

FIGURE 11.14
Retail illustration: transportation costs

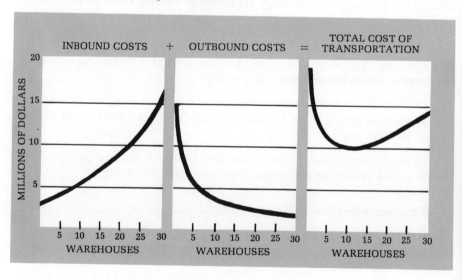

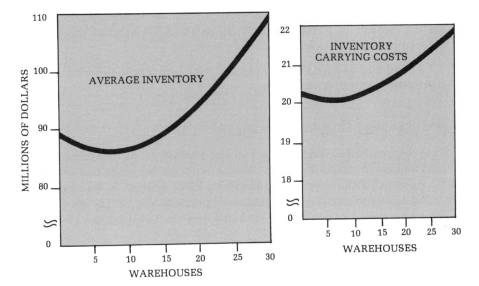

FIGURE 11.15
Retail illustration: inventory carrying costs

FIGURE 11.16
Retail illustration: correlation between inventory level and obsolescence

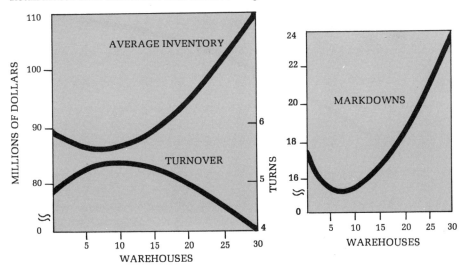

Outbound transportation cost, from warehouses to stores, falls rapidly as the number of warehouses is increased, and levels off as the number of warehouses approaches the number of stores.

Total cost of transportation reaches a minimum at some point (in this illustration, at twelve warehouses).

Inventory-Carrying Costs (Figure 11.15)

Replenishment time changes as the number of warehouses changes, and that in turn causes inventory changes. An inventory model was developed to permit determination of the inventory level required in the stores and warehouses for any given replenishment time—hence, for any given warehouse network. The inventory level was then translated into an inventory-carrying cost.

Inventory Obsolescence (Figure 11.16)

A mathematical correlation was developed to relate average inventory, inventory turnover, and obsolescence or markdown costs. This correlation was used to quantify the expected markdowns, in stores and warehouses,

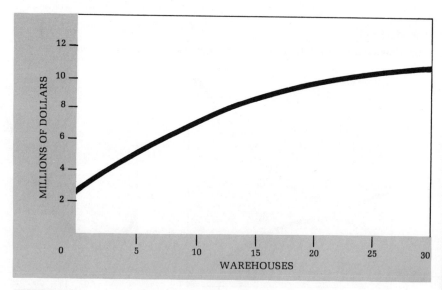

FIGURE 11.17

Retail illustration: value of space released

as a function of the warehouse network. As shown in the left-hand panel of Figure 11.16, inventory and turnover are inversely proportional. The right-hand panel shows that turnover and markdowns are inversely proportional.

Value of Space Released (Figure 11.17)

This relationship is based on the store inventory reduction resulting from shortened replenishment time; the space occupied by inventory in store stockrooms which can be converted to selling areas; and the incremental profits produced by the sales yielded by the additional sales area.

Value of Supply Alternatives (Figure 11.18)

This curve reflects reductions in the cost of merchandise when suppliers can ship in bulk into the retailers' warehouses.

Value of Reduction in Out-of-Stocks (Figure 11.19)

These data are based on actual tests made with selected stores to determine the effect of improved replenishment time. Replenishment time, in turn, was related to the size and composition of the warehouse network.

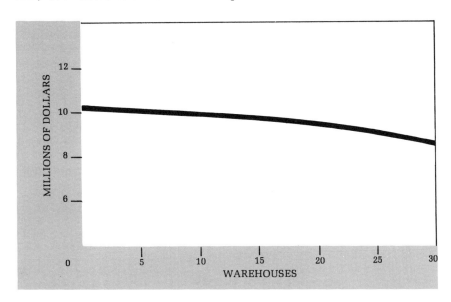

FIGURE 11.18
Retail illustration: value of cost concessions

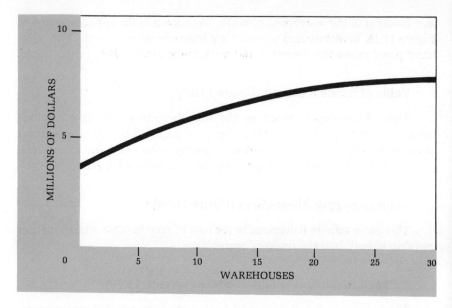

FIGURE 11.19
Retail illustration: value of reduction in out-of-stocks

[3] Trace the Interactions (Figure 11.20)

Figure 11.20 shows the major interactions as the number of warehouses is increased in the system: changes in warehouse and transportation costs; an increase in warehouse inventory, which yields some bulk buying benefits or changes in acquisition costs; and, a reduction in the replenishment time, as well as variability of replenishment time. This gives rise to a decrease in average store inventory which, together with the warehouse increase (in the optimum situation), results in a net reduction of total system inventory. This causes changes in inventory-carrying and obsolescence costs. There are also changes in the use of store space and in the number of stockouts in the stores, which cause changes in sales. All of these effects combine finally to cause a change in profits.

This is essentially a verbal description of the system. These relationships were used to construct a model that would express the interactions in mathematical terms suitable for manipulation through a computer. In the computer, a large number of alternatives could be analyzed, or priced out, to determine which is the optimum solution.

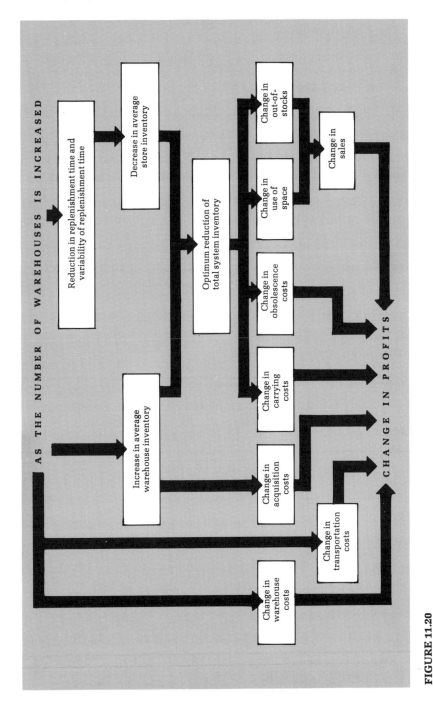

AS THE NUMBER OF WAREHOUSES IS INCREASED

Reduction in replenishment time and variability of replenishment time

Decrease in average store inventory

Increase in average warehouse inventory

Optimum reduction of total system inventory

Change in out-of-stocks

Change in use of space

Change in obsolescence costs

Change in carrying costs

Change in acquisition costs

Change in transportation costs

Change in warehouse costs

Change in sales

CHANGE IN PROFITS

FIGURE 11.20

Retail illustration: trace the interactions

[4]   The Best Solution

Using a simulation approach, it was determined that the optimum distribution network for this retail chain would include five large regional distribution centers. The process also indicated:

Where the warehouses should be located

What stores each warehouse should serve

What products should be handled by each warehouse and what products should be shipped directly from vendors to the stores.

The profit improvement for the optimum solution is shown in Table 11.3. These figures pertain only to that merchandise which would pass through the new warehouse system, and show a pretax profit improvement of $23 million.

The final question deals with the expected return on the investment required to implement the warehouse distribution plan. This computation

TABLE 11.3

Retail Illustration: Optimum Solution

	OLD MODE OF DISTRIBUTION		NEW MODE OF DISTRIBUTION	
	Millions of Dollars	*Per Cent of Sales*	*Millions of Dollars*	*Per Cent of Sales*
Sales	500	100.0	500	100.0
Cost of goods	300	60.0	291	58.2
Gross margin	200	40.0	209	41.8
Expenses:				
Warehousing	0	0.0	10	2.0
Transportation	15	3.0	11	2.2
Cost of carrying inventory	25	5.0	18	3.6
Markdowns	18	3.6	15	3.0
All other cost items	105	21.0	105	21.0
Subtotal	163	32.6	159	31.8
Added profit from increased sales			10[a]	2.0
Pretax profit	37	7.4	60[a]	12.0

[a]An added $10 million in net profit is indicated. This is based on increased sales which result from reduced stockouts and increased selling space because of the new mode of distribution. Thus, the pretax profit figure includes $9 million savings in cost of goods, $4 million savings in expenses (over the old system), and an added $10 million of profit from a $100 million increase in sales.

showed that return on shareholders' equity would be about 22 per cent. The company's average return over the past three years has been about 15 per cent. The evidence indicated clearly that this company should indeed revise its distribution system. Comprehensive analysis had uncovered $23 million of pretax profits.

CONCLUSIONS

Three major conclusions emerge from the analysis of numerous physical distribution problems:

1. *The key factors are essentially the same in each case, although the relative importance varies.* The key cost factors are:

   > Production or supply alternatives
   > Warehousing
   > Transportation
   > Carrying inventory
   > Inventory obsolescence
   > Communications and data processing.

   The key service factors are:

   > Time required to fill customer orders
   > Variability in time required to fill customer orders
   > Percentage of customer orders which can be filled.

   It is essential that tangible values be developed for the service factors. Only then can an optimum balance be developed between cost and service.

2. *Profit will be maximized only when all factors have been considered in an integrated manner.* An examination of individual elements of the problem leads to suboptimization. This is a "bits and pieces" approach. Profits will be greatest only when all of the factors are considered in a systems approach.

3. *Effective action to optimize distribution systems requires top management action.* The distribution elements are arrayed on a typical manufacturing company organization chart in Figure 11.21. In this instance, it is evident that:

   a. Responsibility for distribution costs is scattered organizationally. No one executive is responsible for minimizing this group of costs.

b. Classical accounting and analytical systems have grown up to reflect major organization functions. In each case, distribution cost elements are subordinate items within the main functional groupings. As a consequence, they are almost never grouped together for analysis, but are characteristically "buried" in statements of marketing and manufacturing cost.

c. There are conflicting objectives at different levels in the business. Only top management really seeks maximum return on investment. To illustrate:

> The sales manager wants more inventory, frequent short production runs, fastest possible order processing and delivery, and perhaps field warehousing.

FIGURE 11.21

Distribution responsibilities in a typical manufacturing company

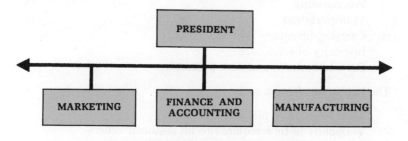

Responsibilities Affecting Distribution

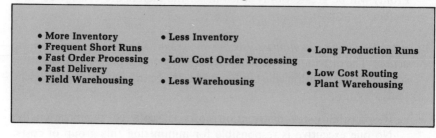

Objectives Affecting Distribution

The financial officer wants less inventory, lower order-processing costs, and less warehousing.

The production manager wants long production runs and more warehousing space.

The traffic manager wants lowest-cost routing and less warehousing.

A change in any one element of distribution cost is likely to affect all others, some of them favorably and some unfavorably. This begins to explain why distribution is a top management problem. A fundamental responsibility of top management is to *coordinate and control activities that cross organizational lines.* Distribution is such an activity, as was shown in Figure 11.21.

The amount of management attention and effort applied to any particular group of activities must, of course, be proportional to its importance (relative to all other activities). *Distribution accounts for a major portion of total value.* The conclusion emerges that effective distribution action must be initiated by top management.

In most companies distribution costs are substantial—and are likely to present the major opportunities for profit improvement. The most promising approach to profit improvement is one that considers and integrates all activities affected by distribution, including those normally regarded as "manufacturing" or "marketing." Only through use of the *profit improvement approach can maximum benefits be achieved.*

APPENDIX

PHYSICAL DISTRIBUTION MANAGEMENT COST COMPONENTS

I. INBOUND RAW MATERIAL COST (PER UNIT)

II. PLANT COST (OR PURCHASE COST OF ITEM IF SECURED FROM VENDOR)

   A. Production Cost   *Cost per Unit*

      1. Rent
        a. Land
        b. Taxes
        c. Capital costs (depreciation and interest costs)

        2. Labor (includes Fringe Benefits)
        3. Utilities and Miscellaneous Costs

  B. Plant Shipping Department Cost   *Cost per Unit*

        1. Depreciation and Interest Cost of Materials Handling Equipment
        2. Labor Cost (includes Fringe Benefits)
        3. Supervision (includes Fringe Benefits)

III. TOTAL TRANSPORTATION COST, INBOUND AND OUTBOUND

  A. Commercial Carriage and Handling

      1. Carriers, Agencies, and Distributors Costs

	COST PER UNIT		
	PLANT		WAREHOUSE*
	Inbound	*Outbound*	*Outbound*
a. Rail			
b. Air freight			
c. Motor carrier			
d. Water			
e. Pipeline			
f. Freight forwarder			
g. Rail express			
h. Air express			
i. Bus express			
j. Parcel post			
k. United Parcel			
l. Shippers Associates			
m. Miscellaneous carriers (includes local cartage, contract carriers, etc.)			
n. Distributor and handling costs at break-bulk points, etc.			

      2. Office and Administration Costs (includes Traffic Department payroll, office expense, etc.)   *Cost per Unit*

---

*Warehouses, bulk plants, etc.

B.   Private Carriage (Company-owned or leased equipment)

1. Fixed Costs

	COST PER UNIT		
	PLANT		WAREHOUSE*
	Inbound	*Outbound*	*Outbound*
a. Entire capital investment			
b. Interest on investment			
c. Finance charges			
d. License fees			
e. Insurance (property damage, public liability, buildings, maintenance, equipment, etc.)			
f. Depreciation on operating equipment			
g. Depreciation on maintenance equipment and buildings			
h. Property taxes			
i. Garage supervision			
j. Garage labor (including all insurance, fringe benefits, social security, etc.)			
k. Garage maintenance costs (including building repairs, heat, gas, light, water, telephone, etc.)			
l. Costs to replace broken, worn-out tools and equipment			
m. Special equipment costs (tarpaulins, heaters, refrigerating units, etc.)			

*Warehouse, bulk plants, etc.

COST PER UNIT

| | PLANT | | WAREHOUSE |
| | *Inbound* | *Outbound* | *Outbound* |

n. Special garage
equipment (racks,
storage bins, etc.)

o. Fleet supervisor
salary and expenses

p. Administration
expense (includes
time management
spends on fleet
operation problems)

q. Costs for maintenance of
records (including
checking, typing,
posting and payment
of bills, postage,
stationery and
supplies, other office
work)

2. Operating Costs

a. Primary maintenance
of equipment
(includes washing,
polishing, greasing,
painting, etc.)

b. Road service costs
(resulting from
breakdowns, wrecks,
or other catastrophes)

c. Repairs outside
company's shop

d. Gasoline and oil

e. Tires and tubes
(replacement
and repairs)

f. Replacement parts
(tractor and trailer)

g. Antifreeze, tire
chains, flares, lamps,
and other vehicle
accessories

	COST PER UNIT	
	PLANT	WAREHOUSE
	Inbound *Outbound*	*Outbound*

    h. Cost of equipment retail (when required due to breakdowns or unusual peak load requirements)

    i. Drivers and helpers salaries (includes all union benefits, insurance, social security, etc.)

    j. Extra drivers and helpers for vacation periods, sick leaves, etc.

    k. Toll road fees

IV. PACKAGING COST   *Cost per Unit*

    A. Cost of Materials
    B. Labor Cost (includes Fringe Benefits)
    C. Supervision (includes Fringe Benefits)
    D. Rental Space Cost (includes Storage Space for Materials)
    E. Depreciation of Packaging Machinery
    F. Interest Cost (Investment in Packaging Materials and Machinery)

V. WAREHOUSE COST

    A. Private Warehouse Cost   *Cost per Unit*

        1. Total Salaries, Wages, and Other Remuneration

            a. General supervision
            b. Maintenance, alteration supervision
            c. Office salaries
            d. Warehouse labor

   e. Packing labor
   f. Shipping labor
   g. Maintenance labor
   h. Alteration labor
   i. Watchman
   j. Nurse
   k. Overtime bonus
   l. Profit-sharing dividend
   m. Incentive pay
   n. Vacation wages
   o. Holiday pay
   p. Pensions
   q. Retirement plan
   r. Other fringe benefits

2. Utilities Expense

   a. Water
   b. Heat
   c. Light and power
   d. Telephone

3. Building and Equipment Materials and Supplies

   a. Building maintenance materials
   b. Building alteration materials
   c. Handling equipment supplies
   d. Packing and shipping materials
   e. Miscellaneous warehouse and shipping supplies

4. Building Rent, Insurance, and Taxes

   a. Rent
   b. Insurance
   c. Taxes

5. Employees' Insurance Expenses

   a. Unemployment
   b. Compensation

Cost per Unit

        c. Liability
        d. Group
        e. Hospitalization
        f. Employees' safety
        g. Medical examination
           fees
        h. Medical office expense

    6. Depreciation

        a. Building depreciation
        b. Handling equipment
           depreciation

    7. Other Warehouse Expenses

        a. Cafeteria expenses
        b. Overage, shortage

    8. Capital Cost Expense

        a. Interest cost

  B. Public Warehouse Cost

    1. Storage Cost
    2. Insurance Cost
    3. Handling Cost
    4. Preparing Stock Report
    5. Physical Inventory Cost

VI. INVENTORY COST

  A. At:

    1. Plant
    2. Warehouse
    3. In-transit

  B. Costs: *Cost per Unit*

    1. Cost of Capital
    2. Obsolescence, Scrap, and Waste
    3. Loss and Damage
    4. Insurance
    5. Taxes

VII. DATA CONTROL, ORDER PROCESSING, AND COMMUNICATIONS COSTS

     A. Equipment Rental, or Depreciation Cost of   *Cost per Unit*
          Equipment

     B. Interest Cost on Investment

     C. Labor Cost and Supervision (includes Fringe
          Benefits)

     D. Communications Cost

     E. Order Preparation

     F. Miscellaneous

VIII. BUSINESS TAX COST

Many states levy a sales tax for all merchandise distributed from a warehouse.

12

Warren Billings

Communications:
The Catalyst

The vitality of a business enterprise depends to a substantial degree on the adequacy and effectiveness of its internal communications system. A progressive and competitive organization will quickly recognize that it must identify and clearly define the communications profile which is best suited to its operations. Such recognition and action by management is vital to the achievement of leadership or the protection of existing leadership in the market place.

In a world of ever-growing technology and specialization; of expanding consumer demand for new products and services; of the diametrically opposed but simultaneous development of organizational decentralization and centralization; of expanding geographical markets; and of tougher competition the fundamental managerial objectives of profitability and high standards of product or service quality assume important new dimensions. This challenge to businessmen offers handsome rewards to those who have the foresight and courage to venture toward the frontiers of new knowledge.

One such frontier is communications. While the concept of the exchange or transmission of information can hardly be considered new knowledge, work to develop new capabilities and far-reaching flexibility and adaptability in the communications field has progressed rapidly in recent years. Technology in the art of telephony, data transmission, and other modes of communications has been at the forefront of progress throughout industry as a whole.

COMMUNICATIONS AND LOGISTICS (Figure 12.1)

What is the meaning of "communications"? A catch-all meaning for "communications" is unthinkable because a great deal can be lost in oversimplification. We can perhaps focus on a more specific definition for our purposes here, if we limit our consideration to "business communications." But even with this qualification our focusing is not sufficiently concentrated. Certain textbooks, dealing with the principles and philosophy of management, devote page after page to discussions of the many forms and techniques of communications necessary within a business organization. The validity and importance of these concepts is recognized, accepted; and, for the most part, their implementation is recommended by astute students of sound management. Few will deny the utility of principles which form the basis for effective and productive communications between management and employees; between superior and subordinate within management; between coordinates at the interdepartmental conference table, and between firm and suppliers, agents, customers, and the general public.

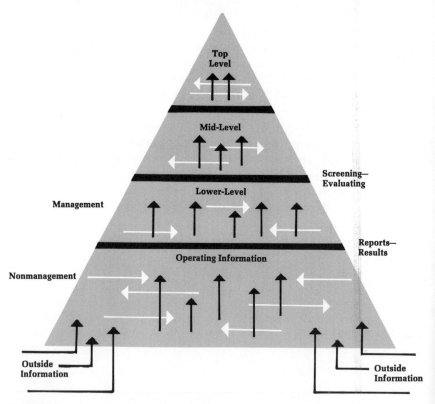

FIGURE 12.1
Communications and logistics

In this discussion, however, we are concerned with communications which serve the needs and objectives of marketing logistics operations; with the physical network which integrates the various elements of the total logistics effort; with the mechanical flow of information—both voice and data—which has an immediate and positive effect on the quality of customer service; and with the exchange and collection of information which increases the reliability of decisions at both the operating and corporate levels of management.

More specifically, attention will be directed to communications systems which provide for effective *coordination* between such logistical functions as transportation, inventory control, warehousing, and distribution; between these logistical activities and other departmental operations such as production and product development, sales and sales promotion, market research, and accounting; and finally, between these departmental operations and the corporate policymaking function. It is well to remember that the essence of communications is coordination.

In an earlier paragraph I mentioned a challenge to businessmen occasioned by modern technology, more sophisticated marketing efforts, and other forces. One effect of the interaction between these forces and of the fundamental complexity of contemporary living is the information explosion. As a result of the widespread availability of and need for myriad types of information, we find ourselves in the century of the Great Paper Blizzard. To accommodate the rapid expansion of man's knowledge (which is manifested in the Great Paper Blizzard), the development of computers and electronic data processing was accelerated. Progress in this field has been swift—probably much faster than would have been predicted a decade ago. The present capabilities and future potential of electronic data processing achieved through continually improved hardware and programing techniques startle the imagination. Computer systems can substantially advance scientific progress and promote efficiency in business. But the central issue in the operation of business-oriented computers is optimum use. An idle computer system is a silent but steady drain on revenues. It can restrain capital that might otherwise produce revenue.

One of the problems in achieving optimum utilization is to make data available for processing when the source of the data is not near the computer installation. The need to move information to EDP centers from distant points of data collection and vice versa sparked the development of *data communications*. To interconnect the point of input (data) generation with computer, computer with output destination, and computer with computer, a sophisticated system of data communications is essential. Machines, it is said, will talk with machines.

Does all this mean the dehumanization of communications? A distressing thought but not at all likely. Data communications will never displace voice communications. On the contrary, voice communications will become increasingly critical in helping to cope with the complexities of data movement and processing. Actually voice and data communications complement each other. The latter permits the transmission of large volumes or small bits of information at tremendous speeds. Voice communications, by means of tone, inflection, and vocabulary, must prevail to meet the daily need for explicitness, clarity, emphasis, immediate exchange, and personal contact. I have said the essence of communications is coordination. While this statement may appear obvious, its validity can be tested by examining the information requirements of various interested groups in a typical, although generalized, business operation:

Customer information requirements:

(1) product design, materials and operating specifications; (2) prices and applicable tax rates; (3) product availability; (4) delivery information; (5) method of billing; (6) credit, discount, and warranty information.

Salesman information requirements:

(1) product specifications; (2) price ranges if negotiable; (3) availability of products in plants and/or warehouses; (4) production schedules; (5) method and date of shipment; (6) credit and billing information; (7) knowledge of current sales promotion activities and advertising; (8) market information including activities of competitors; (9) knowledge of research and product development activities; (10) financial position of the firm represented; (11) over-all sales productivity level; salesman's individual sales productivity rate and those of competing salesmen.

Production information requirements:

(1) production cost data; (2) raw materials and product inventory levels and availability of storage space at warehouses; (3) availability of transportation; (4) knowledge of research and product development activities; (5) material procurement data; (6) product handling requirements; packaging requirements.

Marketing and sales promotion information requirements:

(1) rate of sales and profitability of individual products; (2) customer attitudes toward products; (3) knowledge of research and product development activities; (4) competitive promotional actions.

Financial and higher levels of management information requirements:
(1) over-all effectivenss of sales effort and volume of sales; (2) expense, revenue, and profitability data; (3) macroeconomic trend information; (4) research and product development activities; (5) customer attitude trends toward product or service quality; (6) quality control data; (7) marketing research estimates of possible changes in the market.

Admittedly this brief outline is oversimplified. There are other interested groups and other information matters which have been omitted. Notwithstanding the omissions, the pattern of interdependence; the need for the exchange of information; for coordination—should be clear. The high-speed transmission of information at relatively low cost is in the interest of both a company and the customers it serves. This is the objective of data communications.

Data communications are an inherent part of a total information system; particularly one involving real-time computers. While the field of data communications offers endless possibilities, management should consider the following criteria when determining the data communications facilities and network it requires:[1]

Function The purpose served by the communications system. The types of messages it has to handle.

Distribution The number of places involved in moving information.

Volume The total amount or bulk of information to be moved in a given period of time.

Urgency The speed at which information has to be transmitted.

Language The physical nature of messages—coded tape, handwriting, punched cards, facsimile.

Accuracy The tolerable error performance that will still provide desired results.

Cost The justifiable limit for the system. The cost will always be dependent upon the other criteria and in proportion to their weighting in the design of any system.

---

[1]Edgar Gentle, Jr., "Keying the Executive to Real Time Concepts," *Bell Telephone Magazine*, Summer 1964, p. 8.

The optimum combination of these elements in accordance with the specific requirements of a given application will result in a flexible and completely integrated computer and communications complex.

Thoughtful management, alarmed by diminishing profit margins and recognizing that the physical distribution of goods represents one-quarter to one-third of the sales dollar and that it is the third largest cost of conducting business, is urging greater recognition at corporate levels of physical distribution as a major function in business operations. They see the need for using the tools of quantitative analysis to solve physical distribution problems. They see the need for new and better methods and practices which will promote improved customer service and reduce costs. The relevance of the concept that "the problems of distribution are the opportunities of communications"[2] was never more apparent.

It would appear that efficient and effective *coordination* is the element most critically needed in the logistics of physical distribution. Computers and data communications, properly planned and implemented, can advance physical distribution operations to its rightful place of importance and emphasis in the activities of a business organization. Will the combination of these modern tools meet the specific objectives set by perceptive managers in reappraising the status of physical distribution? Indeed it will. EDP supplemented and integrated by an efficient network of data communications can provide the means for quantitative analysis of complex distribution problems. It can provide the information required at higher levels of management where the execution of the distribution function can be examined and related to other departmental areas of performance for the purpose of long-range planning and decision-making in the formulation of corporate policy and objectives. It can accelerate the physical distribution process itself by transmitting customer orders at fast speeds with a high degree of accuracy. Moreover, the EDP and data communications combination offers these new horizons and capabilities to management at costs, which, when systems are intelligently planned in accordance with function and need, may be easily justified by the potential value of the system.

Thus far I have attempted to conceptualize the role of communications in physical distribution and in the over-all coordination of departmental activities. It is appropriate that I attempt broadly to identify the communications tools themselves.

Basic, of course, is the telephone. Because it is a powerful extension of a human faculty, it should not be taken for granted. Its utility and importance

---

[2]Stanley F. Damkroger, "Phone Power in Action," *Bell Telephone Magazine*, Winter 1964–1965, p. 48.

are not subject to debate. It is absolutely indispensable in the conduct of all human affairs—not the least of which is business activity. The occasions are too numerous and varied to list when there is a critical need for the spoken word. The telephone meets the demand for immediacy which is so frequently vital in matters requiring close coordination where a delay may mean an unsound decision, the loss of revenue, or the loss of customer confidence. The telephone is the omnipresent complement to all other forms of communications including, as previously noted, data communications.

Data communications may be divided into three broad categories: narrowband, voiceband, and wideband transmission. The basic non-technical distinguishing characteristic is transmittal speed and capacity—wideband permitting the fastest transmission speed and the movement of the largest volumes of data. Depending on the type of data communications equipment used, information can be transmitted in various forms: ordinary readable alphabetic and numeric characters, computer code symbols, and graphic displays. Digital data can be transmitted serially (in parts) or in parallel (a combination of parts representing a character). Analog data, the source of facsimile reproduction, can also be transmitted. Input and output to and from the data communications network can be in card, tape, or hard copy format. Moreover, the network can be "on-line," thereby enabling one computer processor to communicate with another computer processor.

This brief enumeration of some of the features of data communications suggests the great flexibility and adaptability of the equipment and the interconnecting network to specific operations. By definition, data communications equipment must be compatible with data processing equipment.

One of the advantages of data communications is its ability to provide automatic and unattended operation. Consider the value of this capacity to those involved in physical distribution. Customer orders can be placed; inventory levels can be ascertained; production orders can be originated based on inventory low limit; shipping route and rate data can be obtained: all without unnecessary delays. At any terminating point in the network transactions can be summarized, merged, collated, correlated, analyzed, and printed out as required.

To illustrate how a data communications network can enhance the physical distribution function of a business, consider the system used by the ABC Steel Corporation—a fully integrated steel-producing firm with its own mills, fabrication plants, custom work shops, sales offices, and two subsidiary distribution depots where 30,000 steel and other industrial items are warehoused. Using computers interconnected by data communications facilities, these operating components are effectively linked together to form a completely coordinated whole.

Data communications orginating equipment located at the various sales offices are used to process customer orders called in by salesmen. The orders are transmitted to a data processing center at the warehouse. After interrogating received transactions and comparing them with certain data stored in its memory, the computer produces a delivery order showing the location in the warehouse where the item is stored, the most desirable method of shipment from the standpoint of cost and speed, the time it should be dispatched, billing information, and other pertinent data. Coincident with the processing of the delivery order, inventory control summaries are updated, and stock reorders are issued. This information is selectively transmitted to the appropriate mill, fabrication plant, and material procurement department over data communications circuits. Related data in somewhat modified form are transmitted over other circuits to administrative groups for market research, sales, and profitability analysis.

What advantages have resulted from the introduction of this data movement and data processing system? ABC's customers enjoy faster order processing and, therefore, better service. Some have realized sizable savings in time and expense because costly expediting headaches have been eliminated and the need for safety stock inventories has been reduced. ABC benefits from improved control over inventory levels, substantial reductions in clerical work, curtailment in manpower requirements, and better material procurement and production scheduling. The company now has the enviable capability of rapidly accumulating basic data for use in (a) evaluating sales effectiveness, (b) long-range planning in marketing and sales promotion, (c) appraising its financial status, and (d) more confident decision-making at top levels of management. ABC has devised a total information system which provides for the horizontal flow of data between operating departments and for the vertical flow of data for use at various levels of management. Utilizing a well-planned data communications network to interlace a series of remotely located EDP configurations, ABC has designed a management tool which permits:

1. A vastly more efficient physical distribution operation

2. Generation of reports on an up-to-the-minute basis

3. A significant degree of scientific management

4. The opportunity to achieve a better profit position

5. The opportunity to serve its customers better.

The search and discovery of new and broader sources of revenue; the capability of greater control over operating expenses; the ability to provide faster and improved service to customers—these are the fundamental criteria for the growth of a business enterprise. The importance of these criteria will intensify in the decades that lie ahead. Sophisticated managerial thinking is vital because managers function in an atmosphere of sophisticated competitors and demanding consumers.

In a rapidly changing world, the methods of operating a business must likewise change merely to keep pace. The commercial or industrial entity seeking to establish its leadership in this environment must distinguish itself by demonstrating managerial ingenuity and the willingness to innovate.

One does not have to be visionary to foresee the expanding role of communications in the economic sphere of the national and even the international community. The facility to identify essentials will adequately serve the businessman in making this observation. While the philosophers and semanticists may debate the view that communications is an *essence* or an *absolute* of human existence, those of us who are less inclined toward abstractions may agree that it is at least *basic* to human existence. We may, perhaps more confidently, agree from practical experience that communications is basic to business. Indeed, it is the nervous system of economic activity. Buying and selling do not occur in a vacuum. The forces of supply and demand do not operate in the market place unless they are communicated. Each responds to the pressure exerted by the other—but only when there is awareness. The same concept of awareness must prevail between business entity and customer and, equally important, among operating groups within the business organization.

The research, development, and engineering of communications devices and the network that interconnects them is well advanced in technology and in practical applications. Moreover, the future promises almost limitless possibilities. Farsighted and progressive marketing management is cognizant of the economic potential that lies within the framework of a well-executed and dynamic communications system. They endorse the idea that the intelligent application of communications and EDP concepts will serve effectively to overcome, or at least minimize, the problems of high cost and antiquated methods generally associated with physical distribution. Their recognition of the inherent utility of the data communications–data processing combination has enabled them to move forward with conviction in organizing for the years that lie ahead. Their foresight permits them the coveted luxury of planning now with some degree of certainty for the always elusive and unpredictable future. Since managerial foresight is, most of us will agree, one of the distinguishing qualities of leadership, it is incumbent upon top management to demand foresight in the area of communications for the single purpose of achieving a competitive position in the market place in terms of both profit and service quality.

13

Martin L. Ernst

Systems Analysis in Logistical Planning

Let us start by considering a very generalized system, which can be represented as a "black box" in the manner used by electronics engineers in their design problems. This black box has certain important characteristics. As in the case of electronics equipment, there obviously will be inputs and outputs. There also are two other characteristics of very great significance that are not so obvious; one concerns the dimensions or extent of the system, and the other the objectives. Within this black box, there may be many subsystems. Each of these should have dimensions smaller than those of the system as a whole, and it must have objectives that are dominated by the common goals of the over-all system.

Let us begin with the characteristic that has received the least attention, that is, the dimension or extent of a system. By extent of a system is meant description of the boundaries which separate those things that are within the system—and therefore a reasonable object of study—from those that are outside. To describe the dimension or extent of the system we may use a simple operational definition: A system starts at the point where you begin to have positive control over operations and functions, and continues to the point where you lose this positive control.

It is fairly easy to find examples which illustrate systems of different extent. Consider, for example, the contrast between a common carrier, which has to plan to accept and move all the cargo delivered to it, whenever it is delivered, and that of an organization which is engaged in a business where it handles the manufacture, the movement, and the marketing of its product. The latter organization has a system of far greater extent; it has freedom to unite, to balance, or to sacrifice parts of the various basic functions. It can vary production rates during different periods, if this is economically desirable, in order to lower transportation costs. It can vary its marketing functions in order to match marketing with transportation or with production. The whole approach to considering a system of this sort is different from that where one has simply to accept and move whatever is brought into the system.

In analyzing such a system, one must consider the elements that are beyond control—that will be controlled by other people or by nature. These form the "inputs" and the "outputs." Often these are predictable, which makes it easier to operate the system, but since they are beyond control, they cannot be varied so as to improve the over-all system performance.

In many cases one may have some degree of cooperation with regard to the uncontrollable elements or inputs. For example, consider the problems of commuter transportation—of taking people to and from their places of business. Cooperation is achieved by arranging for the businesses to stagger their office hours, thereby spreading out the peak load and making for more efficient transportation. However, except in dealing with a government activity, as in the city of Washington, where assured cooperation can be counted on over a long period of time, there is no guarantee that this co-operation will continue. It is a transient arrangement because there may not continue to be common objectives. However, a company that is moving its own people to work on its own premises does have control over the situation. It can stagger the work hours and work load, and thereby achieve a more efficient combination of transportation and work operations.

There are, of course, many gray areas of partial or limited control, but in most specific cases it is not too difficult to determine where control begins and where it is lost. So, it can be maintained that the dimensions of a system are strictly related to the area in which a degree of positive control can be exerted for the sake of achieving specific system objectives.

A major advantage of this definition is that it makes explicit for over-all common objectives and the need for orienting all control procedures to achieve them. We have many practical examples where errors were made— often through historical processes—leading to failures to recognize the extent of systems. As a result, these systems have operated in less than optimum fashion.

For example, there are cases where companies have grown up with decentralized production and transportation functions. The producers prefer to have all the goods they manufacture moved as quickly as possible; they do not want to have to store finished items. From the point of view of the transportation system, it is desirable to have a smooth, steady flow of shipments. Quite often, however, the combination is not possible. Usually, in these cases, some arbitrary rules are established, such as that transportation will provide immediate movement of all production, or that transportation will provide a fixed level of service. These may not be the optimum rules if the problem is looked at from an over-all point of view.

There are also errors of what might be termed the second kind—where management thinks that it has control over situations although it really does not. A number of historical cases can be cited where it appeared that a transportation system had control over the flow of articles to an extent permitting regulation of the entry of shipments. Then technological developments came along that completely changed the pattern by providing alternate means of transportation, and all presumed control was lost.

Failure to recognize the extent or the dimensions of a system generally results in what is called "suboptimizing"; i.e., trying to make each of several components operate in a fashion best for its own set of objectives, without necessarily having an adequate set of unified goals. This whole area forms a very fruitful field for examination because huge gains are often possible through eliminating mismatches between different subsystems within the over-all system.

There is another dimension to transportation systems—in fact to all systems—which is far more difficult to handle and has been much less studied. This is what might be called the temporal extent of a system, covering the questions For how long should it be built? or How rapidly should it become obsolete? As far as I know, very little work has been done on this subject. Yet, when we look around we find many examples and folly in judging the length of time for which an article should be built. Many of the worst slums in the world arose because buildings were made to last too long and are still a little too solid to tear down although they are very out of date as reasonable living places. Among highways and bridges there are many notable cases where advance planning was adequate and incorporated a degree of flexibility that has permitted expansion and change. There are other examples where articles were built in much too limited a style, without recognition of the changes that the future could bring.

In transportation the operators of short-lived vehicles seem to derive considerable advantages from this characteristic. Aircraft and trucks have relatively short lives; the current models can incorporate the latest ideas and concepts of technology and can be designed to meet up-to-date economic needs. I am not trying to specify a cause-and-effect relationship here; short life seems to offer benefits to certain equipment, through providing an ability to employ advanced design features.

This subject raises a variety of interesting questions. For example, most of the rolling stock in our railroad systems is quite old. Would it have been an advantage to the railroads if they had built their equipment to last for a shorter period of time? In recent years, handling costs have increased tremendously in proportion to the total cost of operating a transportation system. A limited number of railroad cars have been designed to open in such a way that the cargo can be handled with great speed and efficiency. However, we have a tremendous backlog of old cars, producing a form of inertia that makes it hard to change and take advantage of the improvements that technology can now provide. There might have been gains if railroad cars had been built to last a shorter period of time.

A similar situation applies to ships. When a ship is designed, it must be done with the anticipation that it will probably still be operating thirty years later. Until the last few decades, progress was sufficiently slow that this caused no particularly severe problems. Ships could be built, as could railroad cars, with a reasonable expectation that the next few decades would find the pattern of events sufficiently unchanged that both the ships and the rail cars would be fairly efficient vehicles.

In recent years, however, our culture has been changing far more rapidly. There is good reason to believe that a ship being designed or built now will be obsolescent long before it has completed its potentially useful life. It might be wise therefore to plan the construction of ships—and other types of vehicles that must be so rugged that they "automatically" have long lives—with the recognition that when they are about halfway through their useful lives, they will have to be taken in for major modifications. Most likely these modifications will be required to achieve compatibility with better materials handling equipment and thereby improve the economy efficiency of the vehicles.

The subject of temporal extent is related to the matter of standardization. Standardization usually provides a sign that a new industry, or a new tool or implement, has come of age, and that its use is about to expand rapidly. For example, the recent agreement of the American Standards Association, establishing standard sizes for American containers, is probably a fairly significant action, and may lead to a rapid increase in the use of these containers.

However, we have to be careful here, for standardization can also be the first sign of death and rigor mortis. Overly detailed and rigid standardization encourages development of systems with too much inertia to move very quickly, and not enough flexibility to permit modifications and changes. The plea here, of course, is for flexibility—for keeping standardization from standardizing too much and for always leaving a certain amount of room for growth and change.

As indicated earlier, little work has been done in the study of optimum depreciation rates. However, one obvious point can be made: A system should not be designed to last longer than the customers which it will serve. Although this is obvious, there are quite a few cases where the point was not applied in the past. One of the major difficulties rail commuter transportation faces these days is that our living places and working places have fragmented. As a result, rail transportation is quite impractical for our needs. The people have scattered, and their work places have scattered; the rail system is still there, but the customers it was built to serve have moved away.

Now let us look at the other characteristics of a system. First, let us examine inputs. There are two elements of interest here: One is the predictability of the inputs, and the other is their stability. If we have a predictable and stable input, it is obviously possible to operate a rigidly scheduled system in an efficient and effective manner. This is characteristic of many modes of transportation. On the other hand, we also have inputs that can be predicted accurately, but that are not stable—for example, inputs provided by seasonal products such as those of agriculture, or by-products that vary daily, such as commuter traffic. Here it is possible—because inputs are predictable—to build up effective scheduled systems, but they will not necessarily be efficient. The transportation requirements will be set by the peak loads, and during the slack periods most of this peak transportation capability will not be used. In cases where a single organization has control over both production and transportation, it is often worthwhile to sacrifice a portion of the peak production for the sake of requiring fewer transportation vehicles, and thereby achieving greater over-all economy. In other cases, this is not possible; we simply have to recognize that we have an inefficient system on our hands. In these situations, the requirements and economics are established by the peak, and the peak periods must essentially pay for the whole system.

We also have inputs that cannot be predicted accurately on any short-term basis. Although their long-term averages often can be estimated accurately, the fluctuations over short periods may be violent. Here the vital question arises whether a scheduled operation should be used rather than one that is dependent on demand. In many cases it is best to use a mixture of a basic schedule plus a limited capability for responding to demand for cargo lift. There is a wide variety of analytical and simulation techniques available to help solve this type of problem, and there have been quite a few individual cases where good solutions have been obtained. Major increases in efficiency have resulted through balancing the scheduled portion and the demand portion of the transportation system to match the input characteristics.

The inputs determine a variety of flow rate and capacity requirements of transportation systems. At some early point in the system there must be enough capacity to handle the inputs even if they fluctuate violently. In most situations, for example, there must be sufficient terminal space to store that portion of a peak input which cannot be moved immediately. Irregular inputs require numerous reservoirs in our national transportation systems, and I do not believe that the extent of these reservoirs has ever been adequately recognized. They appear in the form of a variety of inventories scattered throughout the country, some in warehouses and some awaiting movement in terminals. Staggering quantities of goods are being held in these inventories, to provide a reservoir action between an irregular input and either a regular or irregular output. It is very likely that we have safety factor piled on safety factor in this process, and that major gains in efficiency could be achieved by rationalizing and unifying these requirements. The inputs determine the basic nature of the entire system, and the more extensive a system, the more we are usually able to do to live with difficult inputs.

Outputs of systems also provide a great deal of variety in required flow rates and capacities. In some cases, they directly reflect the input; general cargo movements, for example, in a system that has adequate capacity, will normally reflect the input in simple fashion. Often the input has to be smoothed, either for a transition—where limited carrying capacity prevails— or where the output demands a rather smooth flow of items. Local pickup and delivery services combined with warehouse activity provide an example of this type of operation. We also have outputs that are directly demand-dependent. The movement and storage of equipment spare parts and inventories of many retail goods fit this characteristic. The input-output relationship, as indicated earlier, provides the basis for establishing the reservoir action, which is necessary somewhere in the system.

Finally, we turn to the objectives of the system. A few years ago, the objectives were the least understood and the least considered characteristic of systems. However, the situation has improved, and in recent years much attention has been focused on this subject. It is quite clear that the proper objectives for a system have to be consistent and well defined.

The prime difficulty in determining transportation system objectives is to define the rational relationship between service and economy. It is very seldom that we can ship by a method which is both the fastest and the cheapest. Normally, in a system, we have to pay attention to achieving a proper balance between costs, speed, reliability, and availability of transport. In the case of private enterprise, profit must be balanced with service if the firm is to endure.

In many instances, major inconsistencies in system objectives can be discovered if they are examined in detail. For example, if some systems requirements for fast movement are strongly stressed, but such slow paper work accompanies these movements, they could very well take four or five times as long without appreciable over-all loss of time. This unfortunately is characteristic of certain military logistics problems. For example, it may take forty-five days from the time a spare part is ordered until it is delivered, and yet transportation sections are pressed not to keep an item in their terminals for more than twelve hours. This is a basic inconsistency; the wrong part of the problem has been emphasized.

In some cases movement operations are a mixture of high speed and long delays. Thus the question is raised whether the introduction of diesel engines has speeded up the movement of general cargo on the railroads to the extent which might have been predicted. The diesels can pull longer trains than steam locomotives; they can pull them faster, and they can pull them more cheaply. Unfortunately, to take full advantage of the possible economies, it is necessary to use long trains. However, general cargo inputs are collected at scattered points and delivered to scattered points, and it is necessary to use classification yards, where trains are broken down and built up again. With diesel engines, the delay experienced by the average rail car, while waiting for enough other cars to arrive to build up an adequate length of train, is greater than with steam engines; and average origin-to-destination speed is thereby decreased more than might be anticipated.

The same type of problem occurred during World War II in the area of antisubmarine warfare. In studying this problem, it was noted that one of the best means for saving ships was to sail them in rather large convoys. Submarines, when they attacked, tended to kill a constant number rather than a constant percentage of the ships in a convoy. Therefore, the larger the convoys, the safer the individual ships were apt to be. Unfortunately it takes time to form large convoys. Systems analysis showed that if we had been able to decrease ship turnaround times by a rather small fraction, we would have compensated for all of the ship losses suffered during the war—another case where the full dimensions of a system were not recognized and the proper over-all objectives were not established.

There are also overdefined systems. Take, for example, a transportation organization which had no control over its randomly fluctuating inputs. Nevertheless, the following system objectives had been established:

1. The system should operate with complete, rigid, advance-schedule movements.

2. The vehicles should have high-load factors.

3. There should be only short delays in the terminals.

It is not too hard to prove mathematically that these objectives are incompatible; you can achieve two of the three objectives, but you cannot simultaneously achieve the third. If you wish to exercise real control over the operations, you have to identify the objectives that should be sacrificed, or the degree to which all three of them can be compromised. The organization had overdefined its objectives, and this made it impossible to carry them all out.

In contrast, the objectives may be underdefined. There are, for example, organizations whose products have sharp seasonal variations in demand,

and which have in effect said to their transportation element: "Be prepared to lift all of our production." This is a blank check to the transportation department to have an oversupply of lift capability. They cannot predict accurately what the transportation requirements will be, but they have a blanket order to move everything. They have been given no rational economic and business objectives. The statement of their objective is simply too broad to form a proper definition.

A fourth system characteristic may be carelessly defined objectives. Consider, for example, a maintenance shop which overhauls and repairs transportation vehicles. The vehicles are expensive, and it is desirable to have them out of service for a minimum length of time, say, seven days. This is misguided economy, however. A limit of this type forces the maintenance shop to give priority to that vehicle which requires the most maintenance, simply to insure that they will be able to finish on time. Yet it can be shown mathematically that to minimize the average time out of service, it is often best to pay first attention to repairing the vehicle that requires the least service.

The four systems characteristics I have just described form much of the meat of systems analysis. If the characteristics are once properly defined, the problems of the system can usually be solved. However, these problems have been solved for many years—long before the phrase "systems analysis" was coined. Why, then, has systems analysis become so popular in recent years?

This situation results primarily from the rapid growth in our technology, which has introduced three very critical factors: first, an increased requirement for long lead times in ordering equipment; second, spiraling equipment costs; and third, an increase in the rate of obsolescence. The fundamental aspects of this problem were first encountered by the military services and are shown most clearly there; for example, in the transition from aircraft to missiles.

Similar situations are arising in industry, although they are perhaps not quite as clear-cut. The development of automated warehouses and the use of electronic scheduling and traffic-control systems involve huge investments. They also lead to radical changes in the manner of doing business and must be developed quite rapidly because technological growth will otherwise force early obsolescence.

As a result, both the military and industry have suffered a loss in their capabilities for incremental advance and improvement. They have suffered a loss in ability to experiment with alternatives and to develop experience for making their decisions.

Systems analysis has grown in popularity largely as a substitute for experience. It is not a substitute that we like, but one that is forced on us—

simply because it is the best available of a collection of rather poor alternative techniques. At the moment, however, it would certainly be preferable to make a decision on the basis of experience rather than on the basis of systems analysis. Perhaps in time this choice may be reversed, if we can develop our systems analysis techniques adequately.

We have been applying these techniques consciously to transportation problems for ten to fifteen years, and it would be well to review what has been accomplished to date. There certainly have been a large number of individual successes. But one point deserves special emphasis. This is that, in considering transportation problems, one must regard transportation as simply part of a distribution system, and not as an entity in itself.

There are a lot of reasons why this is so. One is that in recent years shippers have had, for the first time, a real choice available in the mode of transportation that they could employ. Looking back in history, we find that usually one method of transportation completely dominated the field. Fifty years ago, shipping by rail was the fastest, the most efficient, and the cheapest method. This is no longer the case. We now have a variety of systems—aircraft, trucks, ships, pipelines, and others—each of which provides some combination of service, speed, and cost. This might not be important if it were not that we have come to need this variety of choices. Cost per ton-mile is becoming appreciably less significant as the prime factor determining the means of shipping for a very appreciable fraction of the total goods that we move. It still may be the dominating factor for bulk cargoes, but even here there have been cases where methods of shipping with higher costs per ton-mile have been used because their pickup and delivery times were more reliable.

We need a variety of choices largely for what might be called inventory control, in the broadest sense of that term. In recent years, distribution costs have been increasing as a proportion of the total cost of producing and delivering goods. The reason for this is simply that production has tended to become increasingly efficient, and production costs have gone down, while distribution costs—especially those for materials handling—have not. Simultaneously, our needs for transportation have been increasing, because of the much greater number of items used in our daily lives. Competition has forced an increase in variety. The standard household appliances, for example, used to be called "white" goods. Now they appear not only in three or four types, but in five or six colors, leading to perhaps thirty combinations of a single make of washer or drier. This poses quite a problem to a local distributor; he literally cannot afford to have an adequate inventory of all combinations. On the other hand, it is well known to the merchandising field that the distributor must be able to deliver to a customer very promptly. If he cannot provide quick delivery, the customer will spend his available money on something else. So quick delivery is necessary, even though an adequate inventory cannot be stocked. The result is that companies can afford to pay more and more for rapid and reliable transportation.

As the number of items handled increases, it includes a larger and larger fraction that is rather slow moving. In a typical manufacturer's catalog, about 80 per cent of the items listed are responsible for only 10–20 per cent of the sales. As a result, far more planning of the warehouse and distribution structure is needed in order to avoid large unused inventories scattered around the country. The problem is apt to become more severe due to increases in storage costs which are likely to arise in the future. Higher costs will force a move in the direction of automated warehouses in as many locales as at present. At the present time, five well-placed warehouses in the United States can provide goods within one day's travel of about 33 per cent of the population if rapid surface transportation is used. With 25 warehouse points, goods could be within one day of 80 per cent of the population. High prices can be paid for high-speed transportation for the sake of cutting down the enormous investment that automated warehouses may require.

So the whole transportation problem is tied to, and is closely integrated with, the problems of production and marketing. One of the greatest benefits of systems analysis to date—and one of its greatest lessons—has been that these factors do have to be considered in a common problem structure. The system has to cover all of the elements over which control can be exerted, or all of the elements from which allegiance can be demanded for a common set of objectives.

SUMMARY

I have tried to provide a framework from which to begin consideration of possible applications of systems analysis to distribution problems. The five most important considerations of the systems approach are:

First, it is fairly clear that systems analysis is becoming increasingly necessary as a tool for planning, not only for its own virtues, but also because the alternatives are becoming less and less suitable. The rapid advance of technology is forcing us to make decisions far earlier than we would like to on the basis of experience and experimentation, and analysis is the only available substitute.

Second, systems analysis has considerable value in that it can supply a degree of rigor and a framework in our approach to problems that we have dealt with for a long time. Simply recognizing the importance of searching out the characteristics of a system, and simply having a pattern with which to attack these problems, can supply great benefits.

Third, systems analysis offers a bridge by means of which we can seek out and apply the most modern mathematical, analytical, and simulation techniques to practical problems.

Fourth, systems analysis opens up new areas for investigation by the simple process of looking at old problems in new ways. New technical tools have been developed because systems analysis showed a need for them; and new attitudes have been developed by management under the pressure of critical questions posed by analysts.

Fifth, systems analysis will provide increasing potential for improved prediction and control of operations and will help us move toward a state where ever more rigorous methods will be applied to systems planning, in a manner corresponding more closely to the procedure of the physical sciences.

APPENDIX

The following diagrams (Figures 13A.1–13A.5) illustrate various systems approaches.

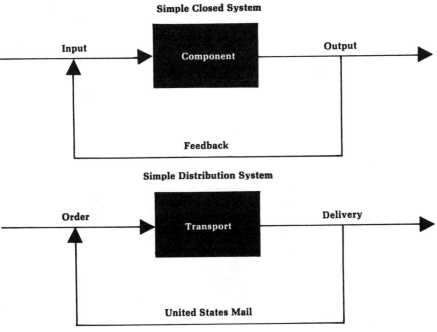

FIGURE 13A.1

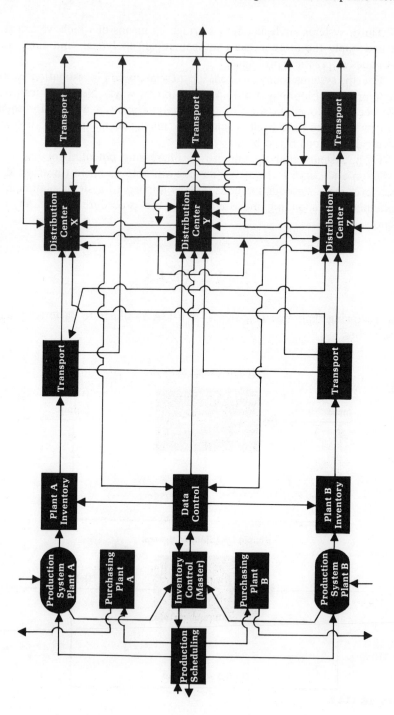

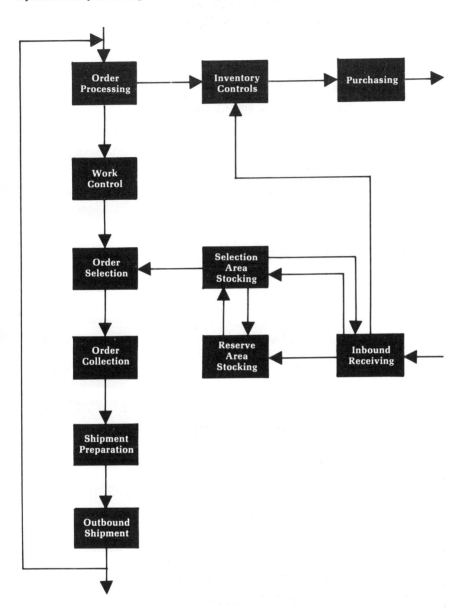

FIGURE 13A.2 (left)
Two plant-three distribution center system

FIGURE 13A.3 (above)
Distribution center subsystem

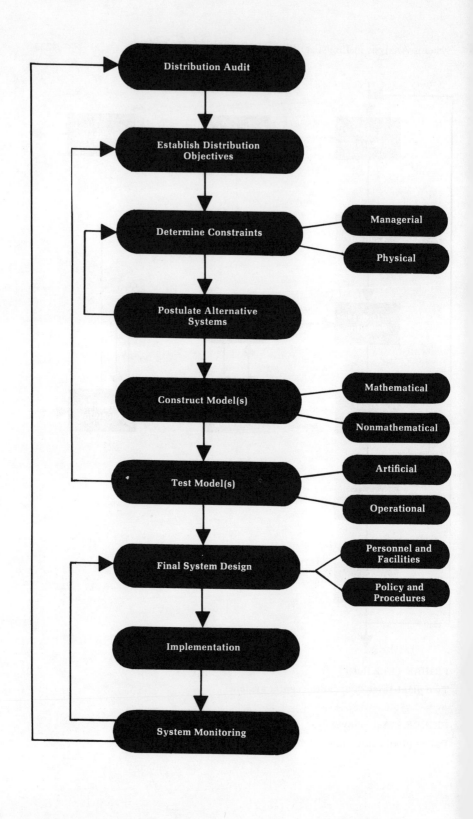

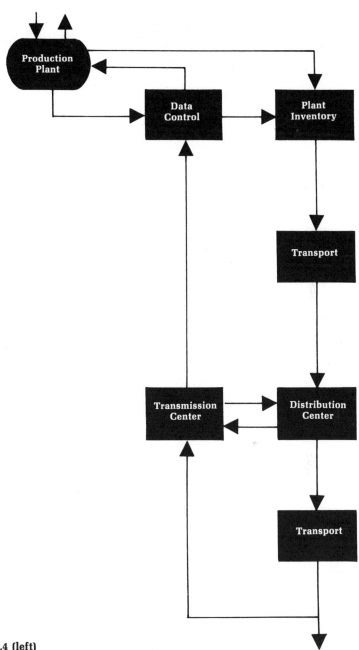

FIGURE 13A.4 (left)
Steps in systems analysis

FIGURE 13A.5 (above)
Distribution center

Part

Four

QUANTITATIVE TECHNIQUES FOR SOLVING LOGISTICAL PROBLEMS

Traditionally, "traffic management"—to the extent it was even considered as a bundle of interrelated concepts, techniques, and controls in the physical movement of commodities through channels of distribution—has been little more than an entrepreneurial art with the possible exception of the elementary algebra used in the selection of routes and the computation of rates. But as was underlined in Chapter 1 and reviewed in detail in subsequent chapters, logistics has in recent years been ''taken over'' by the most sophisticated problem-solvers and techniques—simulation, linear programing, queuing theory, and a host of other methods of operations research.

These new methods have been especially useful in optimizing solutions of problems in transportation, warehousing, materials handling, inventory control, and the transfer of vehicles.

Chapter 14 relates operations research and its applications to problems of marketing logistics; and Chapter 15, more specifically, reviews and explains the use of linear programing tools and techniques.

14

Robert A. Hammond

The Application of Operations Research to Problems in Logistics

In recent years, operations research has developed into one of the most powerful tools for the solution of logistics problems. As business grows in complexity, its logistics operations, too, become more complex and bewildering, less susceptible to intuitive grasp. New techniques are required, techniques that can be used quantitatively to analyze vast and intricate systems of distribution, transportation, and inventory. OR provides such techniques; hence for many companies with wide-scale logistics operations, it has become indispensable.

OPERATIONS RESEARCH APPROACH

Basically, OR is an approach to problemsolving that works by developing descriptive models of business problems; that is, it describes these problems usually in mathematical and economic terms, and then compares the relative profitability of various alternative decisions or policies. By quantitatively analyzing this model, a study team can determine the effects of various policies or decisions, and thus aid management in choosing the right one. It is not the function of such techniques to replace intuition and judgment; they simply furnish management with a more solid basis for its decisions.

OR methods, then, provide means for handling complexities with which the human intuition cannot cope unaided. They permit management to test the implications of new plans, new systems, new ideas; to develop further possibilities; to evaluate the effectiveness of present methods. Naturally, the computer plays a role in this kind of problemsolving. It provides the means for making economic comparisons quickly and accurately. It tests hypothetical decisions by applying them to various possible situations. It provides an information system for monitoring and appraising the effectiveness of such decisions. But the computer is not the basis of the OR approach; it is simply one of the many tools used by OR specialists. The important thing to remember about OR is that it is an *approach* to problemsolving rather than a set of specific techniques.

Actually, the most effective use of OR methods combines more traditional techniques—such as calculus or statistics—with more advanced ones, such as linear programing, simulation, or critical path method. And, as we shall see, the OR approach leaves a great deal of room for considerations of intuition and judgment. This is particularly important in the areas of logistics and marketing in which factors must often be taken into account that cannot easily be reduced to a simple model.

How are OR methods applied to specific problems in logistics? To take a relatively simple example, let us imagine a company interested in minimizing the costs of distributing its product. The company has a single factory and three warehouses; the system is shown in Figure 14.1. Improvement opportunities include modernizing existing warehouses, eliminating one or more of the warehouses, reorganizing the routing from factory to warehouse —or even abandoning the warehouse system altogether and shipping direct to customers. The problem is how to evaluate these alternatives.

Even in this relatively simple problem the number of alternatives can easily get out of hand. First of all, there are eight possibilities involved in the warehouse system itself, from eliminating all three of them to retaining all three. In addition, there are alternatives for improving materials-handling equipment. Finally, there is the possibility of changing the size of any or all of the warehouses in the system. An OR study could easily analyze these alternatives. It might show, for example, that minimum distribution costs could be achieved by eliminating warehouse 3, expanding warehouse 1, and modernizing warehouse 2, and reorganizing the routing. This, of course, would be a relatively simple problem in logistics. But with a 10-warehouse system, the alternatives might run into the thousands; for a 25-warehouse system, into the millions. In such cases, OR methods would be almost essential to obtain a good solution.

OPERATIONS RESEARCH AND
INVENTORY PROBLEMS

One area of logistics in which OR methods have been applied with particular success is in solving problems and developing control systems for supply and

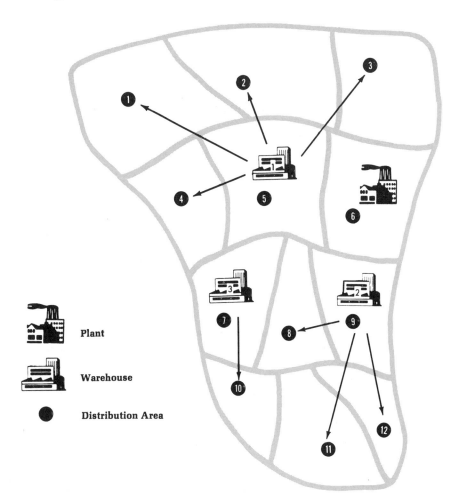

FIGURE 14.1
The present distribution system

distribution of inventory. Companies employ OR techniques usually in conjunction with computer technology—to forecast shifts in demand; to determine the most effective ways of controlling spare parts; to improve purchasing and control of materials; to provide decision rules or policies for reordering stocks.

A typical problem was faced by a manufacturer of a metal tubing used in the construction industry. The company wished to develop a system for distributing its product to franchised dealers, one that would function efficiently, without excessive delays or back orders, and yet would operate at minimum cost. The problem was further complicated by frequent, unexpected price changes in the industry, which often caused the demand for certain product lines to rise or fall drastically. These sudden fluctuations were apt to catch the company short-handed; its inventory and distribution system simply could not keep up with the sudden shifts in demand. In the time it took to rush needed items to the warehouses, the company was missing out on a good many sales.

An OR study group was assigned to the problem. It examined records of sales, production, and inventory, analyzed the effects of price changes, and compared the costs of delivering products at different intervals and in different lot sizes. The study showed, first of all, that the company's efforts to meet surges in demand following price drops were not only futile, but wasteful. Often by the time new shipments were rushed to the warehouses, sales had returned to normal, leaving warehouses with huge inventories of undisposable merchandise.

A survey of the warehouses showed the entire inventory system completely out of balance. Certain product lines were almost constantly out of stock; others, unsold, piled up in ever-growing quantities. In addition, money was being wasted shipping products to the warehouses in small lots. The study showed that considerable amounts could be saved by delivering in full carload lots.

As a solution, the OR group offered two recommendations. First, it urged keeping safety stocks on hand at warehouses that would cover the bulk of sudden increases in demand in the event of price changes. Second, it developed a forecasting system which would project, for each product, an optimum level of supply, based on such factors as the average long-term sales of the product. A computerized central information system was installed automatically to keep the levels of each product up to the required minimum. At all times, this system would keep track of how much of each product was on hand, and on delivery at any moment. Whenever the level of on-hand plus on-delivery dropped below the optimum level, additional shipments of that product would be sent out to bring the supply back to the required level. Finally, the transportation system was revised so that shipments were made in full carload lots rather than smaller ones (see Appendix A at end of this chapter).

The techniques used to solve this particular problem were, by OR standards, not at all sophisticated. Ordinary statistical methods were used to determine optimum levels of inventory. A computer system was installed constantly to recalculate these optimum levels in the light of changing business conditions and to keep inventory up to the required levels, but the data processing techniques involved were not overly elaborate. Gathering accurate data on which to base all these calculations was the most important part of the solution—as it often is in OR problems.

OR techniques are often used to solve problems of inventory supply as well as distribution. For example, an automobile company wished to improve its method of supplying parts to its assembly line and, if possible, to reduce the inventory of parts it was obliged to keep on hand. The company was already using a computer-controlled purchasing procedure in which orders for parts were sent out to vendors each month. Yet, due to fluctuations in supply and usage, some parts were in constant oversupply, while others were subject to severe shortages. Naturally, when the supply of any item ran out, the whole assembly line would be disrupted, resulting in high production costs. And the oversupply of other items was likewise costing the company money in unused inventory.

An OR analysis showed that considerable costs could be saved by instructing the manufacturers of parts exactly when to deliver their shipments, rather than allowing deliveries to come any time in the month. However, to obtain this improvement required extensive design changes in the computer-controlled purchasing system. This involved procedures to calculate the expected values of usage and inventory for each item and automatically determine the optimum delivery time.

The OR team developed a more refined safety stock system that took account of several important factors. For example, it was found that the penalty of running out of supply was very severe even with low-cost items. Also, parts with low average usage tended to go out of stock more frequently than parts with high average usage. By evaluating the costs and statistics, the best policy led to keeping proportionally larger inventories of the low-usage and low-cost items and smaller inventories of others (see Appendix B). The company was able to reduce inventory and yet keep the supply of parts to the assembly line flowing smoothly.

OPERATIONS RESEARCH AND DISTRIBUTION SYSTEMS

Making OR work effectively in a business situation is often more than just a matter of working out a mathematically sound solution. A system that operates at minimum cost may be unacceptable to management in other respects; for example, it may not provide a satisfactory standard of customer service. Hence applying OR to logistics problems involves more than technical solutions; those solutions have to be successfully implemented.

Reducing the Number of Field Warehouses

To take a case in point: A company was interested in reducing the number of warehouses in its distribution system. Over the years, the company had accumulated a number of warehouses in different sales territories, as the need arose. But it had never examined its warehouse system as a whole, with a view toward minimizing total cost. Gradually, management became aware that, although each particular warehouse was functioning efficiently, the system as a whole was not. Some warehouses dealt with too large territories others with too small. Some were equipped differently from others, which meant that separate delivery facilities had to be maintained. Many further problems had arisen, due to the lack of over-all planning.

An OR group assigned to the problem constructed a model that described the warehouse system along with the various costs of maintaining the different warehouses. The group examined the hypothetical costs of eliminating certain warehouses, combining others, or building new ones, and compared these various alternatives. A development of linear programing was used to analyze the possible systems (see Appendix C). A new warehouse system was worked out to replace the old one; the study indicated it was the most efficient and economical system feasible.

But this was far from the whole story. The all-important problem of implementation remained—to translate the technical solution achieved by the OR group into management action.

Before this could be done, two things were necessary. First, the model solution had to be interpreted in terms of the business situation, and the various alternatives had to be presented to management in clear, non-technical language. Secondly, it was necessary to consider the effect that various changes in the system might have on organization, on management responsibilities, on labor problems, on customer relations, and so forth. Possible disruptive effects had to be taken into account. For example, here are just a few of the side effects the proposed solution would have:

1. It would affect customer service. In general, service would be more reliable, but special deliveries to favored customers would be eliminated.

2. A number of warehouses would have to be abandoned, introducing questions of disposal of property, cuts in labor and overhead, etc.

3. Control of distribution would be taken out of the hands of sales managers in the territories and transferred to a central authority.

4. A whole new central distribution department would have to be set up, and its policies and responsibilities defined.

5. More flexibility would be required of the production department in meeting distribution orders.

6. Greater factory warehousing of goods would be required.

7. New administrative techniques would be necessary to run the new system, including data processing equipment, and trained personnel to use it.

8. Top-management direction would be required to implement the plan over a period of a year or more.

These were just some of the major problems involved in implementing the solution. Fortunately, the company had prepared for the implementation stage by having management participate actively during the OR study. This had a double effect. It allowed the company's executives to contribute their understanding to the problem, and thus helped the OR team set up its study in the most meaningful way. It also helped management to interpret the results of the completed study, to anticipate the effects of various changes, and to plan the implementation process in advance. Hence, implementation was carried out relatively smoothly, and in little more than a year the new warehouse system was functioning at top efficiency.

Investment in a New Distribution Channel

We have seen from the previous example the importance of close cooperation between a team of OR specialists and top-level management, especially when major decisions are being contemplated. The following example shows in even greater detail how this cooperation, along each step of the way, can be vital to successful decision-making.

Recently, an industrial firm had to decide whether to expand its distribution facilities to compete with its rivals in the industry. The question was whether the product could be distributed to the new markets effectively enough and at low enough cost to make the expansion worthwhile. The decision was difficult because of the uncertainty of several factors: e.g., estimated sales, product life, etc. Since the company could not afford a severe loss in such a venture, it decided to analyze the risks involved, using OR techniques.

A study team was set up to work with management on the problem. In a series of working sessions, the OR specialists explained their approach to the managers, and outlined the techniques that would be used to analyze the problem. Together, both groups determined the several alternatives to be evaluated. Meanwhile, management furnished the OR specialists with the necessary data. Among other things, the managers had to estimate the possible range within which unknown factors might vary: for example, the lowest possible sales that could be expected, as well as the highest; the maximum and minimum cost estimates of building new distribution centers, and so on. Only when all this had been done could the OR team go to work on the actual analysis of the problem.

Using simulation techniques, the OR group ran tests to show the expected return and risk of loss under various sets of circumstances (see Figure 14.2). The simulation runs were repeated several times, each time substituting different values in place of the unknown factors. The results indicated that success or failure hinged chiefly upon two of these factors: the number of new distribution centers required and the pricing of the product.

Thus, both management and the OR team focused their efforts on reaching more precise estimates for these two variables. An analytical model was developed by the OR team to determine the optimum number of distribution centers; meanwhile, management conducted a pilot test to determine the effect that various prices would have on sales. New estimates were reached for each factor, and the simulation run was repeated again, using the new information (see Figure 14.3). This time the answer was fairly conclusive: The company was relatively safe in going ahead with the expansion.

As it turned out, the prediction was accurate; the expansion was a success. But such a result could never have been predicted by either group working alone. Only by combining the problemsolving techniques of the OR specialists with the practical knowledge and judgment of management could an intelligent solution be achieved.

LOGISTICS IN THE BUSINESS SYSTEM

When applying OR techniques to logistics, it is important to remember that logistics problems can seldom be considered in isolation; they have to be considered as part of a total business system. Changes in distribution systems invariably affect other areas, such as production and marketing. An OR approach must take into account these effects, keeping in mind the functioning of the system as a whole. For example, one must ask such questions as: How will adding new distribution centers affect production planning and costs? Will plants be able to meet the increased demand? How will reorganizing the warehouse system affect transportation costs? Will eliminating warehouses result in a too high factory inventory? And so forth.

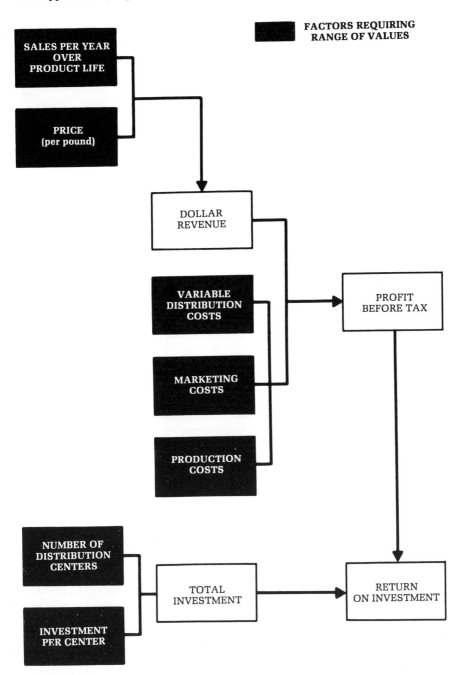

**FACTORS REQUIRING
RANGE OF VALUES**

FIGURE 14.2

Determining return on investment for new distribution channel

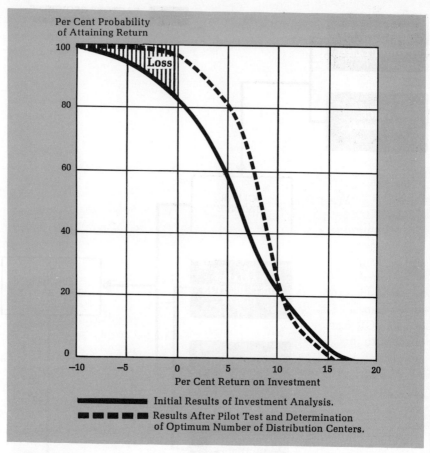

FIGURE 14.3

Comparison of investment analysis before and after pilot test

Because logistics problems are so closely related to other aspects of the total business picture, "trading off" distribution costs with other costs may offer important opportunities for cost reduction. For example, consolidating production in one plant would result in increased distribution costs, but these might be more than offset by the expected increase in profits. On the other hand, expanding the number of warehouses might decrease transportation costs and improve service to customers, yet increase costs of inventory to an even greater extent.

To cope with such complexities, OR techniques are gradually expanding in scope. Thus, OR specialists today seldom study logistics problems without examining other aspects of the total business system, such as marketing, production, sales, customer service, and so on. This broader approach becomes more and more feasible as OR techniques become more sophisticated and as management becomes more aware of the expanding possibilities. In the future, it can safely be said, OR methods will be applied on an ever-broadening scale.

An example of this forward-looking OR approach is found in the oil industry, where all planning must be closely coordinated on a company-wide basis—since a change in the selection of crude oil, for example, may affect refinery operation, which in turn may affect the allocation of finished goods. In order to cope successfully with such complex interrelationships, major oil companies work with logistics models that combine various aspects of the company's operations, from selection and refining of crude oil to distribution and marketing of the finished products (see Figure 14.4).

Summing up, then, what is it that makes an OR program function effectively in the solution of logistics problems? From the examples we have looked at, we can draw several conclusions. First of all, an OR study must consider problems of logistics in relation to the total business picture, rather than in isolation. Secondly, top-level management must work closely with the OR team along each step of the way, from setting up the original problem to implementing the final solution. Finally, both management and OR specialists must bring to the problem all the creativity at their disposal, especially in seeking new alternatives. Success in problemsolving is often more the result of a determined search for alternatives than of analyzing already existing ones. OR techniques are themselves a considerable help in the search for alternatives. Once a quantitative model of a logistics problem has been constructed, it is far easier for both management and OR specialists to visualize new alternatives.

What factors indicate whether a company is likely to benefit from applying OR techniques to logistics problems? The company is apt to be a large one, one whose logistics problems are too complex to be easily comprehended. Typically, companies whose products are bulky, whose operations involve a great deal of transportation, or whose distribution costs are relatively high are most apt to find OR techniques useful. Companies benefiting most from OR usually have a progressive outlook. For example, the company's different branches will be closely coordinated at the management level, so that problems can be considered in their broadest scope. We have seen, for example, that only through interdepartmental cooperation can the advantages of cost trade offs between departments be exploited. The company will have a sound information system to furnish necessary data and to monitor the effects of various policies. And finally, the company's logistics operations will be flexible enough so that changes can be implemented.

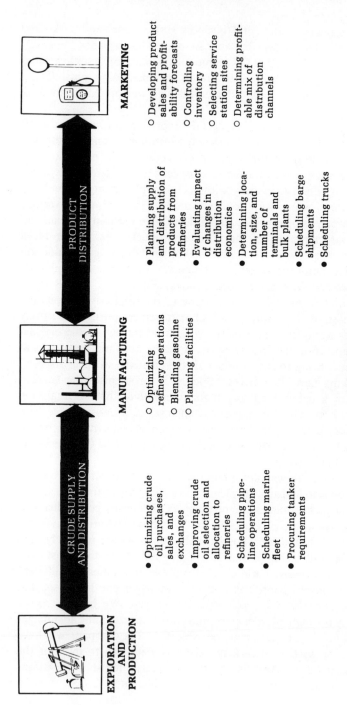

EXPLORATION AND PRODUCTION

CRUDE SUPPLY AND DISTRIBUTION

- Optimizing crude oil purchases, sales, and exchanges
- Improving crude oil selection and allocation to refineries
- Scheduling pipeline operations
- Scheduling marine fleet
- Procuring tanker requirements

MANUFACTURING

○ Optimizing refinery operations
○ Blending gasoline
○ Planning facilities

PRODUCT DISTRIBUTION

- Planning supply and distribution of products from refineries
- Evaluating impact of changes in distribution economics
- Determining location, size, and number of terminals and bulk plants
- Scheduling barge shipments
- Scheduling trucks

MARKETING

○ Developing product sales and profitability forecasts
○ Controlling inventory
○ Selecting service station sites
○ Determining profitable mix of distribution channels

- **LOGISTICS PROBLEMS**
  ○ **RELATED PROBLEMS INVOLVING LOGISTICS COSTS AND EFFECTIVENESS**

FIGURE 14.4

Applications of operations research to an oil company's logistics and related problems

Above all, a company must know how to apply OR techniques to business realities if it is to benefit from its OR investment. OR programs that fail seldom do so from any lack of mathematical or statistical techniques; they fail because these techniques are applied to the wrong problems, or applied to the right problems in the wrong way. The OR approach is merely a tool in the hands of management; ultimately, management is responsible for its success or failure. Hence in the area of logistics, the real key to sucessful operations research lies with those who grasp the complexities of marketing, distribution, inventory control, warehousing—in short, all the aspects of logistics discussed in other chapters of this volume. It is through such understanding, moreover, that opportunities for applying OR techniques to logistics problems are identified.

APPENDIX A

DISTRIBUTION OF ITEMS TO MEET PRICE CHANGES

Let I_{ij} = inventory of item i, on hand at warehouse j, and on delivery.

S_{ij} = forecast of average weekly sales in dollars for item i, at warehouse j.

T_{ij} = level of inventory needed to meet a price change.

F_i = factor to convert requirements to cubic feet of space.

B_i = minimum lot size for item i.

C = capacity of truck in cubic feet.

a_j = lead time in weeks for recording inventory and delivering to warehouse j.

To obtain adequate inventory to meet a price change, the requirement R_{ij} for item i at warehouse j is determined from the following simple relationship:

$$R_{ij} = T_{ij} + a_j S_{ij} - I_{ij}$$

To ship in full carload lots, the distribution rule schedules shipment of a truck to warehouse j when:

$$\Sigma F_i R_{ij} = C$$

Subject to

$$R_{ij} \geq B_i$$

(The shipment for an item must exceed the minimum lot size.)

When the total requirements for distributing items are greater than the availability (immediately after a price change), then a priority system is used so that the amount shipped is in proportion to the need. One rule used is to ship an amount

$$R_{ij}A_i/\Sigma_j R_{ij}$$

where A_i is the total quantity of item i available for distribution.

APPENDIX B

IMPROVING AN INVENTORY CONTROL SYSTEM

An automobile company uses a computer-controlled purchasing system where vendors receive monthly releases to ship specific quantities during the next month and estimates for the following two months. The system is to be changed so that releases specify shipment during a specific week.

To minimize inventory, the computer system must calculate in which week of the month a product should arrive to cover the month's requirements with adequate safety stock for variability in usage and delivery time.

The vendor release system calculates requirements cumulatively from a yearly starting point.

Let I_0 = beginning inventory (at starting point).

D_i = cumulative releases requested up to the end of month i.

U_i = cumulative usage up to the end of the month i.

F_j = forecast for usage of month j.

The expected inventory I_i at the end of month i is equal to: $I_0 + D_i - U_i$.

The shipping week is determined so that a safety stock of value S is expected at the end of the week. If there are w working days in the month, the expected cumulative usage on day n is equal to $U_i + (n/w)F_j$.

Then, the delivery should arrive in month i during the week in which:

$$I_0 + D_i - \left(U_i + \frac{n}{w}F_j\right) = S$$

or simply,

$$I_i - \frac{n}{w}F_j = S$$

The amount to be delivered is calculated from economic lot size considerations.

In calculating the optimum safety stock, the computer showed that the total penalty cost of shortages was proportional to the number of items short and an observed penalty cost per item. Then a simple analysis showed that safety stock should be given by:[1]

$$\int_{sp}^{00} (x)dx = \frac{IC}{Pn}$$

where $p(x)$ is the distribution of usage around the forecast value during the lead time between the request for release and the delivery, and

I = annual inventory rate.
C = cost of part.
p = penalty cost of shortage.
n = number of deliveries per year (based on the economic lot size).

The computer program calculated for each item the expected usage during the lead time, then determined the optimum safety stock, and finally calculated the week when the vendors should deliver.

APPENDIX C

SOLVING THE WAREHOUSE PROBLEM

The problem can be stated as follows: A mix of products is shipped either directly from factories i, or through warehouses j to customers k. A solution is to be found giving the set of warehouses that minimizes the sum of the fixed and variable costs of the system.

$X_{i,j}$ = quantity shipped from factory i to warehouse j.
$X_{i,k}$ = quantity shipped direct from factory i to customer k.
$X_{j,k}$ = quantity shipped from warehouse j to customer k.
$C_{i,j}$ = cost per unit of shipping from factory i to warehouse j.
$C_{i,k}$ = cost per unit of shipping direct from factory i to customer k.

---

[1]Robert B. Fetter and Winston C. Dalleck, *Decision Models for Inventory Management*, Richard D. Irwin, 1961, p. 20.

$C_{j,k}$ = cost per unit of delivery from warehouse j to customer k.

$C_j(W_j)$ = total fixed and variable cost of warehouse operation for a total throughput of W units at warehouse j.

W_j = throughput at warehouse j.

F_j = fixed costs per unit time for warehouse j.

V_j = variable cost per unit for warehouse j.

D_k = demand by customer k.

M_j = maximum throughput of warehouse j.

Y_i = maximum output of factory i.

Z_j = 1 if warehouse j is used, and zero if it is not used.

The problem then is to minimize total costs given by the objective function,

$$F(x) = \Sigma_{ij}C_{ij}X_{ij} + \Sigma_{jk}C_{jk}X_{jk} + \Sigma_{ik}C_{ik}X_{ik} + \Sigma_j C_j(W_j)Z_j$$

subject to the following constraints:

$$\Sigma_j X_{jk} + \Sigma_i X_{ik} = D_k$$

(Sum of deliveries from warehouses plus shipments direct from factories to customer k equals the demand of customer k.)

$$\Sigma_i X_{ij} = \Sigma_k X_{jk} = W_j$$

(Product flowing into warehouse j equals product flowing out.)

$$\Sigma_i X_{ij} \leq M_j$$

(Maximum warehouse throughput cannot be exceeded.)

$$\Sigma_j X_{ij} + \Sigma_k X_{ik} \leq Y_i$$

(Maximum factory output cannot be exceeded.)

There are a number of methods for dealing with this nonlinear problem:

1. In some cases integer programing can be used when the problem is small.

2. If there are only a few alternatives, the variable costs alone can be minimized for each alternative system of fixed costs—that is, each possible warehouse system.

3. A simulation (or Monte Carlo) method can be used to test alternative distribution systems.

4. Heuristic programing can be used. This method involves programing practical rules of thumb which reduce the search for lower-cost systems among the alternatives.

5. An approximation technique to overcome the nonlinearities can be used with linear programing. This method, which is based on successive approximations of the costs in a linear model, is illustrated below.

Approximation Method

The total cost of a warehouse consists of fixed and variable costs. The total cost $C_j(W_j) = F_j + V_j W_j$ is approximated by

$$W_j \left(\frac{F_j}{W_j^n} + V_j \right)$$

where the term in parentheses is the average cost based on an assumed throughput of W_j^n. An initial warehouse throughput W_j^1 is assumed and the first approximation minimizes:

$$F_1(x) = \Sigma_{jk} C_{jk} X_{jk} + \Sigma_{jk} C_{ik} X_{ik} + \Sigma_{ij} \left(C_{ij} + \frac{F_j}{W_j^1} + V_j \right) X_{ij}$$

For the second approximation

$$W_j^2 = \Sigma_i X_{ij}$$

is obtained from the solution of the problem to minimize $F_1(x)$. The second approximation minimizes:

$$F_2(x) = \Sigma_{jk} C_{jk} X_{jk} + \Sigma_{ik} C_{ik} X_{ik} + \Sigma_{ij} \left(C_{ij} + \frac{F_j}{W_j^2} + V_j \right) X_{ij}$$

These approximations are continued until $W_j^n = W_j^{n-1}$ over all j.

In practice it may be possible to reduce the size of a warehouse in economic steps with a different value of fixed cost for each step. In this case, additional constraints are required, for example: If $0 \le W_j \le N_j$, the fixed cost $F_j = F_{j,1}$ and $N_j \le W_j \le M_j$; then $F_j = F_{j,2}$.

15

Jerry Schorr

Special Applications of
Linear Programing

Costs inherent in the physical distribution pipeline have been likened to a leaky garden hose that has been a standard prop for film and television comedians for many years: When the comic pushes down at one leak, the water comes spouting out of another, usually in the dowager duchess's face— and when the least-cost approach is applied to an individual segment of a distribution system, costs are apt to bounce up disproportionately in other segments.

To overcome this problem in physical distribution, the systems approach is used. And this is another way of saying that the interaction of variable cost elements—or the impact of a change in one element on the total system— is measured.

To that end linear programing is an interactive mathematical tool used to obtain the single optimum solution to a problem containing a number of variables. In effect, linear programing makes it possible to state all these interactive elements in graphic form—one may then actually "see" numerically the impact on the total system of changes in individual cost elements.

To demonstrate how linear programing can best be used to solve distribution problems, in this chapter we will construct elementary distribution problems involving distribution centers and market areas. The solving of these distribution problems will be accomplished through the individual use of three linear programing methods, including:

The zero technique
The "stepping stone" technique
    (or the transportation technique or matrix algebra)
Matrix logic

ADVANTAGES OF LINEAR PROGRAMING

Before we commence solving distribution problems let us look at the advantages gained by the use of linear programing. The manual solution of a transportation problem (i.e., without the use of linear programing) dealing with ten or twenty plants and five or ten market areas would take a great deal of time. Linear programing simplifies the solving of a logistics problem, but even more important, it develops a scientific proof for the optimum answer. There is complete confidence that the optimum answer resulting from the use of linear programing is ±0.0 per cent in variance from the true optimum answer.

CONSTRUCTING A MATRIX

All three linear programing techniques described in this chapter involve the use of the matrix. A matrix is very much like a chart or graph in that it allows us to visualize the varying relationship between unlike numerical items—e.g., the relationship between the number of east–west highways and the number of north–south highways which link together, or the relationship between the number of units shipped and the number of dollars of transportation cost as well as their relationship to nonnumerical items such as products, plant locations, and types of transportation. Like a chart or graph, a matrix has both horizontal and vertical dimensions. A simple matrix is a square divided into nine squares or "cells" consisting of three horizontal rows and three vertical columns (Figure 15.1). Actually, a matrix can be either square or rectangular, and it can contain as many rows and columns as are necessary to state all the elements being studied.

The next step in constructing the matrix is to identify each cell. A simple identification system is to use a two-digit number for each cell, the first digit identifying the row number and the second digit identifying the column number. Thus, the cell in the left upper corner is identified as cell 11 and the one in the lower right corner is cell 33 (Figure 15.2).

Next, we should identify each of the distribution centers and market areas, as shown in Figure 15.3. While in Figure 15.3 the market areas are identified as columns and the distribution centers as rows, the designations could as well have been reversed—the market areas designated as rows and the distribution centers as columns.

The next step is to identify the quantities of, say, ZOGs produced at the distribution centers (in this case the distribution centers are plant warehouses) and the average sales of ZOGs in each of the market areas (Figure 15.4).

	Col. 1	Col. 2	Col. 3
Row 1			
Row 2			
Row 3			

FIGURE 15.1

	Col. 1	Col. 2	Col. 3
Row 1	11	12	13
Row 2	21	22	23
Row 3	31	32	33

FIGURE 15.2

DISTRIBUTION CENTER	MARKET AREA		
	Louisville	Cleveland	Pittsburgh
Philadelphia			
Chicago			
Atlanta			

FIGURE 15.3

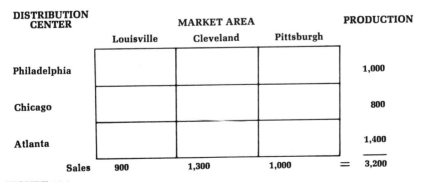

DISTRIBUTION CENTER	MARKET AREA			PRODUCTION
	Louisville	Cleveland	Pittsburgh	
Philadelphia				1,000
Chicago				800
Atlanta				1,400
Sales	900	1,300	1,000	= 3,200

FIGURE 15.4

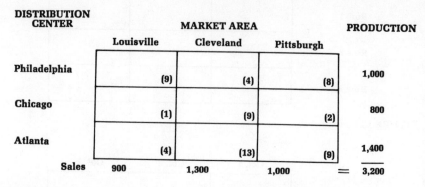

FIGURE 15.5

Distribution Centers	ZOG Production (units)[a]
Philadelphia	1,000
Chicago	800
Atlanta	1,400
TOTAL	3,200

[a]Each unit weighs 100 pounds

Market Areas	ZOG Sales (units)
Louisville	900
Cleveland	1,300
Pittsburgh	1,000
TOTAL	3,200

As the final step in the construction of a matrix, transportation costs per unit of production are developed between each pair of points (9 in this illustration) and are placed at the lower right corner of each cell. It is usual to place parentheses around the cost so as to distinguish the cost from any other numbers placed in the cell (Figure 15.5).

THE ZERO TECHNIQUE

The zero technique is the first of three linear programing tools which we shall use to solve the distribution problem we have constructed. This simple technique is used in production, transportation, and other business areas to solve complex problems. Listed below are the steps which should be used in applying the zero technique:

Step 1: In each column, find the lowest-cost cell and reduce the cost in this cell to zero.

Example (Figure 15.6): The lowest-cost cell in column 1 is $1.00; in column 2 it is $4.00; and in column 3 it is $2.00. Reduce each of these costs to zero.

Step 2: In each column reduce the cost in each of the remaining cells by the exact amount by which the lowest-cost cell was reduced in the previous step.

Example (Figure 15.7): In column 1 reduce the cost of each of the two remaining cells by $1.00; in column 2, by $4.00; and in column 3, by $2.00.

Step 3: In those rows which do not contain a zero, locate the lowest-cost box in the row and reduce the cost in this box to zero.

DISTRIBUTION CENTER	MARKET AREA			PRODUCTION
	Louisville	Cleveland	Pittsburgh	
Philadelphia	(8)	(0)	(6)	1,000
Chicago	(0)	(5)	(0)	800
Atlanta	(3)	(9)	(7)	1,400
Sales	900	1,300	1,000	= 3,200

FIGURE 15.6

DISTRIBUTION CENTER	MARKET AREA			PRODUCTION
	Louisville	Cleveland	Pittsburgh	
Philadelphia	(7)	(0)	(4)	1,000
Chicago	(0)	(1)	(0)	800
Atlanta	(2)	(5)	(5)	1,400
Sales	900	1,300	1,000	= 3,200

FIGURE 15.7

Example (Figure 15.8): Rows 1 and 2 contain boxes which have a zero, but in row 3 the lowest-cost box is $2.00. Therefore, reduce the $2.00 cost to zero.

Step 4: In each row which did not previously contain a zero box, reduce the cost of each of the remaining boxes by the exact amount by which the lowest-cost box was reduced in step 3.

Example (Figure 15.9): In row 3 reduce the cost of the two remaining boxes by $2.00.

Step 5: In all columns and in all rows which contain only *one* box with a zero cost, place the maximum number of ZOGs in the zero box.

Example (Figure 15.10): Column 2 has one zero box (Philadelphia to Cleveland). Place 1,000 units of ZOGs in this box. Column 3 has one zero

DISTRIBUTION CENTER	MARKET AREA			PRODUCTION
	Louisville	Cleveland	Pittsburgh	
Philadelphia	(7)	(0)	(4)	1,000
Chicago	(0)	(1)	(0)	800
Atlanta	(0)	(5)	(5)	1,400
Sales	900	1,300	1,000	= 3,200

FIGURE 15.8

DISTRIBUTION CENTER	MARKET AREA			PRODUCTION
	Louisville	Cleveland	Pittsburgh	
Philadelphia	(7)	(0)	(4)	1,000
Chicago	(0)	(1)	(0)	800
Atlanta	(0)	(3)	(3)	1,400
Sales	900	1,300	1,000	= 3,200

FIGURE 15.9

DISTRIBUTION CENTER	MARKET AREA			PRODUCTION
	Louisville	Cleveland	Pittsburgh	
Philadelphia	(7)	*1000* (0)	(4)	1,000
Chicago	(0)	(1)	*800* (0)	800
Atlanta	*900* (0)	(3)	(3)	1,400
Sales	900	1,300	1,000	= 3,200

FIGURE 15.10

DISTRIBUTION CENTER	MARKET AREA			PRODUCTION
	Louisville	Cleveland	Pittsburgh	
Philadelphia	(7)	*1000* (0)	(4)	1,000
Chicago	(0)	(1)	*800* (0)	800
Atlanta	*900* (0)	*300* (3)	*200* (3)	1,400
Sales	900	1,300	1,000	= 3,200

FIGURE 15.11

box (Chicago to Pittsburgh). Place 800 units of ZOGs in this box. Row 3 has one zero box (Atlanta to Louisville). Place 900 units of ZOGs in this box.

Step 6: Any ZOGs which remain to be distributed will automatically fall into place in the matrix.

Example (Figure 15.11): Atlanta, which has 500 ZOGs remaining, is the only plant which still has to distribute ZOGs. The matrix shows that 300 ZOGs must be distributed to the Cleveland market area and 200 ZOGs must be distributed to the Pittsburgh market area.

Step 7 (Figure 15.12): Calculate the total cost for the entire distribution of 3,000 ZOGs. Notice that we have solved for the lowest possible cost of $12,400. Also notice that the lowest-cost answer is arrived at by not placing

DISTRIBUTION CENTER	MARKET AREA			PRODUCTION
	Louisville	Cleveland	Pittsburgh	
Philadelphia	(8)	*1000* (4)	(6)	1,000
Chicago	(1)	(5)	*800* (2)	800
Atlanta	*900* (3)	*300* (9)	*200* (7)	1,400
Sales	900	1,300	1,000	= 3,200

FIGURE 15.12

DISTRIBUTION CENTER	MARKET AREA			PRODUCTION
	Louisville	Cleveland	Pittsburgh	
Philadelphia	(5)	(3)	(7)	1,000
Chicago	(3)	(1)	(5)	800
Atlanta	(6)	(4)	(8)	1,400
Sales	900	1,300	1,000	= 3,200

FIGURE 15.13

DISTRIBUTION CENTER	MARKET AREA			PRODUCTION
	Louisville	Cleveland	Pittsburgh	
Philadelphia	(0)	(0)	(0)	1,000
Chicago	(0)	(0)	(0)	800
Atlanta	(0)	(0)	(0)	1,400
Sales	900	1,300	1,000	= 3,200

FIGURE 15.14

any ZOGs in the lowest-cost box of $1.00 and placing 300 ZOGs in the highest-cost box of $9.00.

	Units	×	Unit Transporta- tion Cost	=	Total Cost
From Philadelphia	1,000		$4		$ 4,000
From Chicago	800		2		1,600
From Atlanta	900		3		2,700
	300		9		2,700
	200		7		1,400
TOTAL	3,200				$12,400

While the zero technique solved for the lowest-cost answer in the above example, it will not provide the optimum answer for every problem, as shown in Figures 15.13 and 15.14.

The reader should not be discouraged because of the limitations of this technique. In fact, because the zero technique is so fast and so simple, one should use it readily. If the optimum answer cannot be derived by the use of the zero technique, the stepping stone technique or matrix logic should be employed.

THE STEPPING STONE TECHNIQUE

The stepping stone technique is essentially a movement system, using addition, subtraction, and some algebra. The following steps are employed in this technique.

Step 1 (Figure 15.15): Allocate units in any cells as a starting point (and circle the number of allocated units), but make sure that the total number of units in each row and column equals production or sales.

Step 2 (Figure 15.16): Evaluate all cells not containing ZOGs as possible alternatives by using the following movement system: Starting in any one of the cells not containing a circled cost figure, move horizontally to a circled cell. Then alternate vertical and horizontal moves, moving to circled cells only, until the column of the starting cell is reached; then move vertically

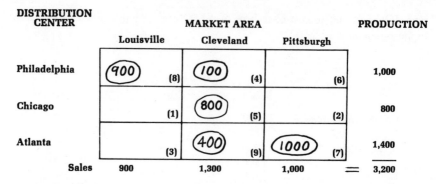

FIGURE 15.15

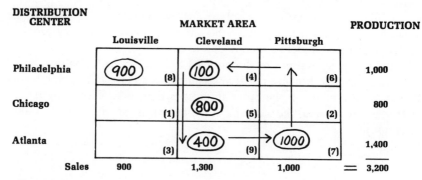

FIGURE 15.16

to that cell. The fewest possible movements should be used in returning to the starting cell; circled cells can be bypassed.

Example: Movement system followed to evaluate cell (Philadelphia to Pittsburgh):

a.   Move horizontally from cell 13 to cell 12.
b.   Move vertically from cell 12 to cell 32 (bypassing cell 22).
c.   Move horizontally from cell 32 to cell 33.
d.   Move vertically from cell 33 to cell 13.

Following the movement path, assign a negative sign to each circled transportation cost (i.e., cost figures in cells 12, 32, and 33). Then, starting with the first cell moved to, multiply the negatively signed costs alternately by +1 and −1. Insert the number arrived at in the cell being evaluated.

Example: Deriving number for cell 13. Cells traversed are: 12, 32, 33, 13 (cell being evaluated). Costs for traversed cells are (letting A be any cell):

$$A_{12} = 4; A_{32} = 9; A_{33} = 7; A_{13} = 6$$

Evaluating number for cell 13:

$$\begin{aligned}
A_{13} &= [+(-A_{12})] + [-(-A_{32})] + [+(-A_{33})] + [-(-A_{13})] \\
&= +(-4) + (+9) + (-7) + (+6) \\
&= -4 + 9 - 7 + 6 \\
&= +4.
\end{aligned}$$

Step 3 (Figure 15.17): Then evaluate all noncircled cells.

Step 4 (Figure 15.18): The optimum solution has been achieved if the noncircled numbers shown in Figure 15.22 are not all negative, i.e., if they

DISTRIBUTION CENTER	MARKET AREA			PRODUCTION
	Louisville	Cleveland	Pittsburgh	
Philadelphia	(900) (8)	(100) (4)	+4 (6)	1,000
Chicago	−8 (1)	(800) (5)	−1 (2)	800
Atlanta	−2 (3)	(400) (9)	(1000) (7)	1,400
Sales	900	1,300	1,000	= 3,200

FIGURE 15.17

DISTRIBUTION CENTER	MARKET AREA			PRODUCTION
	Louisville	Cleveland	Pittsburgh	
Philadelphia	100 (8)	900 (4)	+4 (6)	1,000
Chicago	800 (1)	+8 (5)	+7 (2)	800
Atlanta	−10 (3)	400 (9)	1000 (7)	1,400
Sales	900	1,300	1,000	= 3,200

FIGURE 15.18

are all zero or greater. If one or more of the noncircled numbers is negative, another feasible solution must be found in the following way:

a. Select the cell containing the largest negative number ($A_{21} = -8$).

b. Retrace the path followed in evaluating this number (path is $A_{22}, A_{12}, A_{11}, A_{21}$).

c. Identify in the path the circled cells that were assigned positive signs (A_{22}, A_{11}) and select that cell containing the smallest transportation cost ($A_{22} = \$5$).

d. Shift 800 ZOGs away from cell A_{22} to cell A_{21}.

e. In order to equalize shipments with sales requirements in Louisville and Cleveland, shift 800 ZOGs from cell A_{11} to cell A_{12}.

DISTRIBUTION CENTER	MARKET AREA			PRODUCTION
	Louisville	Cleveland	Pittsburgh	
Philadelphia	+10 (8)	1000 (4)	+4 (6)	1,000
Chicago	800 (1)	−2 (5)	+7 (2)	800
Atlanta	100 (3)	300 (9)	1000 (7)	1,400
Sales	900	1,300	1,000 =	3,200

FIGURE 15.19

Solution A

DISTRIBUTION CENTER	MARKET AREA			PRODUCTION
	Louisville	Cleveland	Pittsburgh	
Philadelphia	+8 (8)	1000 (4)	+2 (6)	1,000
Chicago	500 (1)	300 (5)	−3 (2)	800
Atlanta	400 (3)	+2 (9)	1000 (7)	1,400
Sales	900	1,300	1,000 =	3,200

FIGURE 15.20

Solution B

Step 5 (Figures 15.19–15.22): Continue steps 1–4 until a solution is obtained that has either zeros or positive numbers in all noncircled cells. In this particular example, four more solutions are calculated before achieving the optimum solution.

The stepping stone technique is quite useful for solving distribution problems, but like the zero technique, this linear programing tool has limitations:

1. Total production must equal total sales. If it does not, the problem cannot be solved by the stepping stone technique.

2. In many problems the movement system breaks down; that is, a point is reached where a move cannot be made between circled cells, as shown in Figure 15.23.

DISTRIBUTION CENTER	MARKET AREA			PRODUCTION
	Louisville	Cleveland	Pittsburgh	
Philadelphia	+11 (8)	1000 (4)	+5 (6)	1,000
Chicago	+3 (1)	300 (5)	500 (2)	800
Atlanta	900 (3)	−1 (9)	500 (7)	1,400
Sales	900	1,300	1,000 =	3,200

FIGURE 15.21

Solution C

DISTRIBUTION CENTER	MARKET AREA			PRODUCTION
	Louisville	Cleveland	Pittsburgh	
Philadelphia	+10 (8)	1000 (4)	+4 (6)	1,000
Chicago	+3 (1)	+1 (5)	800 (2)	800
Atlanta	900 (3)	300 (9)	200 (7)	1,400
Sales	900	1,300	1,000	3,200

FIGURE 15.22

Solution D: Optimum solution

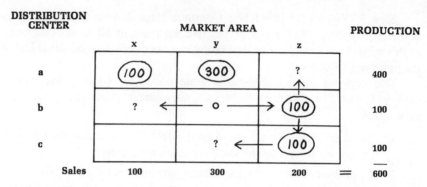

FIGURE 15.23

MATRIX LOGIC TECHNIQUE

The user of the matrix logic technique needs no formal training in linear programing or sophisticated mathematics. All that is needed for the application of this technique is simple logic plus addition and subtraction.

The application of the technique, which takes only a few minutes, achieves the lowest-cost solution for many varieties of logistics problems, including those of dispatching vehicles and containers and routing products.

This is in sharp contrast to many linear programing techniques which are difficult to use, involve complex mathematics, and do not arrive at the lowest-cost solution for many logistics problems.

In order to demonstrate the versatility of the matrix logic technique, the problem will be changed so as to start with an unequal supply and demand emanating from different plants and market areas.

Step 1 (Figure 15.24):

a. First, identify each plant and each market area.
b. At the bottom of each column list the number of ZOGs produced at each plant.
c. To the right of each row show the sales for each market area.
d. Then, insert the transportation cost between each plant and market area into every cell in the matrix.

Step 2 (Figure 15.25):

a. Locate the box with the lowest cost ($2). Into this box insert the maximum number of ZOGs (700) which can be placed in it. Then,

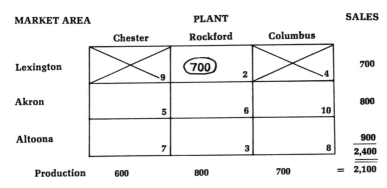

FIGURE 15.25

circle this number. For example, 700 ZOGs are needed at Lexington and 800 are produced at Rockford. Therefore, insert the circled number 700 in the box showing the lowest cost of $2.

b. Since Lexington does not need any more ZOGs, now mark an X in each of the two remaining boxes in row 1.

Step 3 (Figure 15.26):

a. In the remaining six boxes (all of those boxes which do not contain a circled number or an X), find the lowest-cost box ($3). Then follow the same procedure shown in Step 2 until all boxes contain either a circled number or an X.

b. Now add the total number of ZOGs shown in circled numbers in each row (add horizontally) and each column (add vertically).

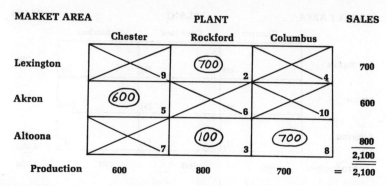

FIGURE 15.26

The total number of ZOGs produced and forwarded to market areas will now be equal. That is, it has been determined that since anticipated sales exceeds production, products will be shipped to those market areas which have the lowest transportation cost. (The absolute profit per unit of product is constant for all market areas). At this point, because of high transportation costs, Akron will receive only 600 ZOGs while its anticipated sales are 800 ZOGs; and Altoona will receive only 800 ZOGs while its anticipated sales are 900 ZOGs.

Sales	Number of ZOGs Supplied	Number of ZOGs Not Supplied
700	700	–
800	600	(200)
900	800	(100)
2,400	2,100	(300)

Then determine the total transportation cost.

Number of ZOGs	Unit Cost	Total Cost
700	$2	$1,400
600	5	3,000
100	3	300
700	8	5,600
	TOTAL	$10,300

Step 4:

a. Although production has been allocated to the three market areas, the solution shown in step 3 may not be the lowest-cost solution. By following steps 4 and 5 the lowest-cost solution can be determined.

Starting in the third column on the right, determine whether a circled number is located in the lowest-cost box in that column. If there is a box with a lower cost in that column, transfer the circled number into the lower-cost box. Notice that while transportation costs are reduced, too many ZOGs are being supplied to one market area (Lexington) and too few to another market area (Altoona).

Example (Figure 15.27): Lexington, with sales of 700 ZOGs, is receiving 400 ZOGs; and 100 ZOGs are going to Altoona, which has sales of 800 ZOGs.

b. Therefore, since Rockford is the only other plant supplying ZOGs to Lexington, forward 700 ZOGs from Rockford to Altoona instead of to Lexington in order to have the circled number of ZOGs equal the sales in each market area. Notice that by forwarding ZOGs from Rockford to Altoona instead of to Lexington, costs have been increased by $1 per unit. Therefore, the net cost reduction equals $3 per unit multiplied by 700 units, or $2,100.

Number of ZOGs	Unit Cost	Total Cost
700	$4	$2,800
600	5	3,000
800	3	2,400
	TOTAL	$8,200

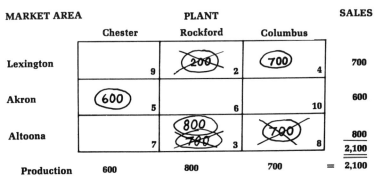

FIGURE 15.27

Step 5 (Figure 15.28): Follow step 4 first by column and then by row. Determine whether it is cheaper to place each ZOG in a lower-cost box first within the column and then within the row in which the circled number of ZOGs is contained. After following step 4 *only once* for each column and row, *the lowest-cost solution will be achieved.*

In Figure 15.28, we have already arrived at the lowest-cost solution in step 4.

Notice the ZOGs are placed in the lowest-cost box in each column (except column 2 where all ZOGs were shifted in step 4, from the box which has a cost of $2 to the box which has a cost of $3; a net cost reduction of $2,100 was thus achieved).

Also, while ZOGs are placed in the lowest-cost boxes in rows 2 and 3, the 700 ZOGs in row 1 are placed in the second-highest-cost box ($4). If we were to shift these ZOGs to the box in row 1 which has the lowest cost of $2 (Rockford to Lexington), we would be reducing our cost by $2 per unit. But, in order to have the circled number of ZOGs equal to production from each plant (1,500 ZOGs are being forwarded from Rockford, which produces only 800 ZOGs, and no ZOGs are being forwarded from Columbus, which produces 700 ZOGs), 700 ZOGs must be forwarded from Columbus to Altoona instead of from Rockford to Altoona, thus raising the cost for each unit of ZOGs by $5 (it will cost $8 instead of $2 to forward each unit of ZOGs to Altoona). Therefore, it would not be wise to place ZOGs in the lowest-cost box ($2) in row 1, because this alternative will yield a net increase in transportation costs of $3 per unit (a reduction of only $2 per unit and an increase of $5 per unit).

The matrix logic technique may be used for solving many types of logistics problems, including the applications shown in Figures 15.29 and 15.30.

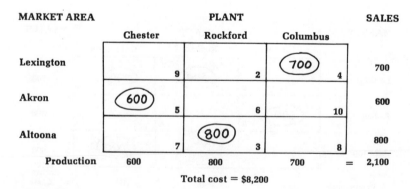

FIGURE 15.28

Lowest-cost solution

CUSTOMER		TERMINAL				SHIPMENT WEIGHT (lbs.)
		1	**2**	**3**		
A		(8)	10,000 (4)	(6)		10,000
B		(1)	(5)	8,000 (2)		8,000
C		9,000 (3)	3,000 (9)	2,000 (7)		14,000
Weight capacity of truck		9,000	13,000	10,000	=	32,000

FIGURE 15.29

Pickup of shipments

DEFICIT TERMINAL		SURPLUS TERMINAL				DEFICIT TRAILERS
		A	**B**	**C**		
D		(8)	10 (4)	(6)		10
E		(1)	(5)	8 (2)		8
F		9 (3)	3 (9)	2 (7)		14
Surplus Trailers		9	13	10	=	32

FIGURE 15.30

Dispatch of tractors and trailers between terminals

Weight lbs.	×	Cost per Cwt.	=	Cost
10,000		4		$400
8,000		2		160
9,000		3		270
3,000		9		270
2,000		7		140
			TOTAL	$1,240

Units	×	Cost per Unit	=	Cost
10		4		$40
8		2		16
9		3		27
3		9		27
2		1		14
			TOTAL	$124

SUMMARY

Linear programing techniques have made the solution of logistics problems economically feasible. In this chapter, we have described three such linear programing techniques—of which matrix logic is easily the most versatile and practical. But in any event, the use of the other two techniques is recommended for the validation of matrix logic solutions.

Part

Five

ISSUES AND
PROBLEMS
OF PUBLIC
POLICY

As is common knowledge, the policies and practices of physical distribution are shaped, in part, by the regulatory agencies of the federal and state governments. Thus, the levels and differentials in rates; the award of routes; many of the decision rules in shipping, packaging, warehousing, and the like are set outside the firm. At best, logisticians can only adjust to these acts of "public policy."

The impact of computerization on government regulation of the transport industry is analyzed in Chapter 16.

Part

Two

ISSUES AND
PROBLEMS
OF PUBLIC
POLICY

16

Robert L. Calhoun / Ernest Weiss

Computers and Government Regulation of the Transportation Industry

The several modes of transportation have seized upon the advantages offered by computers and the related disciplines of "management science," systems analysis, and operations research, paralleling applications by the Interstate Commerce Commission and other government agencies. Considerable benefits have already been derived from a variety of applications.

The operational nature and performance of transportation make it a rich source of uses for electronic data processing (EDP). There are few other industries in which its application holds greater promise for the future. Two significant factors confronting the carriers handling the bulk of the nation's for-hire transportation point this up. First, the movement of goods over any distance generates a large and expensive volume of documentation, supplemented by internal record-keeping requirements and the necessity of preparing numerous reports for public agencies and others. Except for the smaller-size firms, a second major problem is one of inadequate or imperfect communication between various production units and carrier management. While these same problems are faced, in some form, by nearly all enterprises, they are acute in the case of a transport firm whose operations sprawl over a wide geographic area and whose activities are regulated by government authorities.

As in other industries, the use of EDP is largely motivated by a desire to increase operational efficiency and reduce costs. This latter factor looms large in transportation, where rising labor costs, accounting for nearly 60 per cent of total costs, clash with declining, or, at best, stable revenues. Until reversed to some extent in 1964, this problem was particularly acute for many major railroads whose revenues and earnings were caught in a long-term downward spiral. Although this trend has now been largely halted, rail carriers are still far from full recovery of their competitive position and are relying heavily on computers to assist them to do so.

Until recently, the use of computers in the transportation industry was largely confined to the processing of internal paper work, in accounting and similar areas. While such functions still make up the largest proportions of applications, the trend among the carriers is to apply EDP technology to new and more sophisticated uses. A 1964 survey of 52 railroads, accounting for 95 per cent of the industry's mileage and revenues, indicated that roughly 89 per cent of the computer time available was devoted to accounting activities, with the remainder being devoted to "management science" activities, the proportion used for these latter activities being twice that of 1963. Although similar information is not available for the motor carrier industry, individual firms and industry associations, as will be noted, are already deeply involved in similar activities.

As the proportion devoted to management science activities has increased, the variety of uses has grown, expanding into almost every phase of the industry's operations. Faced with the needs to restore its competitive position and to cope with large traffic volumes and plant size, the railroad industry has invested much more in a wide variety of EDP applications than other competing modes. Aside from financial and accounting applications, the principal uses fall into three broad categories: traffic sales; operations; and transportation, meaning in this context those activities dealing with the actual movement of freight and passengers. Applications in traffic sales include traffic and market analysis studies by customer, commodity, and traffic territory, freight rate studies leading to new and improved pricing schemes, cost and statistical analysis, and computerized industrial development studies. In the important operations area, uses include such diverse items as freight car spotting and tracing, control of car supply, purchase order writing, ticket stock control, inventory control over supplies and stores, demurrage records, scheduling of maintenance of way of both track and roadbed, calculating vegetation growth to determine optional cutting and spraying cycles along rights of way, and a complex system that integrates mine production with rail service to a lake port for further shipment by water. Transportation sector uses are planned or underway chiefly in the vital area of yard-to-yard–general office communication, some on a real-time basis, to provide management and traffic, sales, and other nonoperating divisions with advance up-to-the-minute information on train consists, interchange reports, and customer inquiries. Other applications in this area include freight scheduling simulation studies and freight service quality control programs. Beyond these major categories, computers are doing service in engineering studies, analysis and research, simulation studies of yard performance for projected new yards, simulation studies of communication network requirements, personnel records, safety analysis, and freight car purchase programs.[1] In sum, railroad management is revolutionizing the "management" of all railroad activities through the use of computers and related techniques. In all, roughly 80 per cent of the nation's railroads are presently committed to one or more uses of computers.

Computer use in other forms of transportation such as motor carriers, freight forwarders, air carriers (with Eastern being a leader in this field), and REA Express is neither so extensive in terms of the number of firms involved nor so elaborate in terms of the number of uses. A combination of several factors may explain this. Contrasted to the railroad industry, the average motor carrier firm is relatively smaller in size, revenues, and operating territory, although there are a number of large motor carriers whose revenues exceed that of many Class I Railroads. In addition, the rapid development of the motor carrier industry in the last three decades was more rapid than investment of capital in equipment and terminals for expanding service. Without the keen spur of heavy capitalization costs and declining revenues, motor carriers were not under as much pressure to accomplish efficient and economic use of facilities and personnel. A third major factor is environmental, chiefly the avoidance by the industry of costly rights of way and other fixed facilities through the use of a publicly owned and maintained highway system. Along with this are such factors as the smaller maximum size of the producing unit (truckload versus trainload or carload) and a more restricted geographical area of operations.

Except for the third, all of these have been undergoing profound change over the last few years. Mergers, new grants of operating authority, and natural growth have tended to increase the scale size of the average firm. Trucking firms caught in a profit squeeze between rising costs, chiefly wages, and rate-cutting competition from the invigorated railroads and from shipper-controlled private carriage have been searching for ways to trim expenses, including exploitation of computer applications. Like the railroads, the earliest and still primary use of EDP has been in the accounting and payroll fields. More recent applications include traffic flow and load analysis, individual terminal profit and loss reports, billing and collecting, maintenance, control and computerized cost analysis, pricing, studies, and tariff automation.

A new force, which will lead to greater use of computers by medium-sized or small motor carriers is the commercial service bureau or computer services offered by associations of motor carriers.

Having generally listed some of the many varied uses to which data processing systems and skills are being put in transportation, it is useful to discuss a few of them in more detail.

---

[1]For a more elaborate listing, see "Cybernetics—Computers Give Boost to Management Science," *Railway Age*, December 14, 1964, p. 19.

In rail, motor carrier, and air carrier operations, some of the most promising gains have come about with the development of real-time applications of data processing to the complex problem of providing adequate service to the shipping public. For the railroads, a particularly distressing aspect of this for many years has been the dual problem of freight car shortages and efficient utilization of the existing supply.[2] The supply of boxcars has dropped from 726,000 in 1947 to 607,000 in 1964. Total cars in service have decreased almost 200,000 during the same period. Studies indicate that a freight car may stand still as much as 90 per cent of the time, and is empty 6 per cent of the time when moving. As an alternative to expensive car-building programs, a number of rail carriers are studying ways to increase car utilization. In one such study,[3] computer simulation models have been used to examine various alternatives to improved utilization through yards and terminals and over main lines of the study systems. Using car lists which specify arrival date and time, number and tonnage of cars, commodity, etc., and parametric data such as track and yard capacity as input, these models simulate yard and mainline performance factors, generating as output time histories of car movement, motive power utilization, use of fixed facilities, and the like. Such output is then acted upon by special analysis programs which assess the impact of simulated variations in operations upon the carrier's costs and investment programs. Programs of this type are now in effect on two southwestern railroads with more such projects in the planning stage.

Car utilization is also an important aspect of those programs established to provide real-time operating data. Now used by a number of railroads, such techniques enable the firm to maintain accurate up-to-the-minute location and movement information on equipment and motive power. These systems also provide for perpetual car inventory and control and records of the number and type of cars received and delivered on and off the line; they check yard efficiency and compute demurrage charges. One system now underway on a large eastern railroad will also develop forecasts of traffic movements and maintain a continuous check on the movement of priority traffic. Through optical scanning of car number or other indicators, car "spotting" can be accomplished while the cars are underway.

These real-time applications are the heart of various systems moving toward the "total systems" control concept. A typical program is one now in operation on a large southern road, the Louisville & Nashville.[4] This

---

[2]See Ex. Parte No. 241, *Investigation of Adequacy of Railroad Freight Car Ownership, Car Utilization, Distribution, Rules and Practices*, 323 I.C.C. 48 (1964).
[3]Koomanoff, *The Systems Approach and Transportation*, Battelle Memorial Institute, 1964.
[4]"L&N Reaches for Real Time Data," *Railway Age*, April 26, 1965, p. 36.

system, which went into operation in early 1964, is based on an elaborate communications network, using on- and off-line Telex machines and a number of IBM 1050s installed in yard and division offices. Data on car departure movements, consists, and other factors are processed on perforated tape and transmitted via the 1050 to a centralized IBM 1448–1460 computer "switching center." Here, data are compiled, sent to disc storage, and transmitted to receiving yards where a perforated tape is prepared for yard control use. From the disc storage, data can be retrieved via an IBM 7010–1301 random search on a real-time basis or otherwise, furnishing replies to shipper inquiries, using Telex, or, through periodic or daily runs on the 1460, furnishing car and movement data to the several operating departments of the company on a monthly or semimonthly basis. The L&N system will become completely operational in 1969 with the completion of a massive employee training program and the planned conversion of the 1448–1460 and the 7010–1301 systems to IBM's new 360 system. Similar programs are planned or in process on the Western Pacific, New York Central, the "Frisco," and the Pittsburgh and Lake Erie, among others.

In addition to the uses described in discussing the L&N's system, rail carriers, using a "systems" approach, have developed techniques to provide top management as well as traffic and other nonoperating departments with timely information for use in pricing and market decision. Facing intense intermodal competition and increased operating expenses, carrier management has turned to EDP and other new tools to seek out new traffic with an emphasis on increasing dollar return rather than merely increased tonnage, trains, and carloads. To meet a primary need for concise, detailed marketing data, computer programs are now generating detailed reports of inbound and outbound traffic flows by commodity groups, and freight revenues by customer or classes of customers, indicating destination, origin, routing, commodity, equipment type, car miles, total revenues, and characteristics. These statistical data may be applied to a number of profit control activities and may, in addition, improve equipment and plant utilization. Profit and loss statements of major segments of carrier business are a major use.[5] Special cost studies, including customer demand studies, branch line studies, rate research, and merger effect studies, are important supplements to this continuing analysis.

Similar developments are also taking place in the motor carrier industry, where a number of firms have adopted a "total systems" approach to provide information on traffic, operations control, and customer service problems. A system, designed by Honeywell, to be used by a large New England

[5]Cf. "Computers Help Spark a Revolution on the NYC," *Railway Age*, July 12, 1965, pp. 16, 19—a discussion of the EDP program of the New York Central Railroad.

carrier,[6] is illustrative. Using the Honeywell 200 hardware and software series, the program is concerned with three vital areas: operations control, including handling of manifests, shipment tracing, reports, production statistics, and real-time communications; transportation revenue accounting, including revenue tonnage statistics, budget control, sales and budget analysis, claims, and standard accounting uses; and a computerized rating system, known as CART (computerized automatic rating technique), for automatic rating (pricing) of shipments and, through computerized processing of shipment documentation, for providing data inputs to the rest of the system. This last part is tied into an elaborate communications system to provide consignees with advance notification of shipment arrivals.

When completely operational, the basic system will monitor the movement of motor freight from the time it is picked to final delivery. At the same time, it will rate all shipments and produce all statistical and financial report data required by the firm. Upon receipt of a shipment, a paper tape, duplicating the shipment manifest carried by the driver, will be punched at the point of origin. The tape, containing data on origin, destination, shipment weight and density, and commodity, will be transmitted to a central computer which will rate the shipment, the dollar amount of the charges, delivery route, and, where required, any interline settlement required. This information will be forwarded to the destination terminal and will also be stored for future financial and statistical use.

One of the most interesting aspects of the CART technique is its application of computer science to the industry's complex and massive pricing structure, contained in the thousands of tariffs and millions of rates now filed with the I.C.C., and state regulatory bodies by all regulated carriers. Since there can only be one legal published rate at any given time applicable to a given shipment, and this rate must be offered to all shippers able to meet its conditions, rate searching is, in its most basic form, a discrete deterministic problem in which all factors such as origin, destination, weight, etc. are specified, the only unknown being the lowest lawful rate and total charge.

At the present time, almost all freight is "rated" manually by experienced rate clerks. Despite this skill, many millions of dollars are lost each year either by carriers or shippers due to misapplication, misquoting, or other

---

[6]Cf. "St. Johnsbury Order $500,000 Data Processing Machine," *Transport Topics*, March 2, 1964, p. 16. Also, W. A. McPherson, "The Total System—A New Dimension in Trucking Management," unpublished paper presented before the Transportation Research Forum, Ohio Chapter, Canton, Ohio, May 4–6, 1965.

errors. Except in those instances where judgment is required, rating of shipments is largely a clerical task, thus making it a ripe subject for automation.

APPLICATIONS OF EDP TO I.C.C. RATING REQUIREMENTS

The subject of tariff computerization has received extensive attention in the last few years. Space permits only a few brief comments outlining the progress being made in this area.

As noted, the Interstate Commerce Act requires all regulated carriers to publish, and file with the I.C.C., schedules of their tariffs and rates. It is basic law that these schedules must be in such a form that a shipper will "know with certainty what rates he must pay."[7] Over the years, this certainty increasingly has become confined to expert traffic and tariff specialists. Competition has eroded the pristine logic and simplicity of the all-inclusive class rate structure; it has become, instead, a bewildering mass of exceptions ratings and special point-to-point commodity rates. Publishing and filing these millions of rates place a heavy financial burden on the carriers, the shipping public, and the I.C.C. The complexity of the system has generated demands for simplification of rates, of publishing form, procedures, and language.

In this work, EDP is playing a growing role in several areas. Several carriers have already filed "computerized" tariffs with the commission. Illustrative of this is a three-part tariff published at various times over the last three years by the Middle Atlantic Conference.[8] Using IBM equipment, Middle Atlantic has been able to simplify its tariffs and, more importantly, reduce the time lag and expense in making necessary changes. Use of EDP has also aided in eliminating duplicative or overaged material. Similar work is underway in other motor carrier territories. An important project in the Midwest ties together rate computerization with a continuous traffic study of movements, thus providing a basis for relating rates to costs. In addition, this program will eventually provide other useful information on a "total

---

[7]*Speed Van Service Between Md., N.J., N.Y., Pa., and Ill.*, 321 I.C.C. 452, 457 (1963).
[8]Middle Atlantic Conference, Master Tariff 20, MF–I.C.C. A–1500; Tariff 30–Q–A–1478; and Routing Guide MF–I.C.C., A–1430 as supplemented. These tariffs are partly in the form of reproduced printout sheets.

systems" basis for management and shippers in a similar fashion to the system previously described.[9]

The infinitely more complex task of computerizing rail tariffs is already underway at Battelle Institute in conjunction with a broad study authorized by the Department of Commerce. A report, released in January 1964, outlined the progress and expected course of this project. As a "bonus," Battelle included a sample of what may be the tariff of the future, a computer printout of the Akron, Canton, and Youngstown Railroad's Tariff 100–C, I.C.C. 472. Certain aspects of the Battelle study indicate the feasibility of a system that will permit the rapid selection of individual rates, routings, and other information. Several large shippers and REA Express, Inc., have already developed such systems on a smaller scale.[10]

The implications of tariff automation, however, run beyond the computerization of rate schedules. As noted by Joseph Hoffman[11] of the Middle Atlantic Conference, a tariff is more than a mere price list: A tariff indicates such elements as scope of operation and participation of the named carriers, points served, joint and through movements, and the classification and description of thousands of articles. A published tariff thus provides an available basing point upon which to build a multidimensional picture of the transportation industry. Using standardized codes, it will be possible to correlate tariff routings, rates, and commodity descriptions with both the IMCA system and studies of traffic movements derived from waybill samples.

A major step in this direction has already been taken by the commission in Docket No. 34206, Commodity Classification for Transportation Statistics. Beginning with 1964 data, all railroad waybills received by the commission will be coded, punched, and processed according to this modified five-digit code. A similar code, called the Standard Transportation Commodity Code or STCC, has been adopted by the American Association of Railroads for use by the carriers. Both codes are based on the Bureau of the Budget version of the Standard Industrial Classification. In a recent article, Herbert O. Whitten discussed the application of this code to computerized tariffs and other areas.[12] Among the potential uses are tariff item numbers, waybills, revenue statistics, and freight claims. The tariff of

---

[9]Henry A. Fahl, general manager, Eastern-Central Motor Carrier Association, "Data Processing Application in Collective Ratemaking," 32 *I.C.C. Pract. J.* 572 (1965).

[10]See papers collected in *Rates and Tariffs—Automation's Impact*, Transportation Research Forum, Ohio Chapter, 1964.

[11]Joseph V. Hoffman, "Motor Carrier Research in Rates and Tariffs," paper delivered to the Transportation Research Forum, Washington Chapter, January 15, 1964.

[12]"STCC: Big Mouthful with a Big Meaning," *Handling and Shipping*, January and February 1964.

the future, as illustrated by Whitten, would be based on STCC sequences and commodity descriptions. Using EDP, density codes might replace existing column ratings, with minimum weights standardized for given densities. Out of this activity, there may in time come a modernized and simplified uniform freight classification, based on a conceptually simple rate structure that will reflect both the competitive needs of the carriers and the requirements of the computer. As Whitten notes, there are many problems to resolve before the computer comes into its own in transportation. Considerable research and development remain to be done not only in the technical area but in the basic economics of ratemaking itself.

Beyond applications for compiling, storing, and analyzing traffic and operating information and uses tied to measuring and improving performance factors, computers are assisting in the planning of new rates, services, and equipment. Two areas, simulation studies and pricing design, which have public policy implications illustrate this role.

As noted previously,[13] computer techniques have been applied to simulation studies of freight car supply and utilization. Simulated "models" showing the interaction of parts of a system, an organization, or a problem are logical tools for use in transportation, since they permit the duplication in model form of a "real world" situation without the time or expense of actual experimentation while allowing for optional consideration of all relevant variables and alternative solutions.[14] Although simulation is possible without computers, the speed and memory capacity of computers permits more extensive and high-quality research. In addition to freight car utilization studies, computerized simulation studies have been used for plotting traffic flows, measuring elasticity of shipper demand, and, in a "business game" context, balancing equipment shortages and surpluses between motor carrier terminals. One study has been used before the I.C.C. in a pending proceeding. This study, similar to the "shipper preference models," is discussed in the concluding section of this chapter.

In designing new pricing schemes and rate structures, the "what if" questions posed in simulation studies are applied along with other tools to garner new traffic or to improve the revenue potential of existing consists. In designing any new pricing structure, sound economic considerations are primary. These include appraisals of market conditions, transportation conditions, and the all-over objective of profit maximization. One important use of EDP in this area was in redesigning the eastern grain rate structure in

---

[13]See pages 282–283.
[14]See John J. Coyle, "Simulation: Discussion and Application," *Transportation Journal*, Vol. 4, No. 3 (Spring 1965).

1963.[15] Because of the volume of movement and intense market competition, any major commodity structure must be designed for an entire area or group to preserve the integrity of the group and to avoid unlawful market discrimination. The computer is a logical tool for both experimenting with and calculating the complex relationships involved.

Similar studies, relating costs to rates, using computers to design optimal rate scales that will meet the requirements of law and return adequate profits to the carriers, are underway in the motor carrier industry. Such a rate scale, called the COR scale, for "cost-oriented rates," has been proposed as a solution to the pricing of smaller shipments.[16]

Since computers offer a tool for rapid and systematic handling of vast amounts of information, it has been suggested that the entire rate structure be redesigned to meet current competitive conditions.[17] This task, last undertaken over a fifteen-year period between 1939 and 1952 by the I.C.C. and the carriers, would be an enormous undertaking even with the aid of a computer. However, such a study might well assist in restoring some logic to the rate structure and might lead to tariff simplification and to the weeding out of "paper" rates that move little or no traffic. It would thus supplement the work now being done in the Commerce–Battelle study and that of the individual carriers.

In addition to the areas discussed, a number of other computer uses are being explored in transportation, the most important being the application of EDP in the actual operation of trains. Barring serious labor and safety questions, it is likely that EDP may eventually be used, as it is already in Japan, to control and even operate high-speed commuter and intercity passenger trains.

COMPUTER SCIENCE: POLICY INTERACTION AND PROBLEMS

The influence of EDP on public policy may be divided into two more or less arbitrary categories: influences resulting from government use and those flowing from government's role as a regulator of private conduct and a

---

[15]Cf. Joseph Steiner, "Development of the New York Central Grain Mileage Rates," *Papers—Fifth Annual Meeting, Transportation Research Forum*, 1964, p. 1; also, *Corn and Corn Products, Illinois and Indiana to East*, 319 I.C.C. 605 (1963).

[16]Because of its novelty, the COR scale is being investigated by the commission in Docket No. I. & S. M–18455. See also Fahl, *op. cit.*, p. 30.

[17]Herbert O. Whitten, *Mathematics of Rate Structures for Computerized Pricing*, Washington, D.C., 1965.

promoter of the public welfare.   Although oversimplified, it is probably accurate to attribute many positive actions in the second sphere to feedback resulting from the first, since use of EDP has sensitized decision-makers in the public sector to both its promises and its problems.   Having pointed out some of the developments in EDP applications, it is now possible to explore a few of the implications that these applications hold for public policy.

The effects of the computer revolution on transportation policy and law are varied.   It performs routine tasks with greater speed and accuracy and cuts costs of carrier operations in an absolute sense.   Since the computer, judiciously used, can assist in operations control and management decisions and can also provide guidance for future planning, it has become a vital tool in helping the carriers function more efficiently and profitably.   To this extent, the application of EDP to transportation may provide part of the needed cure for improving and strengthening the nation's transportation system.   This economic fact alone would be justification enough, just as more efficient conduct of its internal affairs would provide ample justification for the I.C.C.'s own uses.

In this new field, public agencies such as the I.C.C. and its counterparts in other forms of transportation (the Civil Aeronautics Board and the Federal Maritime Commission), the Department of Commerce, and other agencies charged with responsibilities in transportation are taking a creative role, encouraging innovation to the maximum extent consistent with their legal obligations.   In part, this role may be in creating a favorable environment that encourages not only new thoughts and methods, but also the sweeping away of unnecessary impediments.   This thought is well expressed in a recent speech by Commissioner Virginia May Brown, stating that:

> Carriers must be encourged to experiment and thereby improve their services to the public . . . .   No other agency of Government has a heavier burden than the Commission in supporting progressive innovations in surface transportation.   This means the Commission's policies must be flexible.   For the policies are constantly subject to review and amendment to meet new conditions.

Since this favorable climate, or lack of it, is reflected largely in the commission's decision-making process, the focus is on this area.

To place this in perspective, it is useful to digress briefly and to outline the nature of the I.C.C. and its work.   It is constituted as a "tribunal appointed by law and informed by experience."[18]   Within broad and flexible

---

[18]*Illinois Central RR Co. v. United States*, 206 U.S. 441, 454 (1907).

guides set down by the Congress, it adjudicates particular cases before it. As a "legislator," it establishes general rules and policies, regulating the conduct and business practices of carriers subject to its jurisdiction. The Uniform System of Accounts, regulating carrier accounting and financial practices, is a clear example of the latter.

In the performance of its function, the commission must pour expert substance into the applicable legal standards. To a considerable extent, this process of "putting meat on the bone" rests on the gathering and analysis of information, a procedure usually described as "fact-finding." In formal proceedings, such "facts" are usually derived from the record as made by the parties in order to insure procedural fairness. As noted previously,[19] however, the commission has supplemented this information with numerous economic and statistical studies to provide it with more knowledge about the economic behavior of all modes of transportation. This information leads to improved regulatory techniques, and informed legislative recommendations to the Congress. Most of this information is either published for general circulation or available upon request at the commission. Familiar examples already mentioned include the 1 per cent waybill studies of railroad carloadings and rail and motor carrier territorial cost studies. While there are sensible limitations on the direct use of such data in a particular legal context, much of the information can, and is, offered as "proof" in the form of evidence adduced by interested parties. In this respect, it is helpful here to distinguish between the use of EDP as a tool for processing, deriving, and organizing factual material and its use in the actual rendering of a decision.

The first area is basically concerned with the presentation of computer-produced information as evidence. In discussing both the commission's and the carriers' applications of EDP, a number of areas have been noted where a prime use is the assimilation and analysis of economic, statistical, and other data.

To the extent that such data have in turn been offered to the commission and the courts, the results have been largely positive, particularly in the "big case," where masses of relevant information threaten to exhaust both the litigants and the decision-making body. Substantively, the use of computers permits the development of statistical and economic data that never would have been undertaken at all or, at least, not in such detailed fashion. At the same time, the speed and capacity of the computer permit the assembly of the data in more manageable form. Also, through proper use of probability sampling processed by the computer, the absolute volume of

---

[19]See pages 286–288.

data may be reduced.[20] While sampling, like simulation exercises, can be done without EDP, the increasing use of complex samples and sampling plans is largely the result of the impact of EDP. In one form or another machine-processed evidence and other documentation has been presented to the I.C.C. since 1942, the earliest uses being machine-prepared abstracts of business and accounting records offered in motor carrier application proceedings.[21] In more recent proceedings, computer-prepared evidence has been offered to show carrier cost of service,[22] revenues,[23] traffic movements,[24] and day-to-day operating records.[25] As the industry and the commission grow more familiar with computer applications, the use of EDP can be expected to increase. One indication of this is the movement of simulation techniques and game theory applications from the research and planning departments of the carriers first to the operating departments and recently to the commission itself.

The first known application of these techniques in a formal proceeding was a computer simulation study prepared by Stager and Graves[26] on behalf of the Commonwealth of Pennsylvania[27] for use in the pending Pennsylvania Railroad–New York Central merger proceedings. The general thrust of the study was to show both the beneficial and adverse effects of the merger on service, routing, terminals and yards, and train scheduling. The possible diversion of traffic from the main line of the Pennsylvania to either the New York Central or to other railroads was also measured. The heart of the exercise was a model of the affected railroads and the economy in which they operate. A major product of the study was the charting of a critical-path scheduling operations which initially determined the shortest and, in theory, the most efficient route between two points in the network. While

---

[20]See Thomas Miller, "Legal Questions Relating to the New Aids Used in Preparation of Traffic and Cost Evidence," XXXI *I.C.C. Practitioners Journal* 275, 282–283 (1963); Dession, "The Trial of Economic and Technological Issues of Fact II, 58 *Yale Law Journal* 1242 (1955).

[21]Hebert O. Whitten, *Contract Carrier Applications*, 32 M.C.C. 60, 61 (1942).

[22]*American Colloid Co. v. Akron, Canton & Youngstown R. Co.*, 321 I.C.C. 91 (1963) (rail); *Carbon Blacks, Southwest to Indiana, Ohio, and Missouri*, 325 I.C.C. 138 (1965) (motor).

[23]*LTL. Class Rates & Minimum Charges between Midwest and Central Territories*, 325 I.C.C. 106 (1965).

[24]*Denver Oil Co. v. Platte Pipe Line Co.*, 319 I.C.C. 725 (1963) (oil pipelines).

[25]*Arkansas Best Freight System Inc.–Purchase–Fine*, 90 M.C.C. 858 (1958).

[26]The study is described in James Stagar and John Graves, "Data Processing Analysis of the Penn-Central Merger," *Papers—Fourth Annual Meeting Transportation Research Forum*, 1963, p. 114.

[27]FD 21989 and 21990, Pennsylvania Railroad Company-Merger-New York Central Railroad Company, examiner's report served March 29, 1965.

this study was admitted into evidence, the final determination of its value will be made by the Commission.

A potentially knotty set of problems for users of EDP is posed by the rules of evidence and procedure. To the extent that processing data via the computer adds another link in the chain between the data source and the witness who eventually offers it to a tribunal, these problems are different in form but probably not in substance from the usual legal process. However, the complex and different nature of the computer itself and the "team" approach in most EDP organizations (most members are unknown not only to the opponents but to the users) have created a degree of reluctance in accepting EDP and material prepared with it.

As pointed out by Miller,[28] the basic problems are those of "hearsay," statements offered for their truth that are not subject to cross-examination; the rule against improper opinion evidence; and the "best evidence" rule. Fortunately both the courts and the commission have recognized that rigid application of these rules, originally designed for a fair and orderly jury trial, might defeat the purpose of having an expert body such as the commission pass on a question. Thus, these rules do not apply except where required by statute or where common sense and a decent sense for procedural fair play direct their application.[29] In the United States, the root of the process of giving evidence is the long-standing right of cross-examination of a witness under oath as a method for ascertaining truth.

To date, there have been only a limited number of cases either by the commission or the courts. The most extensive discussions are found in the examiner's recommended reports in No. 33820, *American Colloid Co. v. Akron, Canton and Youngstown R. Co.* and No. 34099, *Bituminous Coal Tenn., Ky. & Va. to N. C., Tenn. & Va.* In the first case, objections were made to cost evidence prepared with an IBM 7090. Specifically, it was suggested that the witness presenting such evidence was not an expert and could not therefore testify of his own knowledge. The examiner, in overruling the objections, discussed at great length the necessity for broad standards of admissibility for EDP evidence.[30] Part of this report is reproduced in Miller's

[28]Miller, *op. cit.*, p. 282.

[29]Cf. *Opp Cotton Mills v. Administrator*, 312 U.S. 126, 155 (1940); Morton Freed, "A Lawyer's Guide through the Computer Maze," *Journal of Machine Accounting*, 1961, p. 1; R. Sigmon, "Rules of Evidence Before the I.C.C.," XXXI *George Washington Law Review* 258 (1962).

[30]In both of these proceedings, the examiner's ruling permitting computer-processed evidence to be admitted was upheld by the commission, Division 2. Cf. *Bituminous Coal, Tenn., Ky. & Va. to N.C., Tenn. & Va.*, 325 I.C.C. 548, 557–558 (1965). For a general discussion of these problems by a prominent federal judge, see Virginia May Brown, "Electronic Brains and the Legal Mind: Computing the Data Computer's Collision with the Law," 71 *Yale Law Journal* 239 (1961).

article. At present, it is probably the rule that if EDP-prepared evidence is objected to as hearsay, it must be shown "who selected the data inputs, the basis of that selection, in what fashion the data were processed, and that the procedures followed [comply with whatever formula or program is used]."[31] While somewhat rigorous and perhaps overly formal, this requirement is fair and reasonably workable.

In addition to the hearsay problem posed in *American Colloid* and other cases, the I.C.C. has also dealt with EDP in the context of the "best-evidence" rule and the "business records as evidence" rule. These can be treated as one. Here, in addition to hearsay to "second-hand" evidence questions, there is the problem of EDP-prepared abstracts purporting to represent shipping documents, waybills, or other routine business records. In an early case, the commission stated that abstracts of bulky records are admissible as "best evidence" to obviate the necessity for physical introduction of documents and to reduce the size of the record. Such abstracts *do not*, however, relieve the party offering them of the obligation to provide authentic copies of the original for inspection and cross-examination. This requirement is not one " . . . which may be relaxed by a quasi-judicial agency on a theory that is but a legal technicality which should be invoked only in a court of law. To the contrary, it is a necessary and reasonable precaution against the introduction of spurious evidence."[32]

Because these and similar expressions in the courts appear to impose unnecessary burdens on both users and developers of EDP, it has been argued that the law should be altered to permit more freedom for EDP, meaning a relaxation of the traditional rules, lest the cost of producing documents and witnesses offset the inherent efficiency of the computer. In these remarks, one detects a certain impatience and restlessness with traditional procedure without a genuine understanding of its purpose. For its part, the legal profession and legal institutions have been restrained in their appreciation, in part because EDP, like other new technology, appears to express an alien philosophy and may lead to an abdication of professional responsibility.[33]

This problem becomes more acute as EDP operations research and similar skills reach beyond the merely mechanical application of the computer to information handling and analysis and into the decisional process itself. Within the I.C.C. and the industry, these stresses are illustrated by the current Budget Bureau–I.C.C. project described earlier and the use of the predictive model in the Penn-Central proceeding.

---

[31]*Glass Bottles from Muskogee, Okla., to Chicago*, 323 I.C.C. 260–261 (1964).
[32]John Dickerson, "Some Jurisprudential Implications of Electronic Data Processing, XXVIII *Law and Contemporary Problems* 53 (Winter 1963).
[33]Cf. Dickerson, *ibid.*

Certain aspects of the project such as the possibility of computer retrieval and digesting of I.C.C. reports are, in part, extensions of work previously described. An important consideration will be the design of suitable programs and language systems. Other aspects are without precedent. At this early stage, it is difficult to assess the possible implications of this project for the I.C.C.'s work. There is no question but that this project and many similar ones being carried on in other areas of the law will have a marked impact on the decision-making process.

Yet these developments are also a cause for reflection. Although the form and the content of the law are logical, involving mixed questions of fact and legal rules in particular cases, the "life of the law," as stated by Justice Holmes, "has not been logic but experience." In his essay, "The Path of the Law," Holmes warned against undue reliance on a closed system based solely on logical analysis. As Holmes stated:

> ... the logical method and form flatter that longing for certainty and for repose which is in every human mind. But certainty generally is an illusion and repose is not the destiny of man. Behind the logical form lies a judgment as to the relative worth of competing legislative grounds, often an inarticulated and unconscious judgment, it is true, and yet the very root and nerve of the whole proceeding.

At the same time, being aware of the problem should not narrow acceptance of EDP; for, as noted by another distinguished jurist, the late Jerome Frank:[34]

> [It] is far more important that [lawyers] catch the *spirit of the creative scientist* [emphasis in the original] which yearns not for safety but risk not for certainty but adventure, which thrives on experiments and novelty and not on nostalgia for the absolute, which devotes itself to new ways of manipulating protean particulars, and not to the quest of undeviating universals.

The notion that a legal system can be worked out like rules of mathematics is, to our mind, false and dangerous reasoning. A similar danger exists in undue reliance upon EDP for the analysis of facts which, in the last analysis, are the "stuff" of a legal decision. As the French mathematician Poincaré pointed out, "A machine can take hold of a fact, but the soul of the fact will always elude it." This suggests the necessity for exploring the limitations of the computer as well as its potential. The EDP specialist and the lawyer need an increased awareness of each other's thinking, values, and

---

[34]*Law and the Modern Mind*, Anchor Edition, 1963, p. 105.

goals. It is, of course, too optimistic to hope that the barriers to mutual understanding will disappear or that cleavages due to differing premises will be reduced.[35] Public policy is not advanced, however, by one-sided criticism of either discipline, and the effort must be made to close the information gap. With increased knowledge of both its potential and its limitation, EDP will become an increasingly valuable tool in the economic regulation of transportation and in all other areas where its capacity may assist in reaching sound decisions.

---

[35]In another context, economics, for discussion of the same problem, see Arthur Massel, *Competition and Monopoly; Legal and Economic Issues*, Anchor Edition, 1964, pp. 166–192.

Part

Six

SELECTED CASES IN MARKETING LOGISTICS

The following nine cases illustrate practical applications of the material contained in this text. Case 1 was contributed by Price Waterhouse & Company; Case 2 and Cases 4 through 9 were written by the editors; and Case 3 is based on materials submitted by the General Foods Corporation.

The "Small-Order" Problem

There are two basic problems in distributing a product from a plant to a customer. First, we must create a demand for the product by means of sales promotion. Secondly, once we have created this demand, we must physically distribute the product. This case is concerned with the physical distribution problem.

The objective in this case is to discuss the factors and principles that are involved in physically distributing a product from a plant to the company's customers in the most economic fashion. To lend substance and clarity to the explanation of the principles involved, the quantitative results of an operations research distribution study are utilized.

We are dealing with a company which sells approximately one million cases of its product each year to customers scattered throughout the entire United States. The company assumes almost the entire physical distribution cost. This firm is quite prosperous and, aside from having an excellent product, one of the main reasons for its success is its reliable customer service. It ships almost immediately to all retailers, whenever they order, with little or no restriction on the order size. This results in many small shipments to customers.

METHOD OF SHIPMENT

Two shipping patterns are simultaneously used in shipping small customer orders to individual customers. These are illustrated in Figure 1.A.

1. Via direct truck. Forty per cent of the orders are trucked direct from the plant near Boston to customers' premises as close as Boston or as

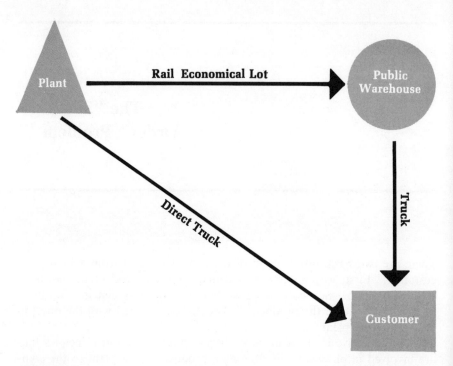

FIGURE 1.A
Shipping patterns

distant as Cleveland, Ohio. Since there is individual delivery, the charge per delivery is based on the weight of the individual shipment.

2. Via rail, public warehouse, and truck. Stocks are shipped by rail at the minimum carload rate from the plant to 38 public warehouses. The customer order in most instances is filled directly from the nearest public warehouse by trucking it from the warehouse to his location. If the customer is located in the same city as the warehouse, the customer assumes the drayage charge from the warehouse. If the customer is located outside the warehouse city, the firm assumes the drayage cost. However, at least two additional charges are incurred in using a public warehouse—a rental or storage charge and a handling charge. The rental charge depends on the size of the inventory that is carried. It is necessary to carry enough inventory in a warehouse to fill the customers' orders and give prompt delivery. There is a fixed charge per case for handling the cases in and out of the warehouse.

OBJECTIVES

In order to integrate all parts of control of the distribution, the following
basic decisions must be made:

1. Which areas or cities should be serviced directly by truck from the
   plant and which via the rail-warehouse-truck route? Warehouses are
   obviously needed as the distance from the plant increases. This is
   illustrated in Figure 1.B which compares truck and rail shipment costs.
   As the distance from the plant increases, direct trucking beomes more
   and more uneconomical as compared to rail shipments. Increased
   distances have a small effect on rail costs if carload quantities are
   shipped.

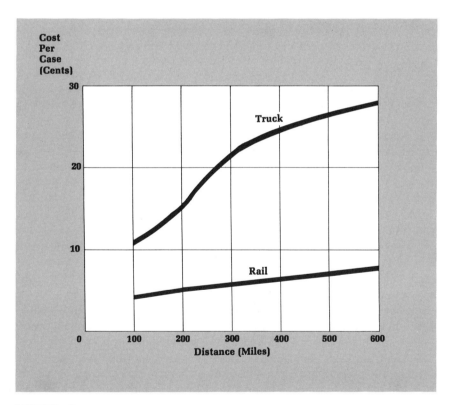

FIGURE 1.B
Truck versus rail shipment costs

2. Are additional, fewer, or the same number of warehouses needed? There could be a few large regional warehouses. This would cut rail costs, and possibly reduce storage expenses. However, would the increase in the drayage cost from the warehouse to the customer offset this reduction?

3. What stock level should be reached at each warehouse before reordering, and how much should be ordered to maintain the same customer service as at present? What shall be the firm's inventory policy?

4. Should there be a change in the warehouse currently servicing certain cities due to (a) a more advantageous location than the one currently being used or (b) a reduced handling or storage charge at another warehouse?

APPROACH

Let us first concern ourselves with two important and interrelated costs—storage and rail freight.

A storage charge in a public warehouse is a rental charge. Rent is paid per case for the period of time that each case is in the warehouse. The average number of months for which storage would be paid on a case is equal to the ratio of the average inventory that is carried divided by the average monthly sales. The inventory that is carried is equal to one-half of the size of the average individual shipment to a warehouse plus the safety stock. Individual-shipment size is related to freight cost.

Freight is a major expense. In order to benefit from rail shipments, it is necessary to ship at one time enough cases to obtain carload rates. At least 3,300 cases must be shipped to warehouses east of Denver. However, two warehouses had sales of less than 3,000 cases in 1957. Fifty-five per cent of the warehouses had annual sales of less than 10,000 cases. Consequently, it would be necessary to ship once or twice a year, at most, to many warehouses to obtain this carload rate. This would result in a relatively large individual shipment compared to sales and would enormously increase the inventory and resulting warehouse storage charge. However, shipments to two or more warehouses can be pooled to obtain this minimum carload rate. The only added expense would be a $17 drop-off charge at each warehouse (except the last warehouse on the line). Thus, inventory can be kept within bounds and yet shipping can be done more frequently and economically.

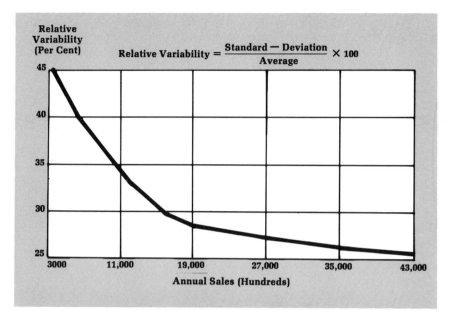

FIGURE 1.C

Relation between number of cases sold annually and relative variability of monthly sales

By using this pooled-car approach, it is not necessary to carry a disproportionately large inventory in warehouses that have relatively small annual sales.

If the annual sales of a warehouse are relatively small, its monthly sales on the average tend to fluctuate more widely on a relative basis than the monthly sales of warehouses with large annual sales. This is illustrated in Figure 1.C. The relative variability of monthly sales is measured by the ratio of the standard deviation of the sales (a measure of variability about the average) divided by the average monthly sales. The relative variability decreases as total sales increase. For example, the average relative variability of warehouses with sales of approximately 9,000 cases is 37 per cent, while the average relative variability of warehouses with sales of approximately 25,000 cases is 28 per cent. Thus, warehouses with small annual sales should on the average carry a relatively larger safety stock than warehouses with relatively large annual sales.

A reorder policy was established for each warehouse. The reorder point was equal to the sum of (1) the average quantity which will be sold during the lead time and (2) the amount of safety stock that is carried. The amount

of safety stock carried would be proportional to the variability of the sales
during the lead-time period; the greater the variability, the greater the safety
stock. The variability of sales was measured by the standard deviation.
The "lead time" is the period from the time when it is noted that an order
should be placed to the time of actual receipt of the shipment.

After discussion with officials, it was determined that the amount of
safety stock to be carried should be sufficient to ensure less than one chance
in a hundred of running out of stock during any one replenishment period.

To test the firm's inventory policy, the same routing and shipment
quantity was maintained that had been established by the firm for each
warehouse. An average inventory level was then computed for each warehouse. Use of the revised inventory policy resulted in a decrease of approximately 30 per cent in the inventory carried in many warehouses with
a comparable decrease in the storage charge. However, the same high-
level customer service was still provided.

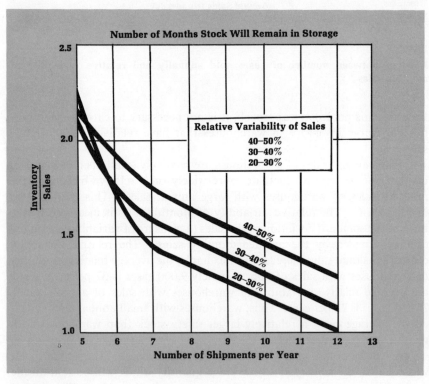

FIGURE 1.D
Factors influencing inventory/sales ratio

Now let us actually see how the relative amount of inventory carried in each warehouse is affected by the *number of shipments* that are made per year to the warehouse *and* the *relative variability* of their sales.

The independent effect of these two factors is illustrated in Figure 1.D. Warehouses were grouped by their relative variability of monthly sales, 20–30 per cent, 30–40 per cent, and 40–50 per cent. Let us first consider those warehouses which had relative sales variability of 20–30 per cent. On the average, those warehouses which had five rail shipments per year had an inventory-to-sales ratio of approximately 2.2. However, those warehouses which had twelve shipments per year had an inventory-to-sales ratio of approximately 1.0. Thus, products in warehouses which had five shipments per year will remain in stock more than twice as long as those in warehouses with twelve shipments per year. There is a marked consistency among the three relative variability groups in the decrease of the inventory-to-sales ratio as the number of rail shipments per year increases. On an over-all basis, increases in the number of shipments per year are more effective in reducing the ratio of inventory to sales than decreases in the relative variability of sales.

Considering this chart and the sales of the various warehouses, an inventory-to-sales ratio of 1.6 appears typical and corresponds to about seven shipments per year.

The third important distribution cost associated with the rail-warehouse-truck system is the drayage expense that is incurred in servicing the customers from the warehouses. Drayage cost is affected by the distances of the customers from the warehouse and the proportion of the sales outside of the city in which the warehouse is located.

The drayage cost per case without regard to shipment size was obtained for each warehouse. The percentage of sales at increasing distances from each warehouse was also obtained. Then an over-all relationship was ascertained by the use of multiple regression techniques between the average cost per case drayed and the percentage of sales at increasing distances from the warehouse (1–50, 51–150, 151–250, and 251–350 miles). Only those sales which were not in the city in which the warehouse was located were considered.

We now have the information necessary to make our basic decisions.

1. *Should a certain area be serviced by direct truck shipments from the plant or via rail, public warehouse, and truck?* We would recommend the use of a public warehouse in an area currently serviced by direct truck if *the current annual trucking cost exceeds:*

    a. Freight charge per case times cases sold per year

plus

b. Drop-off charge of $17 per rail shipment times estimate of 7 shipments per year

plus

c. Storage charge per case times cases sold per year times 1.6 months

plus

d. Handling charge per case times cases sold per year

plus

e. Estimated drayage charge per case times cases drayed per year.

For example, let us assume that our area had sales of 10,000 cases per year. Figure 1.E illustrates the costs that will be incurred if use is made of each of the two shipping patterns. The costs for shipping via a public warehouse are shown for those situations in which either 25 per cent or 75 per cent of the sales will be outside the warehouse city (up to 150 miles), and a drayage expense will be incurred. The point at which it pays to use public warehouses rather than direct trucking, under most circumstances, occurs at a little over 300 miles from the plant. The decision will be unaffected by the number of cases shipped.

2. *What is the minimal number of sales that are required in a city to justify using a public warehouse?* How is this affected by (a) the city's distance to its closest warehouse, (b) the number of rail shipments that are made per year to the warehouse, and (c) the possible increase in inventory that may be required? Instead of one warehouse with a relatively large number of sales servicing an area, we may have two warehouses, each with a relatively small number of sales, servicing the area. Since the relative variability of warehouse sales increases as the annual sales decrease, there may also be an increase in the total inventory carried. We will assume that, if a new warehouse is established in an area, it will pool its shipments in the same rail car as its closest warehouse. Thus we will know the number of shipments per year that will be made to this possible public warehouse. Let us also assume that we would not desire to establish an additional warehouse in an area if it did not result in a minimum savings of $150.

We would recommend the use of a public warehouse in a city now serviced by its closest warehouse *if the reduction in annual drayage cost exceeds:*

a. A minimum savings of $150 per year

plus

b. The number of estimated rail shipments per year times $17

plus

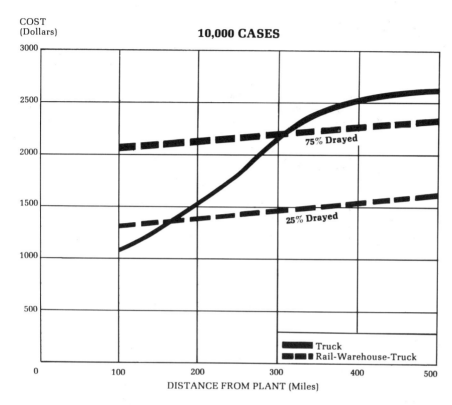

FIGURE 1.E
Shipments by truck or by rail, warehouse, and truck

    c. An increase in warehousing charge per year (caused by increased inventory).

    The minimum number of sales required to justify establishing a new warehouse in a city under these differing conditions is shown in Figure 1.F. The required annual sales to justify establishing a warehouse in a city that is 50 miles, 150 miles, and 250 miles from the closest warehouse are shown in three separate curves. The minimum number of sales is shown for warehouses whose rail shipments may range from six to twelve times per year. For example, let us take a city to which it is estimated that nine rail shipments per year will be made. It is 50 miles from the closest warehouse. From the curve it is estimated that there should be sales of at least 3,500 cases per year in this city to justify establishing a warehouse in it. It can be observed that as the city's distance to its closest warehouse increases, the required number of sales decreases.

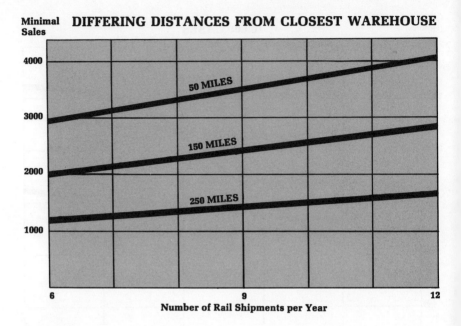

FIGURE 1.F
Minimal number of sales in a city to justify a warehouse installation

3. *Should we remove a warehouse from an area and consolidate its sales with its closest warehouse?* Figure 1.F also helps answer this question. Assume that there are two warehouses less than 50 miles apart, and that shipment is made to each of these warehouses six times per year. If sales of one of the two warehouses are less than 3,000 cases per year, it might pay to close it. An investigation should be made as to what savings are actually being realized by the use of the two warehouses and whether sales will increase.

4. *Which public warehouse should we select in a city, if they all have the same desirable physical characteristics?* It is assumed that it is desirable to establish a public warehouse in a certain city. The present policy of the plant is to use the sum of the handling and storage charges per case as the criterion. If one warehouse had a one-cent handling charge and a three-cent monthly storage charge, it would be considered as desirable as a warehouse which had a one-cent monthly storage charge and a three-cent handling charge. But this rule neglects the effect of inventory and the payment of approximately 1.5 to 2.0 months' storage. The

revised criterion is the sum of the handling charge plus *twice* the monthly storage charge.

RESULTS

We recommended changes in the number of warehouses to be established, their optimal placement, and the method of shipping; and we revised the company's inventory policy. The resulting annual savings should be approximately 8 per cent of their current distribution costs.

In addition, the company will now have "decision-rules" which will enable it to make effective future selections of transportation and warehousing methods.

QUESTIONS

1. What are the basic problems in the distribution of a product from plants or distribution centers to customers?
2. Describe the advantages and disadvantages of shipping small orders by truck; by rail.
3. Discuss the information that is required in order properly to analyze distribution alternatives.
4. Discuss the importance of "safety stock."

CASE

2

The ASME Manufacturing Company—A Sample Study in Logistical Planning

The distribution service of XYZ Transportation Company is representative of a relatively new concept in shipper-carrier relations. Broadly, its designated function has been to help shippers:

—*eliminate* or *reduce expenses* of *transportation, warehousing, inventory financing, materials handling, inventory control, packaging, order processing*, and *other costly functions in the marketing*, production, purchasing, *accounting*, and *administrative areas of distribution.*

—*speed the flow of goods* in more direct movement to widely dispersed customers and retail points of sale, and at the same time enhance the manufacturer's own customer service.

While all of these factors are considered in a distribution study, the weight or importance of each factor in the context of the whole study varies considerably. In one instance, the shipper's primary consideration may be to reduce total distribution costs; in another, improvement in the speed of completing the distribution process may be of greater importance.

Despite certain differences in the individual objectives of distribution studies prepared for shippers, certain "ground rules" or procedures have to be laid out in order to insure effective coordination among all XYZ Transportation Company units contributing to each study and affected by the ultimate distribution plan developed. In short, a programed effort is made to insure that "the left hand knows what the right hand is doing."

To illustrate, a case study is presented here in which the various steps taken to initiate, carry out, and complete a typical study will be described.

This case study involves the preparation of a proposed distribution plan for ASME Manufacturing Company, Kansas City, Missouri.

As will be evident throughout, no study is a one-man or even a one-division project. Results are obtained only through collective research and cooperative effort on the part of a great number of XYZ personnel as well as the shipper himself. The role of the distribution service is essentially to determine the alternative methods of distribution to be examined, to exercise the necessary centralized control over the preparation of data required for study, and, on the basis of the information gathered, to analyze and then recommend to the shipper an optimum distribution plan, that is, an economical and practicable plan.

INITIATING THE STUDY

The study of the ASME distribution system by XYZ's distribution service can be traced back as the direct result of personal contact made between XYZ's sales manager in Kansas City and the regional traffic manager of ASME.

Sales Manager H. E. James forwarded a request to Regional Manager H. J. Ben in Chicago for consideration of such a study to be conducted by the distribution service. Attached to this request was a completed "Preliminary Analysis Form," giving general information about ASME's present distribution pattern and the potential traffic volume.

Since the number of studies that can be undertaken by XYZ's distribution service is necessarily limited owing to manpower requirements, it is the obligation of the regional manager to screen these requests before referring them to the manager of the distribution service in New York. Since Mr. Ben concurred that this request merited further consideration, it was forwarded with the "Preliminary Analysis Form" to the distribution service manager for evaluation as a potential study.

Upon review, the manager of XYZ's distribution service (DS) agreed that a distribution study for ASME appeared to be warranted. He therefore advised ASME's traffic manager of his decision and arranged to meet with him to plan a study designed to speed up the distribution of ASME's product and reduce its distribution costs.

ORGANIZING THE STUDY

Previous to the meeting date with ASME, additional data were secured by the XYZ district manager in Kansas City from the ASME Company, covering a week's sample of the firm's shipments from Kansas City. Included in these data were shipment volume, prevailing rates under which the traffic was presently moving, methods of transportation employed, and a break-down of shipments by pieces, weight, and charges to each break-bulk point to which the traffic was moving.

After formulating some preliminary recommendations on how the study should be structured, a meeting was set up at ASME's offices in Kansas City between ASME's traffic manager and three XYZ representatives—one from Sales, one from Operations, and one from the distribution service. Through collective appraisal of ASME's present shipping situations and of practical alternative methods from a *marketing, operations,* and *distribution economics* standpoint, preliminary agreement was reached as to the structure of the study and the course of action to be taken in realizing the study's objectives.

PLANNING THE STUDY

Nature of Product and Marketing Procedure

In setting up a proposed distribution plan for a firm, first consideration is given to the nature of the product being studied and the general manner in which it is marketed.

ASME is a manufacturer and distributor of home cooking products. These products are sold solely through company representatives who receive deliveries of the products at their homes.

Defining the Geographic Boundaries of the Study

ASME's product distribution is handled and controlled on a regional basis, with shipments moving from five different warehouses nationally. Since the request for a DS study was made by ASME's regional traffic manager in Kansas City, the study was confined from the start to traffic moving within the region served by the Kansas City regional warehouse.

Existing Methods of Distribution

At the time of the study, ASME shipments from Kansas City were made by four different distribution methods as determined by the volume and characteristics of each movement, and varying considerably in cost to ASME.

It was found that under existing rates, XYZ would not be the least-cost carrier for traffic moving by any of these methods. However, the preliminary investigation did show that for the considerable volume of traffic moving by *one* of these methods, a distribution plan might be devised whereby shipper's distribution cost could possibly be reduced and XYZ could secure the traffic.

In the method in question, shipments were consolidated by group destination lots in Kansas City and then forwarded by motor carrier in both truckload and less-than-truckload quantities to post offices in various predesignated, centrally located destinations; from these points shipments were separated and mailed out via parcel post to ASME customers throughout the surrounding area.

Assembling Data for Analysis

In working on the study, a one-day sample of ASME shipments from Kansas City was examined in detail. From these data, shipping characteristics were determined, consisting of averages for weight per shipment, weight per piece, pieces per shipment, density of product, and a projected annual tonnage estimate.

A breakdown of data in this manner was necessary for the costing and pricing of XYZ's service, as well as for determining size and weight limitations governing the handling and transporting of the shipper's products. With these data as a base, alternative methods of distribution could be considered and a proposed method developed.

PROPOSED METHOD OF DISTRIBUTION

Fundamentally, the proposed distribution plan was intended to reduce ASME's present cost of distribution in two ways:

1. By reducing the number of shipper and carrier freight handlings by unitizing shipments in XYZ-furnished disposable containers.

2. By forwarding shipments from Kansas City to post offices closer to final destination than under the existing method. This involved increasing the number of post office ("break-bulk") destinations to permit shipments to be forwarded to final destinations under lower parcel post zone rates.

Since, under the proposed plan, shipments would be moved in smaller lots to an increased number of intermediate destinations with increased line-haul mileage, it was to be expected that the common carrier transportation cost portion of the movement would increase over the existing method. However, to be economical, the alternative plan had to produce savings in parcel post charges exceeding the increase in common carrier transportation costs.

An illustration of the present and proposed methods of distribution studied is shown in Figure 2.A.

Defining the Scope of the Study

Costing out a shipper's entire distribution system is generally too complex and too time-consuming to be practical. Therefore, the initial scope of a study is generally limited to a representative sampling of the shipper's current operations. The findings developed for the sample are ultimately applied, where appropriate, to the remainder of the distribution system.

Thus with ASME, it was agreed to limit the initial analysis of traffic moving to three of the eleven break-bulk points being served by motor freight from the Kansas City warehouse. The three break-bulk points selected were Cheyenne and Casper, Wyoming, and North Platte, Nebraska, and were named by ASME as being representative of the group.

Completing the Study

After a proposed plan is decided upon, it becomes DS's task to determine all the individual intricate details necessary to effect the plan, and then to take whatever action is necessary toward its accomplishment.

Increasing the Number of Break-Bulk Destinations

To begin with, it was necessary to determine the number of break-bulk destinations required effectively to service the study area.

The sample revealed that many destinations within the Cheyenne, Casper, and North Platte study area were receiving shipments of sufficient weight to fill a pallet container. By examining the data, eleven additional destinations were selected as break-bulk points, thus increasing the total number from three to fourteen.

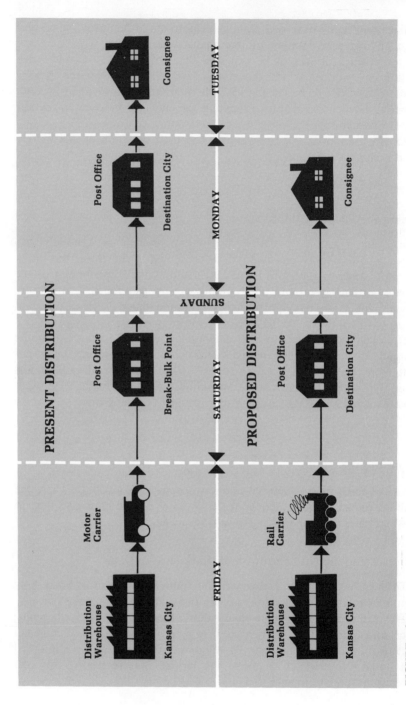

FIGURE 2.A
Present and proposed methods of distribution

Proposed Shipment Handling in Disposable Pallet Containers

Under the proposal, ASME would assemble and band the containers to be used, and XYZ would load them directly onto its vehicles. Shipments consigned to ASME representatives beyond the fourteen break-bulk points would be forwarded (in containers) to the break-bulk point closest to final destination.

At the break-bulk point, the pallet containers would be unloaded from the rail car, loaded into an XYZ delivery truck, and delivered to the post office for mailing to the consignee.

Selection of Size and Type of Containers

Since the proposed plan was predicated on the use of XYZ containers, advice in the selection of the best size and type of container to be used in this program was solicited from the manager, coordinated traffic development.

It was found that because the plan required the grouping of shipments of varying weights and sizes, it would be best to use three different sizes of disposable pallet container—namely, 21-cubic-foot, 33-cubic-foot, and 60-cubic-foot containers. Each of these containers is made of corrugated cardboard and consists of four separate parts—a pallet, a sleeve, a top, and a bottom.

Based on the relationship between the density of the product cartons and the cubic capacity of the containers, average load limits were determined for each size of pallet container.

Proposed Rate Schedule

As a basis for formulating a rate structure for the shipper, present LTL rates on household articles (Class 70) were requested and subsequently furnished by the pricing division of the marketing department.

With this information as a foundation, an effort was made by DS personnel to construct a rate schedule which would be economical for the shipper's use, yet profitable to XYZ. The rate schedule finally developed encompassed rates to those key points from which shipments would be forwarded to the consignee via parcel post. The cost of the disposable pallet containers was included in this rate structure. These rates were equal to the motor carrier less-than-1,000-pound LTL rate, and were subject to a minimum weight aggregation of 5,000 pounds daily.

When combined with the reduced parcel post charges resulting from the proposed distribution plan, these rates were expected to produce a savings to ASME of approximately 16 cents per hundredweight.

In the event that proposed rates are agreeable to the shipper, but are protested when presented before the Interstate Commerce Commission for approval, DS assists the law department in the preparation of protest replies and participates in any associated legal proceedings.

Setting Up Required Service (Routing)

A distribution plan is only an idea until it proves operationally possible and economically practicable. The development of efficient routing schedules to meet the requirements of a proposed distribution plan is the key to transforming this idea into a reality.

TABLE 2.A

ASME Manufacturing Company, Kansas City, Missouri: Present versus Proposed Distribution Time

EXAMPLE I   *Kansas City to Alliance, Nebraska*
    Present shipping distance = 850 miles
    Proposed shipping distance = 650 miles

Movement of Shipment	Present Distribution	Proposed Distribution
Leave Kansas City	Friday	Friday
Arrive Cheyenne	Saturday	–
Leave Cheyenne	Monday	–
Arrive Alliance	Monday	Saturday
Delivery to Consignee	Tuesday	Monday

EXAMPLE II   *Kansas City to Rock Springs, Wyoming*
    Present shipping distance = 1,000 miles
    Proposed shipping distance = 950 miles

Movement of Shipment	Present Distribution	Proposed Distribution
Leave Kansas City	Friday	Friday
Arrive Casper	Sunday	–
Leave Casper	Monday	–
Arrive Rock Springs	Monday	Sunday
Delivery to Consignee	Tuesday	Monday

At the request of DS, the transportation division of the operations department prepared a detailed routing schedule specifically designed to meet the requirements of the proposed plan or, in effect, the needs of the shipper. These schedules were planned with considerable effort to combine available rail and truck service into the most efficient integrated system of transport possible.

Under the prescribed routing, XYZ would load the pallet containers directly onto its trucks at ASME's Kansas City plant and transport them approximately 15 miles to a rail siding, unload them from the trucks directly onto rail cars, transport them to the break-bulk destination cities, and unload them from the rail car directly onto delivery trucks for drop-off at the local post office and subsequent mailing to the consignee.

A comparison of delivery times under the present and proposed methods of distribution is shown in Table 2.A.

Costing of Proposal and Determination of Profitability

Before a plan can be presented to the shipper, a cost simulation has to be prepared by the technical services division of the operations department. When completed, these data are referred to the cost division of the controller's department for auditing against the proposed rate structure and ultimate determination of the level of profitability of these rates to XYZ.

The ASME rates were found to be compatible with costs and sufficiently profitable to XYZ.

CONCLUDING THE STUDY

The proposed distribution plan offers ASME significant reductions in transportation and associated distribution costs, as well as an improvement in transport and customer services.

Transportation Savings

Savings in total transportation costs are primarily the result of the wide variance in rates among the various parcel post shipping zones.

The example in Table 2.B illustrates the extent to which parcel post charges can be reduced by transporting shipments just one zone closer to final destination than under the existing method.

Under the proposed plan, ASME shipments are not split until they are considerably closer to final destination than under the present plan. Note in Table 2.C the proposed change in prevailing parcel post rate zones.

An illustration of how the higher XYZ line-haul and container rates and charges are much more than offset by the reduction in parcel post charges is shown in Table 2.D.

The proposed plan offers ASME a net reduction in transportation costs of approximately 16 cents per hundredweight, based on all movement within the study area.

TABLE 2.B

Parcel Post

Shipment Weight (pounds)	Pieces per Shipment	Third Zone Charge	First Zone Charge	Local Zone Charge	Dollar Savings	Percentage Savings
5	1		$0.48	$0.30	$0.18	38%
10	1		0.73	0.40	0.33	45
20	1		1.13	0.60	0.53	47
40	1		1.93	1.00	0.93	48
20	1	$1.33	1.13		0.20	15
95	5	$1.33	$5.40	$2.30	$2.17	39%

TABLE 2.C

	PRESENT PLAN		PROPOSED PLAN	
Parcel Post Zones	Number of Shipments	Percentage of Shipments	Number of Shipments	Percentage of Shipments
Local	93	26%	186	53%
1 & 2	236	68	164	47
3	21	6		
TOTAL	350	100%	350	100%

TABLE 2.D

ASME Manufacturing Company, Kansas City, Missouri: Present versus Proposed Distribution Cost

EXAMPLE I *Kansas City to Alliance, Nebraska*
55 lb. shipment, 3 pieces
Distance = 650 miles

Cost Elements	Present Lay-Down Cost per Hundredweight	Proposed Lay-Down Cost per Hundredweight
Transportation	$2.74	$2.78
Stop-off	0.15	
Parcel post	2.77	1.31
Container		0.49
TOTAL LAY-DOWN COST	$5.66	$4.58

Savings = $1.08 (19.1% cost reduction)

EXAMPLE II *Kansas City to Rock Springs, Wyoming*
65 lb. shipment, 4 pieces
Distance = 950 miles

Cost Elements	Present Lay-Down Cost per Hundredweight	Proposed Lay-Down Cost per Hundredweight
Transportation	$2.74	$3.03
Stop-off	0.15	
Parcel post	4.07	1.62
Container		0.49
TOTAL LAY-DOWN COST	$6.96	$5.14

Savings = $1.82 (26.1% cost reduction)

Additional Savings Through Improved Service

Besides transportation cost savings, several other cost and service benefits are made available to ASME under the proposed plan:

1. The disposable containers furnished by XYZ substantially reduce the number of ASME shipping personnel man-hours required for materials-handling operations, thus producing an indirect labor savings.

2. The containerized operation also speeds the procedures required for loading and handling goods at the warehouse and in transit. Additionally, the proposed routing plan permits a significant reduction in actual transit time. Both of these factors result in a better customer service to ASME as well as an improvement in inventory turnover with consequent reductions in inventory-carrying costs.

3. A unitized operation will also normally cut down on loss and damage claims, which are expensive to both the shipper and the carrier.

4. The proposed plan for forwarding shipments via XYZ, instead of the existing use of as many as fourteen different motor carriers, results in significant reduction in shipment processing costs, including paper work, and the relief of carrier congestion at the shipping terminal.

SUMMARY

A proposed new plan of distribution was drawn up and developed for ASME through considerable "team" effort at XYZ and full cooperation on the part of the shipper. The resulting plan offers ASME substantial freight savings and an improved transportation service, and provides XYZ with a considerable amount of profitable new business.

QUESTIONS

1. What is wrong with ASME's present distribution system?
2. What alternative distribution systems would you consider?
3. How would you compute the in-transit inventory cost?
4. What types of containerization, other than those described in the study, could be used in ASME's distribution system?
5. What changes in packaging costs would be inherent in container use?

The ABC Corporation

Recently, ABC Corporation set up a new sales distribution operations pattern in the recently created Denver district.

The new pattern offers these specific advantages:

1. Individualized service

2. Improved order-taking and delivery procedures; better shipping and handling of ABC products

3. Receipt of products on a dependable, rapid basis

4. Ready and complete information on the status of orders, shipments, and sales problems

5. Greater inventory turnover with lower capital investment and reduced warehouse space.

Seeking to improve the typical distribution pattern, ABC distribution specialists saw the need for a warehouse that

1. Is located in the specific market it serves.

2. Provides facilities for close coordination between sales and service personnel.

3. Is organized to provide fast, frequent, dependable shipments to customers of all sizes—and with a mix of products from the ABC divisions it acts for.

4. Has one service organization; that is to say, is set up to provide fast, complete, and "one-stop" service on order processing, billing, credits,

reports, as well as all the functions normally thought of as "warehousing and transportation" and to provide individualized customer service, dealing directly with both customers and sales organization as necessary. Customers would get all information from one source.

The directness and simplicity of the market warehouse concept compared to the old concept is seen clearly in Figures 3.A and 3.B.

Before ABC decided to install the new pattern nationally, it was given a year-long practical test in the Boston district, and was studied further as it was extended to the Memphis district, and then to the Youngstown, Atlanta, Minneapolis, and St. Louis districts, and most recently to the Philadelphia district. Every specified cost and performance objective was evaluated from the customer's point of view, from the point of view of ABC, overall and in detail. During the first year particularly the service was checked for flaws virtually every day of its existence.

The five specific advantages of the new service plan are:

[1]   Individualized Service

The new pattern provides a one-step individualized service to each customer in the sales district.

The sales and distribution center, incorporating sales, service, warehousing, billing, and credit activities, handles all sales and service problems. An individualized service plan is set up for each customer, and a complete service record is maintained on his behalf.

Customers need not wait while several offices and warehouses are consulted to find an answer to a question, or to check the progress of an order, since the sales and distribution center is always available to answer questions at once. It is also prepared to answer all the customer's questions about normal modes of transportation.

[2]   Improved Order-Handling and Delivery Procedures; Better Shipping and Handling of ABC Products

Order Handling

Personal selling remains important. ABC sales representatives call regularly on all customers in the sales district both for providing help on merchandising and promotion projects as desired and for order taking.

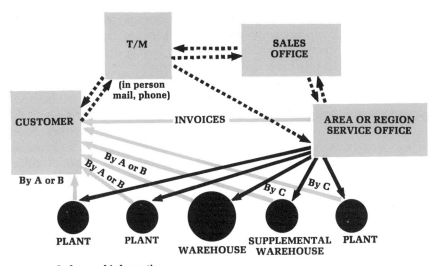

Orders and information
Orders
Shipment by (A) Carload,
(B) Pool Car, and (C) Truck

FIGURE 3.A
Former sales and distribution services pattern

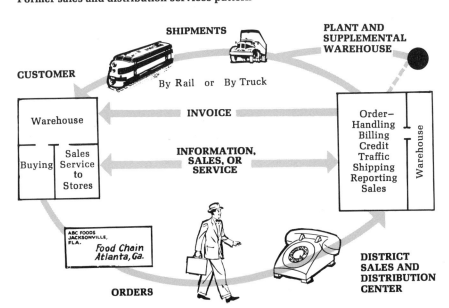

FIGURE 3.B
New sales and distribution services pattern

It is recognized, however, that some customers prefer to review their inventory records and order by mail or telephone on days of their own choosing, rather than tying up the time of the buying organization or the sales representatives with order taking. For their benefit—or for any customer who wishes to place an order by mail or telephone—a new service desk was installed in the sales and distribution center for the expeditious, effective handling of such orders. Regular users of this service, nevertheless, continue to receive personal visits by ABC's sales representatives to help them promote, merchandise, and buy.

Whether taken in person, or sent by mail or telephone, normal or regular orders are processed and shipped within thirty-six hours after receipt at the sales and distribution center. Emergency orders are shipped the same day if possible.

Delivery Procedures

With some exceptions, orders for 40,000 pounds or more received at the center are delivered by rail. Cars are precisely scheduled to arrive on a given date.

Trucks are used to ship orders between 22,000 and 39,999 pounds. Truck shipments are made on a scheduled four-week-cycle basis, with most deliveries to customers on the day following shipment.

Scheduled Service

Within the sales district, scheduled service is established customer by customer for all carload, truckload, and split-truck shipments. The schedule is planned around total elapsed time, broken down into order-processing and loading and delivery times. Shipments are made either on a regular cycle basis, or on a basis of what service is to follow a specific date. All the needs and wants of each customer are considered in establishing these schedules.

Figure 3.C is a customer delivery service record from Memphis, typical of the reports that are kept for every carload, truckload, or split-truck customer.

[3]   Receipt of Products on a Dependable, Rapid Basis

Each shipment is scheduled to arrive at a customer's warehouse within a certain time, agreed upon with the customer in advance. If a car or truck is not able to keep the schedule, ABC transportation service immediately

CUSTOMER'S NAME:	Z
ADDRESS:	293 "D" Street, Boston
RAIL SIDING (R.R. NAME):	New Haven
CAR SPOTS (NUMBER):	15
NORMAL BUYING METHOD & FREQUENCY:	Combined Carloads — Weekly — Inventories updated each Wednesday
MANIFEST TO:	Mail to Charles Elliott

TRAIN SCHEDULE & ROUTING:	Leave Warehouse 64 at 5:00 P.M. Arrive customer's siding next A.M.
SCHEDULED LAPSED TIME:	Cycle Friday — Tuesday — Wednesday
SCHEDULED TRANSIT TIME:	1 day
BACK ORDER POLICY:	None accepted
DESIRED WAREHOUSE INVENTORY LEVEL:	2 weeks

Date Order Taken	*	Date Rec'd at Dist. Off.	Spec. Ship. Date	Actual Ship. Date	Date Avail. to Customer	Weight	Comment
11-7		11-8	11-12	11-12	11-13	40,839	
11-14		11-19	11-20	11-20	11-21	43,396	
11-21		11-25	11-27	11-27	11-28	40,624	
11-27		12-3	12-4	12-4	12-5	40,168	
12-6		12-6	12-11	12-11	12-12	40,860	
12-20		12-20	12-27	12-26	12-27	41,496	
12-31	P	12-31	1-2	1-2	1-3	42,084	
1-9		1-9	1-13	1-13	1-14	40,851	
1-17	P	1-17	1-21	1-21	1-22	40,000	
1-23	P	1-23	1-24	1-24	1-25	41,539	
1-27	P	1-28	1-29	1-29	1-30	40,071	
1-31		1-31	2-4	2-4	2-5	44,167	
2-7		2-7	2-11	2-11	2-12	41,164	
2-13	P	2-17	2-18	2-19	2-21	40,400	Bad Snow. Cust. told A.M. 20th
2-27	P	2-28	3-1	3-1	3-3	40,564	Bad Snow. Cust. told A.M. 2nd
3-6		3-7	3-10	3-10	3-11	40,755	
3-13	P	3-13	3-17	3-17	3-18	41,225	

*P—Palletized

FIGURE 3.C

Scheduled service report

notifies the customer. The customer does not have to inquire. The responsibility to keep him informed is ABC's.

To make this service possible, ABC's distribution-sales service department and the corporate traffic department worked closely with the top operating management of railroad and truck lines to gather all pertinent transportation information: what schedules the railroad can definitely meet, the time it takes a truck to reach certain destinations, and so on.

At the same time, an exhaustive survey was made of the distribution needs of each customer's market, in terms of gross volume of product, seasonal volumes, and rates of turnover. ABC then used these facts to work out schedules to meet—within realistic limits—virtually every customer's need.

To maintain these schedules at the optimum level, the transportation service keeps a record of all shipments to each customer, and each week it studies for correction or revision the customer delivery record which summarizes the movement of every car and truck.

A report covering one week of the Boston district operation is shown in Figure 3.D.

[4]   Ready and Complete Information on Status of Orders, Shipments, Sales Problems

Centralization of all information about sales, orders, shipments, and service is an important advantage of the new market-centered customer service plan.   Over the years, ABC customers had valid complaints about the difficulty of getting fast answers to their questions. The new pattern eliminates the bottlenecks that caused these delays in the old system.

Since every customer's order is scheduled, the sales and distribution center knows exactly when it is to be shipped, what conveyance will carry it, and when it will arrive. And all information on billing, accounts receivable, and credits are readily available.

[5]   Greater Inventory Turnover with Lower Capital Investment and Reduced Warehouse Space

More frequent turnover and greater delivery dependability under the new plan significantly reduces out-of-stock conditions for many customers, both in frequency and length of time.   In addition, customers who previously bought products in separate carloads, truck shipments, or pool cars can now order more frequently from these divisions in combined shipments.

Shipping Point _____ Dorchester   Week Ending 6/12

Order Number	Type Shipment CL - MCL P/C - MPC Full Truck Split Truck	Consignee and Destination	Date Order Taken	Date Received at Shipping Point	*Specified Shipping Date	Date Shipped	Number of Days Late	Date Received by Consignee	Explanation
104424	C/L	Standard Grocery / N. Bedford, Mass.	6/8	6/9	6/10	6/10	0	6/11	
104887	S/T	Barre Who. Groc. / Barre, Vt.	6/1	6/8	6/10	6/10	0	6/11	
104888	S/T	J. A. Santarini / Barre, Vt.	6/1	6/8	6/10	6/10	0	6/11	
104889	S/T	Wood Specialty / Rutland, Vt.	6/2	6/8	6/10	6/10	0	6/11	
104892	S/T	Holbrook Grocery / Woodsville, N. H.	6/4	6/8	6/10	6/10	0	6/11	
198089	T/L	Nashua Who. Groc. / Nashua, N. H.	6/2	6/8	6/10	6/10	0	6/11	
198419	T/L	Burlington Groc. / Burlington, Vt.	6/5	6/8	6/10	6/10	0	6/11	
109254	T/L	Milliken Tomlinson Co. / Portland, Me.	6/10	6/11	6/12	6/12	0	6/12	
155458	C/L	Hannaford Bros. / Portland, Me.	6/10	6/11	6/12	6/12	0	6/15	Week end

NOTE: * If order shows a firm shipping date, enter this date in col. 6
If undated and received A.M., enter following working days date
If undated and received P.M., show date of two working days after receipt

NUMBER OF ORDERS CARRIED OVER [0]

SHIPMENTS RECAPITULATION

Total for week	54	No. two days late	0
No. on schedule	53	No. three or more days late	0
No. one day late	1	No. shipped more than one day prior to schedule	1

FIGURE 3.D
Weekly report of orders shipped

Experience in the New England district, where combined shipments were also made available from the same three ABC divisions, showed a marked reduction of capital investment and warehouse space—several customers reduced their inventory by 25 per cent or more. Some New England customers, however, preferred to make use of the availability of combined shipments to order in larger quantities for price advantages.

QUESTIONS

1. Discuss the importance of communications in the development of ABC's distribution system.
2. Compare the advantages and disadvantages of bypassing the warehouse function.
3. What options are available to ABC for communicating orders to the distribution centers?
4. Analyze the relationship between cost and service in ABC's new distribution system.

4

The Apex Manufacturing Company

The Apex Manufacturing Company, a manufacturer and distributor of industrial safety equipment, ships its products throughout the United States from its plant in Oshkosh, Pennsylvania, via the following two channels of distribution:

1. Direct to customer

2. Through twenty-two private warehouses located in the following states and then to customers (there is one warehouse in each state except as noted in parentheses): Alabama, California (2), Georgia, Illinois, Louisiana, Maryland, Michigan, Minnesota, Missouri (2), New York (2), Ohio, Oklahoma, Pennsylvania, Rhode Island, Texas (2), Utah, Washington, and West Virginia.

A new distribution department has been introduced into the Apex Manufacturing Company. Its ultimate objective is to reduce costs while keeping service at least at its present level. This is to be accomplished without eliminating any of the twenty-two Apex warehouses.

SHIPPING CHARACTERISTICS OF APEX PRODUCTS

Investigation of the average shipping characteristics (Table 4.A) of the subject firm showed the following.

Number of products shipped during average week = 87

Range of common carrier class rates for products = Class 50 to Class 110

TABLE 4.A

Shipping Characteristics of Apex Products

Characteristics	Forwarded to Warehouse	Direct to Customer	Total
Average daily pounds	9,988	18,335	28,323
Average weekly pounds	49,938	91,678	141,616
Annual pounds	2,596,800	4,767,200	7,364,000
Average pounds per shipment	602	310	374
Average pounds per piece	19.9	46.9	31.7
Average pieces per shipment	30.3	6.6	11.8
Average mileage per shipment	1,047	571	675

Most Apex safety products have a weight density ranging from 15 to 80 pounds per cubic foot. However, eight products forwarded by Apex, which account for 33 per cent of total annual shipping weight, have extremely low weight densities, ranging from 1.6 to 7.6 pounds per cubic foot.

PRESENT DISTRIBUTION OPERATION

Under the present distribution operation employed by Apex, shipments are forwarded in LTL quantities via motor truck directly to customers or they are forwarded in LTL quantities via motor truck to the twenty-two Apex-owned warehouses before being distributed to customers.

In many cases, the weight of direct shipments to customers is below 100 pounds (emergency shipments) and the motor truck minimum charge is applied to these low-weight shipments.

Shipments which are forwarded to Apex-owned warehouses are unloaded from motor trucks and stored in the warehouse until they are used to fill customer orders.

In seeking to reduce costs and provide an adequate level of customer service, the new Apex Manufacturing distribution department considered many alternative distribution plans.

Alternative Distribution Plan I: Consolidate and Containerize Shipments to Apex Warehouses[1]

In considering the containerization of consolidated warehouse shipments, the following two alternatives were explored:

1. Containerize all products.

2. Containerize only products having a weight density of more than 15 pounds per cubic foot.

Alternative Distribution Plan II: Consolidate and Containerize Shipments to Apex Customers[2]

The following alternatives were explored for this plan:

1. Containerize all products.

2. Containerize only products having a weight density of more than 15 pounds per cubic foot.

3. Consolidate customer and warehouse shipments being forwarded to the same city.

Alternative Distribution Plan III: Continue the Present Distribution Operation

The following alternatives were explored for this plan:

1. Forward all products via motor carrier.

2. Forward all shipments weighing more than 125 pounds via motor carrier; all shipments weighing less than 125 pounds would be forwarded by Railway Express, United Parcel Service, parcel post, etc.

---

[1]Shipments would be consolidated until there were sufficient pieces to fill a container for a warehouse or customer. Each container has a minimum weight of 800 pounds and a maximum weight of 2,500 pounds.
[2]See note 1, above.

QUESTIONS

1. Comment on each alternative distribution plan, showing the advantages and disadvantages which would be derived through the implementation of each plan and the alternatives within each plan.
2. What distribution plan(s), not already listed, would you consider? What are the advantages and disadvantages of the distribution plan(s)?
3. List the Apex Manufacturing distribution functions which would undergo a change as a result of the use of each distribution plan in questions 1 and 2. Would the distribution cost for each function rise or be lowered (list for each plan)?
4. How important is a plan for balancing present and alternative shipping schedules to warehouses? ("Balancing" means that each warehouse will receive a quantity of products in a week equal to the quantity of products it now receives during an average week.)
5. List the advantages and disadvantages of increasing warehouse safety stocks in order to reduce the high number of emergency shipments.

The Barnes
Manufacturing
Company

The Barnes Manufacturing Company manufactures and distributes a diversified line of industrial and household products, including chemicals, paint lacquers and varnish, plastics, explosives, petroleum, and food items. Barnes Manufacturing distributes its products through 93 plants and 167 warehouses located throughout the United States. Products produced at Barnes plants are either forwarded to company-owned warehouses or directly to the customer.

STATEMENT OF THE PROBLEM

Barnes presently forwards a large number of small-lot packaged goods from its eastern plants directly to West Coast customers and to company-owned warehouses. These small-lot packaged goods shipments have a weight range between 1 and 20,000 pounds, as shown in Table 5.A.

Barnes Manufacturing sustains a high transportation cost for forwarding these shipments to its West Coast distribution areas. Mr. Barnes, the president of the firm, has requested that the S.A.F. Consulting Company propose a plan that will achieve optimum distribution costs and an improved transportation service for the movement of small-lot packaged goods from Barnes's eastern plants to customers and company warehouses located on the West Coast.

The sixteen eastern plants are located in the following states (the number of plants is shown in parentheses): Connecticut (1), Delaware (1), Illinois (1), Massachusetts (1), Michigan (1), New Jersey (5), New York (2),

TABLE 5.A

**Distribution of Small-Lot Packaged Goods Shipments
Forwarded to West Coast**

Weight Range (lbs.)	Per Cent of Shipments
1–30	21.9
31–60	15.3
61–105	9.6
106–500	34.0
501–1,000	7.0
1,001–2,000	5.5
2,001–6,000	3.8
6,001–10,000	2.0
10,001–20,000	0.9
TOTAL	100.0%

Pennsylvania (1), Tennessee (2), and West Virginia (1). The four West Coast distribution centers are in Los Angeles and San Francisco, California; Portland, Oregon; and Seattle, Washington.

PRESENT DISTRIBUTION OPERATION AND CHARACTERISTICS OF SHIPMENTS

Small-lot packaged goods shipments forwarded from the shipper's sixteen eastern plants are presently routed as individual shipments via motor truck, freight forwarder, and express to West Coast distribution areas (Table 5.B).

TABLE 5.B

Shipping Characteristics of Small-Lot Shipments to West Coast

Average pounds forwarded daily	22,973
Annual weight forwarded (lbs.)	5,743,000
Average weight per shipment (lbs.)	661
Average weight per piece (lbs.)	50
Average weight density (lbs. per cubic foot)	19
Average miles per shipment	2,893

Forty-five per cent of the shipments are delivered within twenty miles of the four West Coast distribution centers. The other 55 per cent are delivered beyond twenty miles, but within the metropolitan areas of the four cities.

CONSIDERED DISTRIBUTION ALTERNATIVES

1. Continue Barnes's present operation.

2. Set up a private trucking operation for *all* Barnes shipments.

3. Establish a combined private and common carrier transportation system.

4. Use unitized loads for transporting all small-lot shipments.

5. Bypass warehouses and deliver all shipments directly to customers.

QUESTIONS

1. Comment briefly about the possible cost reductions or cost increases which would be achieved in the following areas by effecting each of the five distribution alternatives: (a) transportation, (b) materials handling, (c) inventory holding, and (d) order processing.
2. Comment briefly about the distribution flexibility to Barnes Manufacturing under each distribution alternative.
3. What other distribution alternatives would you consider? What advantages and disadvantages are inherent in each of these alternatives?
4. What advantages and disadvantages should be considered for distribution alternative 5 regarding bypassing warehouses and delivering all shipments directly to customers?

6

The Alexander Hamilton Electrical Company

The Alexander Hamilton Electrical Company, division of the Hamilton Manufacturing Corporation, manufactures and distributes a diversified line of electrical appliances and parts to retail appliance dealers throughout the United States. The company distributes its electrical products through its Los Angeles, California, plant and its South Bend, Indiana, and Atlanta, Georgia, warehouses.

PROBLEM

The shipper is dissatisfied with his present distribution plan, which is costly and causes numerous service difficulties, and has decided to investigate the idea of eliminating either one or both of his distribution warehouses. Therefore, the shipper has decided to study the pattern of deliveries to retail appliance dealers located in the area served by the South Bend and the Atlanta warehouses.

PRESENT DISTRIBUTION OPERATION AND SHIPMENT CHARACTERISTICS

Alexander Hamilton products are loaded onto trucks, trailers, and trains at the Los Angeles plant and forwarded via approximately sixty different carriers (the majority being motor carriers) directly to retail appliance dealers located west of the Mississippi River or to the South Bend and Atlanta warehouses for ultimate distribution to appliance dealers located in the East.

TABLE 6.A

Characteristics of Shipments Forwarded to Hamilton Warehouses

Characteristics	Atlanta Warehouse	South Bend Warehouse	Total
Average daily weight (lbs.)	1,447	4,539	5,986[a]
Annual weight (lbs.)	361,867	1,134,743	1,496,610
Average weight per shipment (lbs.)	147.3	374.7	272.8
Average weight per piece (lbs.)	44.3	87.9	71.0
Average mileage per shipment	2,917	2,455	2,528
Average weight density (lbs. per cu. ft.)	14.3	14.3	14.3

[a]Daily weight ranges from 1,903 to 13,369 pounds.

TABLE 6.B

	WEIGHT INTERVAL (LBS.)		
	1–200	201–1,000	1,001–2,000
From South Bend			
Per cent of total shipments	35.7%	57.1%	7.2%
Per cent of total weight	10.7	76.3	13.0
From Atlanta			
Per cent of total shipments	84.0	16.0	—
Per cent of total weight	31.0	69.0	—
Total			
Per cent of total shipments	47.3	47.2	5.5
Per cent of total weight	15.6	74.5	9.9

SHIPMENT CHARACTERISTICS

Shipments made directly to retail appliance dealers account for 77 per cent of the total weight of all shipments from the plant. The balance, 23 per cent, is shipped to the warehouses. Characteristics of the shipments to the warehouses are shown in Table 6.A.

Shipments to both warehouses are forwarded from the Los Angeles plant via piggyback service at low "mixed commodity" ratings. The products

TABLE 6.C

Additional Characteristics of Hamilton Warehouse Shipments

PRESENT DISTRIBUTION OF PRODUCTS FROM WAREHOUSES

Motor Carrier Class Rating	Per Cent of Total Weight
85	85.3
92.5	4.9
100	0.8
Misc. (70, 100, and 125)	9.0
TOTAL	100.0%

PER CENT OF WEIGHT BY STATE FORWARDED FROM SOUTH BEND WAREHOUSE

State	Per Cent of Weight
Alabama	2.2
Illinois	14.2
West Virginia	14.0
Georgia	8.7
South Carolina	5.1
Ohio	2.8
Tennessee	25.3
Indiana	9.5
Virginia	10.2
Kentucky	2.2
North Carolina	5.8
TOTAL	100.0%

PER CENT OF WEIGHT BY STATE FORWARDED FROM ATLANTA WAREHOUSE

State	Per Cent of Weight
Florida	10.0
Georgia	5.8
North Carolina	4.2
South Carolina	5.0
New Jersey	15.0
New York	25.5
Massachusetts	4.5
Pennsylvania	14.6
Maryland	15.4
TOTAL	100.0%

are then stored in the warehouses for eventual distribution via motor truck to retail appliance dealers located in the East.

The weight characteristics of shipments forwarded from warehouses to retail appliance dealers are shown in Table 6.B.

Other characteristics of the warehouse shipments are shown in Table 6.C.

QUESTIONS

1. What is wrong with the present distribution operation of Alexander Hamilton Electrical Company?
2. Would you bypass the two present warehouses? If so, where would you locate warehouses (if at all)?
3. Describe the distribution operation you would employ.

CASE

7

**Total
Distribution
Cost**

You are the distribution director for a large eastern manufacturing concern now using a combined rail-warehouse distribution method to forward products to consignees located in the Midwest.

Customers have complained that, too frequently, they have not received ordered merchandise because of stockouts at your Midwest warehouses. You are, therefore, investigating the use of air freight in order to improve service to customers and eliminate the stockout problem.

Table 7.A shows some of the major cost components which vary because of a change in distribution operations:

TABLE 7.A

Total Distribution Cost Approach

Annual sales = 1,000,000 units or 1,000 tons

Rail and Warehouse	Cost per Ton	Total Cost
Transport	$ 58.00	
Warehouse cost	55.20	
Taxes on inventory	4.00	
Interest on inventory, $150,000 at 6%	——	——
COST VIA RAIL WAREHOUSE		

Air Freight	Cost per Ton	Total Cost
Transport	$120.00	
Pickup and delivery	20.00	
Interest on inventory, $50,000 at 6%	——	——
COST VIA AIR FREIGHT		

QUESTIONS

1. What is the inventory cost per ton:
   a. Under the rail-warehouse distribution method?
   b. Under the air freight distribution method?
2. What is the total cost:
   a. Of the rail-warehouse distribution method?
   b. Of the air freight distribution method?
3. What other distribution methods would you explore?

CASE

8

Using Linear
Programing to
Dispatch Vehicles

The following case problem deals with the dispatch of vehicles within the New York metropolitan area. The problem encompasses fifteen hypothetical terminals and the projection of cost savings by the use of linear programing during a 16-hour test period.

HOW LINEAR PROGRAMING SHOULD BE USED
FOR DISPATCHING VEHICLES

[1]   Constructing a Matrix

At the beginning of each day the dispatcher determines the total number of trailers that should be at each terminal by 3:00 P.M. (This is usually a constant number.) All terminals now report their lineup no later than 8:30 A.M. (most terminals report by 7:45 A.M.). Each morning, some terminals have a surplus of trailers, some terminals have a deficit of trailers, and some terminals have exactly the number needed. Terminals which usually have surplus units include the Post Express Terminal (PXT) and Thirty-fifth Street. Terminals usually having a deficit of trailers include Eleventh Avenue, Inland, and Hanson Place. Although the number of deficit and surplus trailers at each terminal may change each day, the terminals having deficits and the terminals having surpluses usually do not change. Therefore, at the start of each day the dispatcher may set up a matrix showing PXT and Thirty-fifth Street as surplus terminals and Eleventh Avenue, Inland, and Hanson Place as deficit terminals.

[2]   Dispatching Tractors to Surplus Terminals

Before trailers can be dispatched from surplus terminals to deficit terminals, a tractor with a driver must be available at the surplus terminal. In many cases, drivers and tractors must be dispatched to surplus terminals from deficit terminals—"clean" terminals.

[3]   Types of Tractors and Trailers

Since Lapeer tractors must be hooked up to Lapeer trailers and Universal tractors must be hooked up to Universal trailers, the dispatching of each type of tractor must be made to surplus terminals which have the same type of trailer. There are 91 Universal tractors and 78 Lapeer tractors. There are available 228 20-foot Lapeer trailers. For Universal, there are available 87 20-foot trailers, 67 26-foot trailers, and 86 35-foot trailers.

[4]   Length of Trailers at Terminals

The three major terminals which cannot accommodate 35-foot trailers are Inland, Hanson Place, and West Side.

ACTUAL DISPATCHES VS. PROPOSED DISPATCH PROGRAM

This section will show how the proposed dispatch program can be used for dispatching during each time period, and the amount of savings that would be gained by using this program.

[1]   Actual vs. Proposed Dispatches
7:00 A.M. – 9:25 A.M.

Matrix Solution for Table 8.A

At 7:00 A.M. it was known that PXT and Thirty-fifth Street were surplus terminals and Eleventh Avenue, Inland, and Hanson Place were deficit terminals. Therefore, the matrix shown in Figure 8.A could have been constructed.

TABLE 8.A

7:00 A.M. to 9:25 A.M. – Actual Dispatches

Time	Type of Movement	Type of Unit	Number of Units	From	To
7:00	MT	Lapeer	1	Hoboken	11th Avenue
7:00	MT	26'	1	PXT	Hanson Place
7:10	MT	Lapeer	1	PXT	Hanson Place
7:15	MT	Lapeer	2	PXT	11th Avenue
8:00	MT	20'	1	West Side	11th Avenue
8:00	MT	Lapeer	2	PXT	Hanson Place
8:10	MT	Lapeer	2	PXT	Hanson Place
8:15	MT	Lapeer	1	PXT	11th Avenue
8:15	MT	26'	1	Walnut Street	Inland
8:15	light	Universal	2	11th Avenue	PXT
9:15	light	Universal	1	11th Avenue	35th Street
9:15	MT	Lapeer	1	35th Street	Grand Central
9:17	MT	35'	1	PXT	11th Avenue

By 8:15 A.M. the number of surplus and deficit trailers was reported for all terminals. The matrix at this time could have been solved as in Figure 8.B.

Figure 8.C shows the number of trailers that should be dispatched from each surplus terminal to each deficit terminal (when a man and a tractor are available for each unit).

By analyzing the dispatches that were made during this time period, notably the 7:00 dispatch of a trailer from Hoboken to Eleventh Avenue, one can see that the use of relative cost charts (see Table 8.E, below) would reduce the dispatching costs. For example, if the dispatcher had consulted the chart showing relative costs between terminals, he would have dispatched a trailer from Hoboken at 7:00 A.M. to Hanson Place instead of to Eleventh

	PXT	35th St.
11th Avenue		
Inland		
Hanson Place		

FIGURE 8.A

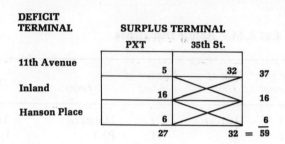

DEFICIT
TERMINAL   SURPLUS TERMINAL
                  PXT   35th St.

	PXT	35th St.	
11th Avenue	5	32	37
Inland	16		16
Hanson Place	6		6
	27	32 = 59	

FIGURE 8.B

DEFICIT
TERMINAL   SURPLUS TERMINAL
                  PXT   35th St.

	PXT	35th St.	
11th Avenue	21	16	37
Inland		16	16
Hanson Place	6		6
	27	32 = 59	

FIGURE 8.C

Avenue. In combination with this movement he would have dispatched one of the units from PXT to Eleventh Avenue, instead of to Hanson Place. The savings gained by using this solution would be $0.9945.

As far as the light movements are concerned, the two tractors forwarded at 8:15 A.M. from Eleventh Avenue to PXT should have instead been forwarded to Thirty-fifth Street. These tractors would have arrived at Thirty-fifth Street at 8:30 A.M., would have taken at least fifteen minutes to hook up, and would have been at Hanson Place no earlier than 9:45 A.M. The relative cost chart shows a savings of $3.0797 per unit or $6.1594 for the two units.

[2]   **Actual vs. Proposed Dispatches**
       9:25 A.M. – 11:00 A.M.

Matrix Solution for Table 8.B

At 9:25, the surplus and deficit terminals reported the following situations: PXT—24 surplus units; Thirty-fifth Street—30 surplus units;

Eleventh Avenue—25 deficit units; Inland—32 deficit units; and Hanson Place—3 deficit units. (Because there are changing circumstances at each of the surplus and deficit terminals, the quantity of surplus and deficit trailers varies many times during the day. That is, some surplus trailers are used for loading at surplus terminals, and some trailers are unloaded at deficit terminals and therefore reduce the terminal's deficit of trailers, etc.) The new matrix setup at 9:25 A.M. is shown in Figure 8.D.

If the dispatcher had used this matrix solution, he would have dispatched five units from PXT to Eleventh Avenue rather than to the Inland terminal.

TABLE 8.B

9:25 A.M. to 11:00 A.M. — Actual Dispatches

Time	Type of Movement	Type of Unit	Number of Units	From	To
9:26	MT	35'	1	PXT	11th Avenue
9:30	light	Lapeer	2	Hanson Place	PXT
9:40	MT	26'	1	35th Street	Inland
9:40	light	Universal	1	11th Avenue	35th Street
9:45	MT	Lapeer	1	Hoboken	Inland
9:52	MT	Lapeer	1	PXT	Inland
10:00	MT	Lapeer	1	35th Street	Inland
10:00	light	Universal	1	11th Avenue	35th Street
10:02	MT	35'	1	PXT	11th Avenue
10:02	MT	Lapeer	2	35th Street	Inland
10:02	light	Universal	2	West Side	35th Street
10:04	MT	Lapeer	1	PXT	Inland
10:08	light	Lapeer	1	Inland	PXT
10:16	MT	Lapeer	1	35th Street	Inland
10:16	light	Lapeer	1	Inland	35th Street
10:25	light	Universal	1	West Side	35th Street
10:25	MT	Lapeer	1	35th Street	Inland
10:27	MT	Lapeer	1	International	Inland
10:34	MT	Lapeer	1	PXT	Inland
10:34	MT	26'	1	PXT	Inland
10:34	MT	Lapeer	1	PXT	Hanson Place
10:46	MT	26'	1	PXT	Inland
10:46	light	Universal	1	11th Avenue	PXT
10:49	MT	35'	1	35th Street	11th Avenue
10:49	light	Universal	1	11th Avenue	35th Street
10:50	light	Universal	1	11th Avenue	35th Street

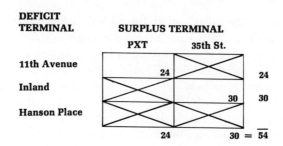

FIGURE 8.D

He would have also dispatched a unit from PXT to Eleventh Avenue rather than to Hanson Place. The resulting savings would have been $7.4185. As far as light movements are concerned, a tractor was forwarded from Inland to PXT at 10:08 A.M. although there were trailers available at Thirty-fifth Street. This tractor was forwarded to PXT in order to maintain a steady flow of manpower to this critical terminal. In keeping with these requirements, the dispatcher should have made the light move from Eleventh Avenue to PXT at 10:00 A.M. and forwarded the Inland tractor to Thirty-fifth Street. (This movement would have been obvious to the dispatcher if he could have consulted the chart showing relative costs between terminals.) The savings resulting from this movement would be $0.1724.

[3]   **Actual vs. Proposed Dispatches**
      11:00 A.M. – 1:00 P.M.

Matrix Solution for Table 8.C

At 11:00 A.M. the following terminals reported the following surplus and deficit conditions: PXT—10 surplus trailers; Thirty-fifth Street—18

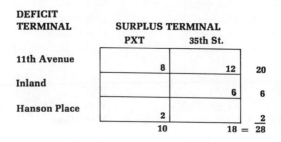

FIGURE 8.E

TABLE 8.C

11:00 A.M. to 1:00 P.M. — Actual Dispatches

Time	Type of Movement	Type of Unit	Number of Units	From	To
11:18	MT	26'	1	PXT	Inland
11:35	MT	26'	2	35th Street	Inland
11:35	light	Lapeer	2	Inland	35th Street
11:58	MT	26'	1	PXT	Englewood
12:04	MT	26'	1	35th Street	Grand Central
12:04	light	Lapeer	1	West Side	35th Street
12:08	MT	35'	1	35th Street	11th Avenue
12:08	light	Universal	1	11th Avenue	35th Street
12:40	MT	35'	1	35th Street	11th Avenue
12:40	light	Lapeer	1	Inland	35th Street
12:42	light	Lapeer	1	Grand Central	35th Street
12:43	MT	Lapeer	1	35th Street	11th Avenue
12:43	MT	Lapeer	1	International	Inland
12:44	light	Lapeer	1	Inland	35th Street
12:45	MT	26'	1	35th Street	Inland
12:57	MT	Lapeer	1	35th Street	Inland
12:57	light	Universal	1	11th Avenue	35th Street

surplus trailers; Eleventh Avenue—20 deficit trailers; Inland—17 deficit trailers; and Hanson Place—2 deficit trailers.

The matrix solution for this time period is shown in Figure 8.E.

If the dispatcher had used the matrix solution shown above he would have dispatched a unit at 11:18 A.M. from PXT to Eleventh Avenue instead of to Inland, and in combination with this movement, he would have dispatched a unit from Thirty-fifth Street to Inland rather than to Eleventh Avenue. The resulting savings from this combination of moves would have been $0.1925. Also, the dispatcher should have forwarded a trailer from Thirty-fifth Street to Englewood rather than from PXT to Englewood, and in combination with this movement, he should have forwarded a trailer from PXT to Eleventh Avenue instead of from Thirty-fifth Street to Eleventh Avenue. The savings resulting from this combination of movements would have been $0.4772. (This movement can be determined by consulting the relative cost chart.)

[4]   Actual vs. Proposed Dispatches
1:00 P.M. – 2:00 P.M.

At 1:00 P.M., the terminals reported the following quantities of surplus and deficit trailers: PXT—10 surplus trailers; Thirty-fifth Street—7 surplus trailers; Hoboken—4 surplus trailers; Eleventh Avenue—18 deficit trailers; Inland—7 deficit trailers.

The actual dispatches made during this time period are shown in Table 8.D.

TABLE 8.D

1:00 P.M. to 2:00 P.M. – Actual Dispatches

Time	Type of Movement	Type of Unit	Number of Units	From	To
1:10	MT	35′	2	PXT	11th Avenue
1:19	MT	Lapeer	1	35th Street	Inland
1:19	light	Lapeer	1	Inland	35th Street
1:23	light	Universal	1	Hanson Place	PXT
1:32	MT	20′	1	PXT	West Side
1:34	MT	Lapeer	1	35th Street	Inland
1:34	light	Universal	1	West Side	35th Street

Matrix Solution for Table 8.D

The matrix solution for this time period is shown in Figure 8.F.

If the dispatcher had used the matrix to forward trailers between terminals, he would have dispatched two trailers from Thirty-fifth Street to Eleventh Avenue, instead of to Inland. The resulting savings would have been $2.1012.

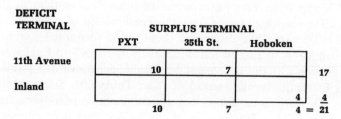

FIGURE 8.F

[5]   Actual vs. Proposed Dispatches
2:00 P.M. – 11:00 P.M.

By using the proposed program instead of the present dispatching system, the following savings would have resulted between 2:00 P.M. and 11:00 P.M. (see Table 8.E):

2:00–4:00 = $2.4862	6:01–7:00	= $1.4838
4:00–4:40 = 3.9700	7:00–8:10	= 2.9676
4:40–5:05 = 1.4838	8:10–9:30	= 1.4838
5:05–6:01 = 2.7840	9:30–11:00	= None

Therefore, by using the proposed program, the total savings between 7:00 A.M. and 11:00 P.M. would have been $34.1749. Multiplying this total by 365 days, the annual savings would have been $12,838.84. (This is a conservative estimate of savings, since this figure is based on a 16-hour rather than a 24-hour period. Also, a relatively small number of dispatches was made during this period.)

TABLE 8.E

ACTUAL DISPATCH		DISPATCH UNDER PROPOSED PROGRAM		
Surplus Terminal	*Deficit Terminal*	*Surplus Terminal*	*Deficit Terminal*	*Savings*[1]
2:00 P.M.–4:00 P.M.				
PXT	Inland	PXT	11th Avenue	$1.2431
PXT	Inland	PXT	11th Avenue	1.2431
				$2.4862
4:00 P.M.–4:40 P.M.				
PXT	Inland	PXT	11th Avenue	$1.2431
PXT	Inland	PXT	11th Avenue	1.2431
PXT	Inland	PXT	11th Avenue	1.2431
PXT	Inland	PXT	11th Avenue	1.2431
West Side	11th Avenue	West Side	Inland	(.5012)
West Side	11th Avenue	West Side	Inland	(.5012)
				$3.9700

[1]Parentheses denote negative figures.

TABLE 8.E (continued)

| ACTUAL DISPATCH | | DISPATCH UNDER PROPOSED PROGRAM | | |
Surplus Terminal	Deficit Terminal	Surplus Terminal	Deficit Terminal	Savings
4:40 P.M.–5:05 P.M.				
PXT	Inland	PXT	11th Avenue	$1.2431
PXT	Inland	PXT	11th Avenue	1.2431
West Side	11th Avenue	West Side	Inland	(.5012)
West Side	11th Avenue	West Side	Inland	(.5012)
				$1.4838
5:05 P.M.–6:01 P.M.				
Hoboken	Hanson Place	Hoboken	Inland	$1.2592
PXT	Inland	PXT	Hanson Place	0.0410
West Side	11th Avenue	West Side	Inland	(.5012)
PXT	Inland	PXT	11th Avenue	1.2431
West Side	11th Avenue	West Side	Inland	(.5012)
PXT	Inland	PXT	11th Avenue	1.2431
				$2.7840
6:01 P.M.–7:00 P.M.				
PXT	Inland	PXT	11th Avenue	$1.2431
PXT	Inland	PXT	11th Avenue	1.2431
West Side	11th Avenue	West Side	Inland	(.5012)
West Side	11th Avenue	West Side	Inland	(.5012)
				$1.4838
7:00 P.M.–8:10 P.M.				
PXT	Inland	PXT	11th Avenue	$1.2431
PXT	Inland	PXT	11th Avenue	1.2431
PXT	Inland	PXT	11th Avenue	1.2431
PXT	Inland	PXT	11th Avenue	1.2431
West Side	11th Avenue	West Side	Inland	(.5012)
West Side	11th Avenue	West Side	Inland	(.5012)
West Side	11th Avenue	West Side	Inland	(.5012)
West Side	11th Avenue	West Side	Inland	(.5012)
				$2.9676
8:10 P.M.–9:30 P.M.				
PXT	Inland	PXT	11th Avenue	$1.2431
PXT	Inland	PXT	11th Avenue	1.2431
West Side	11th Avenue	West Side	Inland	(.5012)
West Side	11th Avenue	West Side	Inland	(.5012)
				$1.4838

CONCLUSION

By observing and simulating the movement of trailers for the subject test period, it is concluded that:

1. The program for priority dispatch of equipment is feasible and the use of the program should substantially reduce movement costs.

2. Other operating areas, including the use of the proposed program for dispatching many different types of equipment and the use of the subject program in major cities other than New York, should be investigated.

QUESTIONS

1. How would you use linear programing for moving goods from distribution centers to marketing areas?
2. Describe the advantages and disadvantages of using manual linear programing techniques.
3. Discuss the advantages and disadvantages of computerizing linear programing techniques.
4. How would you have solved this case problem if two noninterchangeable types of tractors and trailers were being used?

CASE

9

A Short Problem in
Linear Programing
for Distribution Costs

You are the general traffic manager of a soap-manufacturing firm. Your plants are located in the following cities, and each plant produces soap as indicated:

Plant Location	Soap Production (thousands of units)
Philadelphia, Pa.	2,000
Chicago, Ill.	1,800
Atlanta, Ga.	3,400
TOTAL	7,200

You move this product from these manufacturing points to market areas known as Louisville, Kentucky; Cleveland, Ohio; and Pittsburgh, Pennsylvania.

Monthly sales are rather uniform and are expected to be as follows:

Market Area	Sales (thousands of units)
Louisville, Ky.	1,900
Cleveland, Ohio	2,300
Pittsburgh, Pa.	2,000
TOTAL	6,200

You will note that the anticipated total sales exceed production by a thousand units.

Transportation costs from each manufacturing point to each market "area" are as follows:

| TRANSPORTATION COST PER 1,000 UNITS | | |
Philadelphia	Chicago	Atlanta
Louisville	$8	$1	$3
Cleveland	4	5	9
Pittsburgh	6	2	7

PROBLEM: Soap production must be moved to the market areas. Each market area must receive only enough soap to handle its sales. How would you minimize your transportation costs?

Robert J. Franco

A

Introduction and
Background to the
Transportation Function

Winston's Encyclopedic Dictionary defines transportation as "the act of carrying or state of being carried from one place to another—the means of conveyance and also the charge for conveyance."[1]

This chapter will deal with the instruments that enable such conveyance to occur, the cost of the conveyance from the viewpoint of both the carrier and the user, and the regulatory framework in which this actually occurs. I will also attempt to place the transportation function in proper perspective vis-à-vis the total physical distribution concept, so that it can be analyzed as part of the total system.

CHOICES OF TRANSPORTATION
AVAILABLE

There are two primary choices of transportation available to the user in transporting goods. Private carriage or the use of company-owned or leased equipment is the first of these and for-hire transportation or the use of common or contract carriers is the second.

While private carriage is not subject to regulation (excepting safety) it is limited to the movement of products owned by the firm receiving or sending the goods. As a rule (excluding specialty goods) a two-way loaded

---

[1]John C. Winston, 1942, p. 1061.

movement and a high utilization of equipment is necessary to make private carriage economical.

On the other hand, contract carriers offer a specialized service to one or more firms, each act of carriage being supported by a contract. Public Law 85–163 in 1957 defined contract carriage to mean:

> ... any person who engages in transportation by motor vehicle passengers or property in interstate or foreign commerce, for compensation under continuing contracts with one person or a limited number of persons either (a) for the furnishing of transportation services through the assignment of motor vehicles for a continuing period of time to the exclusive use of each person served or (b) for the furnishing of transportation services designed to meet the distinct need of each individual customer.

The availabilities of major common carriage and for-hire carriage may be listed as follows:

Railroad	Freight forwarder
Motor carrier	REA Express
Water	United Parcel
Air freight	Bus
Pipelines	Parcel post

Railroad

Railroads have relatively low line-haul costs in comparison with other modes. One engine can haul a number of cars, each of which is heavily loaded, which makes their ratio of motive unit per lading unit extremely low. This advantage is reflected in their rate structure, for their long-distance rates to shippers are generally lower than all other modes, except waterway carriers.

The railroads also offer a wide range of services including transit privileges, diversion, storage, manufacturing, and refrigeration. They are able to handle heavy and bulky articles with considerable ease when compared with other modes, due to the nature of their car equipment and their roadbeds. Their fixed railways seriously hampered their flexibility (when viewed against other modes) until the introduction of "piggyback," which enables them to move volume door to door.

They generally offer a dependable service but in short-haul movements theirs is generally not the fastest service available to the public. However, as the length of haul increases, their ability to compete "timewise" improves (except against air freight). Adverse weather conditions, which affect transport, are less detrimental to railroads than to other types of carriers.

Restrictions on the interchange of cars are limited, which also permits a comprehensive range of through service, i.e., cars can be interchanged over all lines because of uniformity in rail width, cars, and couplings.

Motor Carriers

Motor carriers provide a flexible, dependable, fast service, particularly on short hauls and for truckload shipments. Their advantage in speed decreases when compared with rail carriers as the length of haul increases; and their less-than-truckload shipments are moved with considerably less speed. Quite often, in terms of time, they do possess a competitive advantage on this type of traffic for short hauls. Also, door-to-door delivery and pickups are standard trucking services that are highly attractive to the shipping public. On long hauls, there is no advantage in transit time on less-than-truckload traffic.

Motor carriers generally have low rates for local and short-haul traffic, particularly on truckload movements. As the distance increases, they gradually lose their cost advantage to railroads.

Water Carriers

Water carriers have the lowest unit cost, predicated on volume and distance, next to pipeline movements. Their services are attractive to a limited public as their main forte is in moving large volumes of nonperishables at a relatively slow rate of speed. This can be used to an advantage, however, in that it supplements warehousing and terminal storage needs.

Air Transport

Speed is the outstanding advantage of air transport, while its relatively high cost is the chief disadvantage.

Changes in distribution technique that reduce the need for warehouses and costly redistribution have caused an accelerated growth of this mode of transport. Additional airports and the use of new types of equipment specifically geared to handle cargo have greatly increased service capabilities and therefore the share of market of airlines.

Pipelines

Pipelines provide the lowest unit cost of any mode in terms of distance and volume. Also, there is no backhaul problem, and the nature of the operation permits low maintenance and labor costs. Finally, the incremental costs of increased volumes handled are extremely low. Their service is limited to a specific market, however, as the product must be "flowable" and must move between fixed points.

Freight Forwarder

Freight forwarders hold themselves out to the general public to transport or provide transportation but are not carriers themselves. They assemble and consolidate (generally small) shipments and provide accessory services, utilizing the services of common carriers subject to the Interstate Commerce Act for the underlying carriage.

REA Express

REA Express is a small-shipment carrier that maintains over 8,000 offices and terminals in the United States. The service provided coordinates all forms of rail, highway, ocean, and air transport to link shipper-consignees. Pickup and delivery service is provided at all principal points in all fifty states, Canada, Puerto Rico, and nations throughout the Free World. Small shipments, as defined by REA, are those weighing less than 10,000 pounds each.

Parcel Post, Bus, and United Parcel

These are specialized carriers that are limited by size and weight restrictions on the shipments they handle. Parcel post is part of the U.S. mail system and is limited to moving packages and parcels.

Packages may be shipped by bus, but this service is restricted to key cities and does not include pickup or delivery service. Because of size and weight restrictions, only small shipments can be handled in this service.

United Parcel has made considerable inroads into the "package" transportation market. It competes directly with parcel post and bus for this type of traffic. It has size and weight restrictions similar to those of parcel post and bus, and it provides its own pickup and delivery service.

REGULATION OF TRANSPORTATION

Transportation is a regulated industry. Intrastate movements of goods are regulated by the individual state agencies variously called Public Utility Commission, Railroad Commission, Public Service Commission, etc. Interstate transportation is regulated by the Interstate Commerce Commission, the Civil Aeronautics Board, and the Federal Power Commission.

Regulation by these agencies embraces not only the cost or charge to the using public but also the areas (routes) individual carriers can serve, commodities permitted to be moved, and safety.

Rates are made by the carriers either on their own initiative or at the request of shippers. Rate bureaus and conferences of the carriers analyze the shipper rate request and, subject to their approval and that of the regulatory body, the rate is published. Independent action by individual carriers can also result in rate changes, but these rates differ from the conference rate published in the tariff in that only the carriers participating in such a rate decision are permitted to move the traffic at the rate shown.

Thousands of rates are filed for publication each day, and the majority are published as submitted. In effect, then, the Interstate Commerce Commission *does not make rates.* If a protest is filed on a rate to be published (and the protest of an interested party may come from a shipper, another carrier, etc.), the commission investigates and decides whether to: Let the rate stand as published; let the rate stand as published pending an investigation so that all parties can be heard; suspend the rate and hold an investigation; or, suspend the rate without an investigation.

There is a great deal of misunderstanding of the role the regulatory agency plays in ratemaking, but from the above it is obvious that rates can be changed and that most of the time this change occurs without the Interstate Commerce Commission becoming involved. The commission can on its own decide to investigate a rate, but without a protest of another party this is rarely done.

Principal Factors Affecting the Level of Transportation Rates

Transportation rates as published in the tariff can be used by any shipper or receiver to whom the rates are applicable. The carrier sets the rates on the basis of certain criteria. Among these criteria are: the carrier's own cost factors for performing the service, the amount of transportation cost that the traffic will bear, and the competitive level of rates in effect. Despite the regulatory constraints within which the carriers must operate the rates are subject to marked and continual change. Shippers and carriers, cognizant of the demand and supply relating to their transportation cost factors, may so exploit them as to effect changes in their transportation rate structure. The principal factors are:

[1] Cost of Service to the Carriers

Transportation carriers strive to make a return on their investment, and attempt to make their service attractive to the shipping public as well as profitable to themselves. They therefore attempt to determine the cost associated with these services or proposed services in order to optimize their rates. Many products move at rates which are below full cost to the individual carriers. The present-day trend, however, is for the carrier to assess all direct and indirect costs attributable to individual movements and set its rates accordingly. (The carrier uses this cost as a rate "floor" and uses "what the traffic will bear" as a rate "ceiling.")

[2] Value of Service to the Shipper

The shipper assesses the transportation rates available to him to serve a particular market, and depending on his competition in that area and on his cost of producing the product, he determines how much he can profitably spend for transportation service. The existing rate structure is not necessarily indicative of the optimum transportation rate, inasmuch as the rate is not static, and can be changed by the carrier for cause. The shipper also may use private carriage if it enables him to serve his market more profitably. In any event, the shipper will investigate the alternative transportation modes available to him and the various levels of rates to determine his optimal level of service for the particular market. The shipper, for example, may decide on air freight or air express, and thus pay more for transportation but less for inventory and warehousing. On the other hand, he may use carload rates and pay substantially less for transportation but considerably more for warehousing, inventory, and break-bulk distribution costs. The carrier, therefore, must assess this factor in terms of comparative value of his service to shippers.

[3] Length of Haul

The cost of performing transportation (other things being equal) is directly related to the length of the movement involved, the unit weight of the product, and the shipment weight. Generally speaking, the unit cost decreases as the length of haul increases. For as the shipping distance increases, the terminal and clerical costs, being relatively constant, are readily absorbed into the total cost.

[4]　Direction of Haul

The concentration of manufacturing plants along the eastern seaboard and east northcentral states during our industrial revolution, in the mid- and late nineteenth century, has naturally keyed the directional flow of goods to and from markets. Raw materials and finished goods have largely retained these patterns over the years. As a result there is considerable imbalance of traffic and therefore much unused capacity in terms of transportation equipment returning empty to points of origin, where new loads can be picked up. Rates which will cause products to move in the direction of the empty movement can be set considerably below the rates in the opposite direction in order to stabilize the movement of loaded equipment. The rates in the direction of the primary flow usually reflect the round-trip cost to the carrier, including the cost of the empty return. Goods moving back in previously empty equipment therefore move at an incremental cost to the carrier.

[5]　Volume of Traffic and Periods of Movement

Traffic which flows in a steady stream is considerably cheaper to handle than blocks of traffic which move on an irregular basis, not only by day of week but by season of year. Carriers that are forced to have peak-period equipment available find its idleness in off-period use considerably expensive, a condition which is ultimately reflected in higher rate levels. Conversely, regularly moving traffic which the carrier can service with a minimum of operating equipment makes for a lower cost, which can be reflected in the rates for this type of traffic.

[6]　Competition Between Centers and Markets

The "lay-down" (total) cost of a product determines the minimum amount of money that must be realized on a sale before a profit is secured. The competitive price for this product in the market represents the "ceiling" and should the lay-down cost exceed this competitive level, the seller may be priced out of this market. The carrier must therefore analyze both the shippers it serves and the "markets" of a particular product in order to determine competitive transportation rates.

[7]   Rates of Competing Carriers

The carrier must determine not only the rates of the other carriers serving shippers in the immediate locale, but also the rates of carriers serving competing customers in other areas. In addition to this criterion of transportation rate-related service, charges must also be considered in this overall analysis of "what the traffic will bear."

[8]   Density (Bulk and Weight of the Product)

Density of the product is one of the most important cost factors to consider in setting rate levels. The weight of the traffic utilizing a given amount of space determines the level of revenue for the carrier. Thus, if a carrier publishes a rate that attracts traffic with a density four times greater than another product (product X) which can be loaded in the same amount of space, he obviously can reduce his rates on a weight basis substantially below the rate on "product X" and realize a considerable increase in revenue. As an example, if a rate of $1.00 per hundredweight is made available on a shipment with a density of 10 pounds per cubic foot and the shipment weighs 10,000 pounds, the carrier will have to provide 1,000 feet of space to accommodate the shipment; and for this will receive $100.00 in revenue or 10 cents per cubic foot (product X). If the shipment weighs 25 pounds per cubic foot, it will only occupy 400 feet of space, releasing 600 feet of space for the carrier to use in loading other products; and the rate could very easily be reduced to 75 cents per hundredweight. Although the revenue generated would be only $75.00, or almost 19 cents per cubic foot, the carrier would have the additional 600 feet of space in which to secure $25.00 of revenue, at four cents per cubic foot, to balance out the first example. Any revenue exceeding $25.00 that is generated for this space would provide incremental profit to the carrier.

[9]   Packaging of the Product

Packaging affects the cost to the carrier in several ways. First, the shape of the package affects loadability; and, second, the strength of the package determines the height of the shipments that can be placed in a given amount of space. Weight of the packaging is another factor, since there often are load limits on the physical capabilities of the equipment. (Besides, regulatory agencies may set a maximum load level.) Heavy packaging means that less of a product can be carried when there is a weight "ceiling" of this type. Claims are another prime cost factor which must be considered, for the extent of claims may be said to vary inversely with the quality (adequacy) of the packaging.

[10]   Other Factors

The fragility and perishability of a product also affect the cost to the carrier, and consequently the rate that is established. In addition, the value and nature of a product—whether it is bulk or packaged, wet or dry, etc.— have a marked bearing on the cost to the carrier.

CLASSIFICATION

Classification of commodities as used in transportation systematically assigns each of the many commodities for shipment to a class and group. A transportation rating, therefore, can be applied to one of these classes or groups and cover a large number of commodities. This technique considerably simplifies the pricing structure of transportation in that a restricted number of rates can be used to cover the movement of goods instead of having an individual rate for each type of goods from each point of origin to each point of destination. The various freight classification lists identify the rating for each commodity. The two main freight classifications are the Uniform Freight Classification used by the railroads and the National Motor Freight classification used by the trucking industry. The class rates which will be covered later in this chapter apply directly to the commodities shown in the freight classifications. In addition to this class rate structure, there are exception ratings (see Transportation Rates, below) which are placed on products that differ in some way from the product's "normal" group or rating.

The classification not only covers the rating for the product in question, but also covers the minimum amount of weight which must be moved. Different ratings are shown on the same product, also varying by weight. Different ratings are also shown for variations in packing.

Inasmuch as the classification of a product determines the rate to be assessed for the movement of a product, it is extremely important for the shipper to pay special attention to matters of classification. An improper classification *will*, of course, mean an improper rate; and even the slightest change in the assembly of the *product*, the container in which it is shipped, or its state of completion can spell the difference between profit and loss in a given market (since the transportation rate will vary considerably, based on the factors indicated above). A change in the classification of a product will change the transportation rate, and many times is considerably easier to achieve than a rate adjustment.

Key Factors Affecting the Classification of a Product

[1]   Value

Generally speaking, the greater the value of a product the higher is its classification and the transportation charge it incurs. This rule ties in directly with the product's susceptibility to damage and/or theft (hence, higher cost to the carrier). If the product were classified solely on the basis of such susceptibility, coal for example, would have an extremely low classification whereas television tubes would have an extremely high classification. The significant difference for purposes of classification, however, is the higher probability of damage (and theft) to television tubes than to coal.

[2]   Susceptibility to Theft

A product which is easy to steal and which has considerable value, if stolen, is subject to a higher classification rating. For example, a portable television set, which is rather easy to carry off, and if carried off is rather easy to dispose of, is considerably more vulnerable to theft than a rolled-up rug (even though the rug may be of high value).

[3]   Type of Packaging

The type of packaging used for the shipment is one of the most important factors in setting the classification rating. In fact, the classification itself tends to vary for a product, given different types of packaging. For example, the less-than-truckload rating on pine needles when shipped in bags, barrels, or boxes is 85, whereas the same pine needles in machine-pressed bales carry a less-than-truckload rating of 65. When the class rate is applied to these ratings it will be seen that the pine needles in machine-pressed bales will be considerably less expensive to ship than those in bags, barrels, or boxes. Two of the other factors used in considering classification—i.e., density and susceptibility to damage—are also directly related to the type of packaging used. Packaging, of course, affects the amount of damage incurred in the movement of a particular type of product. And the packaging itself will have a direct bearing on the over-all density of the shipment (which includes the packaging).

[4] Susceptibility to Damage

The lower the susceptibility to damage, the lower the classification rating will be, all other things being equal. The reason for this, of course, is that the carrier's cost varies directly with damage, which, in turn, is reflected in the rate.

[5] Density

The higher the density of a product (in pounds per cubic foot), the lower its classification rating and, consequently, the lower its transportation rate. In fact, the combination of density and packaging factors outlined above provide the shipper with his greatest opportunity for changing the classification of his product and consequently changing its transportation rate. Thus, if the packaging can be changed to reduce susceptibility to damage or to increase loadability (or in some other way reduce the carrier's cost), the shipper may ask the carrier for a changed classification rating to reduce his transportation rate. Density can be increased by putting the same product in a smaller amount of space and/or in a smaller-sized package. A good illustration of this is the movement of children's bicycles. They previously were moved after assembly, with a resultant low density per carton. Today, very few bicycles are shipped in this manner; most bicycles are shipped unassembled in a rather compact unit. This has caused the density of the bicycle shipment to increase substantially, thereby permitting a lower classification and a lower transportation rate. Also, the higher the weight of a package, the lower the classification rating and transport cost, as demonstrated in the labor savings for handling containers and other types of unitized loads.

TRANSPORTATION RATES

Transportation rates or charges are published in tariffs on file with the various regulatory agencies. They are available to anyone who meets the requirements of the tariff provisions. Generally speaking, the rates in transportation are quoted on the basis of a certain amount of money per hundred pounds (cwt.), and the tariffs are published accordingly. For example, if a rate between two points is $2.20 per cwt. a shipment weighing 10,000 pounds would cost $220.00, which the shipper or consignee would have to pay to the transportation firm performing the movement.

Many types of rates are available to shippers. There are rates on accessory services, which include special handling and packaging. But for present purposes, we will be concerned only with the three prime categories of rates used in transportation. These are class rates, commodity rates, and exception rates.

Class Rates

The class rates are governed by the classification system previously described. The appropriate rating is determined from the classification for a particular commodity; and this classification rating is then applied to the class rate tariff for the rate between any two points. This amount will be shown as a charge per hundredweight; and multiplying the weight of the shipment in hundreds of pounds by the rate indicated will yield the proper transportation charge. The class rate structure greatly simplifies the pricing of transportation. Unfortunately, the majority of transportation prices today are collected on shipments that move under commodity rates and/or exception rates; so the once simple pricing structure is again becoming extremely complex.

Commodity Rates

Commodity rates normally take precedence over exception rates and class rates; however, the tariff itself will indicate whether or not this is the case. The governing rules of the classification and tariff involved indicate precisely whether or not a movement qualifies for a particular rate and whether or not the rate is applicable. Commodity rates are published on particular commodities between specific origins and destinations. They are generally predicated on volume movements, and usually are applicable between key cities. The volume tendered and the regularity of movement have a marked bearing on carrier cost; and when this cost is translated into the charge to the user, the charge can be considerably below the class rate, which is based on "averages." It has been estimated that over 80 per cent of the volume movements made in this country today are on commodity rates.

Exception Rates

Exception rates are used in conjunction with the classification and the class rate structure. The exception may be a lower class or percentage of a class due to the "exception" from the normal procedure as outlined in the classification.

ROUTING

Routing is an important consideration in transportation inasmuch as the route selected may have a direct bearing on transportation charges. Many rates apply only over certain routes. In addition to the routing of freight by a particular mode of transportation, it is equally important that the mode itself be considered. The router therefore must make a preliminary decision as to whether a shipment will move by air, or rail, or truck, or some other mode of transportation. Once this has been determined, he trades off the transportation rate against the service level of each carrier to select the proper route of movement. For example, between New York and Chicago, a router could select one of several rail lines to tender a shipment. The rate will be the same by each of the lines under consideration. His decision, therefore, ought to be based on the service provided by each of the alternative rails; his choice of carrier will be based on experience. The same principle would apply to shipment by truck. In many instances, the rail and truck prices are identical. The router then must determine which of the two modes will meet his service requirements best and which carrier within the mode selected.

Reciprocity

Many shippers use reciprocity extensively as a "club." For example, a rubber manufacturer may let it be known that no shipments will be handled by any truck line not using brand x tires when entering his plant. In this case, the shipper uses his transportation payments as a lever in order to secure sales. The same can be said for the other side, however. This can be illustrated by the carrier who advises a gasoline firm that he will not buy any more of its gasoline unless a certain percentage of the oil company's total shipments is assured. This is an illustration of a carrier using purchasing power as a tool to secure additional sales. Both of these examples are hypothetical; but it can be assumed that reciprocity is fairly common in industry. There is actually nothing wrong with this strategy provided the shipper receives the best transportation for his dollar and provided the carrier is handling and carrying these shipments at a reasonably adequate profit.

Routing Policy

Many traffic departments establish a routing policy based on the services previously rendered, the services of the various carriers that are available, the cost of the service, the carrier's record in paying claims, the carrier's willingness to negotiate rate adjustments, and other key criteria which would have a direct impact on the cost of transportation to the shipper. Basically, most firms have routing policies which stipulate that "where rates and services are equal, the business will be equitably distributed in such a manner as to suit the company's best interest."

SPECIAL SERVICES

There are numerous special services which the various carriers make available to shippers. But they are of such a wide range and so markedly different as to make an enumeration unfeasible in this book. Several key services will be indicated, however, in order to show their range.

Diversion

A diversion may occur any time a shipment is en route, and it merely signifies that the destination point is changed. The carrier is notified of this change, and the shipment is then diverted to the new destination. The carrier charges for this service. Reconsignment, which is often used synonymously with diversion, means that a different consignee is going to receive the shipment. Once again, the carrier is notified of the reconsignment and the shipment is then delivered to the new consignee; and once again a charge is made by the transportation firm. However, both of these services must be applicable in the tariff before they can be used by the shipper.

In-Transit Privileges

It is possible to stop shipments en route (the privilege is primarily used on rail shipments) for further refining, finishing, or for (in some cases) ware-housing. After completion of the in-transit stop, the shipment is sent on its way to its ultimate destination. In many instances, a shipment may be stopped at the in-transit point for days, weeks, and sometimes even months. A charge is made by the carrier for this service.

Tracing and Expediting

These two services, which are provided by almost all transportation firms, are among those available to shippers without charge.   Tracing is the determination of where a shipment is at any particular time. A shipper may need to know the whereabouts of a shipment in order to estimate time of arrival or to determine whether or not to take other remedial action. (Other action, for example, may mean sending a second shipment via air to insure immediate delivery.) In "expediting" a shipment, the carrier is requested to extend every effort to "hurry" a shipment to its destination.

Jerry Schorr

Functional
Components of
Materials Handling

INTRODUCTION

A good starting point in any discussion of materials handling is to define exactly what materials handling involves.

The basic elements include

1. *Time*—assuring that materials will be moved to the right locations at the right time.

2. *Movement*—the physical movement of materials within a location or between locations.

3. *Quantity*—moving the right quantity to the right location at the right time.

4. *Space*—the correct movement of materials assures the optimum use of space and reduces space requirements to a bare minimum.

OBJECTIVES OF MATERIALS HANDLING

Objectives of materials handling are numerous and vary from company to company. But some objectives are nearly universal:

1. To reduce total distribution costs,

2. To achieve optimum space requirements,

3. To reduce damage and waste,

4. To improve efficiency,

5. To improve the distribution pipeline, and

6. To better working conditions.

COSTS OF MATERIALS HANDLING

The cost of materials handling runs extremely high in many companies. In fact, in some companies, materials-handling costs may total as high as 80 per cent of total production costs.

While the above figure may be astonishing to some readers, an inspection of any plant will show the large amount of labor engaged in materials handling, as well as conveyor equipment, fork lifts, dock-levels, hydraulic jacks, etc., all adding up to a huge total cost in the materials-handling area.

In an effort to reduce this high cost in the distribution pipeline, management closely observes materials handling for

1. Inefficient use of manpower,

2. Inefficient use of equipment,

3. Demurrage charges,

4. Lost and damaged material,

5. Bottlenecks in production,

6. Rehandling,

7. Huge inventories,

8. Poor utilization of space, and

9. Excessive maintenance costs.

FUNCTIONS OF MATERIALS HANDLING

The functions of materials-handling activity can be segregated into three broad areas: planning and tooling (or engineering), operations (movement and storing of materials), and training. Each has a series of internal functional elements including

1. Planning and tooling
   a. Method selection and improvement
   b. Equipment selection, design, and purchase
   c. Labor planning and measurement
   d. Plant layout

2. Operations
   a. Transportation in
   b. Receiving
   c. Checking
   d. Storage
   e. Process flow and storage
   f. Finished product storage
   g. Picking
   h. Packaging
   i. Shipping
   j. Transportation out

Further analysis shows that each of these basic functions has several control factors which must be known and used in daily operations:

2a. Transportation in
    Shipment routings and arrival schedules
    Vendor packaging specifications
    Vehicle type (carrier)—common or private

2b. Receiving
    Unload (equipment and labor standards)

2c. Checking
    Count, check, inspect (programs, specifications, standards)
    Transport routing (equipment and labor standards)

2d. Storage
    Place in (equipment and labor standards)
    Take out (equipment and labor standards)
    Transport routing (equipment and labor standards)

2e. Process flow and storage
    Position at point of use (schedule, standards)
    Move between use points (schedule, standards)
    Remove from use point (schedule, standards)
    Transport routing (equipment and labor standards)
    Place in storage (equipment and labor standards)
    Take out of storage (schedule, equipment, and labor standards)

2f. Finished product storage
Place in (equipment and labor standards)
Take out (schedule, equipment, and labor standards)
Transport routing (equipment and labor standards)

2g. Picking
Count, check, inspect (program, specifications, standards)

2h. Packaging
Schedule, specifications (standards)
Supplies (budget, specifications, standards)

2i. Shipping
Load (equipment and labor standards)

2j. Transportation out
Vehicle type (carrier and location)
Loading specifications (dunnaging, etc.)
Load (equipment and labor standards)
Routing, billing (specifications, instructions)

3. Training

Basically the training program geared to materials handling should be directed at the personnel involved in the function:

Manual handler
Hand trucker
Tow tractor operator
Fork truck operator
Platform truck operator
Crane operator
Conveyor operator
Highway truck operator
Material checker
Clerk
Dispatcher

Training of these personnel should include

a. Proper use of equipment
b. Proper maintenance of equipment
c. Safety procedures
d. Duties
e. Procedures
f. Paper work
g. Relationship of jobs to other functions

MATERIALS HANDLING IN THE DISTRIBUTION PIPELINE

Materials handling is an essential function in the distribution pipeline. The materials-handling function enters into plant costs, transportation costs, warehousing costs, inventory costs, and paperwork costs. Thus, materials handling is present in every function of physical distribution.

In addition, when the following critical areas must be planned, materials handling must be considered:

1. Product design
2. Package design
3. Plant layout
4. Warehouse layout
5. Production process
6. Purchasing of raw materials
7. Manpower needs

SUMMARY

While the discussion of materials handling has been brief, principally because it is one of the less dynamic functions within physical distribution, the costs of this function run quite high in most companies.

Great innovations, principally in the area of applying mathematical tools and techniques, are now being introduced into materials handling. In fact, Chapter 15 has a discussion of linear programing applications to materials handling.

These innovations, in what until recently was a static area, are due the recognition of the critical importance of materials handling (without even recognizing the cost element of this function) to all other areas of physical distribution.

BIBLIOGRAPHY

AIR TRANSPORTATION

Lewis, H. T., and J. W. Culliton, *Characteristics of Air Freight and Its Market.* Homewood: Irwin, 1956.

Locklin, D. Philip, *Economics of Transportation*, 6th ed. Homewood: Irwin, 1966.

Meyer, John R., and others, *The Economics of Competition in the Transportation Industries*, 5th ed. New York: McGraw-Hill, 1961.

Norton, Hugh S., *Modern Transportation Economics.* Columbus: Merrill, 1963.

Pegrum, Dudley F., *Transportation Economics and Public Policy.* Homewood: Irwin, 1963.

Ruppenthal, Karl M., *Revolution in Transportation.* Stanford: Stanford University Graduate School of Business, 1960.

U.S. Transportation: Resources, Performance, and Problems. Washington, D.C.: National Academy of Sciences, 1961.

MARKETING AND DISTRIBUTION

Ballantine, Duncan S., *U.S. Naval Logistics in the Second World War.* Princeton: Princeton University Press, 1947.

Beckman, Theodore N., and N. H. Engle, *Wholesaling Principles and Practice.* New York: Ronald Press, 1951.

Brown, Lyndon O., *Marketing and Distribution Research.* New York: Ronald Press, 1955.

"The Changing American Market." *Fortune*, 1955.

Crane, Edgar, *Marketing Communications.* New York: Wiley, 1965.

Diamond, William M., *Distribution Channels for Industrial Goods.* Athens: Ohio State University Bureau of Business Research, 1963.

Falcon, William D. (ed.), *Package: Key Component of Marketing Strategy.* New York: American Management Association, 1964

Fisk, George, *Marketing Systems: An Introductory Analysis.* New York: Harper & Row, 1967.

Heckert, Josiah R., and R. B. Miner, *Distribution Costs*, 2nd ed. New York: Ronald Press, 1953.

Heskett, J. L., and others, *Business Logistics*. New York: Ronald Press, 1964.
Morse, Philip M., *Queues, Inventories, and Maintenance*. New York: Wiley, 1958.
Pricing for Profit and Growth, McGraw-Hill Consultant Report, 1957.
Redding, W. Charles, and George A. Sanborn, *Business and Industrial Communication: A Source Book*. New York: Harper & Row, 1964.
Sevin, Charles H., *Marketing Productivity Analysis*. New York: McGraw-Hill, 1965.
Skillinglaw, Gordon, and J. C. Burton, *Materials Management and the Profit Center Concept*. New York: American Management Association, 1964.
Stewart, Paul W., and J. Frederic Dewhurst, *Does Distribution Cost Too Much?* New York: Twentieth Century Fund, 1939.
Ullman, Edward L., *American Commodity Flow: A Geographical Interpretation of Rail and Water Traffic*. Seattle: University of Washington, 1957.
Wilson, George L., *Transportation and Communication*. New York: Appleton-Century-Crofts, 1954.
Wolfe, Roy I., *Transportation and Politics*. Princeton: Van Nostrand, 1963.

MATERIALS HANDLING

Bolz, H. A., and G. E. Hagemann, *Materials Handling Handbook*. New York: Ronald Press, 1958.
Handbook of Powered Industrial Trucks. Industrial Truck Association, 1957.
Harrington, Carl C., *Materials Handling Manual*. Conover-Mast, 1952.
Haynes, David O., *Materials Handling Equipment*. Philadelphia: Chilton, 1957.
Hudson, W. G., *Conveyors and Related Equipment*, 3rd ed. New York: Chapman, 1954.
Immer, John R., *Materials Handling*. New York: McGraw-Hill, 1953.
Integrated Packaging and Materials Handling. New York: American Management Association, 1958.
Koshkin, S. J., *Modern Materials Handling*. New York: Wiley, 1932.
Morris, William T., *Analysis for Materials Handling Management*. Homewood: Irwin, 1962.
Potts, Matthew W., *Materials Handling Equipment*. New York: Pitman, 1947.
Skillinglaw, Gordon, and J. C. Burton, *Materials Management and the Profit Center Concept*. New York: American Management Association, 1964.
Stocker, Harry E., *Materials Handling*. Englewood Cliffs: Prentice-Hall, 1943.

MATHEMATICS

Arkin, Herbert, and R. R. Colton, *Statistical Methods*. New York: Barnes & Noble, 1950.

Bacon, Harold M., *Differential and Integral Calculus*. New York: McGraw-Hill, 1955.

Boehm, George A. W., *The New World of Math*. New York: Dial Press, 1959.

Chernoff, Herman, and L. E. Moses, *Elementary Decision Theory*. New York: Wiley, 1959.

Constantin, James A., *Principles of Logistics Management*. New York: Appleton-Century-Crofts, 1966.

Crowder, N. A., *The Arithmetic of Computers*. New York: Doubleday, 1960.

Feller, William, *Introduction to Probability Theory and Its Applications*. New York: Wiley, 1950.

Heskett, J. L., and others, *Business Logistics*. New York: Ronald Press, 1964.

Hilton, Alice Mary, *Logic, Computing Machines, and Automation*. Cleveland: World, 1964.

Kemeny, J. G., and others, *Introduction to Finite Mathematics*. Bailey, 1957.

———, and others, *Finite Mathematics with Business Applications*. Englewood Cliffs: Prentice-Hall, 1965.

Koopmans, T. C., *Activity Analysis of Production and Allocation*. New York: Wiley, 1951.

Newman, James R. (ed.), *The World of Mathematics*, 4 vols. New York: Simon and Schuster, 1956.

Smith, Edward S., and others, *Unified Calculus*. New York: Wiley, 1947.

Snedecor, George W., *Statistical Methods*, 5th ed. Ames: Iowa State College, 1956.

Theodore, Chris A., *Applied Mathematics: An Introduction*. Homewood: Irwin, 1965.

Wiener, Norbert, *Cybernetics*. New York: Wiley, 1949.

MOTOR CARRIERS

Brewer, Stanley H., *The Utilization of Motor Common Carriers of General Freight in Distribution Patterns*. Seattle: University of Washington, 1957.

Conroy, Bernard F., *Motor Freight Workshop*. Exposition Press, 1952.

Heskett, J. L., and others, *Business Logistics*. New York: Ronald Press, 1964.

Locklin, D. Philip, *Economics of Transportation*, 6th ed. Homewood: Irwin, 1966.

Meyer, John R., *The Economics of Competition in the Transportation Industries*. Cambridge: Harvard University Press, 1959.

Morse, Philip M., *Queues, Inventories, and Maintenance*. New York: Wiley, 1958.

Mossman, Frank H., and Newton Morton, *Logistics of Distribution Systems*. Boston: Allyn & Bacon, 1965.

Norton, Hugh S., *Modern Transportation Economics*. Columbus: Merrill, 1963.

Pegrum, Dudley F., *Transportation Economics and Public Policy*. Homewood: Irwin, 1963.

Plowman, E. Grosvenor, *Plowman Lectures on Business Logistics*. Stanford: Stanford University Graduate School of Business, 1964.

Ruppenthal, Karl M., *Business Logistics: Appraisal and Prospect*. Stanford: Stanford University Graduate School of Business, n.d.
―――, *Developments in Business Logistics*. Stanford: Stanford University Graduate School of Business, n.d.
―――, *New Dimensions in Business Logistics*. Stanford: Stanford University Graduate School of Business, 1963.
―――, *Revolution in Transportation*. Stanford: Stanford University Graduate School of Business, 1960.
Shinn, G. L., *Reasonable Freight Rates*. Washington, D.C.: Traffic Service Corporation, 1952.
Smykay, Edward W., and others, *Physical Distribution Management*. New York: Macmillan, 1961.
Taft, Charles A., *Commercial Motor Transportation*. Homewood: Irwin, 1951.
―――, *Operating Rights of Motor Carriers*. Dubuque: W. C. Brown, 1953.
U.S. Transportation: Resources, Performance, and Problems. Washington, D.C.: National Academy of Sciences, 1961.
Wilson, G. L., *Industrial Traffic Management*. Washington, D.C.: Traffic Service Corporation, 1949.

OFFICE AUTOMATION

Bell, William D., *A Management Guide to Electronic Computers*. New York: McGraw-Hill, 1957.
Crowder, N. A., *The Arithmetic of Computers*. New York: Doubleday, 1960.
Electronic Data Processing in Industry. New York: American Management Association, 1953.
Electronics at Work. New York: American Management Association, 1950.
Hilton, Alice Mary, *Logic, Computing Machines, and Automation*. Cleveland: World, 1964.
Levin, Howard S., *Office Work and Automation*. New York: Wiley, 1956.
A New Approach to Office Mechanization: Integrated Data Processing Through Common Language Machines. New York: American Management Association, 1954.

OPERATIONS RESEARCH

Adlinger, G. R., and others, *Operations Research: Challenge to Modern Management*. Cambridge: Harvard University Press, 1954.
Alderson, Wroe, and Stanley J. Shapiro, *Marketing and the Computer*. Englewood Cliffs: Prentice-Hall, 1963.

Charnes, Abraham, and others, *An Introduction to Linear Programming*. New York: Wiley, 1953.

Churchman, C. West, and others, *Introduction to Operations Research*. New York: Wiley, 1957.

Ferguson, R. O., and L. F. Sargent, *Linear Programming*. New York: McGraw-Hill, 1958.

Greenwald, D. V., *Linear Programming*. New York: Ronald Press, 1957.

Heskett, J. L., and others, *Business Logistics*. New York: Ronald Press, 1964.

Koopmans, T. C., *Activity Analysis of Production and Allocation*. New York: Wiley, 1951.

Lindsay, Franklin A., *New Techniques for Management Decision-Making*. New York: McGraw-Hill, 1963.

Morse, P. M., *Queues, Inventories, and Maintenance*. New York: Wiley, 1958.

Mossman, Frank H., and Newton Morton, *Logistics of Distribution Systems*. Boston: Allyn & Bacon, 1965.

Operations Research: Explained and Applied. New York: American Management Association, 1958.

Plowman, E. Grosvenor, *Plowman Lectures on Business Logistics*. Stanford: Stanford University Graduate School of Business, 1964.

Research Techniques in Maritime Transportation. Washington, D.C.: National Academy of Sciences, 1959.

Ruppenthal, Karl M., *Business Logistics: Appraisal and Prospect*. Stanford: Stanford University Graduate School of Business, n.d.

————, *Developments in Business Logistics*. Stanford: Stanford University Graduate School of Business, n.d.

————, *New Dimensions in Business Logistics*. Stanford: Stanford University Graduate School of Business, 1963.

Sasieni, M., and others, *Operations Research—Methods and Problems*. New York: Wiley, 1959.

Smykay, Edward W., and others, *Physical Distribution Management*. New York: Macmillan, 1961.

Symonds, G. H., *Linear Programming: The Solution of Refinery Problems*. Esso Standard Oil Company, 1955.

Terborgh, George W., *Business Investment Policy*. Cleveland: Machinery and Allied Products Institute, 1958.

Vazsonyi, Andrew, *Scientific Programming in Business and Industry*. New York: Wiley, 1958.

PACKAGING

Brown, Kenneth, *Package Design Engineering*. Chapman, 1959.

Constantin, James A., *Principles of Logistics Management*. New York: Appleton-Century-Crofts, 1966.

Falcon, William D. (ed.), *Package: Key Component of Marketing Strategy.* New York: American Management Association, 1964.

Friedman, W. F., and J. J. Kipnees, *Industrial Packaging.* New York: Wiley, 1960.

Integrated Packaging and Materials Handling. New York: American Management Association, 1958.

Package Design and Its Management. New York: American Management Association, 1965.

PLANT LAYOUT

Apple, James M., *Plant Layout and Materials Handling.* New York: Ronald Press, 1950.

Immer, John R., *Layout Planning Techniques.* New York: McGraw-Hill, 1950.

Mallick, R. W., and A. T. Gaudreau, *Plant Layout: Planning and Practice.* New York: Wiley, 1951.

Means, R. S., *Building Construction Cost Data.* R. S. Means (publisher), 1963.

Melnitsky, B., *Industrial Storeskeeping Manual.* Bailey, 1956.

Muther, Richard, *Practical Plant Layout.* New York: McGraw-Hill, 1955.

Robichaud, Beryl, *Selecting, Planning, and Managing Office Space.* New York: McGraw-Hill, 1955.

PLANT LOCATION

Greenhut, Melvin L., *Plant Location in Theory and Practice.* Chapel Hill: University of North Carolina Press, 1956.

Heskett, J. L., and others, *Business Logistics.* New York: Ronald Press, 1964.

Hoover, Edgar M., *The Location of Economic Activity.* New York: McGraw-Hill, 1948.

Locklin, D. Philip, *Economics of Transportation*, 6th ed. Homewood: Irwin, 1966.

Mossman, Frank H., and Newton Morton, *Logistics of Distribution Systems.* Boston: Allyn & Bacon, 1965.

Norton, Hugh S., *Modern Transportation Economics.* Columbus: Merrill, 1963.

Pegrum, Dudley F., *Transportation Economics and Public Policy.* Homewood: Irwin, 1963.

Plowman, E. Grosvenor, *Plowman Lectures on Business Logistics.* Stanford: Stanford University Graduate School of Business, 1964.

Ruppenthal, Karl M., *Business Logistics: Appraisal and Prospect.* Stanford: Stanford University Graduate School of Business, n.d.

————, *Developments in Business Logistics.* Stanford: Stanford University Graduate School of Business, n.d.

————, *New Dimensions in Business Logistics.* Stanford: Stanford University Graduate School of Business, 1963.

————, *Revolution in Transportation.* Stanford: Stanford University Graduate School of Business, 1960.

Smykay, Edward W., and others, *Physical Distribution Management.* New York: Macmillan, 1961.

U.S. Transportation: Resources, Performance, and Problems. Washington, D.C.: National Academy of Sciences, 1961.

INVENTORY CONTROL

Bethel, Lawrence L., and others, *Industrial Organization and Management.* New York: McGraw-Hill, 1956.

Boulding, Kenneth E., and W. Allen Spivey, *Linear Programming and the Theory of the Firm.* New York: Macmillan, 1960.

Bowman, Edward H., and Robert B. Fetter, *Analysis for Production and Operations Management.* Homewood: Irwin, 1967.

Brown, R. G., *Statistical Forecasting for Inventory Control.* New York: McGraw-Hill, 1959.

Carson, Gordon B., *Production Handbook*, 2nd ed. New York: Ronald Press, 1958.

Heskett, J. L., and others, *Business Logistics.* New York: Ronald Press, 1964.

Holt, Charles C., *Planning Production, Inventories, and Work Force.* Englewood Cliffs: Prentice-Hall, 1960.

Lewis, H. T., and Wilbur B. England, *Procurement Principles and Cases*, 3rd ed. Homewood: Irwin, 1957.

Lindsay, F. A., *New Techniques for Management Decision Making.* New York: McGraw-Hill, 1958.

Magee, John F., *Production Planning and Inventory Control.* New York: McGraw-Hill, 1958.

Melnitsky, Benjamin, *Management of Industrial Inventory.* Conover-Mast, 1951.

Morse, P. M., *Queues, Inventories, and Maintenance.* New York: Wiley, 1958.

Mossman, Frank H., and Newton Morton, *Logistics of Distribution Systems.* Boston: Allyn & Bacon, 1965.

Plowman, E. Grosvenor, *Plowman Lectures on Business Logistics.* Stanford: Stanford University Graduate School of Business, 1964.

Pritzker, Robert A., and R. A. Gring, *Modern Approaches to Production Planning and Control.* New York: American Management Association, 1960.

Ritchie, William E., *Production and Inventory Control.* New York: Ronald Press, 1951.

Ruppenthal, Karl M., *Business Logistics: Appraisal and Prospect.* Stanford: Stanford University Graduate School of Business, n.d.
————, *Developments in Business Logistics.* Stanford: Stanford University Graduate School of Business, n.d.
————, *New Dimensions in Business Logistics.* Stanford: Stanford University Graduate School of Business, 1963.
Smykay, Edward W., and others, *Physical Distribution Management.* New York: Macmillan, 1961.
Vazsonyi, Andrew, *Scientific Programming in Business and Industry.* New York: Wiley, 1958.
Welch, W. Evert, *Tested Scientific Inventory Control.* Stanford: Management Publications Corporation, 1956.
Whitin, T. M., *Theory of Inventory Management*, 2nd ed. Princeton: Princeton University Press, 1957.

QUALITY CONTROL

Dodge, Harold F., and H. G. Romig, *Sampling Inspection Tables.* New York: Wiley, 1944.
Grant, Eugene L., *Statistical Quality Control*, 2nd ed. New York: McGraw-Hill, 1952.
Shewhart, Walter A., *Economic Control of Quality of Manufactured Product.* New York: Macmillan, 1932.

RAIL TRANSPORTATION

Bigham, Truman C., *Transportation Principles and Problems.* New York: McGraw-Hill, 1947.
Constantin, James A., *Principles of Logistics Management.* New York: Appleton-Century-Crofts, 1966.
Heskett, J. L., and others, *Business Logistics.* New York: Ronald Press, 1964.
Locklin, D. Philip, *Economics of Transportation*, 6th ed. Homewood: Irwin, 1966.
Meyer, John R., and others, *The Economics of Competition in the Transportation Industries.* Cambridge: Harvard University Press, 1959.
Mossman, Frank H., and Newton Morton, *Logistics of Distribution Systems.* Boston: Allyn & Bacon, 1965.
Norton, Hugh S., *Modern Transportation Economics.* Columbus: Merrill, 1963.
Pegrum, Dudley F., *Transportation Economics and Public Policy.* Homewood: Irwin, 1963.

Plowman, E. Grosvenor, *Plowman Lectures on Business Logistics.* Stanford: Stanford University Graduate School of Business, 1964.

Ruppenthal, Karl M., *Business Logistics: Appraisal and Prospect.* Stanford: Stanford University Graduate School of Business, n.d.

——, *Developments in Business Logistics.* Stanford: Stanford University Graduate School of Business, n.d.

——, *New Dimensions in Business Logistics.* Stanford: Stanford University Graduate School of Business, 1963.

——, *Revolution in Transportation.* Stanford: Stanford University Graduate School of Business, 1960.

Shinn, G. L., *Reasonable Freight Rates.* Washington, D.C.: Traffic Service Corporation, 1952.

Smykay, Edward W., and others, *Physical Distribution Management.* New York: Macmillan, 1961.

Ullman, Edward L., *American Commodity Flow: A Geographical Interpretation of Rail and Water Traffic.* Seattle: University of Washington, 1957.

U.S. Transportation: Resources, Performance, and Problems. Washington, D.C.: National Academy of Sciences, 1961.

Wilson, G. L., *Industrial Traffic Management.* Washington, D.C.: Traffic Service Corporation, 1959.

STATISTICAL ANALYSIS

Arkin, Herbert, and R. R. Colton, *Statistical Methods,* 4th ed. New York: Barnes & Noble, 1950.

Brown, R. G., *Statistical Forecasting for Inventory Control.* New York: McGraw-Hill, 1959.

Chernoff, H., and L. E. Moses, *Elementary Decision Theory.* New York: Wiley, 1959.

Deming, W. Edwards, *Sample Design in Business Research.* New York: Wiley, 1960.

Frank, Ronald E., and others, *Quantitative Techniques in Marketing Analysis.* Homewood: Irwin, 1962.

Heskett, J. L., and others, *Business Logistics.* New York: Ronald Press, 1964.

Moroney, M. J., *Facts from Figures,* 3rd ed. Baltimore: Penguin, 1955.

Mossman, Frank H., and Newton Morton, *Logistics of Distribution Systems.* Boston: Allyn & Bacon, 1965.

Peck, L. G., and R. N. Hazelwood, *Finite Queuing Tables.* New York: Wiley, 1953.

Research Techniques in Maritime Transportation. Washington, D.C.: National Academy of Sciences, 1959.

Schlaifer, Robert O., *Probability and Statistics for Business Decisions.* New York: McGraw-Hill, 1959.

Snedecor, George W., *Statistical Methods.* Ames: Iowa State College, 1956.

TRAFFIC MANAGEMENT

Bigham, Truman C., *Transportation Principles and Problems*. New York: McGraw-Hill, 1947.

Bryan, Leslie A., *Traffic Management in Industry*. New York: Holt, Rinehart & Winston, 1953.

Colton, Richard C., *Practical Handbook of Industrial Traffic Management*, 2nd ed. New York: Funk & Wagnalls, 1953.

Cooley, Henry B., *Transportation Management*. Ithaca: Cornell University Press, 1946.

Flood, Kenneth U., *Traffic Management*. Dubuque: W. C. Brown, 1963.

Hay, William W., *An Introduction to Transportation Engineering*. New York: Wiley, 1961.

Heskett, J. L., and others, *Business Logistics*. New York: Ronald Press, 1964.

Meyer, John R., and others, *The Economics of Competition in the Transportation Industries*. Cambridge: Harvard University Press, 1959.

Morton, Newton, and Frank H. Mossman, *Industrial Traffic Management*. New York: Ronald Press, 1954.

Mossman, Frank H., and Newton Morton, *Logistics of Distribution Systems*. Boston: Allyn & Bacon, 1965.

Murr, Alfred, *Export-Import Traffic Management and Forwarding*. Cambridge: Cornell Maritime Press, 1957.

Shinn, Glenn L., *Reasonable Freight Rates*. Washington, D.C.: Traffic Service Corporation, 1952.

Smykay, Edward W., and others, *Physical Distribution Management*. New York: Macmillan, 1961.

Taft, Charles A., *Management of Traffic and Physical Distribution*, 3rd ed. Homewood: Irwin, 1964.

Wilson, G. L., *Industrial Traffic Management*, Washington, D.C.: Traffic Service Corporation, 1949.

———, *Traffic Management: Industrial, Commercial, Governmental*. Englewood Cliffs: Prentice-Hall, 1956.

WAREHOUSING

Bowman, Edward H., and Robert B. Fetter, *Analysis for Production and Operations Management*. Homewood: Irwin, 1967.

Briggs, Andrew J., *Warehouse Operations Planning and Management*. New York: Wiley, 1960.

Constantin, James A., *Principles of Logistics Management*. New York: Appleton-Century-Crofts, 1966.

Frederick, John H., *Using Public Warehouses*. Philadelphia: Chilton, 1957.

Heskett, J. L., and others, *Business Logistics*. New York: Ronald Press, 1964.

Mossman, Frank H., and Newton Morton, *Logistics of Distribution Systems*. Boston: Allyn & Bacon, 1965.

Smykay, Edward W., and others, *Physical Distribution Management*. New York: Macmillan, 1961.

INDEX

Air transport, 361
  break-bulk for parcel post, 42
  costs and services, 34, 361
  use of computers, 281
Albers, Henry H., 12n
Alderson, Wroe, 8n, 11n, 28n
ALDO Inc., 81–5
  concept of standard ratio, 87–9
  inventory management system, 82–5
  inventory standards, 81–97
  management evaluation, 93–7
Alexander, Milton, 3–16, 17–30, 129–55
Alternative decisions
  production or supply, 173–74
  use of operations research, 239–55
*American Colloid Co. v. Akron, Canton
  and Youngstown R. Co.*, 292–93
American Standards Association, 166
Attchison, J., 90n

Balderston, F. E., 59n
Batelle Institute, 286
Baum, W. J., 57n
Beckman T., 50n
Billings, Warren, 211–19
*Bituminous Coal Tenn., Ky. & Va. to
  N.C., Tenn. & Va.*, 292
Bowersox, Donald J., 45–59
Break-bulk point, 38–9
Break-bulk techniques, 41–2
  air parcel post, 42
  containerization, 42
  transportation problems, 41–2
Brown, J. A. C., 90n
Brown, Robert G., 70, 71, 74

Brown, Virginia May, 289
Bushes, shipments by, 362
Business systems, operations research
  techniques, 246–51

Calhoun, Robert L., 279–95
Carr, L. H., 21n
CART (computerized automatic rating
  technique), 284
Case studies, 297–379
  ABC Corporation, 323–30
  Apex Manufacturing Company, 331–34
  ASME Manufacturing Company—A
    Sample Study in Logistical
    Planning, 311–22
  Barnes Manufacturing Company,
    335–37
  Alexander Hamilton Electrical
    Company, 339–41
  Short Problem in Linear Programing
    for Distribution Costs, 357–58
  The "Small-Order" Problem, 299–309
  Total Distribution Cost, 343–44
  Using Linear Programing to Dispatch
    Vehicles, 345–55
Channels of distribution; *see* Distribution
  channels
Cherington, Paul, 51
Civil Aeronautics Board, 289, 363
Clark, Fred, 51
Classification of commodities, 367–68
Codes for products, 110
Commerce, Department of, 288, 289
Common Market, 13
Communications, 8, 9, 211–19

Communications *(Cont.)*
  advances in, 13
  computer systems; *see* Computer
    systems coordination of
    departmental activities, 216
  coordination of logistical functions,
    213
  costs, 178–80, 210
  data communications, 213–15
    ABC Steel Corporation, 217–18
    advantages, 218–19
    equipment, 216–17
    narrowband, voiceband, and
      wideband transmission, 217
    research and development, 219
  definition, 211–12
  electronic data processing; *see*
    Electronic data processing
  gap in internal, 15, 28
  information explosion and, 213
  information requirements, 214–15
    customers, 214
    financial and management, 215
    marketing and sales promotion, 214
    production, 214
    salesmen, 214
  meaning of, 211–18
  physical distribution and, 9, 211–19
  research and development, 219
  role in logistics, 211–19
  total information systems, 215
Competition, in marketing, 16
Computer systems
  communication problem, 15
  costs, 117–18
  data communication, 213–15
  government regulation of
    transportation industry, 279–95
  influence on public policy, 288–95
  integrated information systems, 127
  master file approach, 127
  motor carriers, 281, 283–84
  optimum use, 213
  order-processing, 115–22
    advantages, 124–25
    batch processing, 123
    future trends, 125–27
    large systems, 117–22
    random access, 123–24
    small systems, 115–17
    summary of differences, 122–24

profit improvement approach, 178–80
  "total systems" approach, 215,
    282–83
  transportation industry, 279–95
    accounting activities, 280
    management science activities, 280
    traffic flow and load analysis, 281
  types of, 117–18
Conglomerates and mergers, 6, 23
Containerization, 13, 157–68
  advantages, 38–41, 160–61
  break-bulk, 42
  Conex system, 161
  containers, 138, 157
  cost reduction possibilities, 160–65
  efficiency of, 160–65
  historical background, 157–60
  labor problems, 168
  leasing plans, 167
  liquid products, 162–63
  military use, 160–61
  ownership of containers, 167
  rates, 167–68
  reasons for, 160–65
  research projects, 165, 167–68
  standardized equipment, 165–66, 224
  trailer-on-flat-car operations, 158–60
  transportation problem, 38–41
  unitized loads, 161–62
Contract carriage, 359–60
COR scale (cost-oriented rates), 288
Costs, 173–80, 216
  air transport, 34
  communications and data processing,
    178–80, 210
  customer service, 180
  distribution cost elements, 5, 171–210,
    216
    examples, 182–200
    linear programing for, 357–58
  effect of distribution on, 173–80
  inbound raw material, 203
  indirect labor, 5
  interdependence of, 173–80
    carrying inventory, 176–80
    production or supply alternatives,
      173–74
    transportation, 176
  inventory, 34, 176–80, 209–10
  materials handling, 376
  motor carriers, 34

opportunity, 3, 5, 7, 68
order processing, 107, 210
packaging, 34, 207
physical distribution, 203–10
plant costs, 203–04
profit improvement approach, 173–80;
    see also Profit improvement
    approach
railroads, 34
transportation, 175–76, 204–07
    commercial carriage, 204
    operating costs, 206–07
    private carriage, 205–06
warehousing, 34, 174–75, 207–09
Coyle, Arthur, 287n
Critical path method, 240
Customer service, 6, 11
    cost and value of, 172, 180–82
    distribution centers location and, 49
    information requirements, 214
    inventory control and, 96
    location analysis and, 49, 67
    order-processing and, 100–01, 180–81
    time required to fill orders, 180–81
Cybernetics, 26

Damkroger, Stanley F., 216n
Data communications
    advantages, 218–19
    equipment, 217
    narrowband, voiceband, and wideband
        transmission, 217
    research and development, 219
Davidson, W., 50n
Decision-making, 8
    optimization in, 13
    probabilistic options, 23
Dickerson, John, 293n
Dispatching vehicles, linear
    programing used for, 345–55
Distribution; see Physical distribution
Distribution centers
    consolidation of shipments, 46, 49, 50
    determining if fewer are needed, 62–3
    determining if more are needed, 64–7
    determining total annual costs, 62, 67
    differentiated products, 48–9
    intermediately positioned, 55
    location analysis, 44, 65–7; see also
        Location analysis

logic of, 50–3
market extension by use of, 46–8
market-oriented, 53–4
marketing strategy and, 50–4
multiple-location solutions, 57–9
multiple products, 49–50
nondifferentiated products, 46–8
optimization of, 61–7
production-oriented, 55
for retail stores, 50
retailer-owned, 54
single-location solution, 56–7
in space islands, 47
warehousing and storage, 50–3
Distribution channels, 23, 29
    investments in, 245–46, 247
    manufacturing case, 182–92
    operations research and, 243–46
    retail chains, 192–201
Distribution study, 311–12
    assembling data for analysis, 314
    cost and profitability of, 319–22
    initiating, 312
    organizing, 312–13
    planning, 313–14
    proposed method of distribution,
        314–17
    proposed rate schedule, 317–18
Diversion of shipments, 372
Dorfman, Robert, 57n

Electronic data processing, 7, 13
    admissibility as evidence, 287–93
    costs, 178–80, 210
    data communications, 217–19
        ABC Steel Corporation, 217–18
    EAM (electric accounting
        machines), 113–15, 122–23
    equipment, 217
        requirements, 215
    forecasting inventory, 75
    government regulations, 279–95
    influence on public policy, 288–95
    I.C.C. rating requirements, 285–88
    optimum use, 213
    order-processing cycle, 101–07, 113–22;
        see also Order-processing profit
        improvement approach, 178–80
    transportation problems, 42–3,
        279–80

Eneborg, C. G., 56n
Ernst, Martin L., 221–35
Expediting shipments, 373
Exponential smoothing techniques,
    72–3
  forecasting inventory, 68, 72–3, 75–7

Fahl, Henry A., 286n, 288n
Fayerweather, John, 13n
Federal Maritime Commission, 289
Federal Power Commission, 362
Fish, Lounsbury S., 7n, 23n, 27n
Flaks, Marvin, 171–210
For-hire carriage, 359–60
Forecasting, 69–80
  inventory control and, 69–80
  methods, 71–2
    exponential smoothing, 72–3
    judgment and prediction, 73–5
Forms, order-processing, 112–13
Franco, Robert J., 33–44, 359–73
Frank, Jerome, 294
Frederick, John H., 47
Fredericks, Ward A., 14n
Freed, Morton, 292n
Freight forwarders, 362
  use of computers, 281

Game theory applications, 291
Gargiulo, Granville R., 81–97
Gentle, Edgar, Jr., 215n
Gomez, Henry, 13n
Gordon, Wendell C., 13n
Government regulations, 279–95
  effect on computer use, 279–95
  factors affecting level of rates, 363–67
  influence of EDP on, 288–95
  transportation, 363–72
Graves, John, 291n
Green, Paul E., 8n
Greenhut, Melvin L., 49n
Greenwald, Dakota Ulrich, 57n

Hammond, Robert A., 239–55
Hoggatt, A. C., 59n
Holden, Paul E., 7n, 23n, 27n
Holmes, Oliver Wendell, 294
Hoover, Edgar M., 53

Horn, Paul V., 13n
Howard, John H., 8n
Hultman, Charles W., 13n

Information explosion, 213
Ingersoll, Wilbur, 51
Innovations, marketing, 6, 11
International marketing, logistical
    problems, 13
Interstate Commerce Commission, 166,
    363
  applications of EDP to rating
    requirements, 285–88
  EDP-prepared evidence, 293
  functions of, 289–95
  impact of EDP on, 289–95
In-transit privileges, 372
Inventory control, 3–5, 8, 9, 69–80
  aggregate inventory investment
    standards, 81–97
  ALDO, Inc., 81, 82–5
  alternative methods of stock
    replenishment 97
  annual investments in, 85–6
  concepts, 69–70
    of standard ratio, 87–9
  costs 34, 176–78 209–10
    of carrying inventory, 176–78
    relationship of inventory to ordering
      costs, 82–3
  cycle stocks, 68, 85–6
    computing, 92–3
  definition, 69
  distribution of items to meet price
    changes, 251–52
  economic-order quantities, 82–3
  effect of changing number of items
    in line, 97
  effect of customer service, 96
  electronic data processing, 75, 179
  establishing investment standards,
    90–3
  evaluating past performance, 97
  forecasting requirements, 69–80
    examples of, 75–80
    exponential smoothing technique,
      68, 72–3, 75–7
    future demands, 70–1
    judgment and prediction, 73–5
    methods, 71–7

projection by fitting trend line and
  extrapolating into future, 80
projection of four-point moving
  average, 77–8
projection of simple average, 77–8
projection of weighted moving
  average, 77, 79
use of computers, 75
inventory investment standards, 81–7
management evaluation, 82–5, 93–7
  comparison of actual investment
    against standard, 94
  effect of customer service, 96
  effect of sales on turnover, 95
  effect on product line, 97
mathematical techniques for
  determining optimum levels,
  81–97
obsolescence, 178
operations research and, 240–43,
  251–52
  distribution of items to meet price
    changes, 251–52
  improving control systems, 252–53
opportunity costing, 68
reorder-point concepts, 83–5
safety stocks, 68, 85–6, 242–53
statistical techniques, 82–5
  relationship of inventory costs to
    ordering costs, 82–3
tools and techniques, 81–97
turnover and, 95–6, 178
warehouse stocks, 68
Investments
  comparison of analysis before and
    after pilot test, 248
  inventory standards, 81–7
  for new distribution channel, 247–48
Invoices and invoicing, 99–100
  forms, 112–13
  handling, 179

Jantzen, Nelson R., 129–55

Kantor, Harold H., 58n
Killough, Hugh B., 50n
Klem, Walter, 15n

LaLonde, Bernard J., 46n
Legal decisions on EDP evidence, 287–93

Levitt, Theodore, 22n
Linear programing, 237, 257–76
  advantages of, 258
  location analysis, 57
  matrix logic technique, 270–75
    construction of, 258–60
    dispatch of tractors and trailers,
      275, 345–55
    lowest-cost solution, 274
  in minimizing transportation costs, 9,
    274
  to solve distribution problems, 57,
    257–76, 345–55
  special applications, 257–76
  stepping stone technique, 265–70
  for transportation problems, 35–6,
    257
  zero technique, 260–65
Liquids, containers for, 162–63
Location analysis, 45–59
  compass method, 63, 64
  costs that influence, 45, 58–9, 62, 67
    alternate service policies, 58–9
  determining if fewer are needed, 62–3
  determining if more are needed, 64–7
  determining optimum locations, 65–7
  differentiated products, 48–9
  distribution centers, 44, 45–8
    to extend market coverage, 47
    intermediately-positioned, 55
    market-positioned, 53–4
    with multiple products, 49–50
    nondifferentiated products, 46–8
    product distribution and, 50–3
    production-positioned, 55
  manufacturing facilities, 46
  marketing process and, 50–3
  mathematical programing technique,
    56–7, 61–7
  multiple-location solution, 57–9
  optimization of, 61–7
    distribution cost, 62–5
    locations, 65–7
    number and size, 62–7
  quantitative technique for, 61–7
  selection of locations, 45
  simulation used for, 57–8
  single-location analysis, 56–7
  studies, 46
  "systemic" questions, 44
  warehousing and storage, 5, 50–3

Logistics in marketing, 10*n*, 237
  communications and, 211–18
  conceptualization of organization, 21–2
  containerization, 157–68
  evolution of, 3–16
  functional approach, 31
  influence of, 16
  inventory control, 68, 69–80
  location analysis, 44, 45–59
  operations research, 239–55
  order-processing, 99–127
  organization and, 17–30
  packaging, 129–55
  profit improvement approach, 171–210
  quantitative techniques for, 28, 237–76
  systems analysis, 221–35
  transportation, 33–44
Lösch, August, 46*n*, 48
Louisville and Nashville railroad, 282–3

McDonough, Adrian W., 28*n*
McPherson, W. A., 284*n*
Management
  attitudes toward physical distribution,
    7–8
  change in orientation of, 6–7
  evaluation of inventory control, 93–7
  information requirements, 215
  operational, 15
Management science, 7–8, 10, 14,
    279–80
  forecasting and inventory control,
    69–80
  physical distribution and, 23
  probabilistic options in
    decision-making, 23
Manufacturing companies
  distribution network, 182–92
  responsibilities affecting distribution,
    202
Marketing management
  concept of, 10, 12, 26–7
  effect of physical distribution, 6
  functions, 52–3
  information requirements, 214
  organization of distribution, 20–1, 27
  physical distribution under, 29
  scientific, 12
  White's conception of marketing
    process, 52–3

Massel, Arthur, 295*n*
Materials handling, 375–79
  automated, 13
  costs, 376
  definition, 375
  functions, 376–78
    operations, 377–78
    planning and tooling, 377
    training, 378
  objectives, 375–76
  physical distribution and, 5, 8, 9
  role in distribution pipeline, 379
Matrix logic techniques, 270–75
  dispatch of tractors and trailers
    between terminals, 275, 345–55
  linear programing tool, 258–60,
    270–75
  lowest-cost solution, 274
  pickup of shipments, 275
Matson Navigation Company, 160
Maynard, H. H., 50*n*
Mergers and conglomerates, 6, 23
Miller, David W., 69
Miller, Thomas, 291*n*, 292–93
Modern Packaging Encyclopedia, 143*n*
Moore, Russell F., 13*n*
Mossman, Frank H., 46*n*, 47*n*, 56*n*
Motor carriers, 361
  break-bulk methods, 41–2
  computer programs, 281, 283–84
  costs and services, 34, 361
  linear programing to dispatch vehicles,
    345–55
  rate scales, 288
Muller, Fred, Jr., 157

National Motor Freight Classification,
    367
New products, introduction of, 11
New York Central Railroad, 160, 283

Oil companies, use of operations
    research, 249–50
Operations research, 7, 10, 239–55
  approach to problem-solving, 239–40
  case studies, 251–54
    distribution of items to meet price
      changes, 251–52
    improving inventory control system,
      252–53

solving warehouse problems, 253–54
computers required, 239–40
distribution systems and, 243–46
  investment in new channels, 245–47
  reducing number of warehouses,
    244–45
evaluating alternatives, 240
for inventory problems, 240–43, 251–52
logistics in business system, 246–51
methods of, 237
physical distribution and, 10, 243–47
in relation to total business picture,
  249–51
simulation techniques, 246
"small order" problem, 299–309
for solving logistical problems, 239–55
statistical methods, 242–53
Optimization solutions, 13
of distribution centers, 61–7
  location of, 65–7
  optimum number, 61–5
  procedures, tools, and techniques,
    61–7
operations research methods, 237
Order-processing, 99–127
accounts receivable, 99–100
automated, 13
back orders, 109
coding orders, 110
contract sales, 109
costs, 107, 210
customer service, 100–01, 180–81
cycle, 101–07
department, 108–10
direct shipments, 109–10
electronic data processing, 42–3,
    113–15, 125–217
  advantages of computers, 124–25
  batch processing, 123
  EAM system, 113–15
  future trends, 125–27
  large computer systems, 117–22
  punched card systems, 113–15
  random access, 123–24
  small computer systems, 115–17
  summary of differences, 122–24
forms, 112–13
future shipments, 109
government orders, 109
invoicing, 99–100, 102–06
legible copies, 111

order analysis, 99–100, 102
order entry, 99
order writing, 99–100, 101, 108
overseas sales, 109
physical distribution and, 5, 8, 9
problem areas, 107–13
  forms, 112–13
  order-processing department,
    108–10
  traffic and shipping departments,
    110–12
  use of codes, 110
profit improvement approach, 179
punched cards, 6
rush orders, 108
sales analysis, 99–100
split orders, 109
time cycle, 107, 180–81
time required to fill customer orders,
  180–81
Organization structure, 17–30
charts, 29
communication gaps, 15, 28
distribution as an entity, 21
distribution under manufacturing,
  18–9, 27
distribution under marketing, 20, 26,
  27, 29
effect of industrial revolutions, 17,
  20–1
evolutionary development, 23–8
"human equation," 30
line structure, 21
logistics, 21–2, 27
marketing management concepts, 21,
  26–7
need for managerial coordination, 26
physical distribution, 6, 10, 12–3,
  21–5, 27, 29–30
product flow and, 23
production-oriented approach, 18–9,
  26–7
systems approach to packaging,
  141–42, 143–44
theory and practice, 17–30
transition from "transportation" to
  "physical distribution," 27

Packaging, 129–55
bulk product treatment, 129

Packaging (*Cont.*)
  closing or scaling components, 129
  costs, 34, 207
  customer unit packages, 129
  designs, 138–40, 143–55
  development program, 143–55
    auditing the package, 154–55
    design considerations, 150–52
    determining product needs, 144–46
    piloting program, 143–44
    production and handling
      considerations, 152–54
    selecting the package, 148–50
    selecting the target, 146–48
  handling unit, 129
  historical background, 129–31
  interior components, 129
  physical distribution and, 3–5, 6, 8, 9,
    130–32, 136–37
  problems of, 129–31
  questionnaire on, 143–55
  shipping containers, 139
  systems approach to, 131–32
    contributions of, 142
    design, 132–34
    effect on distribution system, 136
    external influences, 135–36
    general applications, 134–40
    organizational effectiveness,
      141–44
    "total" or "multiple" packaging
      systems, 129
  tote containers, 138
  unit packages, 129, 138
  utility factors, 129
Parcel post, shipping by, 362
  break-bulk shipments, 42
Penn-Central merger, 291
Pennsylvania Railroad, 157
Persuasion, 23, 28, 29
  function of, 6
Philosophy, business, 10–2
  in marketing innovations, 11
  in marketing planning, 11
Physical distribution
  aims of management, 5, 7–8, 10, 14
  analysis of problems, 201
  automation, 6
  business philosophy, 10–2
  communications and, 13
  conceptual nature of, 3–16

cost components, 3, 203–10
  definition, 3
  discipline, 8
  dynamism of, 6, 14
  effect on decision-making, 8
  effectiveness of, 14–6
  functions, 6–9, 23–6, 51
  historical development, 7–8
  interrelated activities, 9–10, 171–73
  "management science" and, 7–8, 10,
    14, 279–80
  marketing orientation, 3–6, 20, 27
  operations research techniques, 7, 10,
    239–58
  opportunity costs, 3, 5, 7
  organization structure, 6, 10, 12–3,
    17–30
  packaging and, 3, 130–32, 136–37
  pipeline flow, 3–4, 9
  product flow and, 23–4
  profitability of, 10, 14, 171–210
  "transportation" compared to, 6–8, 27
  warehousing and storage, 3, 7, 8, 9
Pipelines, 362
Prange, Charles J., 14*n*
Predictions, forecasting inventory,
    70–1, 75–80
Product flow, 3–4, 9
  effect on physical distribution, 23
Product lines, 6, 97
Profit improvement approach, 169,
    171–210
  case studies, 182–201
    manufacturing case, 182–92
    retail case, 192–201
  communications and data processing,
    178–80
  cost elements, 173–80, 203–10
    carrying inventory, 176–78
    inventory obsolescence, 178
    production or supply alternatives,
      173–74
  transportation costs, 10, 175–76
  warehousing, 174–75
  customer service factors, 180–82
    time required to fill orders, 180–82
  integration of distribution activities,
    171–73
  order-processing, 179
  physical distribution key to, 10
  systems approach to, 171–210

Public policy
  influence of computers on, 288–95
  issues and problems of, 277
Public Service Commission, 363
Public Utility Commission, 363
Punched card system, 113–15
  order-processing, 104

Railroad Commission, 363
Railroads, 360–61
  computer systems, use of, 280–83
    analysis of traffic and operating
      information, 282–87
    for car utilization, 282
    real-time applications, 282–83
    systems approach, 283
    tariffs and rates, 285–86
  costs and services, 360–61
  "piggyback," 360
  systems analysis, 223–24, 283
  transportation costs, 34
  use of simulation model, 287
Rates and rate making, 369–72
  CART (computerized automatic
    rating technique), 284
  class rates, 370
  classification of commodities, 367–68
    density of product, 369
    factors affecting, 368–69
    susceptibility to damage, 369
    susceptibility to theft, 368
    types of packaging, 368
    value of product, 368
  commodity rates, 370
  computer systems, 285–88
  containerization, 38, 40, 167–68
  exception rates, 370–71
  factors effecting level of, 363–67
    competition between centers and
      markets, 365
    cost of service to carriers, 364
    density of product, 366
    direction of haul, 365
    length of haul, 364–65
    packaging of product, 366–67
    rates of competing carriers, 366
    value of service to shipper, 364
    volume of traffic, 365
  government regulation, 363–72
  intercity, 5

motor carriers, 288
publishing and filing, 285, 369
simulation studies, 287–88
transportation, 369–72
REA Express, 362
  container tariffs, 38, 40
  use of computers, 281
Reinfeld, Nyles V., 57n
Research, on containerization, 165,
  167–68
Retail chains, distribution network,
  192–201
Robinson, Richard D., 13n
Routing policy, 372

Salesmen
  information requirements, 214
  order-writing, 99–100, 101, 108
Samuelson, Paul A., 57n, 99–128
Saunders, Paul R., 99–127
Schorr, Jerry, 33–44, 61–7, 257–76,
  375–79
Shapiro, Stanley, 28n
Shipments
  containers, 139
  diversion of, 372
  in-transit privileges, 327
  tracing and expediting, 373
Shipper-carrier relations, 311–22
  initiating the study, 312
  logistical planning, 311–22
Shipping departments, 110–12
  legible documents, 111
  pool shipments, 110–11
  stock availability status reports, 111
Shubik, Martin, 48n
Shycon, Harvey N., 58n
Simulation methods
  communication issue, 15
  freight car supply and utilization, 287
  in I.C.C. cases, 291
  location analysis, 57–8
    advantages, 58–9
  operations research and, 246
  Pennsylvania-New York Central
    merger, 291–92
  transportation problems, 37–8
"Small-order" problems, 299–309
  approach, 302–09
  method of shipment, 299–300

"Small-order" problems, (*Cont.*)
  objectives, 301–02
  operations research, 299–300
Smith, Hubert L., 7*n*, 23*n*, 27*n*
Smykay, Edward W., 46*n*, 47*n*, 56*n*
Solow, Robert M., 57*n*
Stagar, James, 291*n*
Standard metropolitan areas, 5
Standard Transportation Commodity
    Code (STCC), 286–87
Standardization
  container-type systems, 165–66
  systems analysis, 224
Starr, Martin K., 69
Staudt, Thomas A., 49*n*
Steiner, Joseph, 288
Stepping stone technique, 265–70
Storage
  distribution center location, 50–3
  importance in marketing process, 52–3
  physical distribution and, 3, 7, 8, 9
Systems analysis, 221–35, 257
  characteristics, 225–26
  dimension or extent of, 221–24
  inputs and outputs, 222, 225–26
  objectives, 226–28
  organizational effectiveness, 141–42
  packaging design, 131–33
    effect on distribution system, 136,
      137–40
    external influences, 135–36
    general applications, 134–40
  profit improvement approach, 171–210
  steps in, 234
  techniques, 229, 234
  tool for planning, 221–25, 230
  total systems approach, 141–42
  variety of choices, 229

"Trading off" distribution costs, 10–2,
    21, 169, 248
Traffic congestion, 5*n*
Traffic departments, 110–12
  function, 105
Traffic management, 10*n*, 13–4
  functions, 31, 105, 237
Trailers and tractors
  linear programing for dispatching,
    345–55

Transportation; *see also* Physical
    distribution
  air transport, 361
  alternative methods, 39
  break-bulk point, 38–9, 41–2
  choices available, 359–62
  contract carriers, 360
  costs, 33–5
    effect on distribution costs, 33,
      175–76
  freight forwarders, 362
  function, 359–73
  government regulation, 363–72
  logistical factors, 33–44
  motor carriers, 361
  physical distribution compared to,
    3–4, 6–8, 27
  pipelines, 362
  private carriage, 359–60
  problem-solving techniques, 33–44
    break-bulk, 41–2
    containerization, 38–41
    electronic data processing, 42–3
    linear programing, 35–6
    simulation method, 37–8
  railroads, 360–61
  special services, 372–73
  water carriers, 361

Uniform Freight Classification, 367
United Parcel, 362
Unitization, 157; *see also*
    Containerization

Vesley, Allan, 69–80
Vogel, William R., 57*n*

Warehouses and warehousing
  automated, 13, 230
  costs, 34, 174–75, 207–09
  determining optimum locations, 65–7
  distribution center location, 50–3
  location analysis, 5, 45–53, 65–7;
    see also Location analysis
  operations research techniques, 253–55
  reducing number of, 62–3, 244–45
  transportation costs, 176
Wasserman, Max J., 13*n*

Water carriers, 361
  costs and services, 361
Weiss, Ernest, 279–95
Wester, Leon, 58n
White, Percival, 51–3
Whitten, Herbert O., 286–87, 288n, 291n

Wolf, P., 57n

Zero techniques, linear programing
  tool, 260–65
Zionts, Stanley, 57n